A D V A N C E D

MSDOS®

P R O G R A M M I N G

RAY DUNCAN

ADVANCED

MSDOS®

PROGRAMMING

The

Microsoft®

guide for

Assembly

Language

and C

programmers.

PUBLISHED BY
Microsoft Press
A Division of Microsoft Corporation
16011 N.E. 36th Way, Box 97017, Redmond, Washington 98073-9717

Library of Congress Cataloging in Publication Data
Duncan, Ray, 1952–
Advanced MS-DOS programming.
Includes index.
1. MS-DOS (Computer operating system)   2. Assembler language (Computer
program language)   3. C (Computer program language)   I. Title.
QA76.76.063D857   1988   005.4'46   88-1251
ISBN 0-914845-77-2

Printed and bound in the United States of America.

 9 10 11 12   FGFG   8 9 0 9 8

Distributed to the book trade in the
United States by Harper & Row.

Distributed to the book trade in
Canada by General Publishing Company, Ltd.

Distributed to the book trade outside the
United States and Canada by Penguin Books Ltd.

Penguin Books Ltd., Harmondsworth, Middlesex, England
Penguin Books Australia Ltd., Ringwood, Victoria, Australia
Penguin Books N.Z. Ltd., 182–190 Wairau Road, Auckland 10, New Zealand

British Cataloging in Publication Data available

UNIX™ is a trademark of AT&T Bell Laboratories.
Compaq® is a registered trademark of COMPAQ Computer Corporation.
Periscope™ is a trademark of Data Base Decisions.
PDP-11® is a registered trademark of Digital Equipment Corporation.
Concurrent DOS®, CP/M-80®, CP/M-86®, and Digital Research® are registered trademarks
of Digital Research, Incorporated.
HP™ is a trademark of Hewlett-Packard.
Intel® is a registered trademark and iRMX-86™ is a trademark of Intel Corporation.
IBM® is a registered trademark, and PC/AT™, PC-DOS™, PC/XT™, and TopView™ are
trademarks of International Business Machines Corporation.
PC/FORTH is a trademark of Laboratory Microsystems Incorporated.
Volkswriter® is a registered trademark of Lifetree Software, Incorporated.
Lotus® is a registered trademark of Lotus Development Corporation.
WordStar® is a registered trademark of MicroPro International Corporation.
Microsoft®, MS-DOS®, and XENIX® are registered trademarks of Microsoft Corporation.
Advanced Trace-86™, Disk Toolkit™, and Trace-86™ are trademarks of Morgan Computing
Company, Incorporated.
Motorola® 6845 is a registered trademark of Motorola, Incorporated.
Norton Utilities™ is a trademark of Peter Norton, Incorporated.
TeleVideo® 950 is a registered trademark of TeleVideo Systems, Incorporated.

For Carolyn

CONTENTS

ACKNOWLEDGMENTS

It has been a real pleasure, and an education in many different ways, to be associated with the fine people at Microsoft Press during the creation of *Advanced MS-DOS*. It has also been a bit sobering to realize the large number of skilled editors, craftsmen, designers, typographers, and proofreaders that a publishing house must deploy to transform a technically complex manuscript of this sort into an attractive, accurate, and marketable book. Collectively, their contribution makes my part look easy; sadly enough, you (and I) will never know most of their names. But special thanks are due to:

Claudette Moore, who got the whole project in motion and was truly tireless in her efforts to get me the necessary software, consultants, and reference materials;

Salley Oberlin, who helped organize and develop the manuscript, and who pointed out all the gaps and hidden assumptions with a blizzard of yellow tags;

Jeff Hinsch, who spent countless hours with the figures and program listings, and validated the reference section against Microsoft sources;

Dori Shattuck, who performed the principal editing and translated the manuscript into English;

Jim Beley, who picked up the project at the end and shepherded it off to the printer;

and Mark Zbikowski of the Microsoft Systems and Languages division, one of the fathers of MS-DOS version 2, who took time out from his many other responsibilities to review the manuscript, and contributed a host of invaluable corrections and suggestions.

Ray Duncan
Los Angeles, California
June 1986

INTRODUCTION

Advanced MS-DOS is written for the experienced assembly-language or C programmer who is already familiar with the architecture of the Intel 8086/8088/80286 family of microprocessors. It supplies the detailed information necessary to write robust, high-performance applications under MS-DOS and its derivatives.

Advanced MS-DOS explores the functions and special features of MS-DOS in detail, comparing and contrasting the various extant versions along the way. It is my belief (based upon experience) that working, well-documented programs are worth far more as learning tools than narrative exposition and tables, so I have used detailed programming examples extensively throughout the book—both isolated code fragments performing specific functions, and complete utility programs. All examples in this book were developed using the Microsoft Macro Assembler version 4.00 or the Microsoft C Compiler version 3.00, and IBM PC hardware.

MS-DOS offers a large number of diverse operating-system services to programs running under its control. These services, which isolate application programs from the hardware environment, are discussed in Section 1 under the following categories:

- Character I/O: keyboard and serial-port input, video display, serial-port and line-printer output

- Mass storage: maintenance of directories and files on removable or fixed disks

- Memory allocation and management

- Loading and execution of one program task under the control of another

This section also discusses the structures of filters, device drivers, and interrupt handlers—features of special interest to programmers writing system tools or extensions to MS-DOS itself—and hardware-dependent programming on the IBM family of personal computers for those areas where such programming is necessary in order to obtain acceptable performance (particularly the video display).

Section 2 provides a complete reference guide to the MS-DOS interrupts, organized so that you can see at a glance the register contents required to call a particular function and the values returned after either successful or unsuccessful execution of the function. Where relevant, I have also included notes about a function's quirks and about differences in its behavior under different versions of MS-DOS. Each entry includes a brief assembly-language program example that you can use as a skeleton for setting up your own calls.

Section 3 provides a reference to the most commonly used IBM PC BIOS interrupts, and Section 4 provides a complete reference to the Lotus/Intel/Microsoft Expanded Memory Specification. These sections are organized in the same manner as Section 2.

Your comments, suggestions, and queries about this book and the programming examples included in it and the companion disk are welcome. You can contact me via MCI Mail (user name *LMI*), CompuServe (user ID *72406,1577*), or by leaving a note on the Laboratory Microsystems RBBS at (213)306-3530. This RBBS supports 300, 1200, or 2400 baud, and is available from 6:00 p.m. to 9:00 a.m. Pacific Time on weekdays, and 24 hours a day on weekends and holidays.

Special Offer
COMPANION DISK TO ADVANCED DOS

Save yourself the time and frustration of typing and compiling the many C and assembly-language programs that appear throughout this book. The COMPANION DISK TO ADVANCED MS-DOS offers you the programs and important coding examples in ASCII text format, as well as the programs in executable form. Other helpful programs and coding examples, written by Ray Duncan, are also included. The COMPANION DISK TO ADVANCED MS-DOS is available only be ordering directly from Microsoft Press. To order, use the special bind-in card at the back of the book. If the card has already been used, you can send $15.95 for each disk ordered (California residents add $.96 sales tax per disk; Washington State residents add $1.29 per disk) to: Microsoft Press, ADVANCED MS-DOS COMPANION DISK OFFER, 13221 SE 26th, Suite L, Bellevue, WA 98005. Add $1.00 per disk for domestic postage and handling; $2.00 per disk for foreign orders. Payment must be in U.S. funds. You may pay by check or money order (payable to Microsoft Press), or by American Express, VISA, or MasterCard; please include both your credit card number and the expiration date. Allow four weeks for delivery.

SECTION I

Chapter 1

Genealogy of MS-DOS

MS-DOS is an operating system that is rapidly evolving. A new major or minor version has been released at least once a year for the last three years (Figure 1-1), and more versions are known to be on the way. Due largely to its adoption by IBM, and to the enormous wave of third-party software that followed the success of the IBM PC, MS-DOS has become the dominant operating system for personal computers that use the Intel 8086 family of microprocessors. With several million licensed copies in use, the number of users of MS-DOS dwarfs the total number of users of all of its competitors (CP/M-86, Concurrent DOS, P-system, iRMX-86, XENIX, and UNIX).

From the programmer's point of view, the current versions of MS-DOS (versions 2 and 3) are robust, rich, and powerful development environments. A broad selection of high-quality programming tools is available from both Microsoft and other software houses. Porting existing applications into the MS-DOS environment is relatively simple, since the programmer can choose to view MS-DOS as either a superset of CP/M or a subset of UNIX.

The progenitor of MS-DOS was an operating system called 86-DOS, which was written by Tim Paterson for Seattle Computer Products in mid-1980. At that time, Digital Research's CP/M-80 was the operating system most commonly used on microcomputers, and a decent though not extensive range of application software (word processors, database managers, and so forth) was available for use with it. In order to ease the process of porting 8-bit CP/M-80 applications into the new 16-bit environment, 86-DOS was originally designed to mimic CP/M-80 in both functions available and style of operation. Consequently, the structures of 86-DOS's file control blocks, program segment prefixes, and executable files were nearly identical to those of CP/M-80. Existing CP/M programs could be converted mechanically (by processing their source-code files through a special translator program) and, after conversion, would run under 86-DOS either immediately or with very little hand editing.

Because 86-DOS was marketed as a proprietary operating system for Seattle Computer Products' line of S-100 bus, 8086-based microcomputers, it made very little impact on the microcomputer world in general. Other vendors of 8086-based microcomputers were understandably reluctant to adopt a competitor's operating system, and continued to wait impatiently for the release of Digital Research's CP/M-86.

In October 1980, IBM approached the major microcomputer-software houses in search of an operating system for the new line of personal computers it was designing. Microsoft had no operating system of its own to offer (other than a stand-alone version of Microsoft BASIC), but paid a fee to Seattle Computer Products for the right to sell Paterson's 86-DOS.

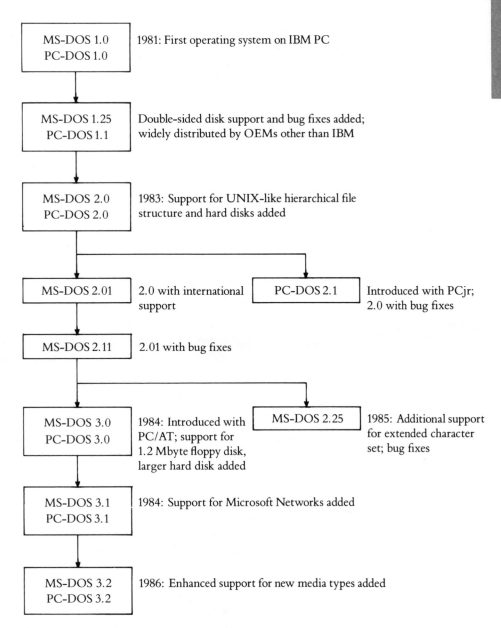

Figure 1-1. The evolution of MS-DOS.

(At that time, Seattle Computer Products received a license to use and sell Microsoft's languages and all 8086 versions of Microsoft's operating system.) In July 1981, Microsoft purchased all rights to 86-DOS, made substantial alterations to it, and renamed it MS-DOS. When the first IBM PC was released in the fall of 1981, IBM offered MS-DOS (referred to as PC-DOS 1.0) as its primary operating system.

IBM also selected Digital Research's CP/M-86 and Softech's P-system as alternative operating systems for the PC. However, they were both very slow to appear at IBM PC dealers, and suffered the additional disadvantages of higher prices and lack of available programming languages. IBM threw its considerable weight behind PC-DOS by releasing all the IBM-logo PC application software and development tools to run under it. Consequently, most third-party software developers targeted their products for PC-DOS from the start, and CP/M-86 and P-system never became significant factors in the IBM PC-compatible market.

In spite of some superficial similarities to its ancestor CP/M-80, MS-DOS version 1.0 contained a number of improvements over CP/M, including:

- An improved disk-directory structure that included information about a file's attributes (such as whether it was a system or hidden file), its exact size in bytes, and the date that the file was created or last modified

- A superior disk-space allocation and management method, allowing extremely fast sequential or random record access and program loading

- An expanded set of operating-system services, including hardware-independent function calls to set or read the date and time, a filename parser, multiple-block record I/O, and variable record sizes

- An AUTOEXEC batch file to perform a user-defined series of commands when the system was powered up or reset

IBM was the only major computer manufacturer (sometimes referred to as OEM, for *original equipment manufacturer*) to ship MS-DOS version 1.0 (as PC-DOS 1.0) with its products. MS-DOS version 1.25 (equivalent to IBM PC-DOS 1.1) was released in June 1982 to fix a number of bugs, and also to support double-sided disks and improved hardware independence in the DOS kernel. This version was shipped by several vendors besides IBM, including Texas Instruments, Compaq, and Columbia, who all entered the personal-computer market early. Today, due mainly to the increasing prevalence of hard-disk-based systems, MS-DOS version 1 is no longer in common use.

MS-DOS version 2.0 (equivalent to PC-DOS 2.0) was first released in March 1983. It was, in retrospect, a totally new operating system (though great care was taken to maintain compatibility with MS-DOS version 1). It contained many significant innovations and enhanced features, including:

- Support for both larger-capacity flexible disks and hard disks
- Many UNIX-like features, including a hierarchical file structure, file handles, I/O redirection, pipes, and filters
- Background printing (print spooling)
- Volume labels, plus additional file attributes
- Installable device drivers
- A user-customizable system-configuration file that controlled the loading of additional device drivers, the number of system disk buffers, and so forth
- Maintenance of program environment blocks that could be used to pass information between programs
- An optional ANSI display driver that allowed programs to position the cursor and control display characteristics in a hardware-independent manner
- Support for the dynamic allocation, modification, and release of memory blocks by application programs
- Support for customized user command interpreters (shells)
- System tables to assist application software in modifying its currency, time, and date formats (known as *international support*)

MS-DOS version 2.11 was subsequently released to improve international support (table-driven currency symbols, date formats, decimal-point symbols, currency separators, and so forth), to add support for 16-bit Kanji characters throughout, and to fix a few minor bugs.

As this book is being written, MS-DOS version 2.11 is the base version being shipped for 8086/8088-based personal computers by nearly all major OEMs, including Hewlett-Packard, Wang, DEC, Texas Instruments, Compaq, and Tandy. It is therefore the version that applications should be designed to run with.

In MS-DOS version 2.25, released in October 1985, the international support was extended even further for Japanese and Korean character sets, additional bugs were repaired, and many of the system utilities were made compatible with MS-DOS version 3.0.

MS-DOS version 3.0 was first introduced by IBM in August 1984, with the release of the 80286-based PC/AT machines and, at the time of this writing, it is gradually becoming available from other OEMs as well. It includes the following major new features:

- Direct control of the print spooler by application software

- Further expansion of international support over version 2.11 (but not as extensive as the expansion for 2.25)

- Extended error reporting, including a code that suggests a recovery strategy to the calling program

- Support for file and record locking and sharing, facilitating the creation of networked applications

- Support for larger hard disks

Additional support for Microsoft Networks and some bug fixes were incorporated in MS-DOS version 3.1, which was released in November 1984, shortly after version 3.0.

By mid-1986, Microsoft had released MS-DOS version 3.2, to support 3½-inch floppy disks and to integrate formatting into the peripheral device driver.

It is interesting to observe the steady growth of MS-DOS since its humble beginnings. Version 1 of the operating system occupied about 16K of RAM and would run applications nicely on a 64K machine. MS-DOS version 2 consumed about 24K of RAM (or more, if there were any installed device drivers) and required a 128K machine to do anything useful. MS-DOS version 3 occupies 36K of RAM and can require considerably more with the file-sharing support and some user-installed drivers loaded (it is usually run on machines with at least 512K of RAM).

Looking to the future, a special version of MS-DOS is reported to be a full multitasking operating system, and another version is expected by industry pundits to be capable of running on the 80286 processor in protected mode, while providing upward compatibility for most existing MS-DOS applications. Such a technically complex operating system will open the door to full exploitation of the 80286's ability to address 16 megabytes of physical memory and 1 gigabyte of virtual memory.

MS-DOS in Operation

It is unlikely that you will ever be called upon to configure the MS-DOS software for a new model of computer. Still, an acquaintance with the general structure of MS-DOS can often be very helpful in understanding the behavior of the system as a whole. In this chapter, we will discuss how MS-DOS is organized and how it is loaded into memory when the computer is turned on.

The Structure of MS-DOS

MS-DOS is partitioned into several layers that serve to isolate the kernel logic of the operating system, and the user's perception of the system, from the hardware it is running on. These layers are:

- The BIOS (Basic I/O System)
- The DOS kernel
- The command processor (shell)

We'll discuss the functions of each of these layers separately.

The BIOS Module

The BIOS is specific to the individual computer system and is provided by the manufacturer of the system. It contains the default resident hardware-dependent drivers for the following devices:

- Console display and keyboard (CON)
- Line printer (PRN)
- Auxiliary device (AUX)
- Date and time (CLOCK)
- Boot disk device (block device)

The MS-DOS kernel communicates with these device drivers through I/O request packets; the drivers then translate these requests into the proper commands for the various hardware controllers. In many MS-DOS systems, including the IBM PC, the most primitive parts of the hardware drivers are located in read-only memory (ROM), so that they can be used by stand-alone applications, diagnostics, and the system boot program.

The terms *resident* and *installable* are used to distinguish between the drivers built into the BIOS and the drivers installed during system boot-up by DEVICE commands in the CONFIG.SYS file. (Installable drivers will be discussed in more detail later in this chapter and in Chapter 12.)

The BIOS is read into random-access memory (RAM) during system initialization as part of a file named IO.SYS (in PC-DOS 2, the file is called IBMBIO.COM instead). This file is marked with the special attributes *hidden* and *system*.

The DOS Kernel

The DOS kernel implements MS-DOS as it is seen by application programs. The kernel is a proprietary program supplied by Microsoft Corporation, and provides a collection of hardware-independent services called *system functions*. These functions include:

- File and record management
- Memory management
- Character device input/output
- "Spawning" of other programs
- Access to the real-time clock

Programs can access the system functions by loading registers with function-specific parameters and then transferring to the operating system via a call, or *software interrupt*.

The DOS kernel is read into memory during system initialization from the MSDOS.SYS file on the boot disk (in PC-DOS systems, the file is called IBMDOS.COM). This file is marked with the attributes hidden and system.

The Command Processor

The command processor, or shell, is the user's interface to the operating system. It is responsible for parsing and carrying out user commands, including the loading and execution of other programs from a disk or other mass-storage device.

The default shell provided with MS-DOS is found in a file called COMMAND.COM. Although COMMAND.COM's prompts and responses constitute the ordinary user's complete perception of MS-DOS, it is important to realize that COMMAND.COM is *not* the operating system, but simply a special class of program running under the control of MS-DOS.

COMMAND.COM can be replaced with a shell of the programmer's own design by simply adding a line to the system-configuration file (CONFIG.SYS) on the boot disk. For example, the Hewlett-Packard MS-DOS computers (the TouchScreen HP-150, the Portable HP-110, and the Vectra) are sold with a powerful screen-oriented proprietary shell called the Personal Applications Manager. Most Hewlett-Packard microcomputer owners have never even seen the MS-DOS *A>* prompt that is so familiar to IBM PC users.

More about COMMAND.COM

The default MS-DOS shell, COMMAND.COM, is divided into three parts:

- A resident portion
- An initialization section
- A transient module

The resident portion is loaded in lower memory, above the DOS kernel and its buffers and tables. It contains the routines to process Ctrl-Cs and Ctrl-Breaks, critical errors, and the termination (final exit) of other transient programs. This part of COMMAND.COM issues error messages and is responsible for the familiar prompt:

Abort, Retry, Ignore?

It also contains the code required to reload the transient portion of COMMAND.COM when necessary.

The initialization section of COMMAND.COM is loaded above the resident portion when the system is booted. It processes the AUTOEXEC batch file (the user's list of commands to execute at system boot time) if one is present, and is then discarded.

The transient portion of COMMAND.COM is loaded at the high end of memory, and its memory can also be used for other purposes by application programs. The transient module issues the user prompt, reads the commands from the keyboard or batch file, and causes them to be executed. When an application program terminates, the resident portion of COMMAND.COM does a checksum of the transient module to determine whether it has been destroyed, and fetches a fresh copy from the disk if necessary.

The user commands accepted by COMMAND.COM fall into three categories:

- Internal commands
- External commands
- Batch files

Internal commands, sometimes called *intrinsic* commands, are those carried out by code embedded in COMMAND.COM itself. Commands in this category include COPY, REN(AME), DIR(ECTORY), and DEL(ETE). The routines for the internal commands are included in the transient part of COMMAND.COM.

External commands, sometimes called *extrinsic* commands or *transient programs*, are the names of programs stored in disk files. Before these programs can be executed, they must be loaded from the disk into the *transient program area* (TPA) of memory (see "How MS-DOS Is Loaded" in this chapter). Familiar examples of external commands are CHKDSK, BACKUP, and RESTORE. As soon as an external command has completed its work, it is discarded from memory; hence, it must be reloaded from disk each time it is invoked.

Batch files are text files that contain lists of other intrinsic, extrinsic, or batch commands. These files are processed by a special interpreter that is built into the transient portion of COMMAND.COM. The interpreter reads the batch file a line at a time and carries out each of the specified operations in order.

In order to interpret a user's command, COMMAND.COM first looks to see if it is the name of a built-in (intrinsic) command that it can carry out directly. If not, it searches for an external command (executable program file) or batch file by the same name. The search is carried out first in the current directory of the current disk drive, then in each of the directories specified in the environment's PATH string. In each directory inspected, COMMAND.COM first tries to find a file with the extension *.COM*, then *.EXE*, and finally *.BAT*. If the search fails for all three file types in all of the possible locations, COMMAND.COM will display the familiar message:

Bad command or file name

If a COM file or EXE file is found, COMMAND.COM uses the MS-DOS EXEC function to load and execute it. The EXEC function builds a special data structure called a *program segment prefix* (PSP) above the resident portion of COMMAND.COM, in the transient program area. The PSP contains various linkages and pointers needed by the application program. Next, the EXEC function loads the program itself, just above the program segment prefix, and performs any relocation that may be necessary. Finally, it sets up the registers appropriately and transfers control to the entry point for the program. (Both the PSP and the EXEC function will be discussed in more detail in Chapters 3 and 10.) When the transient program is finished with its job, it calls a special MS-DOS terminate function that releases its memory and returns control to the program that caused it to be loaded (COMMAND.COM, in this case).

Under MS-DOS 2 and 3, an external command has nearly total control of the system's resources while it is executing. The only other tasks that get accomplished are those performed by interrupt handlers (such as the keyboard-input driver and the real-time clock) and operations the transient program requests from DOS. There is nothing in these two versions of MS-DOS that allows sharing of the central processor among several tasks executing concurrently, or that can wrest control away from a program when it crashes or executes for too long.

How MS-DOS Is Loaded

When the system is reset or powered up, program execution begins at address 0FFFF0H. This is a feature of the 8086 family of microprocessors and has nothing to do with MS-DOS. Systems based on these processors are designed so that address 0FFFF0H lies within an area of ROM and contains a jump machine instruction to transfer control to system test code and the ROM bootstrap routine (Figure 2-1).

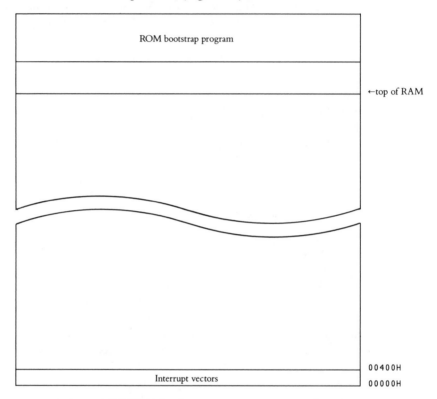

Figure 2-1. A typical 8086/8088-based computer system immediately after power-up or a reset. Execution begins at location 0FFFF0H, which contains a jump instruction that directs program control to the ROM bootstrap routine.

The ROM bootstrap reads the disk bootstrap program from the first sector of the disk (the *boot sector*) into memory at some arbitrary address, and then transfers control to it (Figure 2-2). (The boot sector also contains a table of information about the disk format.)

The disk bootstrap program checks to see if the disk contains a copy of MS-DOS. It does this by reading the first sector of the root directory and determining whether the first two files are IO.SYS and MSDOS.SYS, in that order. If these files are not present, the operator is prompted to change disks and strike any key to try again. If the two system files are

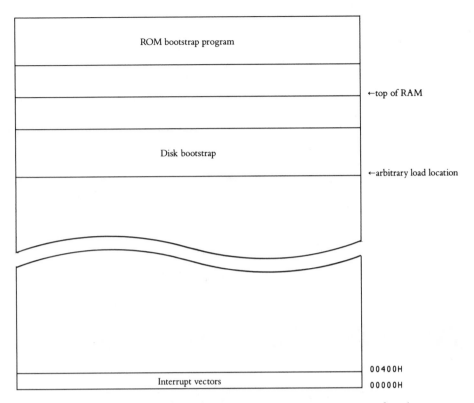

Figure 2-2. The ROM bootstrap routine loads the disk bootstrap program into memory from the first sector of the system-disk device, and then transfers control to it.

found, the disk bootstrap reads them into memory and transfers control to the initial entry point of IO.SYS (Figure 2-3). (In some implementations, the disk bootstrap reads only IO.SYS into memory, and IO.SYS is in turn responsible for loading the MSDOS.SYS file.)

The IO.SYS file that is loaded from the disk actually consists of two separate modules. The first is the BIOS, which contains the linked set of resident device drivers for the console, auxiliary port, printer, and block devices, plus some hardware-specific initialization code that is run only at system boot time. The second module is called SYSINIT. It is supplied by Microsoft and linked into the IO.SYS file, along with the BIOS, by the computer manufacturer.

SYSINIT is called by the manufacturer's BIOS initialization code. It determines the amount of contiguous memory present in the system and then relocates itself to high memory. Then it moves the DOS kernel, MSDOS.SYS, from its original load location to its final memory location, overlaying the original SYSINIT code and any other expendable initialization code that was contained in the IO.SYS file (Figure 2-4).

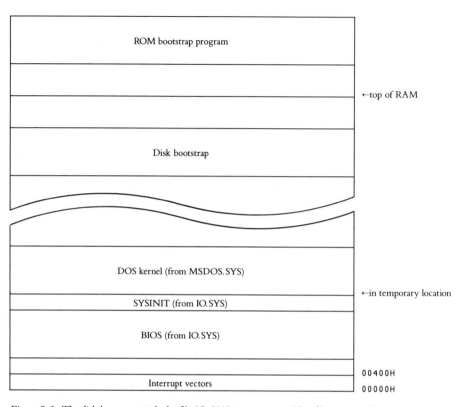

| ROM bootstrap program |
| Disk bootstrap |
| DOS kernel (from MSDOS.SYS) |
| SYSINIT (from IO.SYS) |
| BIOS (from IO.SYS) |
| Interrupt vectors |

←top of RAM

←in temporary location

00400H
00000H

Figure 2-3. The disk bootstrap reads the file IO.SYS into memory. This file contains the MS-DOS BIOS (resident device drivers) and the SYSINIT module. Either the disk bootstrap or the BIOS (depending upon the manufacturer's implementation) then reads the DOS kernel into memory from the file MSDOS.SYS.

Next, SYSINIT performs a call to the initialization code in MSDOS.SYS. The DOS kernel initializes its internal tables and work areas, sets up the interrupt vectors 20H through 2FH, and traces through the linked list of resident device drivers, calling the initialization function for each (see Chapter 12). These driver functions are responsible for determining the equipment status and performing any necessary hardware initialization, as well as for setting up the vectors for any external hardware interrupts the drivers will service.

As part of the initialization sequence, the DOS kernel examines the disk-parameter blocks returned by the resident block-device drivers, determines the largest sector size that will be used in the system, builds some drive-parameter blocks, and allocates a disk sector buffer. The MS-DOS copyright message is then displayed, and control returns to SYSINIT.

Now that the DOS kernel has been initialized and all resident device drivers are available, SYSINIT can call on the normal MS-DOS file services

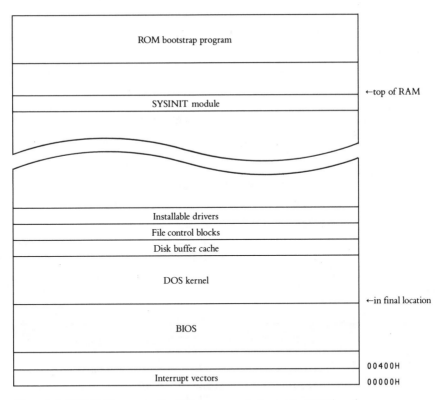

ROM bootstrap program

SYSINIT module ←top of RAM

Installable drivers
File control blocks
Disk buffer cache

DOS kernel

←in final location

BIOS

00400H
Interrupt vectors 00000H

Figure 2-4. SYSINIT moves itself to high memory and relocates the DOS kernel, MSDOS.SYS, downward to its final address. The MS-DOS disk buffer cache and file control block areas are allocated, and then the installable device drivers specified in the CONFIG.SYS file are loaded and linked into the system.

to open the CONFIG.SYS file. This optional file can contain a variety of commands that enable the user to customize the MS-DOS environment.

For instance, the user can specify additional hardware-device drivers, the number of disk buffers, the maximum number of files that can be open at one time, and the filename of the command processor (shell).

If it is found, the entire CONFIG.SYS file is loaded into memory for processing. All lowercase characters are converted to uppercase, and the file is interpreted a line at a time to process the commands. Memory is allocated for the disk buffer cache and the internal file control blocks used by the extended, or *Handle*, file and record system functions (see Chapter 6). Any device drivers indicated in the CONFIG.SYS file are sequentially loaded into memory, initialized by calls to their *init* modules, and linked into the device-driver list. The *init* function of each driver tells SYSINIT how much memory to reserve for that driver.

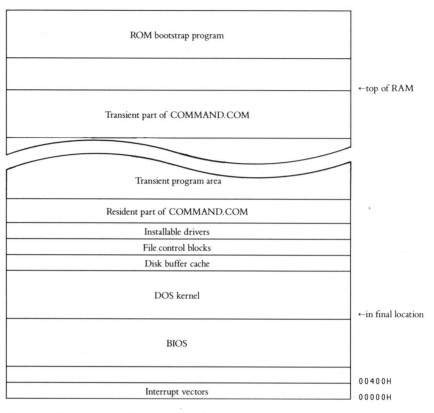

ROM bootstrap program

←top of RAM

Transient part of COMMAND.COM
Transient program area
Resident part of COMMAND.COM
Installable drivers
File control blocks
Disk buffer cache
DOS kernel
BIOS
Interrupt vectors

←in final location

00400H
00000H

Figure 2-5. The final result of the MS-DOS boot process for a typical system. The resident portion of COMMAND.COM lies in low memory, above the DOS kernel. The transient portion containing the batch-file processor and intrinsic commands is placed in high memory, where it can be overlaid by extrinsic commands and application programs running in the transient program area.

After all the installable device drivers have been loaded, SYSINIT closes all file handles and reopens the console (CON), printer (PRN), and auxiliary (AUX) devices as the standard input, standard output, standard error, standard list, and standard auxiliary devices. This allows a user-installed character-device driver to override the BIOS's resident drivers for the standard devices.

Finally, SYSINIT calls the MS-DOS EXEC function to load the command interpreter, or shell (You will recall that the default shell is COMMAND.COM, but another shell can be substituted via the CONFIG.SYS file.) Once the shell is loaded, it displays a prompt and waits for the user to enter a command. MS-DOS is now ready for business, and the SYSINIT module is discarded (Figure 2-5).

Programming for the MS-DOS Environment

Programs that run under MS-DOS come in two basic flavors: There are COM programs, which have a maximum size of approximately 64K, and EXE programs, which can be as large as available memory. In Intel 8086 parlance, COM programs fit the "small model," in which all segment registers contain the same value; that is, code and data are mixed together. EXE programs fit the "medium" or "large model," in which the segment registers contain different values; that is, the code, data, and stack reside in separate segments. There may even be multiple code and data segments, which EXE programs address by long calls and by manipulation of the data segment (DS) register, respectively.

A COM-type program resides on the disk as an absolute memory image, in a file with the extension *.COM*. The file does not have a header or any other internal identifying information. An EXE program, on the other hand, resides on the disk in a special type of file with a unique header, a relocation map, a checksum, and other information that is (or can be) used by MS-DOS.

Both COM and EXE programs are brought into memory for execution by the same mechanism: the EXEC function, which constitutes the MS-DOS loader. EXEC can be called with the filename of a program to be loaded by COMMAND.COM (the normal MS-DOS command interpreter), by other shells or user interfaces, or by another program that was previously loaded by EXEC. As discussed in Chapter 2, if there is sufficient free memory in the transient program area, EXEC allocates a block of memory to hold the new program, builds the program segment prefix at its base, and then reads the program into memory immediately above the PSP. Finally, EXEC sets up the segment registers and the stack, and transfers control to the program.

When it is invoked, EXEC can be given the addresses of additional information, such as a command tail, file control blocks, and an environment block; if supplied, this information will be passed on to the new program. (The exact procedure for using the EXEC function in your own programs is discussed, with examples, in Chapter 10.)

COM and EXE programs are often referred to as *transient programs*. A transient program "owns" the memory block it has been allocated and has nearly total control of the system's resources while it is executing. When the program terminates, either because it is aborted by the operating system or because it has completed its work and systematically performs a final exit back to MS-DOS, the memory block is then freed (hence the term *transient*) and can be used by the next program in line to be loaded.

The Program Segment Prefix

A thorough understanding of the program segment prefix is vital to successful programming under current versions of MS-DOS. It is a reserved area, 256 bytes long, that is set up by MS-DOS at the base of the memory block allocated to a transient program. The PSP contains some linkages to MS-DOS that can be used by the transient program, some information that is being saved by MS-DOS for its own purposes, and some information that is being passed from MS-DOS to the transient program—to be used or not, as the program requires (Figure 3-1).

In the first versions of MS-DOS, the program segment prefix was designed to be compatible with a control area that was built beneath transient programs under Digital Research's venerable CP/M operating system, so that programs could be ported to MS-DOS without extensive logical changes.

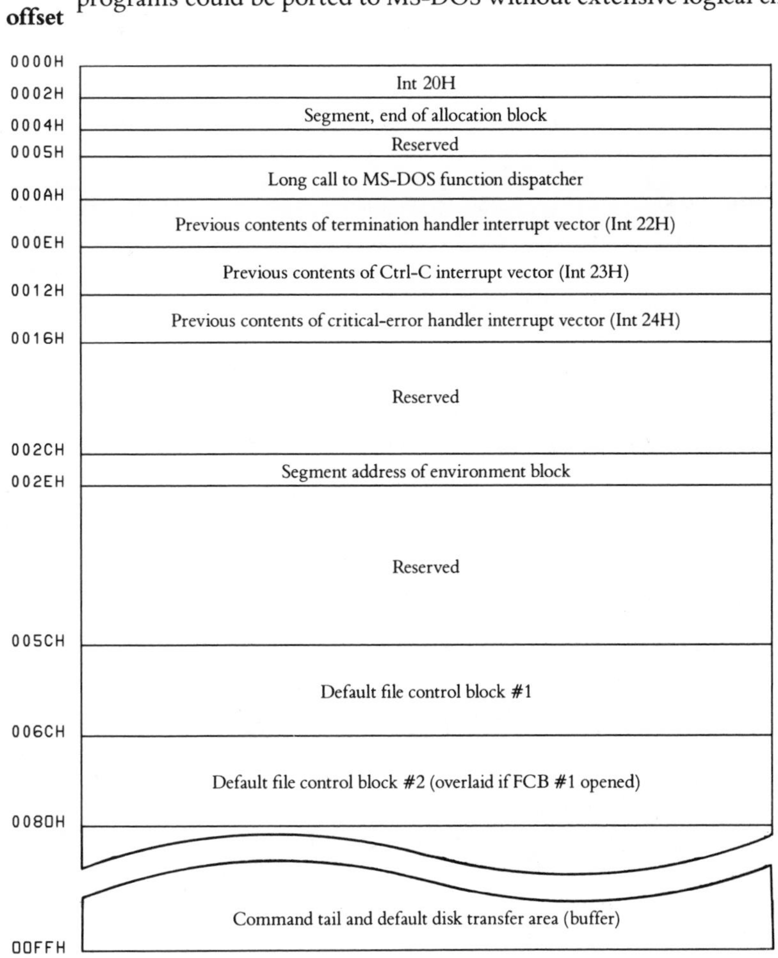

offset

offset	
0000H	Int 20H
0002H	Segment, end of allocation block
0004H	Reserved
0005H	Long call to MS-DOS function dispatcher
000AH	Previous contents of termination handler interrupt vector (Int 22H)
000EH	Previous contents of Ctrl-C interrupt vector (Int 23H)
0012H	Previous contents of critical-error handler interrupt vector (Int 24H)
0016H	Reserved
002CH	Segment address of environment block
002EH	Reserved
005CH	Default file control block #1
006CH	Default file control block #2 (overlaid if FCB #1 opened)
0080H	Command tail and default disk transfer area (buffer)
00FFH	

Figure 3-1. The structure of the program segment prefix.

Although MS-DOS has evolved considerably since those early days, the structure of the PSP is still recognizably similar to its CP/M equivalent. Programmers who are familiar with CP/M file control blocks and calling conventions should feel at ease here.

Offset 0000H in the PSP contains a linkage to the MS-DOS process termination handler, which cleans up after the program has finished its job and performs a final exit. Similarly, offset 0005H in the PSP contains a linkage to the MS-DOS function dispatcher, which performs disk operations, console input/output, and other such services at the request of the transient program. Thus, for the benefit of mechanically translated application programs, calls to *PSP:0000* and *PSP:0005* have the same effect as *CALL 0000* and *CALL 0005* under CP/M (these linkages are not the "approved" means of obtaining these services, however).

The word at offset 0002H in the PSP contains the segment address of the top of the transient program's allocated memory block. The program can use this value to determine whether it should request more memory to do its job, or whether it has extra memory that it can release for use by other processes.

Offsets 000AH through 0015H in the PSP contain the previous contents of the interrupt vectors for the termination, Ctrl-C, and critical error handlers. If the transient program alters these vectors for its own purposes, MS-DOS will restore the original values saved in the PSP when the program performs its final exit.

The word at PSP offset 002CH holds the segment address of the environment block, which contains a series of ASCIIZ strings (sequences of ASCII characters terminated by a null or zero byte). The environment block is inherited from the program that called the EXEC function to load the currently executing program. It contains such information as the current search path used by COMMAND.COM to find executable programs, the location on the disk of COMMAND.COM itself, and the format of the user prompt used by COMMAND.COM.

The *command tail*—the remainder of the command line that invoked the transient program, after the program's name—is copied into the program segment prefix starting at offset 0081H . The length of the command tail, not including the return character at its end, is placed in the byte at offset 0080H. Redirection or piping parameters and their associated filenames do not appear in the portion of the command line (the command tail) that is passed to the transient program, because redirection is supposed to be transparent to applications.

To provide compatibility with CP/M, MS-DOS parses the first two parameters in the command tail into two default *file control blocks* (FCBs) at PSP:005CH and PSP:006CH, under the assumption that they may be filenames. However, if the parameters are filenames that include a path specification, only the drive code will be valid in these default FCBs, since FCB-type file- and record-access functions do not support hierarchical file structures. Although the default FCBs were an aid in earlier years, when compatibility with CP/M was more of a concern, they are essentially useless in modern MS-DOS application programs that must provide full path support. (File control blocks are discussed in detail in Chapter 6 and hierarchical file structures are discussed in Chapter 7.)

The 128-byte area from 0080H through 00FFH in the PSP also serves as the default *disk transfer area* (DTA), which is set by MS-DOS before passing control to the transient program. If the program does not explicitly change the DTA, any file read or write operations requested with the FCB group of function calls will automatically use this area as a data buffer. This is rarely useful, and is another facet of MS-DOS's handling of the PSP that is present only for compatibility with CP/M.

Warning: Programs must not alter any part of the PSP below offset 005CH.

Introduction to COM Programs

Programs of the COM persuasion are stored in disk files that hold an absolute image of the machine instructions to be executed. Since the files contain no relocation information, they are much more compact, and are loaded for execution slightly faster, than equivalent EXE files. Note that MS-DOS does not attempt to ascertain whether a COM file actually contains executable code (there is no signature or checksum, as in the case of an EXE file); it will simply bring anything with the COM extension into memory and jump to it.

Since COM programs are loaded immediately above the program segment prefix and do not have a header that can specify another entry point, they must always have an origin of 0100H, which is the length of the program segment prefix. Location 0100H must contain an executable instruction. The maximum length of a COM program is 65536 bytes, minus the length of the PSP (256 bytes) and a mandatory word of stack (2 bytes).

When control is transferred to the COM program from MS-DOS, all of the segment registers point to the program segment prefix (Figure 3-2). The stack pointer (SP) register contains 0FFFEH if memory allows; otherwise, it is set as high as possible in memory minus 2 bytes (MS-DOS pushes a zero word on the stack before entry).

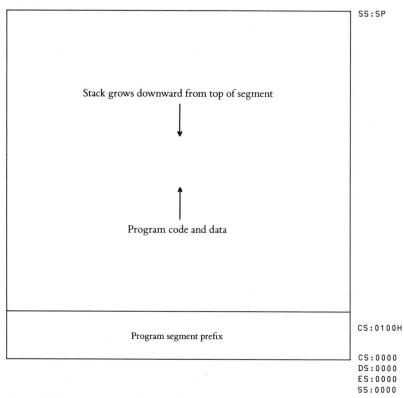

```
                                                          SS:SP



              Stack grows downward from top of segment

                            │
                            ▼




                            ▲
                            │

              Program code and data




                                                          CS:0100H
              Program segment prefix

                                                          CS:0000
                                                          DS:0000
                                                          ES:0000
                                                          SS:0000
```

Figure 3-2. A memory image of a typical COM-type program after loading. The contents of the COM file are brought into memory just above the program segment prefix. Program code and data are mixed together in the same segment, and all segment registers contain the same value.

Although the size of an executable COM file can't exceed 64K, the current versions of MS-DOS allocate all of the transient program area to COM programs when they are loaded. Since many such programs date from the early days of MS-DOS and are not necessarily "well-behaved" in their approach to memory management, the operating system simply makes the worst-case assumption and gives COM programs everything that is available. If a COM program wants to use the EXEC function to invoke another process, it must first shrink down its memory allocation to the minimum memory it needs to continue, taking care to protect its stack. (This is discussed in more detail in Chapter 10.)

When a COM program is finished executing, it can return control to MS-DOS by several means. The preferred method is Int 21H function 4CH, which allows the program to pass a return code back to the program, shell, or batch file that invoked it. However, if the program is running under MS-DOS version 1, it must exit via Int 20H, Int 21H function 0, or a NEAR RETURN. (Since a word of zero was pushed onto the stack at entry, a NEAR RETURN causes a transfer to PSP:0000, which contains an Int 20H instruction.)

A COM-type application can be linked together from many separate object modules. All of the modules must use the same code-segment name and class name, and the module with the entry point at offset 0100H within the segment must be linked first. In addition, all of the procedures within a COM program must have the NEAR attribute, since all executable code resides in one segment.

When linking a COM program, the Linker will display the message:

Warning: no stack segment

which can be ignored. The Linker output is an EXE file, which must be converted into a COM file with the MS-DOS EXE2BIN utility before execution. The EXE file can then be deleted. (An example of this process is provided in Chapter 4.)

An Example COM Program

The *HELLO.COM* program listed in Figure 3-3 demonstrates the structure of a simple assembly-language program that is destined to become a COM file. (You may find it helpful to compare this listing with the *HELLO.EXE* program later in this chapter.) Since this program is so short and simple, a relatively high proportion of the source code is actually Assembler directives that do not result in any executable code.

The NAME statement on line 1 simply provides a module name for use during the linkage process. If the NAME command is not present in the source file, the first six characters of the text provided in the TITLE statement are used as the module name. If neither of these is present, the Linker will simply use the filename. So the NAME statement is far from mandatory; but it's good practice to use it, not only as an aid to documentation and to understanding the map produced by the Linker, but also to avoid the possiblity of the module name defaulting to something that will cause trouble later.

The PAGE command, when used with two operands as in line 2, defines the length and width of the page. These default to 66 lines long and 80 characters wide, respectively. If you use the PAGE command without any operands, it causes a form feed to be sent to the printer and a heading to be printed. In larger programs, use the PAGE command liberally, to place each of your subroutines on separate pages for easy reading.

The TITLE command, in line 3, specifies the text string (limited to 60 characters) to be printed at the upper left corner of each page. The TITLE command is optional and cannot be used more than once in each assembly-language source file.

```
1              name     hello
2              page     55,132
3              title    'HELLO.COM --- print Hello on terminal'
4      ;
5      ; HELLO.COM utility to demonstrate various parts
6      ; of a functional COM-type assembly-language program.
7      ;
8      ; Ray Duncan, September 1983
9      ;
10                                     ;show use of some EQUATES:
11     cr     equ      0dh             ;ASCII carriage return
12     lf     equ      0ah             ;ASCII line feed
13                                     ;
14     ;
15                                     ;begin the "Code" segment
16                                     ;containing executable
17                                     ;machine code.
18     cseg   segment  para public 'CODE'
19     ;
20            org      100h            ;COM files always have
21                                     ;ORIGIN of 100H.
22
23            assume   cs:cseg,ds:cseg,es:cseg,ss:cseg
24     ;
25     print  proc     near            ;actual program code
26                                     ;is completely contained
27                                     ;in the "procedure" named
28                                     ;"PRINT".  At entry all
29                                     ;segment registers are =,
30                                     ;SP contains FFFEH,
31                                     ;and there is a zero on
32                                     ;top of the stack.
33                                     ;
34                                     ;put the offset of the
35                                     ;message text into DX.
36            mov      dx,offset message
37                                     ;now DS:DX specifies the
38                                     ;full address of the message.
39            mov      ah,9            ;use the MS-DOS function 9
40            int      21h             ;to print the string.
41                                     ;
42            mov      ax,4c00h        ;exit back to MS-DOS
43            int      21h             ;with a "return code" of zero.
44                                     ;
45     print  endp                     ;end of the "procedure"
46                                     ;named "PRINT"
47                                     ;
48                                     ;for COM programs,
49                                     ;constants and variables
```

(continued)

Figure 3-3. The HELLO.COM *program listing.*

```
50                              ;are in the same segment as
51                              ;the executable code.
52                              ;
53  message  db       cr,lf,'Hello!',cr,lf,'$'
54                              ;
55  cseg     ends             ;end of the code segment
56                              ;containing executable
57                              ;program
58
59                              ;the final "End" statement
60                              ;signals the end of this
61                              ;program source file, and gives
62                              ;the starting address of
63                              ;the executable program.
64           end      print
```

Figure 3-3 continued.

Dropping down past a few comments and EQUATE statements, we come to a declaration of a code segment that begins in line 18 with a SEGMENT command and ends in line 55 with an ENDS command. The code segment is given the name *cseg* by the label in the leftmost field of line 18, and is given certain attributes—*para*, *public*, and *'CODE'*—by the operand fields at the right end of the line. (You might find it helpful to read the Microsoft Macro Assembler manual for detailed explanations of each possible segment attribute.)

Since this program is going to be converted into a COM file, all of its executable code and data areas must lie within one code segment. The program must also have its origin at offset 0100H (immediately above the program segment prefix), which is taken care of by the ORG statement in line 20.

Following the ORG instruction, we encounter an ASSUME statement on line 23. The concept of ASSUME often baffles new assembly-language programmers. In a way, ASSUME doesn't "do" anything; it simply tells the Assembler which segment registers you are going to use to point to the various segments of your program, so that the Assembler can provide segment overrides when they are necessary. It's important to notice that the ASSUME statement doesn't take care of loading the segment registers with the proper values; it just notifies the Assembler of *your* intent to do that within your program. (Remember that in the case of a COM program, the segment registers are all initialized by MS-DOS before entry to point to the program segment prefix.)

Within the code segment, we come to another type of block declaration that begins with the PROC command on line 25 and closes with ENDP on line 45. These two instructions declare the beginning and end of a *procedure*, a block of executable code that performs a single distinct function. The procedure is given a name by the label in the leftmost field of the PROC statement (in this case, *print*) and an attribute in the operand field. If the procedure carries the NEAR attribute, it can be called only by other code in the same segment, whereas if it carries the FAR attribute, it can be called by code located anywhere in the 8086/8088's memory-addressing space. In COM programs, all procedures carry the NEAR attribute.

For the purposes of this example program, I have kept the *print* procedure almost ridiculously simple. The offset of the string containing the message *Hello!* is loaded into the DX register, and then MS-DOS function 9, which displays strings, is called via the standard MS-DOS Int 21H to send the message to the video screen. Finally, the procedure calls function 4CH to terminate the program.

The END statement in line 64 tells the Assembler that it has reached the end of the source file, and also specifies the entry point for the program. If the entry point is not a label located at offset 0100H, the EXE file resulting from the assembly and linkage of this source program cannot be converted into a COM file.

Introduction to EXE Programs

We have just discussed a program that was written in such a way that it could be assembled into a COM file. Such a program is simple in structure, so a programmer who needs to put together this kind of quick utility can concentrate on the program logic and do a minimum amount of worrying about control of the Assembler. However, programs of the COM type have some definite disadvantages and, as a result, most serious assembly-language efforts for MS-DOS are written to be converted into EXE files.

While COM programs are effectively restricted to a total size of 64K for machine code, data, and stack combined, EXE programs can be practically unlimited in size (up to the limit of the computer's available memory). EXE programs also place the code, data, and stack in separate modules for the loader. At present, since MS-DOS does not support multiple concurrent tasks, this is only marginally important. But when multitasking versions of MS-DOS appear on the scene, the ability to load different parts of large programs into several separated memory fragments, as well as the opportunity to designate a "pure" code portion of your program that can be shared by several tasks, will become very significant.

An EXE program is always brought into memory by the MS-DOS loader immediately above the program segment prefix, although the order of the code, data, and stack segments may vary (Figure 3-4). The EXE file has a *header*, or block of control information, that has a characteristic format (Figures 3-5 and 3-6 on pages 30 and 31). The size of this header varies

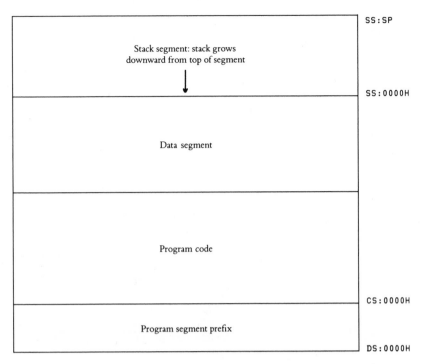

Figure 3-4. A memory image of a typical EXE-type program just after loading. The contents of the EXE file are relocated and brought into memory above the program segment prefix. Code, data, and stack reside in separate segments and need not be in the order shown here. The entry point can be anywhere in the code segment, and is specified by the END statement in the main module of the program. When the program receives control, the DS and ES registers point to the program segment prefix; the program usually saves this value and then resets the DS and ES registers to point to its data area.

according to the number of program instructions that need to be relocated at load time, but is always a multiple of 512 bytes.

Before MS-DOS transfers control to the program, the initial values of the code segment (CS) register and instruction pointer (IP) register are calculated from the entry-point information in the EXE file header and the program's load address. This information derives from an END statement in the source code for one of the program's modules. The data segment (DS) and extra segment (ES) registers are made to point to the program segment prefix, so that the program can access the environment-block pointer, command tail, and other useful information contained there.

The initial contents of the stack segment (SS) and stack pointer (SP) registers come from the header. This information derives from the declaration of a segment with the attribute STACK somewhere in the program's source code. The memory space allocated for the stack may be initialized or uninitialized, depending upon the stack-segment definition; many

Offset	Description
0000H	
0001H	First part of EXE file signature (4DH)
0002H	Second part of EXE file signature (5AH)
0004H	Length of file MOD 512
0006H	Size of file in 512-byte pages, including header
0008H	Number of relocation table items
000AH	Size of header in paragraphs (16-byte units)
000CH	Minimum number of paragraphs needed above program
000EH	Maximum number of paragraphs desired above program
0010H	Segment displacement of stack module
0012H	Contents of SP register at entry
0014H	Word checksum
0016H	Contents of IP register at entry
0018H	Segment displacement of code module
001AH	Offset of first relocation item in file
001BH	Overlay number (0 for resident part of program)
	Variable reserved space
	Relocation table
	Variable reserved space
	Program and data segments
	Stack segment

Figure 3-5. The format of an EXE load module.

programmers like to initialize the stack memory with a recognizable data pattern, so that they can inspect memory dumps and determine how much stack space is actually used by the program.

When an EXE program has finished processing, it should return control to MS-DOS through Int 21H function 4CH. Other methods are feasible, but offer no advantages and are considerably less convenient (since they usually require the CS register to point to the program segment prefix). They also may not be compatible with future versions of MS-DOS.

```
C>DUMP HELLO.EXE

Record 0001
        0  1  2  3  4  5  6  7  8  9  A  B  C  D  E  F
0000   4D 5A 2B 00 02 00 01 00 20 00 09 00 FF FF 03 00   MZ+..... .......
0010   80 00 22 58 00 00 00 00 1E 00 00 00 01 00 01 00   .."X...........
0020   00 00 00 00 00 00 00 00 00 00 00 00 00 00 00 00   ...............
0030   00 00 00 00 00 00 00 00 00 00 00 00 00 00 00 00   ...............
0040   00 00 00 00 00 00 00 00 00 00 00 00 00 00 00 00   ...............
0050   00 00 00 00 00 00 00 00 00 00 00 00 00 00 00 00   ...............
                                      //
Record 0005
        0  1  2  3  4  5  6  7  8  9  A  B  C  D  E  F
0200   B8 02 00 8E D8 BA 00 00 B4 09 CD 21 B8 00 4C CD   ...........!..L.
0210   21 00 00 00 00 00 00 00 00 00 00 00 00 00 00 00   !..............
0220   0D 0A 48 65 6C 6C 6F 21 0D 0A 24 00 00 00 00 00   ..Hello!..$.....
```

Figure 3-6. A hex dump of the HELLO.EXE *program, demonstrating the contents of a simple EXE load module. Note the following interesting values: the EXE signature in bytes 0000H and 0001H, the number of relocation table items in bytes 0006H and 0007H, the minimum extra memory allocation (MIN—ALLOC) in bytes 000AH and 000BH, the maximum extra memory allocation (MAX—ALLOC) in bytes 000CH and 000DH, and the initial IP (instruction pointer) register value in bytes 0014H and 0015H. See also Figure 3-5.*

The input to the Linker for an EXE–type program can be many separate object modules. Each module can use a unique code-segment name, and the procedures can carry either the NEAR or the FAR attribute, depending upon naming conventions and the size of the executable code. The programmer must take care that the modules linked together contain only one segment with the STACK attribute and only one entry point defined with an END Assembler directive. The output from the Linker is a file with an *.EXE* extension. This file can be executed immediately.

An Example EXE Program

The *HELLO.EXE* program in Figure 3-7 demonstrates the fundamental structure of an assembly-language program that is destined to become an EXE file. At minimum, it should have a module name, a code segment, a stack segment, and a primary procedure that receives control of the computer from MS-DOS after the program is loaded. The *HELLO.EXE* program also contains a data segment to provide a more complete example.

The NAME, TITLE, and PAGE directives were covered in the *HELLO.COM* example program, and are used in the same manner here, so we'll move to the first new item of interest. After a few comments and EQUATE statements, we come to a declaration of a code segment that begins on line 19 with a SEGMENT command and ends on line 49 with an ENDS command. As in the *HELLO.COM* example program, the code segment is given the name *cseg* by the label in the leftmost field of the line, and is given the attributes *para*, *public*, and *'CODE'* by the operand fields at the right end of the line.

```
 1              name     hello
 2              page     55,132
 3              title    'HELLO.EXE --- print Hello on terminal'
 4      ;
 5      ; HELLO.EXE utility to demonstrate various parts
 6      ; of a functional EXE-type assembly-language program,
 7      ; use of segments, and a DOS function call.
 8      ;
 9      ; Ray Duncan, September 1983
10      ;
11                                        ;show use of some EQUATES:
12      cr      equ      0dh              ;ASCII carriage return
13      lf      equ      0ah              ;ASCII line feed
14                                        ;
15      ;
16                                        ;begin the "Code" segment
17                                        ;containing executable
18                                        ;machine code.
19      cseg    segment  para public 'CODE'
20      ;
21              assume   cs:cseg,ds:dseg,ss:stack
22      ;
23      print   proc     far              ;actual program code
24                                        ;is completely contained
25                                        ;in the "procedure" named
26                                        ;"PRINT".
27                                        ;
28                                        ;set Data Segment Register
29                                        ;to point to the Data Segment
30                                        ;of this program, so that the
31                                        ;message we want to print is
32                                        ;addressable.
33              mov      ax,dseg
34              mov      ds,ax
35                                        ;now put the offset of the
36                                        ;message text into DX.
37              mov      dx,offset message
38                                        ;now DS:DX specifies the
39                                        ;full address of the message.
40              mov      ah,9             ;use the DOS function 9
41              int      21h              ;to print the string.
42                                        ;
43              mov      ax,4c00h         ;exit back to DOS with
44              int      21h              ;"return code" of zero.
45
46      print   endp                      ;end of the "procedure"
```

Figure 3-7. The HELLO.EXE *program listing.*

(continued)

```
47                              ;named "PRINT"
48                              ;
49    cseg     ends            ;end of the code segment
50                              ;containing executable
51                              ;program
52                              ;
53                              ;now we define a data segment
54                              ;containing our program's
55                              ;constants and variables.
56    dseg     segment  para 'DATA'
57                              ;
58    message  db       cr,lf,'Hello!',cr,lf,'$'
59                              ;
60    dseg     ends
61                              ;
62                              ;lastly, we define a Stack
63                              ;Segment which contains
64                              ;a scratch area of memory
65                              ;for use by our program's stack.
66    stack    segment  para stack 'STACK'
67                              ;allow 64 words in this case.
68             dw       64 dup (?)
69
70    stack    ends
71                              ;the final "End" statement
72                              ;signals the end of this
73                              ;program source file, and gives
74                              ;the starting address of
75                              ;the executable program.
76             end      print
```

Figure 3-7 continued.

Following the code-segment instruction, we find an ASSUME statement on line 21. Notice that, unlike the equivalent statement in the *HELLO.COM* program, the ASSUME statement in this program specifies several different segment names. Again, remember that this statement has no direct effect on the contents of the segment registers, but affects only the operation of the Assembler itself.

Within the code segment, the main *print* procedure is declared by the PROC command on line 23 and closed with ENDP on line 46. Since the procedure resides in an EXE file, we have given it the FAR attribute as an example, but the attribute is really irrelevant since the program is so small and the procedure is not called by anything else in the same program.

Within the *print* procedure, we first initialize the DS register as we told the Assembler we would do in the earlier ASSUME statement, loading it with a value that causes it to point to the base of our data area. (The CS and SS registers were automatically set up by MS-DOS.) Notice that by this action we have lost the address of the program segment prefix, which was passed in DS; in real life, programs usually save the contents of the DS register at entry, before changing it.

Next, we load the offset of the message string *Hello!* into the DX register, and use MS-DOS function 9 to display the message on the screen, just as we did in the *HELLO.COM* program.

Finally, the *print* procedure performs a final exit back to MS-DOS with an Int 21H function 4CH on lines 43 and 44, passing a return code of zero (which by convention is considered a success).

Now let's examine lines 56 through 60. Here we declare a data segment named *dseg*, which contains the variables and constants used by our program. The Linker knows that this portion of the program does not include any executable machine code. If the various modules of your program contain multiple data segments with the same name, they will all be collected together by the Linker and placed in the same physical memory segment.

Lines 66 through 70 establish a stack segment; PUSH and POP instructions will access this area of scratch memory. Before MS-DOS transfers control to an EXE program, it sets up the SS and SP registers according to the declared size and location of the stack segment. Make sure you allow enough room for the maximum stack depth that can occur at runtime, plus a safe number of extra words for registers pushed onto the stack during an MS-DOS service call. If the stack overflows, it may damage your other code and data segments and cause your program to behave strangely or crash altogether!

The END statement on line 76 winds up our brief *HELLO.EXE* program, telling the Assembler that it has reached the end of the source file and providing the label of the program's point of entry from MS-DOS.

The differences between COM and EXE programs are summarized in Figure 3-8.

	COM program	**EXE program**
Maximum size	65536 bytes minus 256 bytes for PSP and 2 bytes for stack	No limit
Entry point	PSP:0100H	Defined by END statement
CS at entry	PSP	Segment containing module with entry point
IP at entry	0100H	Offset of entry point within its segment
DS at entry	PSP	PSP
ES at entry	PSP	PSP
SS at entry	PSP	Segment with STACK attribute
SP at entry	0FFFEH or top word in available memory, whichever is lower	Size of segment defined with STACK attribute
Stack at entry	Zero word	Initialized or uninitialized
Stack size	65536 bytes minus 256 bytes for PSP and size of executable code	Defined in segment with STACK attribute
Subroutine calls	NEAR	NEAR or FAR
Exit method	Int 21H function 4CH preferred, NEAR RET if MS-DOS version 1	Int 21H function 4CH preferred
Size of file	Exact size of program	Size of program plus header (multiple of 512 bytes)

Figure 3-8. Summary of the differences between COM and EXE programs.

Using the MS-DOS Programming Tools

For the purposes of this chapter, and indeed the remainder of this book, we assume a certain level of familiarity with the architecture and instruction set of the Intel 8086 microprocessor family, and with assembly-language programming in general. Readers who wish a detailed introduction to assembly language or to the 8086/8088 microprocessors should see one of the tutorial works mentioned in the bibliography near the end of this chapter.

Preparing an assembly-language or C program to run under MS-DOS is an iterative cycle with four basic steps:

1. Use of an editor to create or modify a source-code file

2. Use of an assembler or compiler to translate the source file into relocatable object code

3. Use of a linker to transform the relocatable object code into an executable MS-DOS load module

4. Use of a debugger to methodically test and debug the program

Additional utilities frequently used by the MS-DOS assembly-language programmer include EXE2BIN (which converts one type of load module into another), CREF (which generates a cross-reference listing), and LIB (the Library Manager).

All of the examples included in this book were developed using the Microsoft Macro Assembler (MASM), Microsoft C Compiler, Microsoft Linker, and associated utilities, so this chapter is devoted to an operational survey of these tools. This overview, together with the example programs themselves, should provide the experienced programmer with sufficient information to begin writing useful programs immediately. In general, the information provided here also applies to the IBM Macro Assembler or C Compiler and their associated utilities, since these are really the Microsoft products with minor variations and different version numbers.

File Types

The Microsoft assembly-language and C programming tools can process, and create, many different file types. By convention, these have been assigned the following specific extensions:

Extension	File type
.ASM	The assembly-language source program used as the input to the Assembler.
.C	The C source program used as the input to the Microsoft C Compiler

(continued)

Extension	File type
.H	A C *header,* or source-library, file that contains C source code for constants, macros, and functions. This file is merged into other C programs with the *#include* directive.
.OBJ	The relocatable object-code output from the Assembler or C Compiler. This code is then passed through the system Linker to create an executable program file.
.CRF	A file created by the Assembler, containing information that can be processed later by the Cross Reference Utility.
.LST	The program listing created by the Assembler. The listing includes memory locations, machine code, the original program text, and any error messages. This file can be copied to the printer to obtain a hard copy.
.MAP	A listing of symbols and their locations within a load module, produced by the Linker.
.EXE	An executable MS-DOS load module that can contain multiple segments and requires additional relocation at runtime.
.COM	A memory-image executable MS-DOS load module that requires no additional relocation at runtime.
.LIB	A program library that is a collection of OBJ files in a special format manipulated by the Library Manager. The library can be searched by the Linker to resolve program references.
.REF	The cross-reference listing produced by the Cross Reference Utility from the information in a CRF file.

Creating an Assembly-Language Source File

The file that is input to the Assembler is called the *source program*. Source programs consist of lines of standard ASCII text, each line terminated by a carriage-return, linefeed sequence.

Although all of the examples in the Microsoft and IBM manuals use the EDLIN line-oriented editor supplied with MS-DOS to create source files, you can use most of the commonly available screen-oriented editors to write programs. Be careful to set the screen editor's mode so that no unusual control characters or formatting commands are embedded in the text file, as they may cause the Assembler to behave erratically or produce spurious error messages.

A source program is a mixture of comments, assembly-language statements that are translated to executable machine code, and commands that affect the operation of the Assembler itself. Each line of the program consists of up to four fields, in the following format:

name   operation   operand   ;comment

The Name Field

The *name* field is usually optional. The name is made up by the programmer and gives a symbolic identity to a location in the source program. The Assembler later associates this symbol with a numeric value or an actual physical memory address in the object program. In the Microsoft Macro Assembler, a name given to a memory location that contains executable code is called a *label*; a name applied to a data item is called a *variable name*.

A name is created from a combination of the characters A through Z, the digits 0 through 9, and the special characters *?* @ _ . and *$*. The only restrictions on the formation of names are:

- The first character cannot be a numeric digit.

- If a period is used, it must be the first character.

- Only the first 31 characters of a name are significant.

You should avoid using the underscore character (_) as the first character of a name, unless you are specifically writing assembly-language modules for use with the Microsoft C Compiler.

The Operation Field

The *operation* field contains a contracted, symbolic term called a *mnemonic*, which usually must match a predefined list built into the Assembler. Mnemonics may be either assembler instructions, each of which stands for a specific machine instruction and is translated to executable code, or assembler directives called *pseudo-ops*, or *pseudo-operations*.

Pseudo-ops have many diverse actions, including definition of data items, assignment of portions of the program to different segments, control of the format of the program listing, association of values with names, and definition of the limits and attributes of a procedure. The important thing to remember about pseudo-op statements is that they have their effect at assembly time and do not usually result in the generation of any executable code for the final program. (An exception to this is a particularly powerful type of pseudo-op called a *macro definition*, which can be used by the programmer to temporarily extend the Assembler itself with new assembly instructions for special applications.)

The Operand Field

The content of the *operand* field is heavily dependent upon the type of instruction or pseudo-op found in the operation field. The operand field usually consists of one or more operands, separated by commas. Each operand can be a simple or complex expression combining register names, numeric constants, and symbolic values or addresses. When the operation is one of the microprocessor's arithmetic/logical or memory-access instructions, the first part of the operand field is called the *destination* and the second part the *source*. For example, the instruction:

```
ADD    AX,BX
```

means, "Add the contents of BX to the contents of AX, leaving the result in register AX." In this case, AX is the destination operand and BX is the source operand. Unlike some other processors (notably the PDP-11 and, for some instructions, the 68000), the 8086 and 8088 will not let you specify memory locations as both the source and destination of a single instruction. For instance, to move a piece of data from one spot in memory to another, you must load it from the first location into a register as one instruction, and then store it from the register into the desired location as the second instruction—you cannot move the data directly in one action.

The Comment Field

The *comment* field begins with a semicolon (;) and contains free text that is ignored by the Assembler. Comments are used to document and explain the assembly code proper. If the first character in a line is a semicolon, the entire line is treated as a comment. The COMMENT pseudo-op can also be used to delimit multiple lines of comment text.

Each of the four parts of an assembly-language statement (name, operation, operand, and comment) is separated from the next by at least one blank or tab character. The appearance and readability of your programs will be vastly improved if names always start in the first character of a line and if tabs are employed to align the fields of the statements vertically. Although the Assembler allows your source-code lines to be as long as 128 characters, in practice you should keep them much shorter, so that they will not be truncated or wrap around on the program listing, making it less readable.

Using the Microsoft Macro Assembler

When beginning a program translation, the Macro Assembler needs the following information:

- The name of the file containing the source program
- The filename for the object program to be created

- The destination of the program listing

- The filename for the information that is later processed by CREF

The Assembler can be invoked in two ways. If you enter the name of the Assembler alone, you will be prompted for the names of each of the various input and output files. The Assembler will supply reasonable defaults for all of the responses except the source-file name. For example, if you wish to assemble the file *HELLO.ASM* and enter:

MASM <Return>

at the C> prompt, the following dialogue will ensue:

```
C>MASM
Microsoft (R) Macro Assembler  Version 4.00
Copyright (C) Microsoft Corp 1981, 1983, 1984, 1985.  All rights reserved.

Source filename [.ASM]: HELLO
Object filename [HELLO.OBJ]:
Source listing  [NUL.LST]:
Cross-reference [NUL.CRF]:

  51004 Bytes symbol space free

     0 Warning Errors
     0 Severe  Errors

C>
```

If you end any response with a semicolon, the remaining responses are all assumed to be the default. Note that the default for the listing and cross-reference files is the NUL device—that is, no file is created.

When you become comfortable with the Macro Assembler, you will find that it is much more efficient to specify all the input and output files on the command line. The format is:

MASM <source>,<object>,<listing>,<crossref> <Return>

For instance, exactly the same result as in the preceding example could have been obtained by entering:

MASM HELLO,,NUL,NUL <Return>

or

MASM HELLO; <Return>

which would use the file *HELLO.ASM* as source, generate the object file *HELLO.OBJ,* and send the listing and cross-reference files to the NUL device (sometimes called the "bit bucket"—that is, the output is simply thrown away).

You can use a logical device name (such as PRN: or COM1:) at any of the Macro Assembler prompts, to send any of the specific outputs of the Assembler to a character device rather than a file.

The Switches

The Macro Assembler accepts a number of optional parameters (*switches*) on the command line, following the file specifications. These parameters influence the arrangement of segments, the generation of symbol tables, the generation of code for the 8087 numeric coprocessor, and the format of listings. Microsoft's version 4.0 of the Macro Assembler accepts the following switches:

Switch	Meaning
/A	Arrange segments in alphabetical order (default).
/B*number*	Set size of source-file buffer (in 1-Kbyte units).
/C	Force creation of cross-reference (CRF) file and add line numbers to program listing.
/D	Produce listing on both passes (to find phase errors).
/D*symbol*	Define *symbol* as null text string (symbol can be referenced by conditional assembly directives in file).
/E	Assemble for 8087 or 80287 emulator using real format.
/I*path*	Set search path for INCLUDE files.
/L	Force creation of program-listing file.
/ML	Preserve case sensitivity in all names (uppercase distinct from lowercase equivalent).
/MX	Preserve lowercase in external names only (names defined with PUBLIC or EXTRN directives).
/MU	Convert all lowercase names to uppercase.
/N	Suppress generation of tables of macros, structures, records, segments, groups, and symbols at end of listing.
/P	Check for impure code in 80286 protected mode.
/R	Assemble for 8087 or 80287 numeric coprocessor.
/S	Arrange segments in order of occurrence.
/T	Suppress all messages unless errors are encountered during assembly.
/V	"Verbose" mode; report number of lines and symbols at end of assembly.
/X	Include false conditionals in listing.
/Z	Display source lines containing errors on screen.

For example, the following command line:

```
MASM /C /S /V HELLO,,HELLO; <Return>
```

would assemble the file *HELLO.ASM,* create the object file *HELLO.OBJ* with segments arranged in the same order as they occur in the source file, produce the listing file *HELLO.LST* (with line numbers) and the cross-reference file *HELLO.CRF,* and report the number of lines and symbols on the screen at the end of the assembly.

In other versions of the Microsoft Macro Assembler, additional or fewer switches may be available. For exact instructions, see the manual for the version you are using.

Remember that the Assembler allows you to override the default extensions on any file. This can be a bit dangerous when you are suffering from lack of sleep! For instance, if in the preceding example you had responded to the *object filename* prompt with *HELLO.ASM,* the Assembler would have happily destroyed your source file. This is not to likely to happen in the interactive command mode, but you must be very careful not to supply the extension when specifying a source-file name as a parameter to a batch file.

Creating a C Source File

As with the Macro Assembler, the source files processed by a C compiler consist of lines of standard ASCII text, each line terminated by a carriage-return, linefeed sequence. You can use virtually any text editor or word processor in non-document mode to create your C source files.

Unlike assembly-language source files, however, C programs can be quite flexible in format. For example, C compilers care nothing about physical ends of lines—they are sensitive only to white space (spaces and tabs) and end-of-statement delimiters (;). Consequently, and perhaps inevitably, the proper formatting of C programs is a hotly debated issue with nearly religious overtones. I would prefer not to venture into those stormy waters in this book; instead, I have used a Microsoft "pretty-printing" program to give the C programs the same style found in other Microsoft Press books.

Running the Microsoft C Compiler

The C programs in this book have been developed and tested using version 3.0 of the Microsoft C Compiler. I selected this compiler over its competitors for my own work at Laboratory Microsystems Incorporated because of its speed, code optimization, support for the 8087 numeric coprocessor, smooth integration with the MS-DOS services, and excellent documentation. However, I have carefully avoided using any implementation-specific tricks or unusual coding practices in this book, so that the example programs should be readily portable to the other C compilers that are available for MS-DOS.

The Microsoft C Compiler consists of four executable files (P0.EXE, P1.EXE, P2.EXE, P3.EXE) that implement the C preprocessor and language translator. Two different control programs—MSC.EXE and CL.EXE—are provided to execute these four files, in the order listed, passing each the necessary information about filenames and compilation options. The MSC control program will be used for the examples in this book, since it closely follows the style of user interaction employed by the Microsoft Macro Assembler and the other Microsoft programming tools. (The CL program has an arcane command syntax designed for compatibility with the UNIX/XENIX C compiler.)

Before using the Compiler and Linker, you need to set up four *environment variables*:

Variable	Action
PATH = *path*	Tells MSC.EXE where to look for the four executable files (P0, P1, P2, P3) if they are not found in the current directory.
INCLUDE = *path*	Tells the Compiler where to look for *#include* files (with the extensions .H) if they are not found in the current directory.
LIB = *path*	Tells the Linker where to look for object-code libraries if they are not found in the current directory.
TMP = *path*	Tells the Compiler and Linker where temporary working files should be placed (*path* can specify a different logical drive from the ones containing the Compiler, the libraries, and the C source files).

These environment variables are most conveniently defined with PATH and SET commands in your AUTOEXEC.BAT file.

When beginning a program translation, the Compiler needs the following information:

- The name of the file containing the source program

- The filename for the object program to be created

- The destination of the program listing

Like the Macro Assembler, the C Compiler can be run with either a dialog-type interaction or a simple command line providing the Compiler with all necessary names and switches. To have the Compiler prompt you for all needed information, simply enter:

MSC <Return>

at the DOS prompt. The Compiler will ask you for the names of the C source file, the resulting object file, and the file or device to receive the object listing, proposing the reasonable default answers for all but the source filename.

For example, if you wished to use the interactive method to compile the file *HELLO.C* into the object file *HELLO.OBJ*, the following dialog would occur:

```
C>MSC
Microsoft C Compiler  Version 3.00
(C)Copyright Microsoft Corp 1984 1985
Source filename[.C]: HELLO
Object filename[HELLO.OBJ]:
Object listing [NUL.COD]:

C>
```

To run the Compiler more quickly, or to use it within batch files, you may wish to supply all necessary information on the command line:

MSC <source file>,<objectfile>,<listingname>

As with the Macro Assembler, if you put a semicolon after any of the file-names, the defaults are taken for the remainder. You could obtain the same result as in the preceding example by entering:

MSC HELLO;

The Microsoft C Compiler supports a vast variety of options that are triggered by switches in the command line or responses to prompts. These switches control optimization, production of listings, generation of 8087 support code, and the like. The following table lists the most commonly used Compiler switches (this is only a partial list of the many options available):

Switch	Meaning
/A*x*	Select memory model for compiled program. Value of *x* may be *S* (for small), *M* (for medium), or *L* (for large). (More complex variant of this switch, with *x* replaced by a string, allows explicit control of code-pointer and data-pointer sizes and segment setup at load time.)
/D*name[= string]*	Define *name* to preprocessor.
/Fa*[filename]*	Produce assembly-language listing (*filename* optional).
/Fc*[filename]*	Produce combined source/assembly-language listing (*filename* optional).
/Fl*[filename]*	Produce object listing (*filename* optional).
/Fo*filename*	Override previously assigned object filename with *filename*.
/FP*string*	Control compilation of floating-point code. Value of *string* generates call to alternate floating-point library, emulator, 8087/80287 library, or in-line 8087/80287 code.
/G*n*	Select code generator for 8086/8088 ($n = 0$), 80186/80188 ($n = 1$), or 80286 ($n = 2$).
/I*directory*	Add *directory* to top of directory list to be searched for *#include* files.
/ND*name*	Set data-segment name.
/NM*name*	Set module name.
/NT*name*	Set text-segment name.
/O*string*	Control optimization via *string* consisting of one or more characters *d* (to disable optimization), *a* (to relax alias checking), *s* (to optimize for minimum code size), and *t* (to optimize for minimum execution time).
/Zd	Include line-number information in object file (for symbolic debugging).

For detailed information on the various switches, refer to the User's Manual for the particular version of Microsoft C you are using.

Using the Linker

The object module produced from a source file by the Macro Assembler or C Compiler is in a form that contains relocation information and may also contain unresolved references to external locations or subroutines. It is written in a common format that is also produced by the various other high-level compilers (such as FORTRAN and Pascal) that run under MS-DOS. Object modules are not suitable for execution by the computer without further processing.

The Linker accepts one or more of these object modules, resolves external references, includes any necessary routines from designated libraries, performs any offset relocations that might be necessary, and writes a file that can be loaded and executed by MS-DOS. The output of the Linker is always in the EXE load-module format (see Chapter 3). However, the system's EXE2BIN utility can be used to convert EXE files that meet certain prerequisites into COM files, which are somewhat more compact (this is discussed in more detail later in the chapter).

Like the Macro Assembler, the Linker can be given its parameters either interactively or by entering all the required information on a single command line. If you simply enter:

LINK <Return>

you will enter a session such as the following:

```
C>LINK

Microsoft (R) 8086 Object Linker  Version 3.05
Copyright (C) Microsoft Corp 1983, 1984, 1985.  All rights reserved.

Object Modules [.OBJ]: HELLO
Run File [HELLO.EXE]:
List File [NUL.MAP]: HELLO
Libraries [.LIB]:
Warning: no stack segment

C>
```

The only input file for this run of the Linker was the file *HELLO.OBJ*; the output files were *HELLO.EXE* (the executable program) and *HELLO.MAP* (the load map produced by the Linker after all references and addresses were resolved; see Figure 4-1).

The equivalent result could have been obtained more efficiently by entering all parameters on the command line in the format:

LINK <object>,<exe>,<map>,<libraries> <Return>

Thus, the linkage command for the *HELLO.OBJ* file could have been entered:

LINK HELLO,HELLO,HELLO,, <Return>

or

LINK HELLO,HELLO,HELLO; <Return>

Note that the entry of a semicolon as the last character of the command line causes the Linker, like the Assembler, to assume the default values for all further parameters.

```
Stack Allocation = 128 bytes


Start  Stop   Length Name                    Class
00000H 00010H 00011H CSEG                    CODE
00020H 0002AH 0000BH DSEG                    DATA
00030H 000AFH 00080H STACK                   STACK



   Address         Publics by Name



   Address         Publics by Value



Program entry point at 0000:0000
```

Figure 4-1. Map produced by the Linker during generation of the HELLO.EXE program in Chapter 3. The program contains one CODE segment, one DATA segment, and one STACK segment. The first instruction to be executed lies in the first byte of the CODE segment. No groups are declared in this simple program. The Start addresses given in the left column are byte offsets relative to the first segment, and are not physical addresses (the latter cannot be known until load time).

A third method of commanding the Linker is through a *response file*. The response file contains lines of text that correspond to the responses you would give the Linker interactively. The name of the response file is specified on the command line with a leading @ character:

LINK @filename <Return>

When entering Linker commands, multiple object files can be specified with the + operator or with spaces. For instance,

LINK HELLO + VMODE + DOSINT,MYPROG,,, <Return>

would link the files *HELLO.OBJ*, *VMODE.OBJ*, and *DOSINT.OBJ*, leaving the result in the file named *MYPROG.EXE*.

If multiple library files are to be searched, they too are connected by + operators. A maximum of eight libraries can be specified. Default libraries are provided with each of the high-level language compilers and will be searched automatically during the linkage process (if the Linker can find them), unless they are explicitly excluded with the /NOD option. The Linker first looks for the default libraries in the current directory of the default disk drive, then along any paths that were given in the command line, and finally along the path(s) specified by the LIB variable, if it is present in the environment block.

The Linker accepts a number of optional parameters as part of the command line or at the end of any interactive prompt. For Microsoft version 3.05 of the Linker, the options are:

Switch	Long form	Meaning
/C:n	/CPARMAXALLOC:number	Set maximum number of 16-byte paragraphs needed by program when loaded; default is 65535.
/D	/DSALLOCATE	Load all data defined in DGROUP at high end of group.
/DO	/DOSSEG	Order segments according to MS-DOS conventions; i.e., class CODE segments, followed by any segments not belonging to DGROUP, followed by all DGROUP segments.
/E	/EXEPACK	Pack executable file, removing sequences of repeated bytes to produce smaller, faster-loading EXE file.
/HE	/HELP	Display information about available options.
/H	/HIGH	Instruct MS-DOS loader to place program as high in memory as possible.
/LI	/LINENUMBERS	Write starting address of each source-code line to map file for use by symbolic debugger.
/M	/MAP	List each public symbol defined in input modules, with its value and segment-offset location in resulting EXE file (list is placed at end of Linker MAP file).
/NOD	/NODEFAULTLIBRARYSEARCH	Skip search of any default compiler libraries specified in OBJ file.
/NOI	/NOIGNORECASE	Do not ignore case in names.
/NOG	/NOGROUPASSOCIATION	Ignore group associations when assigning addresses to data and code items; i.e., fix up external long addresses off segment base even if symbol was defined in segment that is part of a group.
/O:n	/OVERLAYINTERRUPT:number	Set interrupt number used by the overlay manager (normally 03FH).

(continued)

Switch	Long form	Meaning
/P	/PAUSE	Pause during linking, allowing change of disks before EXE file is written.
/SE:*n*	/SEGMENTS:*number*	Set maximum number of segments in linked program (default = 128).
/ST:*n*	/STACK:*number*	Set stack size of program in bytes; ignore stack segment size declarations within program.

For example, the following command line would link *HELLO.OBJ* to create an executable file named *HELLO.EXE*, also create the map file *HELLO.MAP*, and pack the executable file to remove sequences of repeated bytes:

```
LINK /E /M /ST:128 HELLO;  <Return>
```

The number of options available and their actions vary among different versions of the Microsoft Linker. See your Linker instruction manual for detailed information about your particular version.

Using the EXE2BIN Utility

The EXE2BIN utility transforms an EXE file created by the Linker into an executable COM file, if the program meets certain prerequisites:

- It cannot contain more than one declared segment, and cannot define a stack.

- It must be less than 64 Kbytes in length.

- It must have an origin at 0100H.

- The first location in the file must be specified as the *start* address in the END statement.

Since COM programs occupy less disk space than EXE programs, and load slightly faster, it is sometimes convenient to convert small, frequently used utilities into this format. It should be noted, though, that COM files by their very nature are likely to be incompatible with future multitasking versions of MS-DOS.

Another use for the EXE2BIN utility is to convert an installed device driver, after assembly and linking into an EXE file, into a memory-image BIN or SYS file with an origin of zero. This is required in order for the driver to be integrated into the operating system at boot time. The process of writing an installable device driver is discussed in more detail in Chapter 12.

Unlike the other programming utilities, EXE2BIN does *not* have an interactive mode. It always takes its source and destination filenames, separated by spaces, from the MS-DOS command line:

EXE2BIN <sourcefile> <resultfile> <Return>

For example, to convert the file *HELLO.EXE* into *HELLO.COM*, you could enter:

EXE2BIN HELLO.EXE HELLO.COM <Return>

If the source-file extension is not supplied, it defaults to EXE; the destination-file extension defaults to BIN.

The EXE2BIN program also has other capabilities (such as pure binary conversion with segment fixup), but since these are very rarely used, we will not discuss them here.

Using the CREF Utility

The Cross Reference Utility (CREF) processes the CRF file that is optionally produced by the Assembler. It creates a cross-reference listing containing a sorted list of all symbols declared in the program and the line numbers where those symbols are referenced (Figure 4-2). Such a listing is very useful when debugging large assembly-language programs with many interdependent procedures and variables. The cross-reference listing is normally written into a file with the same name as the CRF file, but with the extension *.REF*.

Like the other programming utilities, (except EXE2BIN), CREF may be given its parameters interactively or on a single command line. If you enter

CREF <Return>

the following dialogue appears:

```
C>CREF
Microsoft (R) Cross-Reference Utility  Version 4.00
Copyright (C) Microsoft Corp 1981, 1983, 1984, 1985.  All rights reserved.

Cross-reference [.CRF]: HELLO
Listing [HELLO.REF]:

9 Symbols

C>
```

The parameters may also be entered on the command line in the form:

CREF <cross_ref_file>,<listing_file> <Return>

For example, the same result as in the example above could have been obtained more efficiently by entering:

CREF HELLO,HELLO <Return>

```
Microsoft Cross-Reference  Version 4.00
'HELLO.EXE --- print Hello on terminal'

    Symbol Cross-Reference        (# is definition)                    Cref-1

CODE . . . . . . . . . . . . .   19
CR . . . . . . . . . . . . . .   12    12#    58    59
CSEG . . . . . . . . . . . . .   19    19#    21    49

DATA . . . . . . . . . . . . .   56
DSEG . . . . . . . . . . . . .   21    33     56    56#    61

LF . . . . . . . . . . . . . .   13    13#    58    59

MESSAGE. . . . . . . . . . . .   37    58     58#

PRINT. . . . . . . . . . . . .   23    23#    80

STACK. . . . . . . . . . . . .   21    67     67#    67    74


9 Symbols
```

Figure 4-2. Cross-reference listing HELLO.REF produced by the CREF utility from the file HELLO.CRF (for the HELLO.EXE program example in Chapter 3). The symbols declared in the program are listed on the left in alphabetical order. To the right of each symbol is a list of all of the lines where that symbol is referenced. The line number with a # sign after it denotes the line where the symbol is declared. (The line numbers given in the cross-reference listing correspond to the line numbers that are generated by the Macro Assembler in the program-listing (LST) file, not to any physical line count in the original source file.)

If CREF cannot find the CRF file, an error message will be displayed. Otherwise, the cross-reference listing is left in the specified file on the disk, and can be sent to the printer with the command:

COPY <listing_file> PRN: <Return>

It can also be sent directly to the list device as it is generated, by specifying *PRN* in response to CREF's *Listing* prompt.

Using the Library Manager

As you will recall, the object modules that are produced by the Macro Assembler or by high-level language compilers can be linked directly into load modules for execution by MS-DOS. They can also be collected into special files called *object module libraries*, indexed in such a way that they can be found and extracted when needed by the Linker to resolve references from another program.

The Microsoft Library Manager (LIB.EXE) creates and maintains program libraries, adding, updating, and deleting object files as needed. It is also capable of checking a library file for internal consistency, or printing a table of its contents (Figure 4-3).

The Library Manager (also sometimes called the Librarian) follows the command conventions of the other Microsoft programming tools. You must supply it with the name of the library file to operate on, one or more commands, the name of a listing file or device, and the name of the new library to be produced by the Library Manager session. If no name is specified for the new library, it is given the same name as the old library, and the extension on the previous library file is changed to *.BAK*.

The commands in this case are simply the names of object files, with a prefix character that specifies the action to be taken:

Prefix	Meaning
–	Delete an object module from the library.
*	Extract a module and place it in a separate OBJ file.
+	Add an object module or the entire contents of another library to the program library.

The command prefixes can also be combined. For instance, – + has the effect of replacing a module, while *– has the effect of extracting a module into a new file and then deleting it from the library.

When the Librarian is invoked with its name alone, it will request the other information it needs interactively. For example, the interactive session:

```
C>LIB

Microsoft (R) Library Manager  Version 3.02
Copyright (C) Microsoft Corp 1983, 1984, 1985.  All rights reserved.

Library name: SLIBC
Operations: +VIDEO
List file: SLIBC.LST
Output library: SLIBC2

C>
```

adds the object module *VIDEO.OBJ* to the library SLIBC.LIB, writes a library table of contents into the file *SLIBC.LST*, and leaves the resulting new library in the file *SLIBC2.LIB*.

The Library Manager can also be used in a non-interactive mode by supplying all necessary information on the command line:

```
LIB <library> <commands>,<list>,<newlibrary> <Return>
```

```
_abort...........abort          _abs.............abs
_access..........access         _asctime.........asctime
_atof............atof           _atoi............atoi
_atol............atol           _bdos............bdos
_brk.............brk            _brkctl..........brkctl
_bsearch.........bsearch        _calloc..........calloc
_cgets...........cgets          _chdir...........dir
_chmod...........chmod          _chsize..........chsize

                    .
                    .
                    .

abort           Offset: 00000DC0H  Code and data size: 40H
  _abort

abs             Offset: 00000EE0H  Code and data size: 17H
  _abs

access          Offset: 00000FA0H  Code and data size: 1FH
  _access

aldiv           Offset: 00001040H  Code and data size: 20H
  __aldiv

                    .
                    .
                    .
```

Figure 4-3. Extract from the table-of-contents listing produced by the Library Manager for the Microsoft C library SLIBC.LIB. The first part of the listing is an alphabetical list of all public names declared in all of the modules in the library; each name is associated with the object module to which it belongs. The second part of the listing is an alphabetical list of the object modules in the library, each name followed by its offset within the library file and the actual size of the module in bytes. The name entry for each module is followed by a summary of the public names declared within it.

For example, the following command line would have an effect equivalent to the interactive example just given:

LIB SLIBC + VIDEO,SLIBC.LST,SLIBC2 <Return>

As with the other Microsoft utilities, a semicolon at the end of the command line causes the default responses to be used for any unspecified parameters.

The Librarian is also capable of accepting its commands from a response file containing lines of text that correspond exactly to the responses you would give the Librarian interactively. As with the Linker, the name of the response file is specified on the command line with a leading @ character:

LIB @filename <Return>

The only relevant option for the Library Manager is the switch

/PAGESIZE:*number*

which can be placed immediately after the library filename. The library
page size is in bytes and must therefore be a power of 2 between the values
16 and 32768 (16, 32, 64 . . .); the default is 16 bytes. The page size defines the
size of a unit of space allocation for a given library. Since the index to a
library is always a fixed number of pages, setting a larger page size will
allow you to store more object modules in that library; on the other hand, it
will result in more wasted space within the file.

Debuggers

An object-program debugger named DEBUG.COM is supplied with all
MS-DOS systems. This is a compact, line-oriented utility that allows you
to display and alter memory, assemble or disassemble small portions of
code, set breakpoints, and trace program execution. A simple hex cal-
culator and the capability to read or write I/O ports and logical disk sectors
are also included. The MS-DOS DEBUG program serves the experienced
assembly-language programmer well for quick-and-dirty debugging tasks.
However, its somewhat limited capabilities and lack of screen support
make it unsuitable for extensive use in program development.

A much more powerful and elaborate debugger named SYMDEB is supplied as part of the Microsoft Macro Assembler package. It is capable of
reading MAP files produced by the Linker, displaying the high-level
language source-code lines associated with a particular sequence of object
code, and maintaining separate screens for the output from the debugger
and the output from the traced program. SYMDEB is compatible with all of
the Microsoft assemblers and compilers, though only the most recent
versions of Microsoft C, Pascal, and FORTRAN support the source-line
display option. The SYMDEB commands are a superset of those in
DEBUG.COM, and are easy to learn and use.

There are also a number of innovative and versatile debugging utilities for
the MS-DOS environment available from other software vendors. The most
significant and popular are listed below (the opinions presented here are
completely subjective and purely my own):

- The IBM Resident Debug Tool (RDT) is a full-screen, window-oriented,
  interactive utility that supports the 8087 coprocessor. This is a flexible,
  powerful tool with many runtime options. Unfortunately, very few
  stores carry it. On the negative side, it does suffer from an overly busy
  display and a typically convoluted IBM command syntax.

- Trace-86 from Morgan Computing is a fast, friendly, and robust window-oriented debugging tool that is easy to learn. It was written by Neil Bennett, the author of Professional BASIC. Trace-86 has clean, elegantly designed displays, excellent command syntax checking, and good on-line help. The most recent version of Trace-86 includes 8087 support, the ability to capture screen output by the traced program, and the ability to decompile 8087 mnemonics.

- Advanced Trace-86 from Morgan Computing, although it carries a similar name, is a completely different product, written by Murray Sargent. Advanced Trace-86 has many unusual features, including the ability to breakpoint on specific register contents or instruction opcodes, set conditional breakpoints, track modified memory contents, back up program execution by as many as 20 steps, and add labels to program disassemblies.

- Codesmith-86, written by Eric Osborne and marketed by Visual Age, is a screen-oriented debugger with some interesting features. It is particularly strong in the area of disassembling, labeling, and commenting object code, and then writing the resulting listing into a disk file. However, Codesmith has problems with overly complex displays and an unpredictable command syntax.

- Periscope is a combination hardware/software debugger developed by Brett Salter and sold by Data Base Decisions. The plug-in board includes protected memory and a resident debugger. A remote-breakout switch (which triggers the nonmaskable interrupt) allows the programmer to recover control in almost any conceivable circumstance.

- PDT-PC from Answer Software Corporation and PC-PROBE from Atron are high-performance, professional, combination hardware/software debugging tools. These tools are, unfortunately, very expensive ($1775 and $2495, respectively, at this writing) and thus out of the reach of the casual or freelance programmer.

Finally, you will probably want some type of disk inspection and patching utility. There are many of these available, both commercially and in the public domain. The two best commercial programs I have encountered in this category are The Norton Utilities (Peter Norton, Inc.) and Disk Toolkit (Morgan Computing). Both will allow you to examine or modify the contents of disk sectors, "un-erase" files, and so forth. The Norton program is oriented toward the nontechnical user, and the latest version (3.0) is driven by many layers of menus that can become somewhat cumbersome. The Morgan product is less friendly, but quite efficient.

Reference Books

In addition to the completely indispensable book you are now reading, you will also need access to additional reference materials. I suggest a judicious selection of a few from the following list, after you have browsed through them at your local bookstore. (This list does not reflect any endorsement by Microsoft Corporation.)

- *The 8086 Book*, by Russell Rector and George Alexy. 1980. Osborne/McGraw-Hill, 630 Bancroft Way, Berkeley, CA 94710. ISBN 0-931988-29-2.

- *iAPX 86,88 Programmer's Reference Manual*. 1986. Intel Corporation, Literature Department, 3065 Bowers Ave., Santa Clara, CA 95051. Order No. 210911-003.

- *iAPX 86,88 Hardware Reference Manual*. 1985. Intel Corporation, Literature Department, 3065 Bowers Ave., Santa Clara, CA 95051. Order No. 210912-003.

- *Microsoft Macro Assembler User's Guide*. 1984, 1985. Microsoft Corporation, Box 97017, Redmond, WA 98073. This manual, supplied with the Macro Assembler software, covers the operating instructions for the Assembler and its associated utilities, but also contains much 8086-related programming information of general interest.

- *Microcomputer Systems, The 8086/8088 Family*, by Yu-Cheng Liu and Glenn A. Gibson. 1984. Prentice-Hall, Inc., Englewood Cliffs, NJ 07632. ISBN 0-13-580944-4.

- *IBM PC and XT Assembly Language: A Guide for Programmers*, by Leo Scanlon. 1985. Brady Communications Co., Inc., Simon and Schuster Bldg., 1230 Avenue of the Americas, New York, NY 10020.

- *The IBM Personal Computer from the Inside Out*, by Murray Sargent and Richard L. Shoemaker. 1984. Addison-Wesley Publishing Company, Reading, MA 01867.

- *Assembly Language Primer for the IBM PC and XT*, by Robert Lafore. 1984. The Waite Group, Inc., New American Library, 1663 Broadway, New York, NY 10019. ISBN 0-452-25711-5.

- *IBM PC Technical Reference*. 1985. IBM Corporation, Boca Raton, FL 33432.

- *IBM DOS Technical Reference*. 1985. IBM Corporation, Boca Raton, FL 33432.

- *Programmer's Guide to the IBM PC*, by Peter Norton. 1985. Microsoft Press, Box 97017, Redmond, WA 98073. ISBN 0-914845-46-2.

- *Microsoft MS-DOS Programmer's Reference Manual*, available in several OEM versions (Intel, Hewlett-Packard, Zenith, and others). Microsoft Corporation, Box 97017, Redmond, WA 98073.

If you are programming for 80286-based personal computers, you will also find the following references helpful:

- *iAPX 286 Hardware Reference Manual*. 1983. Intel Corporation, Literature Department, 3065 Bowers Ave., Santa Clara, CA 95051. Order No. 210760.

- *iAPX 286 Programmer's Reference Manual*. 1985. Intel Corporation. Literature Department, 3065 Bowers Ave., Santa Clara, CA 95051. Order No. 210498.

- *iAPX 286 Operating Systems Writer's Guide*. 1983. Intel Corporation. Literature Department, 3065 Bowers Ave., Santa Clara, CA 95051. Order No. 121960.

A Complete Example

Let's demonstrate all the steps needed to assemble and link a simple assembly-language program. Use your favorite program editor to type the source code for the program *HELLO.EXE* in Chapter 3 into a file named *HELLO.ASM*. Once the source file has been created, you can assemble and link it as follows:

```
MASM HELLO,HELLO,HELLO,HELLO <Return>
```

```
LINK HELLO,HELLO,HELLO,, <Return>
```

If no error messages were displayed during the assembly or linking, you will find the file *HELLO.EXE* on your disk. You can execute the file by simply entering:

```
HELLO <Return>
```

If everything went right, you will see a display like this:

```
C>HELLO

Hello!

C>
```

as the file named *HELLO.EXE* is loaded into memory, prints a message via the MS-DOS function calls, and then returns control to COMMAND.COM.

Other files that were created during this process are:

Filename	Contents
HELLO.OBJ	The object code that was used as input to the Linker.
HELLO.LST	The program listing produced by the Assembler.
HELLO.CRF	The raw cross-reference data produced by the Assembler, to be used as input to the CREF utility.
HELLO.MAP	The load map produced by the Linker.

Making Assemblies Easier with Batch Files

The Macro Assembler and Linker always exit back to MS-DOS with a return code that indicates whether or not their task was completed without errors. This return code can be tested in a batch file, to automate the process of producing an executable program from a source-code file.

As an example, the batch file named *MAKECOM.BAT*, shown in Figure 4-4, will create an executable COM file from the ASM file named in the command line, deleting all intermediate files. When this batch file is on your working disk, the command

MAKECOM MYFILE <Return>

will assemble and link the source file *MYFILE.ASM* into the executable program file *MYFILE.EXE*, which is then converted into the executable COM file *MYFILE.COM*. All intermediate files produced during the process are deleted.

Note that the EXE2BIN utility itself does not exit with a return code. To test whether the conversion process was successful, you must delete any pre-existing COM file (line 11) before running EXE2BIN (line 12), and then test for the existence of a new COM file afterwards.

```
echo off
rem    This batch file MAKECOM.BAT is used in the form
rem        C>MAKECOM myfile
rem    and will use the Macro Assembler, Linker, and
rem    EXE2BIN utility to create an executable COM file.
rem
masm %1; >nul
if errorlevel 1 goto asmfail
link %1; >nul
if errorlevel 1 goto linkfail
if exist %1.com  del %1.com
exe2bin %1.exe %1.com
if not exist %1.com  goto comfail
echo *
echo * Assembly and Link successful, COM file created.
echo *
goto exit

:asmfail
echo *
echo * Error detected during Assembly, no files created.
echo *
goto exit

:linkfail
echo *
echo * Errors detected during LINK process, no files created.
echo *
goto exit

:comfail
echo *
echo * Can't convert EXE to COM file, no files created.
echo *

:exit
if exist %1.obj  del %1.obj
if exist %1.exe  del %1.exe
echo on
```

Figure 4-4. Batch file MAKECOM.BAT *used to automate the creation of an executable COM file from an assembly-language source file (ASM).*

Programming the Character Devices

Peripheral devices—that is, devices that supply data to or accept data from the central processing unit—are broadly grouped into character devices and mass-storage devices. In general, character devices supply or accept data one character (or byte) at a time in a serial fashion. The character devices supported by the current versions of MS-DOS are:

- Keyboard
- Video display
- Printer
- Serial port

In contrast, mass-storage devices (block devices) transfer data in blocks of many characters and these blocks are frequently randomly accessible. We will leave discussion of the mass-storage devices for Chapter 6.

The character I/O support in MS-DOS is designed to provide compatibility with both CP/M and UNIX/XENIX. Consequently, there are two more-or-less equivalent groups of MS-DOS function calls to provide hardware-independent communication with the various character devices.

We will refer to the first group of functions as the *traditional* character I/O services. These are a superset of the character I/O functions that were present in the Digital Research CP/M operating system, and facilitate easy porting of programs from that environment.

We will refer to the second group as the *Handle* character I/O functions. A program uses these services by supplying a token, or handle, for the desired output device and the address and length of a memory buffer for the data, in a manner very similar to that used under UNIX/XENIX. Handles are predefined for the commonly used character devices, although a program can also explicitly open these devices for I/O as though they were files, using their logical names. The Handle functions support redirection of input and output, allowing your program to take its input from a file instead of the keyboard (for example) or to write its output to a file instead of the video display.

In addition, if your application program is going to run on an IBM PC or close compatible, there are usually several methods of addressing each character device that can provide increased speed, but do so at the expense of hardware independence and portability to other present or future operating systems. These techniques bypass the MS-DOS services altogether.

Keyboard Input

There are two major classes of keyboard input techniques that can be used by programs written for the IBM PC family and for the MS-DOS environment in general. High-level methods performing character input from the keyboard through standard MS-DOS service calls (Int 21H) allow essentially complete hardware independence and compatibility with other operating systems. MS-DOS is rich in functions that provide keyboard input a character or a line at a time, with or without echo to the screen, and with or without Ctrl-C (Break key) detection.

Alternatively, on machines with known hardware characteristics, such as the IBM PC family, programs can resort to low-level methods of keyboard input that rely on machine firmware (software permanently resident in read-only memory) or on direct access to the keyboard's controller. Programs that use such techniques are nonportable and may cause interference with other tasks in multitasking environments; many of the popular keyboard enhancers and DOS utilities fall into this category.

High-Level Keyboard Functions

One high-level method of keyboard input involves use of the Handle stream I/O functions that were introduced in MS-DOS version 2.0. When an application program receives control, it has already been assigned five handles, or channel numbers, that have been opened to the character devices as follows (we will ignore I/O redirection for the moment):

Handle	Name	Opened to
0	Standard input device	CON
1	Standard output device	CON
2	Standard error device	CON
3	Standard auxiliary device	AUX
4	Standard list device	PRN

These handles can be used, without further preliminaries, to perform read and write operations on their associated logical devices.

As an example, let's use the Handle read system call (function 03FH) to input a line from the keyboard (you will find a more detailed explanation of this function in Section 2):

```
          mov    ah,3fh              ;Fxn 3FH = Read from file or device
          mov    bx,0                ;Handle 0 = standard input device
          mov    cx,80               ;maximum bytes to read
          mov    dx,seg buffer       ;DS:DX = buffer address
          mov    ds,dx
          mov    dx,offset buffer
          int    21h
            .
            .
buffer    db     80 dup (?)
```

When using function 03FH to read from a character device, the exact result depends upon whether the device is in *cooked* or *raw* mode. In cooked mode, the operating system inspects each character as it is received or transmitted, performing special actions when certain characters are detected—therefore, we say that the character stream is *filtered*. In raw mode, the operating system does not take any special action on any characters in the input stream. All the character devices perform their input or output in cooked mode by default, though raw mode can be selected by a program as needed.

In our example, if the standard input is in the default cooked mode, a 128-byte buffer internal to MS-DOS is filled as characters are read from the keyboard. The user is able to edit the input using the Backspace key and any other special function keys, and Ctrl-C will be detected. Once the user presses Enter or Return, the requested number of characters (or the number of characters entered, if less) are copied out of the internal buffer into the calling program's buffer, up to and including the Return at the end. If the standard input is in raw mode, however, the requested number of characters are read regardless of Return, Ctrl-C, or any other control codes. The number of bytes actually read is always returned in register AX.

The standard input is redirectable, so the example code is not a foolproof way of obtaining input from the keyboard. Depending upon whether a redirection parameter was placed on the command line by the user, your input stream might be from the keyboard, a file, another character device, or even the bit-bucket (NUL device)! To bypass redirection and be absolutely sure where your input is coming from, you can ignore the predefined standard input handle and open the console as another file, using the handle obtained from that open to perform your keyboard input. For example:

```
        mov     ah,3dh                  ;function 3DH = OPEN
        mov     al,0                    ;mode = read
        mov     dx,seg fname            ;DS:DX = addr of device name
        mov     ds,dx
        mov     dx,offset fname
        int     21h                     ;transfer to DOS.
        jc      error                   ;jump if device couldn't be opened.
        mov     handle,ax               ;save handle for CON.
          .
          .
          .
        mov     ah,3fh                  ;Fxn 3FH = Read from file or device
        mov     bx,handle               ;get token returned by Open.
        mov     cx,80                   ;maximum bytes to read
        mov     dx,offset buffer        ;DS:DX = addr of buffer
```

(continued)

```
                    int    21h
                           .
error:                     .
                           .
buffer              db     80 dup (?)
fname               db     'CON',0
handle              dw     0
```

(By the way, if you choose not to use the predefined standard devices, you can close those handles (using Int 21H function 3EH), and so free them for use when opening other files or devices.)

The other high-level, machine-independent method of keyboard input is to use the traditional functions that are present in all versions of MS-DOS. Use of this set of system functions simplifies porting applications from CP/M into the MS-DOS environment. These operations have slightly different actions under MS-DOS version 1 than they do under later versions, due to the introduction of I/O redirection in MS-DOS version 2.0. The traditional calls can be summarized as follows:

Function	Action	Ctrl-C checking
01H	Keyboard input with echo	yes
06H	Direct console I/O	no
07H	Keyboard input without echo	no
08H	Keyboard input without echo	yes
0AH	Read buffered line	yes
0BH	Read input status	yes
0CH	Reset input buffer and input	varies

All these calls are affected by redirection of the standard input in MS-DOS version 2.0 or later. The character input calls (01H, 06H, 07H, and 08H) all return a character in the AL register. For example, the following sequence waits until a key is pressed and then returns it in register AL:

```
                    mov    ah,1             ;function 1 = read keyboard
                    int    21h              ;transfer to DOS.
```

The character input calls differ in whether the input is echoed to the screen and whether they are sensitive to Ctrl-C interrupts. Although there is no pure keyboard status call that is immune to Ctrl-C, keyboard status can be read (somewhat circuitously) without interference using function 06H. Extended keys, such as the IBM PC's special function keys, require two calls to a character input function.

As an alternative to use of the single-character input, a program can use a buffered-line input function to read an entire line from the keyboard in one operation. Buffered lines are built up in an internal MS-DOS buffer and are not passed to the calling program until the user presses the Return key. While the line is being entered, all the usual editing keys are active and are handled by the MS-DOS keyboard driver. The traditional buffered-line input function (0AH) is used as follows:

```
          mov   ah,0ah             ;function number
          mov   dx,seg my_buff     ;DS:DX = address of
          mov   ds,dx              ;          input buffer
          mov   dx,offset my_buff
          int   21h                ;transfer to DOS.
          .
          .
          .
my_buff   db    81                 ;max length of input
          db    0                  ;actual length (from DOS)
          db    81 dup (0)         ;buffer for text string
```

This is nearly equivalent to the Handle-type read function discussed on page 65, except that in this case the actual length of the input from the keyboard is returned in the buffer, rather than in register AX.

Ctrl-C checking, which is mentioned in the table of traditional input functions, is discussed in more detail at the end of this chapter. For now, just note that the application programmer can substitute a custom handler for the default MS-DOS Ctrl-C handler, and thereby avoid having the application program lose control of the machine when the user enters a Ctrl-C or Ctrl-Break.

Both the Handle and the traditional keyboard functions are standard features of MS-DOS versions 2 and 3. Programs written using these functions will operate properly on any computer running these levels of MS-DOS, regardless of the hardware configuration.

Low-Level Keyboard Functions

Programmers writing applications for the IBM PC and compatibles can also choose from two hardware-dependent methods of keyboard input.

The first hardware-dependent method, which requires that your software run on a machine with IBM PC ROM BIOS compatibility, is to call the ROM BIOS's keyboard input driver directly via Int 16H. For example, the following sequence will read a single character from the keyboard input buffer and return it in AL:

```
          mov   ah,0
          int   16h
```

The keyboard scan code is also returned in register AH. Other services available from this driver read the keyboard status or return the keyboard status byte (from the ROM BIOS data area 0000:0417H). The ROM BIOS keyboard driver functions are discussed in more detail in Section 3.

In my opinion, there are no real advantages to calling the ROM BIOS keyboard driver rather than the standard MS-DOS keyboard functions. Although you can bypass any I/O redirection that may be in effect, there are other ways to do this without introducing dependence on the PC BIOS. And there are real disadvantages to calling the BIOS keyboard driver:

- It always bypasses I/O redirection, which sometimes may not be desirable.

- It is dependent on IBM PC ROM BIOS compatibility, and will not work correctly, unchanged, on machines such as the Hewlett-Packard Touch-Screen or the Wang Professional Computer.

- It may introduce complicated interactions with resident DOS utilities such as Sidekick and ProKey.

The other and most hardware-dependent method of keyboard input on an IBM PC is to write a new handler for Int 09H and service the keyboard controller's interrupts directly. This involves translation of scan codes to ASCII characters and maintenance of the type-ahead buffer. In ordinary PC applications, there is no reason to take over keyboard I/O at this level; therefore, we will not discuss it further here. If you are curious about the techniques that would be required, the best reference is the listing for the ROM BIOS keyboard driver, included in the *IBM PC Technical Reference Manual*.

Display Output

There are three distinct techniques for video-display control that can be used by programs written for the IBM PC family and MS-DOS in general. The methods offer varying degrees of hardware dependence and performance. Let's begin by examining each of them briefly and discussing their individual benefits and disadvantages.

The high-level methods, which perform all character I/O to the screen through standard MS-DOS service calls (Int 21H), allow essentially complete hardware independence. Under MS-DOS version 1, only teletype-like output capabilities were supported. In version 2, an optional ANSI console driver was added, to allow the programmer to clear the screen, position the cursor, and select colors and attributes via standard escape sequences in the output stream. The throughput using this method is only a fraction of that attainable with direct control of the video hardware, but programs that employ this technique can be executed unchanged on any machine running MS-DOS.

An intermediate low-level approach that performs direct calls to the IBM PC ROM BIOS video driver through a software interrupt results in reasonably fast displays and also provides primitive graphics capabilities. Programs that use the ROM BIOS can write text or individual pixels, as well as selecting display mode, video pages, palette, and foreground/background colors. Such programs will run unchanged on any IBM PC or compatible, but they may not operate properly on other MS-DOS-based computers.

Finally, on computers with a known hardware configuration, programs can control the video display by writing directly to the video controller's registers and *regen buffer* (a dedicated memory area that holds information controlling the appearance of the display). This yields the highest performance of all (good examples are Lotus 1-2-3, PC/FORTH, and the Microsoft Flight Simulator), but essentially locks the program to the hardware configuration. Such programs written for the IBM PC family will not run properly on any but the most compatible of the "clones" (such as the Compaq or the Zenith Z-150). They are also incapable of coexisting in any reasonable manner with other programs in a multitasking environment.

Now let's look at each of these methods more closely.

High-Level Display Functions

The most machine-independent method of display output involves use of the Handle I/O calls that were added in MS-DOS version 2.0. When your application program receives control, it has already been assigned handle 1 for the standard output device and handle 2 for the standard error device. These handles can be used to send strings to the display. For example, you can use function 40H (write to file or device) to send the message *hello* to the screen, as follows:

```
        mov   ah,40h              ;function 40H = write
        mov   bx,0001            ;handle 1 = standard output
        mov   cx,5               ;length of string to write
        mov   dx,seg buffer      ;DS:DX = addr of string
        mov   ds,dx
        mov   dx,offset buffer
        int   21h
        jc    error
        .
        .
        .
buffer  db    'hello'
```

Upon return from the function, AX will contain the number of characters actually transferred. This should be equal to the number of characters requested, except in the case where the output is redirected to a disk file and the disk is full.

As in the case of keyboard input, the fact that the user can specify command-line redirection parameters that are invisible to the application means that, if you use the predefined standard output handle, you can't always be sure where your output is going! However, to make sure your output actually goes to the display, you can use the predefined standard error device handle, which is *always* opened to the CON (logical console) device and is not redirectable.

As an alternative to using the standard output and standard error devices, you can bypass any output redirection and open a separate channel to CON, using the handle obtained from that open operation for character output.

For example, the following code will open the console display for output, and then write the string *hello* to it:

```
        mov     ah,3dh          ;function 3DH = OPEN
        mov     al,2            ;mode = read/write
        mov     dx,seg fname    ;DS:DX = addr of device name
        mov     ds,dx
        mov     dx,offset fname
        int     21h             ;transfer to DOS.
        jc      error           ;jump if device couldn't be opened.
        mov     handle,ax       ;save handle for CON.
        .
        .
        .
        mov     ah,40h          ;function 40H = write
        mov     bx,handle       ;use handle returned from OPEN.
        mov     cx,5            ;length of string to write
        mov     dx,offset buffer ;DS:DX = buffer addr
        int     21h
        jc      error
        .
error:  .
        .
buffer  db      'hello'
fname   db      'CON',0
handle  dw      0
```

Another high-level, hardware-independent method of writing to the display is use of the traditional character output calls. These functions work slightly differently under MS-DOS version 1 than under later versions, because they too are susceptible to redirection of the standard output device under MS-DOS versions 2.0 and above. There are three function calls in this category:

- Function 02H, character output, sends the character in DL to the standard output device. It is sensitive to Ctrl-C interrupts and handles carriage returns, linefeeds, bell codes, and backspaces appropriately.

- Function 06H, raw console I/O, transfers the character in DL to the standard output device, but it is not sensitive to Ctrl-C interrupts. Care must be taken when using this function, since it can also be used for input and for status requests.

- Function 09H, character string output, is passed the address of a string in DS:DX, which is then sent to the standard output device. The string is terminated by the character *$*.

For example, the following code uses the traditional string output function to write the string *hello* to the video display:

```
            mov     dx,seg buffer         ;DS:DX = buffer address
            mov     ds,dx
            mov     dx,offset buffer
            mov     ah,9                  ;function 9 = write string
            int     21h
            .
            .
            .
buffer      db      'hello$'
```

The traditional function calls are slightly faster than the Handle calls when used for single-character output; this advantage disappears, however, when longer strings are sent to the display in a single operation. The Handle calls are to be preferred because of their symmetry with the Handle class of file and record calls covered in Chapter 6.

As with keyboard input, Ctrl-C interrupts can cause problems during output to the display if not properly provided for. This is discussed in detail later in the chapter.

Setting the Raw Output Mode

Substantially increased display speeds for well-behaved application programs can be obtained on many MS-DOS version 2 or 3 systems, without compromising hardware independence, by simply setting the raw output mode bit in the driver's *device information word*. This bit tells MS-DOS not to check for a Ctrl-C from the keyboard between each character it transfers to the output device, and turns off filtering of the output string for other control characters.

The device information word is accessed via the IOCTL function (44H):

```
; Select Raw Output Mode on Standard Output Handle
;
            mov     bx,1                  ;I/O Control Read for
            mov     ax,4400h              ;"device information", using
            int     21h                   ;handle for Standard Output
```

(continued)

```
              mov    dh,0              ;set upper byte of DX = 0.
              or     dl,20h            ;set raw mode bit in DL.

              mov    bx,1              ;I/O Control Write of
              mov    ax,4401h          ;"device information", using
              int    21h               ;handle for Standard Output
```

Note that the program should reset this mode when it exits, if it changes the mode on any inherited handle (such as the five standard device handles). IOCTL is discussed in more detail in Section 2.

Both the Handle and the traditional display output functions are standard features of MS-DOS versions 2 and 3. Programs written using these functions will run properly on any computer running these levels of MS-DOS, regardless of the hardware configuration.

Low-Level Display Functions

Applications written for a known machine environment can often achieve dramatic improvements in throughput to the display, the amount of improvement varying directly with the amount of hardware dependence introduced into the code. In this section, we will briefly discuss some hardware-dependent display techniques for the IBM PC family (a more detailed exposition can be found in Peter Norton's *Programmer's Guide to the IBM PC*). The same general approaches are applicable to machines with other hardware architectures (such as the Hewlett-Packard, Wang, and Texas Instrument personal computers).

On the IBM PC, the first, and most conservative, hardware-dependent display technique is to perform calls on the ROM BIOS's video driver. This will improve display speeds significantly relative to the use of standard MS-DOS output calls, but also means that the program will run only on machines that offer IBM PC ROM BIOS compatibility.

The ROM BIOS video driver is accessed through Int 10H and supports a number of different functions, including display-mode changes, character output, scrolling, and control of the cursor position. For example, we can send the string *hello* to the screen with the following sequence:

```
              mov    si,seg buffer     ;let DS:SI = buffer address.
              mov    ds,si
              mov    si,offset buffer
              mov    cx,buf_len        ;let CX = length of string.

next:         lodsb                    ;get next character into AL.
              push   si                ;save pointer to string.
              mov    ah,0eh            ;Int 10 Fxn 0EH is write char.
              mov    bh,0              ;assume video page 0.
```

(continued)

```
                    mov    bl,color         ;(use in graphics modes only)
                    int    10h              ;call ROM BIOS video driver.
                    pop    si               ;restore string pointer.
                    loop   next             ;loop until entire string done.
                      .
                      .
                      .
      color         db     0
      buffer        db     'hello'
      buf_len       equ    $-buffer
```

The services available from the ROM BIOS video driver through Int 10H
vary among the different members of the IBM PC family and the types of
display adapters. Here is a summary of the functions that are supported on
all of the IBM PCs:

Function	Action
Display mode control	
00H	Set mode
0FH	Get mode
Cursor positioning	
02H	Set cursor position
03H	Get cursor position
Writing to the display	
09H	Write character and attribute at cursor
0AH	Write character only at cursor
0EH	Write character in teletype mode
Reading from the display	
08H	Read character and attribute at cursor
Graphics support	
0CH	Write pixel
0DH	Read pixel
Scroll or clear display	
06H	Scroll up or initialize window
07H	Scroll down or initialize window
Miscellaneous	
01H	Set cursor start and end lines
04H	Read light pen
05H	Select display page
0BH	Set palette/border color

Under TopView, or on the Enhanced Graphics Adapter (EGA) or PCjr, additional services are available. See Section 3 for detailed explanations of the ROM BIOS video driver functions.

Memory-Mapped Techniques

Maximum display performance can be achieved on memory-mapped video machines such as the IBM PC by taking over direct control of the video controller and the video refresh buffer. Needless to say, programs written in this way are extremely nonportable! For example, such programs written for the commonly available IBM PC Monochrome or Color/Graphics Adapters will not work on any other brand of personal computer except the most compatible of the PC clones, and in fact won't necessarily work on some of the more exotic IBM models (such as the 3270PC or the EGA).

The programmer writing applications for the IBM PC family needs to be concerned with two basic models of video controller: a monochrome adapter providing an 80-column by 25-line text-only display, and a color/graphics adapter with both text and bit-mapped graphics capabilities. Both are memory mapped; software drives the displays by simply writing character codes or bit patterns directly into a designated area of RAM. The memory is dual ported and is accessed "from the back" by the Motorola 6845 chip that controls the monitor. Other IBM microcomputers, such as the PCjr or the 3270PC, generally have display modes that emulate one of these two adapters.

The memory diagram in Figure 5-1 shows that the video refresh buffer for the Monochrome Display Adapter occupies 4 Kbytes starting at 0B0000H (B000:0000H) and that the refresh buffer for the Color/Graphics Adapter is assigned 16 Kbytes starting at B8000H (B800:0000H). Other video adapters, such as the EGA or the 3270GX display controller, use various amounts of memory located between 0A0000H and 0C0000H.

IBM PC High-Resolution Text Modes

Since the memory layouts for the IBM Monochrome Display Adapter and for the Color/Graphics Adapter in 80-column text mode are essentially identical (although they are based at different memory addresses), they will be discussed together.

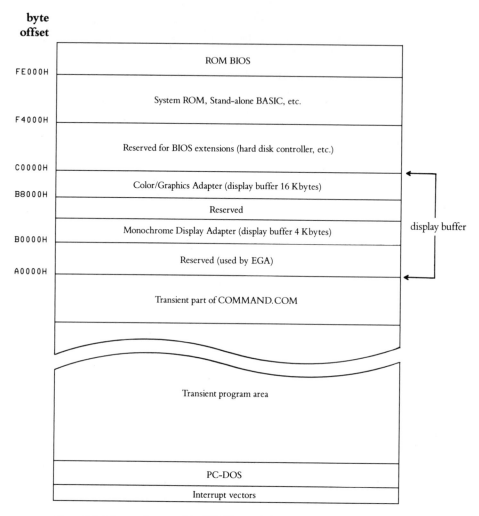

byte
offset

	ROM BIOS
FE000H	System ROM, Stand-alone BASIC, etc.
F4000H	Reserved for BIOS extensions (hard disk controller, etc.)
C0000H	Color/Graphics Adapter (display buffer 16 Kbytes)
B8000H	Reserved
	Monochrome Display Adapter (display buffer 4 Kbytes)
B0000H	Reserved (used by EGA)
A0000H	Transient part of COMMAND.COM

Figure 5-1. Memory diagram of the IBM Personal Computer, showing the display buffers.

Both have an 80-column by 25-line text area. On the Monochrome Display Adapter, characters are 7-by-9 dot patterns defined in a 9-by-14 box; on the Color/Graphics Adapter, characters are 5-by-7 dot patterns defined in an 8-by-8 box, with one line of descender for lowercase. The character set is the same for both. The cursor home position — $(x, y) = (0,0)$ — is considered to be the upper left corner of the screen (see Figure 5-2).

Each character display position is allotted 2 bytes in the RAM buffer. The first byte (even address) contains the ASCII code of the character, which is translated by a special hardware character generator into a dot matrix

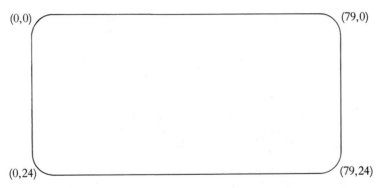

(0,0) ... (79,0)

(0,24) ... (79,24)

Figure 5-2. Cursor addressing for the Monochrome Display Adapter or the Color/Graphics Adapter in high-resolution text mode. 25 lines, 80 columns.

pattern for the screen. The second byte (odd address) is called the *attribute byte*. Several bit fields in this byte control such features as blinking, highlighting, and reverse video (Figure 5-3).

A hex and ASCII dump of part of the video map for the Monochrome Display Adapter is shown in Figure 5-4. Each screenful of text requires 80 columns times 25 lines times 2 bytes per character, or 4000 bytes. The Monochrome Display Adapter has only 4 Kbytes of on-board memory and thus can display exactly one page of text. In contrast, the Color/Graphics Adapter has 16 Kbytes of on-board memory, which in 80-by-25 text mode is divided into four 4-Kbyte pages.

7	6	5	4	3	2	1	0
BL	background			I	foreground		

BL = Blink

I = Intensity or highlight

Background	Foreground	Display
000	000	No display
000	001	Underline
000	111	Normal video
111	000	Reverse video

Figure 5-3. Attribute byte for each displayable character on the Monochrome Display Adapter. Blink, intensity, and foreground/background attributes can be used in any combination. In reverse video, the intensity bit has the opposite sense—that is, the contrast of the character is halved rather than doubled. Attribute bytes for the Color/Graphics Adapter in text mode are similar, except that underlining is not available and the foreground and background fields simply contain color codes in the range 0 through 7.

```
B000:0000 3e 07 73 07 65 07 6c 07|65 07 63 07 74 07 20 07
B000:0010 74 07 65 07 6d 07 70 07|20 07 20 07 20 07 20 07
B000:0020 20 07 20 07 20 07 20 07|20 07 20 07 20 07 20 07
B000:0030 20 07 20 07 20 07 20 07|20 07 20 07 20 07 20 07
B000:0040 20 07 20 07 20 07 20 07|20 07 20 07 20 07 20 07
B000:0050 20 07 20 07 20 07 20 07|20 07 20 07 20 07 20 07
B000:0060 20 07 20 07 20 07 20 07|20 07 20 07 20 07 20 07
B000:0070 20 07 20 07 20 07 20 07|20 07 20 07 20 07 20 07
B000:0080 20 07 20 07 20 07 20 07|20 07 20 07 20 07 20 07
B000:0090 20 07 20 07 20 07 20 07|20 07 20 07 20 07 20 07
```

Figure 5-4. Example dump of the first 160 bytes of the Monochrome Display Adapter's refresh buffer. This corresponds to the first visible line on the screen. Note that ASCII character codes are stored in even bytes and their respective attributes in odd bytes; all the characters in this example line have the attribute normal video.

The portion of memory currently being displayed is called the *active page*. While the user is viewing one portion of text, a program can build up a new text image in another page of the buffer, and then cause a different image to appear instantaneously by simply changing the active page.

The memory offset of any character in the display can be calculated as the line number (y coordinate) times 80 characters per line times 2 bytes per character, plus the column number (x coordinate) times 2 bytes per character, plus (if the Color/Graphics Adapter is being used) the current active page number times the size of the page:

offset = ((y * 50H + x) * 2) + (page * 1000H)

Of course, the segment register that is also being used to address the video buffer must be set appropriately, depending upon the type of display adapter in use.

As a simple example, assume that we have the character to be displayed in register AL, the desired attribute byte for the character in AH, the x coordinate (column) in BX, and the y coordinate (row) in CX. The following code will store the character and attribute byte into the Monochrome Display Adapter's video refresh buffer at the proper location:

```
push  ax              ;save character and attribute.
mov   ax,160
mul   cx              ;find Y * 160, result in DX:AX.
shl   bx,1            ;multiply X by 2.
add   bx,ax           ;BX = (Y * 160) + (X * 2)
mov   ax,0b000h       ;set segment of Monochrome Adapter
mov   es,ax
pop   ax              ;restore character and attribute.
mov   es:[bx],ax      ;write it into video buffer.
```

More frequently, we wish to move entire strings into the refresh buffer, starting at a given coordinate. In the next example, assume that registers DS:SI point to the source string, registers ES:DI point to the starting position in the video buffer (calculated as shown in the previous example), register AH contains the attribute byte to be assigned to every character in the string, and register CX contains the length of the string. Then the following simple code sequence will move the entire string into the refresh buffer:

```
xfer:        lodsb              ;fetch char from source string.
             stosw              ;store character + attribute
             loop   xfer        ;until entire string moved.
```

Of course, the video drivers written for actual application programs must take into account many additional factors, such as checking for special control codes (linefeeds, carriage returns, tabs), line wrap, and scrolling.

Programs that write characters to the Color/Graphics Adapter's buffer in alphanumeric (text) modes must deal with an additional complicating factor—they must examine the video controller's status port, and access the refresh buffer only during the *horizontal retrace* or *vertical retrace* intervals. Otherwise, the contention for memory between the CPU and the video controller will manifest as unsightly "snow" on the display.

Note: If you are writing programs for the IBM PC Monochrome Display Adapter, the Compaq (all display modes), or the PCjr, you can skip the next few paragraphs: Snow is not a problem with these video controllers, and the retrace intervals can be ignored.

As another simple example, assume that the offset for the desired character position has been calculated as in the example above and placed in register BX, the segment for the Color/Graphics Adapter's refresh buffer is in register ES, and an ASCII character code to be displayed is in register CL. The following code will wait for the horizontal retrace status flag and then write the character into the buffer:

```
             mov    dx,03dah    ;controller's status port address
             cli                ;disable interrupts.
wait1:       in     al,dx       ;read status port.
             and    al,1        ;wait for horizontal retrace to end.
             jnz    wait1       ;if one is already in progress
wait2:       in     al,dx       ;read status port.
             and    al,1        ;wait for horizontal retrace
             jz     wait2       ;interval to start.
             mov    es:[bx],cl  ;write the character.
             sti                ;enable interrupts.
```

The first wait loop "synchronizes" the code to the beginning of a horizontal retrace interval. If only the second wait loop were used (that is, if a character were written when a retrace interval was already in progress), you would occasionally begin the write so close to the end of a horizontal retrace "window" that you would partially miss the retrace, resulting in scattered snow at the lefthand edge of the display. It is also important to disable interrupts during accesses to the video buffer, so that service of a hardware interrupt won't ruin the synchronization process.

Note that programs that are running from RAM have only enough time during a single horizontal retrace to write 1 byte to the buffer without causing interference. Therefore, character codes and their corresponding attribute bytes must be written during separate retrace intervals. If you study the program listing for the ROM BIOS video driver (found in the *IBM PC Technical Reference Manual*), you will notice that its routines write the character and attribute together in a single 16-bit store operation. The BIOS driver can get away with this because, due to a peculiarity of the IBM PC's design, programs running from ROM execute slightly faster than RAM-based programs.

Due to the retrace interval constraints outlined above, the rate at which you can update the color/graphics display is severely limited when updating is done a character at a time. Better results can be obtained by calculating all the relevant addresses and setting up the appropriate registers, disabling the video controller by writing to register 3D8H, moving the entire string to the buffer by a REP MOVSW operation, and then re-enabling the video controller. If the string is of reasonable length, the user will not even notice a flicker in the display. Of course, this introduces additional hardware dependence into your code because it requires much greater knowledge of the 6845 controller. (Remember that snow is a potential problem for the Color/Graphics Adapter only in text modes; it does not occur in graphics modes.)

IBM PC High-Resolution Graphics Mode

The high-resolution graphics mode of the IBM Color/Graphics Adapter provides 640 by 200 resolution in black and one other color only. Each bit of the memory map is a pixel, which is either on or off and corresponds directly to a dot on the screen. When addressing the display, the x coordinate giving the horizontal displacement must be in the range 0 through 639, and the y coordinate giving the vertical displacement must be in the range 0 through 199. The home position — $(x, y) = (0,0)$ — is the upper left corner of the screen (Figure 5-5).

Figure 5-5. Point addressing with the Color/Graphics Adapter in high-resolution graphics mode (ROM BIOS mode 6). Two-color display, 640 by 200 resolution.

Each successive group of 80 bytes (640 bits) represents one horizontal scan line. Within each byte, the bits map one-for-one onto points, with the most significant bit corresponding to the leftmost displayed pixel of a set of 8 pixels, and the least significant bit corresponding to the rightmost displayed pixel of a set of 8 pixels. The memory map is set up so that all the even y coordinates are scanned as a set, alternating with all the odd y coordinates; this is referred to as the *memory interlace*.

To find the byte address for a particular (x, y) coordinate, you would use the following formula:

offset = ((y AND 1) * 2000H) + (y/2 * 50H) + (x/8)

This can be implemented in assembly language as:

```
                                    ;assume AX = Y, BX = X.
            shr    bx,1             ;divide X by 8.
            shr    bx,1
            shr    bx,1
            push   ax               ;save copy of Y.
            shr    ax,1             ;find (Y / 2) * 50H.
            mov    cx,50h
            mul    cx
            add    bx,ax            ;add product to X / 8.
            pop    ax               ;now add (Y AND 1) * 2000H.
            and    ax,1
            jz     there
            add    bx, 2000h
            .
there:      .                        ;now BX = offset into
            .                        ;video buffer.
```

Once the correct byte address is calculated, you can use the following formula to calculate the bit position for a given pixel coordinate:

bit number = 7 − (x MOD 8)

where bit 7 is the most significant bit and bit 0 is the least significant bit. It is easiest to build an 8-byte table, or array of bit masks, and use the function *x AND* 7 to extract the appropriate entry from the table:

(x AND 7)	Bit mask	(x AND 7)	Bit mask
0	80H	4	08H
1	40H	5	04H
2	20H	6	02H
3	10H	7	01H

This can be implemented in assembly language as:

```
              and    bx,7              ;assume BX = X coordinate.
              mov    al,[bx+table]     ;now AL = pixel mask from table.
              .
              .
              .
table         db     80h               ; X AND 7 = 0
              db     40h               ; X AND 7 = 1
              db     20h               ; X AND 7 = 2
              db     10h               ; X AND 7 = 3
              db     08                ; X AND 7 = 4
              db     04                ; X AND 7 = 5
              db     02                ; X AND 7 = 6
              db     01                ; X AND 7 = 7
```

IBM PC Medium-Resolution Graphics Mode

The medium-resolution mode of the Color/Graphics Adapter provides 320 by 200 bit-mapped graphics in four colors. Each consecutive 2 bits of the memory map constitute a pixel, which contains a value from 0 through 3 and corresponds directly to a dot on the screen. When addressing the display, the x coordinate giving the horizontal displacement must be in the range 0 through 319, and the y coordinate giving the vertical displacement must be in the range 0 through 199.

Each successive group of 80 bytes (640 bits) represents one horizontal scan line. Within each byte, the bits map two-for-one onto points, with the most significant 2 bits corresponding to the leftmost displayed pixel of a set of 4 pixels, and the least significant 2 bits corresponding to the rightmost displayed pixel of a set of 4 pixels. As in the high-resolution graphics mode, the memory map is interlaced so that all the even y coordinates are scanned as a set, alternating with all the odd y coordinates.

The byte address containing a particular (x,y) coordinate can be calculated as:

offset = ((y AND 1) * 2000H) + (y/2 * 50H) + (x/4)

Once the correct byte is located, masks for the bit fields can be extracted from a table, as follows:

(x AND 3)	Bit mask	(x AND 3)	Bit mask
0	C0H	2	0CH
1	30H	3	03H

This can easily be implemented in assembly language using the approach previously shown on page 82.

Printer Output

MS-DOS has built-in support for a list device, or printer, which has the logical device name PRN. Programs that wish to produce printed output can send a character stream to this logical device and be reasonably assured that it will end up on a corresponding physical printer device—although it may get there circuitously (the output may be spooled or temporarily stored in a disk file before printing, or may be redirected across a network to a printer hooked to another computer altogether).

In most MS-DOS systems, the printer is interfaced to the computer through a parallel port. This is a relatively high-speed type of interface that transfers data 8 bits at a time, in contrast to a serial interface's 1 bit at a time. The printer controller's parallel ports are usually unidirectional for data, although one or two status signals may be available to tell the computer interface when the printer is off line or out of paper.

As with the keyboard and the display, printer output can be handled in a number of ways that offer different degrees of flexibility and hardware independence.

MS-DOS provides two distinct high-level methods of sending data to the printer device: a Handle method and a traditional method. Programs using either of these methods will work unaltered on any MS-DOS system.

Programs can also be customized for specific computers to use low-level, hardware-dependent printer output facilities—either calls to primitive drivers in ROM, provided by the computer's manufacturer, or direct control of the printer interface. We will touch on the low-level methods only briefly, because the printers that are attached to microcomputers aren't usually fast enough to require these techniques anyway.

High-Level Printer Output

The preferred high-level method of printer output is to use the Handle calls with the predefined handle 0004H for the standard list device. For example, you could write the string *hello* to the printer as follows:

```
                mov    ah,40h              ;function 40H = write to device
                mov    bx,0004             ;handle 4 = standard list device
                mov    cx,5                ;length of string
                mov    dx,seg buffer       ;DS:DX = addr of string
                mov    ds,dx
                mov    dx,offset buffer
                int    21h
                jc     error
                  .
error:            .
                  .
buffer          db     'hello'
```

Upon return from the write function, register AX contains the number of characters actually transferred to the list device. Under normal circumstances, this should always be the same as the length requested, and the carry flag indicating an error should never be set. However, the output will be terminated early if your data contains an end-of-file mark (Ctrl-Z). An unexpected carry flag probably indicates a severe error in your program or damage to the operating system itself.

You can write independently to several list devices (e.g., LPT1, LPT2) by issuing a specific open (Int 21H function 3DH) for each device and using the handles returned by the opens to access the printers individually with write function 40H. These general methods were illustrated earlier, in the keyboard and video-display sections of this chapter.

Another high-level method of printer output is to use the traditional function 05H, which transfers the character in register DL to the printer. (This function is sensitive to Ctrl-C interrupts.) For example, the following sequence of assembly code would write the string *hello* to the line printer:

```
                mov    bx,segment buffer   ;let DS:BX = addr of string.
                mov    ds,bx
                mov    bx,offset buffer
                mov    cx,buf_len          ;let CX = length of string.
next:           mov    dl,[bx]             ;get next character.
                mov    ah,5                ;function 5 = list output
                int    21h                 ;transfer to DOS.
                inc    bx                  ;bump pointer to string.
                loop   next                ;loop until string done.
                  .
                  .
buffer          db     'hello'
buf_len         equ    $-buffer
```

Both the Handle and traditional list-device output functions are standard features of MS-DOS versions 2 and 3. Programs written using these functions will operate properly on any computer running these versions of MS-DOS, regardless of the hardware configuration.

Low-Level Printer Output

Programs written for the IBM PC family can obtain some increase in printer speed by bypassing MS-DOS and calling the ROM BIOS printer driver directly. This driver is accessed via Int 17H, and its functions are documented in detail in Section 3.

The advantages of using the ROM BIOS calls for the printer are:

- Printer status can be obtained (though it is reliable only if the printer is plugged in and on line).

- The throughput to the printer is considerably better than when using the MS-DOS function calls.

For example, the following sequence of instructions will call the ROM driver to send the character X to the line printer:

```
        mov     ah,0            ;function 0 = print character
        mov     al,'X'          ;AL = character to transmit to printer
        mov     dx,0            ;printer number
        int     17h             ;call the ROM.
        and     ah,1            ;was character printed?
        jnz     error           ;jump if transmit failed (timed out).
```

As mentioned earlier, the printers usually purchased for microcomputers aren't capable of printing fast enough to require these low-level techniques. Printers capable of outrunning MS-DOS (say, 300 lines per minute or so) are more expensive than the computer itself. On the other hand, if the program in question is already hardware dependent because of video-display techniques, the small amount of additional hardware dependence introduced by using ROM BIOS calls to drive the printer is hardly anything to worry about. You should keep in mind, however, that such BIOS calls may cause conflicts with print spoolers or multitasking environments such as Microsoft Windows.

Finally, the most hardware-dependent technique of printer output is to access the printer controller directly. Considering the functionality already provided in MS-DOS and the IBM PC ROM BIOS, and the speeds of the devices involved, I cannot see any justification for using direct hardware control in this case. The disadvantage of introducing such extreme hardware dependence for such a low-speed device would far outweigh any small performance gains that might be obtained.

The Serial Port

Serial ports, which are used to interface the computer to a modem, another computer, or certain types of printers, are rapidly becoming a standard feature on personal computers. Serial interfaces are so called because they accept data 8 bits at a time from the central processor, but send it out serially to the peripheral device over a single wire, 1 bit at a time.

The most commonly used type of serial interface follows a standard called RS-232. This standard specifies a 25-wire interface with certain electrical characteristics, and a standard DB-25 connector. Only two of the wires actually carry data (a Transmit bit stream and a Receive bit stream); one wire is a ground; the remainder carry certain handshaking signals, most of which are optional. Other serial interface standards exist—for example, the RS-422, which is capable of considerably higher speeds than the RS-232—but are rarely used in personal computers (except for the Apple Macintosh) at this time.

In MS-DOS manuals, the serial interface is called the auxiliary device and is given the logical device name AUX. There may be two or more serial controllers in the system, attached to separate peripheral devices (for example, the IBM PC's COM1 and COM2), but only one of them is accessible to programs as the AUX device at any given time. The MS-DOS MODE command is provided to configure the serial ports and select between them.

MS-DOS support for the auxiliary device is weak compared with the keyboard, video display, and printer support discussed earlier in this chapter. This is one area where the application programmer is frequently justified in making programs hardware dependent to extract adequate performance.

High-Level Serial Port I/O

As with the other character devices we have already discussed, the preferable high-level method of serial port I/O is use of the Handle read and write function calls with the predefined handle 0003H for the standard auxiliary device. For example, the following code would write the string *hello* to the serial port that is currently defined as the AUX device:

```
            mov   ah,40h              ;function 40H = write
            mov   bx,0003             ;handle for standard auxiliary dev
            mov   cx,5                ;length of string
            mov   dx,seg buffer       ;DS:DX = addr of string
            mov   ds,dx
            mov   dx,offset buffer
            int   21h                 ;transfer to DOS.
            jc    error               ;jump if error.
                  .
error:            .
                  .
buffer      db    'hello'
```

Similarly, you can use Int 21H function 3FH (read file or device) and the predefined handle 0003H to input strings from the auxiliary device.

Alternatively, you can ignore the predefined handle for the standard auxiliary device and issue function 3DH (open handle) requests for specific serial ports (e.g., COM1, COM2), using the handles returned by these opens to selectively read and write more than one serial port. Examples of this procedure were provided earlier, in the sections dealing with keyboard input and display output.

(To avoid problems that can occur when using the Handle read call in cooked mode with character devices other than CON, such as the auxiliary device, make sure that both the buffer and the value passed in CX are larger than the longest line you expect to read. Due to a bug in MS-DOS, if you issue a read command for the exact number of characters waiting in the driver's input buffer, AX will sometimes return the actual number of characters less one. This problem can be always circumvented by placing the driver into raw mode, if you are not concerned that MS-DOS recognize the special control characters, such as end-of-file or Ctrl-C.)

Another high-level, hardware-independent method of accessing the serial port is to use the traditional auxiliary-device calls:

- Function 03H inputs a character and returns it in AL.

- Function 04H transmits the character in DL to the serial device.

For example, the following code would send the string *hello* to the auxiliary device using the traditional function 04H:

```
            mov   bx,segment buffer   ;let DS:BX = addr of string.
            mov   ds,bx
            mov   bx,offset buffer
            mov   cx,buf_len          ;let CX = length of string.

next:       mov   dl,[bx]             ;get next character.
            mov   ah,4                ;function 4 = aux. output
            int   21h                 ;transfer to DOS.
            inc   bx                  ;bump pointer to string.
            loop  next                ;loop until string done.
            .
            .
            .
buffer      db    'hello'
buf_len     equ   $-buffer
```

The traditional auxiliary-device functions are translated into calls on the same device driver used by the Handle calls. Therefore, it is generally preferable to use the Handle calls, both because they allow very long strings to be read or written in one operation and because they are structurally symmetrical with the Handle video display, keyboard, and printer I/O methods described earlier in the chapter and with the Handle file and record functions discussed in Chapter 6. Both the Handle and the traditional auxiliary-device functions are standard features of MS-DOS versions 2 and 3. Programs written using these functions will run properly on any computer running those versions of MS-DOS, regardless of the hardware configuration (assuming that the serial port has been properly initialized for baud rate, stop bits, word length, and parity).

Low-Level Serial Port I/O

Although the Handle or traditional auxiliary-device function calls allow you to write programs that will run on any MS-DOS machine without change, they have a number of disadvantages:

- The built-in MS-DOS auxiliary device driver is slow and is not interrupt driven.

- The I/O is not buffered.

- Determining the status of the auxiliary device requires a separate call to the IOCTL function (44H)—if you request an input and no characters are waiting, your program will just hang.

- There is no standardized way to configure the serial port from within a program.

For programs that are going to run on the IBM PC or compatibles, a more hardware-dependent but, paradoxically, more flexible technique for serial port I/O is to call the IBM PC ROM BIOS serial port driver via Int 14H. This driver can be used to initialize the serial port to a desired configuration and baud rate, examine the status of the controller, and read or write characters.

For example, the following sequence would send the character *X* to the first serial port (COM1):

```
        mov    ah,1          ;function 1 = transmit character
        mov    al,'X'        ;AL = character to transmit
        mov    dx,0          ;use first serial port.
        int    14h
        and    ah,80h        ;did transmit fail?
        jnz    error         ;jump if couldn't send character.
```

The functions available by calling the ROM BIOS serial port driver are documented in Section 3 of this book.

Unfortunately, like the MS-DOS auxiliary-device driver, the BIOS serial port driver isn't interrupt driven. Although it will support higher transfer speeds than the MS-DOS functions, at rates greater than 2400 baud it may still lose characters. And of course, using the ROM BIOS serial port driver means that your program may not run on machines that are not IBM PC compatible. Even more important, it also means that you will bypass any device redirecton that has been put into effect with the MODE command at the MS-DOS level. Since systems with two serial ports are relatively common these days, this last consideration should not be taken too lightly.

It is only fair to reiterate that most programmers writing high-performance applications that use a serial port (such as communications or fast file transfer programs) end up taking complete control of the serial port controller and providing their own interrupt driver. The built-in functions provided by MS-DOS, and by the ROM BIOS in the case of the IBM PC, are just not adequate.

Writing such programs requires a good understanding of the hardware. In the case of the IBM PC, the chips to study are the INS8250 Asynchronous Communications Controller and the Intel 8259A Programmable Interrupt Controller. The *IBM Technical Reference* documentation of these chips is a bit disorganized, but most of the necessary information is there if you look for it. More readable and more detailed information can be found in Peter Norton's *Programmer's Guide to the IBM PC*. For those of you who like to learn by doing, see the *TALK* program at the end of this chapter. This program illustrates interrupt-driven control of the IBM PC Asynchronous Communications Adapter.

Ctrl-C Handlers

While we were discussing keyboard input and display output earlier in the chapter, we made some passing references to the the fact that Ctrl-C (Break key) entries can interfere with the expected behavior of those functions.

Whenever MS-DOS detects a Ctrl-C (03H) waiting at the keyboard or in an input stream, it executes the routine whose address is saved in the vector for Int 23H. Ordinarily, this vector points to a routine that simply terminates the currently active process and returns control to the parent process—usually the MS-DOS command interpreter.

In other words, if your program is executing and you accidentally (or intentionally) enter a Ctrl-C, your program is simply aborted. Any files you have opened using file control blocks will not be closed properly, any interrupt vectors you have altered may not be restored correctly, and if you are performing any direct I/O operations (for example, if your program contains an interrupt driver for the serial port), all kinds of unexpected events may occur.

There are a number of measures that you can include in your program to avoid losing control upon entry of a Ctrl-C. These include:

- Performing all keyboard input and status checks through functions 06H and 07H, and turning on the raw mode for the console driver (as described under Display Output).

- Performing all display output through MS-DOS function 06H or by direct writes to the ROM BIOS or to the video controller's refresh buffer.

- Setting the other character devices (AUX, PRN) into raw mode.

- Disabling Ctrl-C checking with function 33H, for MS-DOS operations other than character I/O (this function doesn't affect I/O operations involving the standard input, standard output, auxiliary, or list devices).

Unfortunately, these partial measures are not bombproof. A more elegant way to disable Ctrl-C checking is simply to let it occur, but substitute your own Ctrl-C handler that either does nothing or does something appropriate for your application.

Here is an example of an application substituting a Ctrl-C handler that does nothing. The first part of this code (which alters the contents of the Int 23H vector) would be executed in the initialization part of the application. The handler named *Brk_Routine* would get control whenever MS-DOS detects a Ctrl-C at the keyboard or in a file or device character stream. The handler in this example does nothing except perform an immediate INTERRUPT RETURN. Since the handler took no special action, the Ctrl-C will simply remain in the keyboard input stream and will be passed to the application the next time it requests a character from the keyboard (appearing on the screen as ^C):

```
        mov     ah,25h          ;function 25H = set interrupt
        mov     al,23h          ;Int 23H is the vector for
                                ;the Ctrl-C handler.
                                ;let DS:DX = addr of handler.
        mov     dx,seg Brk_Routine
```

(continued)

```
         mov    ds,dx
         mov    dx,offset Brk_Routine
         int    21h                    ;call DOS to change vector.
         .
Brk_Routine:   .                       ;this is the handler that is
         .                             ;called when DOS detects
         iret                          ;a Ctrl-C.
```

When an application terminates, MS-DOS automatically restores the pre-vious contents of the Int 23H vector from information saved in the program segment prefix.

Note: The Int 23H Ctrl-C handler is a standard feature of MS-DOS and is not limited to the IBM PC family. The code given above is portable to any MS-DOS machine.

On the IBM PC family (and compatibles), there is an additional interrupt handler that is called by the ROM BIOS keyboard driver when it detects the special key combination Ctrl-Break. The address of this handler is saved in the vector for Int 1BH. Under MS-DOS, this vector normally points to a simple interrupt handler that does nothing but set a flag and perform an INTERRUPT RETURN. Taking over this interrupt vector is extremely useful (and somewhat dangerous). Since the keyboard is interrupt driven, a press of Ctrl-Break will regain control under almost any circumstance—many times it will work even if the program has crashed or is in an endless loop.

You cannot, in general, use the same handler for Int 1BH that you wrote for Int 23H. The Int 1BH handler is more limited in what it can do, because it has been called as a result of a hardware interrupt and MS-DOS may have been executing a critical section of code at the time the interrupt was ser-viced. Consequently, all registers except CS:IP are in an unknown state; they may need to be saved and then modified before your interrupt handler can execute. Similarly, the depth of the stack in use when the Int 1BH han-dler is called is unknown, and if the handler wishes to perform stack-intensive operations, it may need to save the stack segment and stack pointer and switch to a new stack that is known to have sufficient depth.

I have found by experience that the Int 1BH handler *can* retain control of the system and branch to some point in the application directly; however, there are a few points you need to consider when using this technique:

● The hardware interrupt automatically disables *all* interrupts, so it is critical that you re-enable interrupts as soon as possible by executing the instruction *sti*.

- Compaq Portable computers with the Compaq ROM revision C have a bug in the ROM keyboard driver that will cause the system to go dead if the Int 1BH handler retains control, unless your application executes the following code:

```
in    al,61h
or    al,80h
out   61h,al
and   al,7fh
out   61h,al
```

(I have included the Compaq code here because of the large number of Compaq machines in use.)

- On the PCjr, if the Int 1BH handler retains control, it must execute

```
in    al,0a0h
```

to reset the keyboard controller; otherwise, the system will appear to go dead (it is still running, but the keyboard interrupts are not being serviced, so it is effectively dead).

- Since the interrupt was hardware generated, your handler must issue an end-of-interrupt (EOI) to the 8259A interrupt controller (see Chapter 11) or the system will appear to die. In the IBM PC family, this is accomplished by the following code:

```
mov   al,20h
out   20h,al
```

- The IBM implementation of MS-DOS (PC-DOS) does not automatically restore the contents of the Int 1BH vector when your program terminates, since this vector belongs to the ROM BIOS and not to MS-DOS proper. If you are going to supply a handler for Int 1BH, you must save the previous state of the vector before you modify it, and then restore it to its original state before your program exits.

Ctrl-Break Handlers and High-Level Languages

As illustrated in the preceding pages, capturing the Ctrl-C and Ctrl-Break interrupts is straightforward when you are programming applications in assembly language. The process is only slightly trickier with high-level languages. The *BREAK.ASM* listing that follows (Figure 5-6) contains source code for a Ctrl-Break handler that can be linked with Microsoft C programs running on the IBM PC family. A short C program (Figure 5-7) that demonstrates use of the handler is also provided. (This code should be readily portable to other C compilers.)

```
1              page    55,132
2              title   Ctrl-Break handler for Microsoft C programs
3              name    break
4
5      ;
6      ; Ctrl-Break Interrupt Handler for Microsoft C programs
7      ; running on IBM PCs (and ROM BIOS compatibles)
8      ;
9      ; Ray Duncan, May 1985
10     ;
11     ; This module allows C programs running on the IBM PC
12     ; to retain control when the user enters a Ctrl-Break
13     ; or Ctrl-C.  This is accomplished by taking over the
14     ; Int 23H (MS-DOS Ctrl-C) and Int 1BH (IBM PC
15     ; ROM BIOS Keyboard Driver Ctrl-Break) interrupt
16     ; vectors.  The interrupt handler sets an internal
17     ; flag (which must be declared STATIC INT) to TRUE within
18     ; the C program; the C program can poll or ignore this
19     ; flag as it wishes.
20     ;
21     ; The module follows the Microsoft C parameter passing conventions.
22     ;
23     ; The Int 23H Ctrl-C handler is a function of MS-DOS
24     ; and is present on all MS-DOS machines; however, the Int 1BH
25     ; handler is a function of the IBM PC ROM BIOS and will not
26     ; necessarily be present on other machines.
27     ;
28
29     args     equ     4               ;offset of arguments, small model
30
31     cr       equ     0dh             ;ASCII carriage return
32     lf       equ     0ah             ;ASCII line feed
33
34
35     _TEXT    segment byte public 'CODE'
36
37              assume cs:_TEXT
38
39              public _capture,_release        ;function names for C
40
41              page
42     ;
43     ; The function CAPTURE is called by the C program to
44     ; take over the MS-DOS and keyboard driver Ctrl-
45     ; Break interrupts (1BH and 23H).  It is passed the
46     ; address of a flag within the C program which is set
47     ; to TRUE whenever a Ctrl-Break or Ctrl-C
```

Figure 5-6. BREAK.ASM: *A Ctrl-C and Ctrl-Break interrupt handler that can be linked with Microsoft C programs.* (continued)

```
48  ; is detected.  The function is used in the form:
49  ;
50  ;                   static int flag;
51  ;                   capture(&flag);
52
53  _capture proc    near                ;take over Ctrl-Break.
54
55           push    bp                  ;interrupt vectors
56           mov     bp,sp
57           push    ds                  ;save registers.
58           push    di
59           push    si
60
61           mov     ax,word ptr [bp+args]
62           mov     cs:flag,ax          ;save address of integer
63           mov     cs:flag+2,ds        ;flag variable in C program.
64
65                                       ;pick up original vector contents
66           mov     ax,3523h            ;for interrupt 23H (MS-DOS
67           int     21h                 ;Ctrl-C handler).
68           mov     cs:int23,bx
69           mov     cs:int23+2,es
70
71           mov     ax,351bh            ;and interrupt 1BH
72           int     21h                 ;(IBM PC ROM BIOS keyboard driver
73           mov     cs:int1b,bx         ;Ctrl-Break interrupt handler).
74           mov     cs:int1b+2,es
75
76           push    cs                  ;set address of new handler
77           pop     ds
78           mov     dx,offset ctrlbrk
79           mov     ax,02523h           ;for interrupt 23H
80           int     21h
81           mov     ax,0251bh           ;and interrupt 1BH.
82           int     21h
83
84           pop     si
85           pop     di
86           pop     ds                  ;restore registers and
87           pop     bp                  ;return to C program.
88           ret
89
90  _capture endp
91           page
92  ;
93  ; The function RELEASE is called by the C program to
94  ; return the MS-DOS and keyboard driver Ctrl-Break
95  ; interrupt vectors to their original state.  Int 23H is
96  ; also automatically restored by MS-DOS upon the termination
```

Figure 5-6 continued.

```
97     ; of a process; however, calling RELEASE allows the C
98     ; program to restore the default action of a Ctrl-C
99     ; without terminating.  The function is used in the form:
100    ;
101    ;              release();
102    ;
103
104    _release proc   near            ;restore Ctrl-Break interrupt
105                                    ;vectors to their original state.
106            push    bp
107            mov     bp,sp
108            push    ds              ;save registers.
109            push    di
110            push    si
111
112            mov     dx,cs:int1b     ;set interrupt 1BH
113            mov     ds,cs:int1b+2   ;(IBM PC ROM BIOS keyboard driver
114            mov     ax,251bh        ;Ctrl-Break interrupt handler).
115            int     21h
116
117            mov     dx,cs:int23     ;set interrupt 23H
118            mov     ds,cs:int23+2   ;(MS-DOS Ctrl-C
119            mov     ax,2523h        ;interrupt handler).
120            int     21h
121
122            pop     si
123            pop     di
124            pop     ds              ;restore registers and
125            pop     bp              ;return to C program.
126            ret
127
128    _release endp
129
130            page
131    ;
132    ; This is the actual interrupt handler which is called by
133    ; the ROM BIOS keyboard driver or by MS-DOS when a Ctrl-C
134    ; or Ctrl-Break is detected.  Since the interrupt handler
135    ; may be called asynchronously by the keyboard driver, it
136    ; is severely restricted in what it may do without crashing
137    ; the system (e.g. no calls on DOS allowed).  In this
138    ; version, it simply sets a flag within the C program to
139    ; TRUE to indicate that a Ctrl-C or Ctrl-Break has
140    ; been detected; the address of this flag was passed
141    ; by the C program during the call to the CAPTURE function.
142    ;
143
144    ctrlbrk proc    far             ;Ctrl-Break interrupt handler
145
```

Figure 5-6 continued.

```
146            push    bx              ;save affected registers
147            push    ds
148
149            mov     bx,cs:flag      ;set flag within C program
150            mov     ds,cs:flag+2    ;to "True"
151            mov     word ptr ds:[bx],-1
152
153            pop     ds              ;restore registers and exit
154            pop     bx
155
156            iret
157
158    ctrlbrk endp
159
160
161    flag    dw      0,0             ;long address of C program's
162                                    ;Ctrl-Break detected flag
163
164    int23   dw      0,0             ;original contents of MS-DOS
165                                    ;Ctrl-C Interrupt 23H
166                                    ;vector
167
168    int1b   dw      0,0             ;original contents of ROM BIOS
169                                    ;keyboard driver Ctrl-Break
170                                    ;Interrupt 1BH vector
171
172    _TEXT   ends
173
174            end
```

Figure 5-6 continued.

```
/*
        TRYBREAK.C

        Try Microsoft C Ctrl-Break interrupt handler

        Ray Duncan, May 1985

*/

#include <stdio.h>

main(argc, argv)
    int     argc;
    char    *argv[];
```

(continued)

Figure 5-7. A simple Microsoft C program that demonstrates use of the interrupt handler BREAK.ASM in Figure 5-6.

```
{   int hit = 0;                        /* flag for keypress */
    int c = 0;                          /* character from keyboard */
    static int flag = 0;                /* true if Ctrl-Break or
                                           Ctrl-C detected */

    puts("\n*** TRYBREAK.C running ***\n");
    puts("Press Ctrl-C or Ctrl-Break to test handler,");
    puts("Press the Esc key to exit TRYBREAK.\n");

    capture(&flag);                     /* pass address of flag */

    puts("TRYBREAK has CAPTUREd interrupt vectors.\n");

    while ( (c&127) != 27 )             /* watch for Esc key */
    {   hit = kbhit();                  /* check for keypress */
        if (flag != 0)
                { puts("\nCtrl-Break detected.\n");
                  flag=0;
                }
        if (hit != 0)                   /* read key if ready */
        { c=getch();
          putch(c);                     /* and display it */
        }
    }
    release();
    puts("\nTRYBREAK has RELEASEd interrupt vectors.");

}
```

Figure 5-7 continued.

The function named *capture* is called with the address of an integer variable within the C program. It saves the address of the variable, points the Int 1BH and Int 23H vectors to the new interrupt handler, and then returns.

When a Ctrl-C or Ctrl-Break is detected, the interrupt handler sets the integer variable within the C program to true (1) and returns. The C program can then poll this variable at its leisure. (Of course, if the program wishes to detect more than one Ctrl-C, it must reset the variable to zero again.) The function named *release* simply restores the Int 1BH and Int 23H vectors to their original values, thereby disabling the interrupt handler.

Although in this example the Int 23H vector is restored by the *release* function, this is not strictly necessary, since MS-DOS will restore the vector automatically when any application terminates. Int 1BH, however, is an IBM PC-specific interrupt handler and is not known to MS-DOS, so it is absolutely mandatory that your program restore this vector properly before exiting, if it modifies it. Otherwise, the vector will be left pointing to some random area in the next program that runs, and the next time the user presses Ctrl-Break a system crash is the best you can hope for.

The *TALK* Program

The source code for a simple terminal-emulator program called *TALK.ASM* (Figure 5-8) is included in this chapter as an example of a useful program that performs screen, keyboard, and serial-port I/O. *TALK* uses the IBM PC's ROM BIOS video driver to put characters on the screen, to clear the display, and to position the cursor; it uses the MS-DOS character input calls to read the keyboard; and it contains its own interrupt driver for the serial port controller.

```
1               name      talk
2               page      55,132
3               .lfcond               ;list false conditionals too
4               title     'TALK --- IBM PC terminal emulator'
5   ;
6   ; TALK.ASM --- a simple terminal emulator for the IBM PC
7   ;
8   ; Copyright (c) 1983, 1984, 1985 Ray Duncan
9   ;
10  ; To assemble, link, and convert this program into
11  ; a COM file, follow these steps:
12  ;
13  ;       C>MASM TALK;
14  ;       C>LINK TALK;
15  ;       C>EXE2BIN TALK.EXE TALK.COM
16  ;       C>DEL TALK.EXE
17  ;
18  ; Ignore the message "Warning: no stack segment" from the Linker.
19
20  cr        equ      0dh            ;ASCII carriage return
21  lf        equ      0ah            ;ASCII line feed
22  bsp       equ      08h            ;ASCII backspace
23  esc       equ      1bh            ;ASCII escape code
24
25  dattr     equ      07h            ;display attribute to use
26                                    ;while in emulation mode.
27
28  echo      equ      0              ;0 = full-duplex, -1 = half-duplex
29
30  comm_port equ      0              ;set = 0 for COM1, <> 0 for COM2
31
32  pic_mask  equ      21h            ;port address, 8259 mask register
33  pic_eoi   equ      20h            ;port address, 8259 EOI instr.
34
35            if       comm_port      ;define physical port assignments
36  comm_data equ      02f8h          ;for COM2.
37  comm_ier  equ      02f9h
```

(continued)

Figure 5-8. TALK.ASM: *A simple terminal-emulator program for the IBM PC.*

```
38    comm_mcr  equ   02fch
39    comm_stat equ   02fdh
40    com_int   equ   0bh
41    int_mask  equ   08h              ;Mask for 8529, COM2 is IRQ3.
42          else
43    comm_data equ   03f8h            ;port assignments for COM1
44    comm_ier  equ   03f9h
45    comm_mcr  equ   03fch
46    comm_stat equ   03fdh
47    com_int   equ   0ch
48    int_mask  equ   10h              ;Mask for 8259, COM1 is IRQ4.
49          endif
50          page
51
52    cseg  segment para public 'CODE'
53
54          org   100h
55
56          assume  cs:cseg,ds:cseg,es:cseg,ss:cseg  ;COM file...
57
58    talk  proc  far                  ;entry point from PC-DOS
59
60                                     ;initialize display for
61                                     ;terminal emulator mode.
62
63          mov   ah,15                ;determine display width
64          int   10h                  ;using get mode function of ROM
65          dec   ah                   ;BIOS video driver; save it for use
66          mov   columns,ah           ;by the screen clear routine.
67          cmp   al,7                 ;make sure display is text mode.
68          je    talk2                ;mode 7 ok, proceed.
69          cmp   al,3
70          jbe   talk2                ;modes 0-3 ok, proceed.
71          mov   dx,offset msg1
72          jmp   talk6                ;print error message and exit.
73
74    talk2:
75          mov   bh,dattr             ;now clear screen with special
76          call  cls                  ;attribute if needed, home cursor.
77
78          call  asc_enb              ;set up communications interrupt
79                                     ;service routine and enable int.
80
81    talk3: call  pc_stat             ;check character waiting
82                                     ;from the IBM PC keyboard.
83          jz    talk4                ;nothing waiting, jump.
84          call  pc_in                ;read char. from PC keyboard.
85          cmp   al,0                 ;is it a function key?
```

Figure 5-8 continued.

```
86              jne     talk32          ;not function key, jump.
87              call    pc_in           ;read and discard the 2nd char
88                                      ;of function key sequence,
89              jmp     talk5           ;then exit the terminal emulator.
90
91      talk32:                         ;character received from PC keyboard
92              if      echo
93              push    ax              ;if running half-duplex, echo
94              call    pc_out          ;the character to the PC display.
95              pop     ax
96              endif
97              call    com_out         ;write char. to the comm port.
98
99      talk4:  call    com_stat        ;check if character waiting
100                                     ;from the comm port.
101             jz      talk3           ;no, loop.
102             call    com_in          ;read char. from comm port.
103
104             cmp     al,20h          ;is it control code?
105             jae     talk45          ;no
106             call    ctrl_code       ;yes, process it.
107             jmp     talk3           ;check local keyboard.
108
109     talk45:
110             call    pc_out          ;write it to the PC display.
111             jmp     talk4           ;see if any more waiting.
112
113     talk5:                          ;ESC key detected, prepare
114                                     ;to exit the terminal emulator.
115             mov     bh,07h          ;clear screen & home cursor
116             call    cls             ;with "normal" video attribute.
117             mov     dx,offset msg2  ;print farewell message.
118
119     talk6:  push    dx              ;save message addr.
120             call    asc_dsb         ;disable controller and
121             pop     dx              ;release interrupt vector.
122             mov     ah,9            ;print message.
123             int     21h
124             mov     ax,4c00h        ;exit with ret code = 0.
125             int     21h
126
127     talk    endp
128
129
130     com_stat proc   near            ;Check asynch status, returns
131                                     ;Z = false if character ready
132                                     ;Z = true if nothing waiting.
133             push    dx
```

Figure 5-8 continued.

```
134     mov     dx,asc_in       ;compare ring buffer pointers.
135     cmp     dx,asc_out
136     pop     dx
137     ret
138 com_stat endp
139
140
141 com_in  proc    near            ;get a char from asynch line.
142         push    bx              ;returns char in AL.
143 com_in1:                        ;if no char waiting, loop
144         mov     bx,asc_out      ;until one is received.
145         cmp     bx,asc_in
146         je      com_in1
147         mov     al,[bx+asc_buf]
148         inc     bx
149         cmp     bx,asc_buf_len
150         jne     com_in2
151         xor     bx,bx           ;reset ring pointer.
152 com_in2:
153         mov     asc_out,bx      ;store updated pointer.
154         pop     bx
155         ret
156 com_in  endp
157
158
159 com_out proc    near            ;write character in AL to COM port.
160         push    dx
161         push    ax              ;save char.
162         mov     dx,comm_stat    ;check TBE status.
163 com_out1:
164         in      al,dx
165         and     al,20h
166         jz      com_out1
167         pop     ax              ;write char.
168         mov     dx,comm_data
169         out     dx,al
170         pop     dx
171         ret
172 com_out endp
173
174
175 pc_stat proc    near            ;read status for the IBM
176                                 ;PC's keyboard; returns
177                                 ;Z = false if character ready
178                                 ;Z = true if nothing waiting.
179                                 ;register DX destroyed
180         mov     al,in_flag      ;if a character is already
181         or      al,al           ;waiting, just return status.
```

Figure 5-8 continued.

```
182            jnz      pc_stat1
183            mov      ah,6               ;otherwise call PC-DOS to
184            mov      dl,0ffh            ;determine status.
185            int      21h
186            jz       pc_stat1           ;jump, nothing ready.
187                                        ;got a char, save it for
188                                        ;"pc_in" routine.
189            mov      in_char,al
190            mov      in_flag,0ffh
191    pc_stat1:                           ;return to caller with
192            ret                         ;Z flag set appropriately.
193    pc_stat endp
194
195
196    pc_in   proc     near               ;read a character from the
197                                         ;IBM PC's keyboard, return
198                                         ;it in AL.  DX may be destroyed.
199            mov      al,in_flag
200            or       al,al              ;any character waiting?
201            jnz      pc_in1             ;yes, return it to caller.
202            call     pc_stat            ;try and read a character.
203            jmp      pc_in
204    pc_in1: mov      in_flag,0          ;clear char waiting flag.
205            mov      al,in_char         ;exit with AL = char.
206            ret
207    pc_in   endp
208
209
210    pc_out  proc     near               ;write the character in AL
211                                         ;to the PC's display.
212            mov      ah,0eh             ;use ROM BIOS TTY output fxn.
213            push     bx                 ;save register.
214            xor      bx,bx              ;assume page 0.
215            int      10h                ;call ROM BIOS video driver.
216            pop      bx                 ;restore register.
217            ret
218    pc_out  endp
219
220
221    cls     proc     near               ;clear the display and set
222                                         ;it to the attribute in BH.
223                                         ;registers AX, CX, DX destroyed
224            mov      dl,columns
225            mov      dh,24              ;DL,DH = X,Y of lower right
226                                         ;corner of "window"
227            mov      cx,0               ;CL,CH = X,Y of upper left
228                                         ;corner of "window"
229            mov      ax,600h            ;AH = 6 for "scroll or initialize
```

Figure 5-8 continued.

```
230                                    ;window" function, AL = 0 for
231                                    ;number of lines to scroll
232              int     10h           ;call ROM BIOS video driver.
233              call    home          ;set cursor at (0,0).
234              ret
235    cls      endp
236
237
238    clreol   proc    near          ;clear from cursor to end of line
239                                    ;using the attribute in BH.
240                                    ;registers AX, CX, DX destroyed
241              call    getxy
242              mov     cx,dx         ;current position = "upper left"
243                                    ;corner of window
244              mov     dl,columns    ;for "lower right", X is max columns,
245                                    ; Y is the same.
246              mov     ax,600h       ;AH = 6 for "scroll or initialize
247                                    ;window" function, AL = 0 for
248                                    ;number of lines to scroll.
249              int     10h           ;call ROM BIOS video driver.
250              ret
251    clreol   endp
252
253
254    home     proc    near          ;home cursor (set X,Y = 0,0).
255              mov     dx,0
256              call    gotoxy
257              ret
258    home     endp
259
260
261    gotoxy   proc    near          ;position the cursor, call
262                                    ;with (DL,DH) = (X,Y).
263              push    bx            ;save registers.
264              push    ax
265              mov     bh,0          ;assume page 0.
266              mov     ah,2
267              int     10h           ;call ROM BIOS video driver.
268              pop     ax            ;restore registers.
269              pop     bx
270              ret
271    gotoxy   endp
272
273
274    getxy    proc    near          ;get the current cursor position,
275                                    ;returns (DL,DH) = (X,Y).
276              push    ax            ;save registers.
277              push    bx
```

Figure 5-8 continued.

```
278                 push    cx
279                 mov     ah,3
280                 mov     bh,0                    ;assume page 0.
281                 int     10h                     ;call ROM BIOS video driver.
282                 pop     cx                      ;restore registers.
283                 pop     bx
284                 pop     ax
285                 ret
286     getxy       endp
287
288
289     ctrl_code proc   near                       ;process a control code character.
290                                                 ;call with AL = char.
291                 cmp     al,cr                   ;if linefeed or carriage
292                 je      ctrl8                   ;return, just send it.
293                 cmp     al,lf
294                 je      ctrl8
295                 cmp     al,bsp                  ;or if backspace, just send it.
296                 je      ctrl8
297
298                 cmp     al,26                   ;is it clearscreen?
299                 jne     ctrl7                   ;no, jump.
300                 mov     bh,dattr
301                 call    cls                     ;clear screen and home cursor.
302                 ret
303
304     ctrl7:
305                 cmp     al,esc                  ;is it escape char?
306                 jne     ctrl9                   ;no, throw it away.
307                 call    esc_seq                 ;yes, emulate CRT terminal.
308                 ret
309
310     ctrl8:      call    pc_out                  ;send CR or LF to display
311
312     ctrl9:      ret                             ;and exit.
313
314     ctrl_code endp
315
316
317     esc_seq proc     near                       ;decode Televideo 950 escape
318                                                 ;sequence to control the screen.
319                 call    com_in
320                 cmp     al,84                   ;clear to end of line.
321                 jne     esc_seq1
322                 mov     bh,dattr
323                 call    clreol
324                 ret
325     esc_seq1:
326                 cmp     al,61                   ;cursor positioning
```

Figure 5-8 continued.

```
327              jne      esc_seq2
328              call     com_in        ;get Y.
329              sub      al,33         ;remove offset.
330              mov      dh,al
331              call     com_in        ;get X.
332              sub      al,33         ;remove offset.
333              mov      dl,al
334              call     gotoxy        ;set cursor.
335  esc_seq2:
336              ret
337  esc_seq endp
338
339
340  asc_enb proc     near          ;set up communications interrupt
341                                 ;vector, and enable interrupt.
342              mov      ah,35h        ;get current address of asynch
343              mov      al,com_int    ;port's interrupt handler.
344              int      21h           ;ES:BX = addr
345              mov      intc_seg,es   ;save segment.
346              mov      intc_offs,bx  ;save offset.
347
348              mov      dx,offset asc_int
349              mov      ah,25h        ;set address of new handler.
350              mov      al,com_int
351              int      21h
352
353              mov      dx,comm_mcr   ;modem controller DTR & OUT2
354              mov      al,0bh
355              out      dx,al
356
357              mov      dx,comm_ier   ;interrupt enable register
358              mov      al,1          ;on asynch controller
359              out      dx,al
360
361              in       al,pic_mask   ;read current 8259A int. mask.
362              and      al,not int_mask ;reset mask for this COM port.
363              out      pic_mask,al   ;write back 8259A int. mask.
364
365              ret
366
367  asc_enb endp
368
369  asc_dsb proc     near          ;disable interrupt and release
370                                 ;service vector
371                                 ;and enable interrupt.
372
373              in       al,pic_mask   ;read current 8259A int. mask.
374              or       al,int_mask   ;set mask for this COM port.
375              out      pic_mask,al   ;write int. mask back to 8259A.
```

Figure 5-8 continued.

```
376
377           push      ds
378           mov       dx,intc_offs        ;saved offset
379           mov       ds,intc_seg         ;saved segment
380           mov       ah,25h              ;restore address of original
381           mov       al,com_int          ;com port interrupt handler.
382           int       21h
383           pop       ds
384           ret
385   asc_dsb endp
386
387
388   asc_int proc      far                 ;interrupt service routine
389                                         ;for asynch controller
390
391           sti                           ;turn interrupts back on.
392           push      ax                  ;save all necessary registers.
393           push      bx
394           push      dx
395           push      ds
396           mov       ax,cs
397           mov       ds,ax
398           mov       dx,comm_data
399           in        al,dx               ;read this character.
400           cli                           ;clear interrupts for
401                                         ;pointer manipulation.
402           mov       bx,asc_in           ;get buffer pointer.
403           mov       [asc_buf+bx],al     ;store this character.
404           inc       bx                  ;bump pointer.
405           cmp       bx,asc_buf_len      ;time for wrap?
406           jne       asc_int1            ;no, jump.
407           xor       bx,bx               ;yes, reset pointer.
408   asc_int1:
409           mov       asc_in,bx           ;store back updated pointer.
410           sti                           ;turn interrupts back on.
411           mov       al,20h              ;send EOI to 8259A.
412           out       pic_eoi,al
413           pop       ds                  ;restore all registers
414           pop       dx
415           pop       bx
416           pop       ax
417           iret                          ;and exit handler.
418   asc_int endp
419
420
421   in_char db        0                   ;PC keyboard input char.
422   in_flag db        0                   ;<>0 if char waiting
423
424   columns db        0                   ;highest numbered column in
```

Figure 5-8 continued.

```
425                                          ;current display mode (39 or 79)
426
427   msg1           db       cr,lf,'Display must be text mode.'
428                  db       cr,lf,'$'
429
430   msg2           db       cr,lf,lf,'Exit from terminal emulator.'
431                  db       cr,lf,'$'
432
433   intc_offs      dw       0        ;original contents of Int OCH
434   intc_seg       dw       0        ;service vector
435
436   asc_in         dw       0        ;input pointer to ring buffer
437   asc_out        dw       0        ;output pointer to ring buffer
438
439   asc_buf_len    equ      16384
440
441   asc_buf        equ      this byte
442
443   cseg    ends
444
445           end      talk
```

Figure 5-8 continued.

The *TALK* program is a good illustration of the methods that an application should use to take over and service interrupts from the serial port without running afoul of MS-DOS conventions.

The program begins with some equates and conditional assembly statements that configure the serial port controller for half- or full-duplex and for the desired serial port (COM1 or COM2). Next, the main routine of the program—the procedure named *talk*—checks the status of the serial port, initializes the display, and calls the routine *asc_enb* to take over the serial port interrupt vector and enable interrupts. The *talk* procedure then enters a loop that reads the keyboard and sends the characters out the serial port, reads the serial port, and puts the characters on the display—in other words, it causes the PC to emulate a simple CRT terminal.

The *TALK* program intercepts and handles control codes (carriage return, linefeed, and so forth) appropriately. It detects escape sequences and handles them as a subset of the Televideo 950 terminal capabilities. When one of the PC's special function keys is pressed, the program disables serial port interrupts, releases the serial port interrupt vector, and exits back to MS-DOS.

There are several TALK program procedures that merit close study. These are listed in the table on the next page.

Procedure	Action
asc—enb	Takes over the serial port interrupt vector and enables interrupts by writing to the modem control register of the INS8250 and the interrupt mask register of the 8259A.
asc—dsb	Restores the original state of the serial port interrupt vector and disables interrupts by writing to the interrupt mask register of the 8259A.
asc—int	Services serial port interrupts, placing received characters into a ring buffer.
com—stat	Tests whether characters from the serial port are waiting in the ring buffer.
com—in	Removes characters from the interrupt handler's ring buffer and increments the buffer pointers appropriately.
com—out	Sends one character to the serial port.
cls	Calls the ROM BIOS video driver to clear the screen.
clreol	Calls the ROM BIOS video driver to clear from the current cursor position to the end of the line.
home	Places the cursor in the upper left corner of the screen.
gotoxy	Positions the cursor at the desired position on the display.
getxy	Obtains the current cursor position.
pc—out	Sends one character to the PC's display.
pc—stat	Gets status for the PC's keyboard.
pc—in	Returns a character from the PC's keyboard.

Chapter 6

MS-DOS File and Record Manipulation

As discussed in previous chapters, MS-DOS is largely compatible with both UNIX/XENIX and Digital Research's CP/M, and was designed this way to ease the porting of applications into MS-DOS from those two environments. Consequently, MS-DOS supports a large battery of disk file- and record-management calls with considerable functional overlap—in general, there are at least two distinct operating-system calls for each major file or record function. In this chapter, we will factor this overlapping set of functions into separate and easily understandable groups, summarize the advantages and disadvantages of each group, and point out which of the functions are most important and which are used infrequently.

We will refer to the set of file and record functions that are compatible with CP/M as *FCB functions*. These functions rely on a data structure called a *file control block* (hence, FCB) to maintain certain bookkeeping information about open files. This structure resides in the application program's memory space. The FCB functions allow the programmer to create, open, close, and delete files, and to read or write records of any size at any record position within such files. These functions do not support the hierarchical (tree-like) file structure that was first introduced in MS-DOS version 2.0, which means that they can be used only to access files in the current subdirectory for a given disk drive.

We will refer to the set of file and record functions that provide compatibility with UNIX/XENIX as the *Handle functions*. Using these functions, files are opened or created by passing MS-DOS a null-terminated string that describes the file's location in the hierarchical file structure (the path), the file's name, and its extension. If the open or create is successful, MS-DOS returns a 16-bit token, or *handle*, that is saved by the application program and used to specify the file in subsequent operations.

When the Handle functions are used, the data structures that contain bookkeeping information about the file are maintained by the operating system inside its own memory space, and are not accessible to the application program. The Handle functions fully support the hierarchical file structure, allowing the programmer to create, open, close, and delete files in any subdirectory on any disk drive, and to read or write records of any size at any byte offset within such files.

Using the FCB Functions

Understanding the structure of the file control block is the key to success with the FCB family of file and record functions. An FCB is a 37-byte-long data structure allocated within the application program's memory space; it is divided into many fields (Figure 6-1). Typically, an FCB is initialized by the program with a drive code, a filename, and an extension (conveniently accomplished with the parse-filename service, Int 21H function 29H), and the address of the FCB is then passed to MS-DOS to open or create the file.

If the file is successfully opened or created, MS-DOS fills in certain fields of the FCB with information from the file's entry in the disk directory. This information includes the file's exact size in bytes and the date the file was created or last updated. Certain other information is also placed within a reserved area of the FCB; however, this area is used by the operating system for its own purposes and varies among different versions of MS-DOS. The reserved area should never be modified by application programs.

For compatibility with CP/M, MS-DOS automatically sets the record-size field of the FCB to 128 bytes. If the program does not want to use this default record size, it must place the desired size (in bytes) into the record-size field. Subsequently, when the program needs to read or write records from the file, it must pass the address of the FCB to MS-DOS; MS-DOS, in turn, keeps the FCB updated with information about the current position of the file pointer and the size of the file. If the application program wishes to perform random record access, it must set the record number into the file control block *before* issuing each function call; when sequential record access is being used, MS-DOS maintains the FCB and no special intervention is needed from the application.

In general, MS-DOS calls that use file control blocks accept the full address of the FCB in registers DS:DX and pass back a return code in register AL (Figure 6-2). For file-management calls (open, close, create, and delete), this return code is zero if the function was successful and 0FFH (255) if the function failed. For the FCB-type record read and write functions, the success code returned in register AL is again zero, but there are several different failure codes. Under MS-DOS version 3.0 or above, more detailed error reporting can be obtained by calling function 59H (get extended error) after a failed FCB function call.

When a program is loaded under MS-DOS, the operating system sets up two file control blocks in the program segment prefix, at offsets 005CH and 006CH. These are often referred to as the *default FCBs*, and they are included to provide upward compatibility from CP/M. The first two parameters in the command line that invokes the program (excluding any redirection directives) are parsed by MS-DOS into the default FCBs, under the assumption that they may be file specifications. It is the responsibility of the application to determine whether they really *are* filenames or not. In addition, since the default FCBs overlap and are not in a particularly convenient location (especially for EXE programs), they usually must be copied elsewhere in order to be used safely (see Chapter 2).

byte
offset

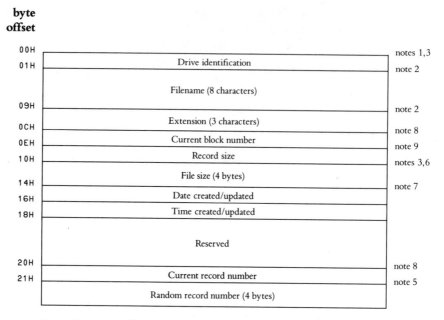

Figure 6-1. Normal file control block. Total length is 37 bytes (25H bytes). See notes on page 114.

It should be noted that the structures of FCBs under CP/M and MS-DOS are not identical. However, the differences lie chiefly in the reserved areas of the FCBs, which should not be manipulated by application programs in any case, so well-behaved CP/M applications should be relatively easy to port into MS-DOS. It seems, however, that few such applications exist. Many of the tricks that were played by clever CP/M programmers to increase performance or circumvent the limitations of that operating system

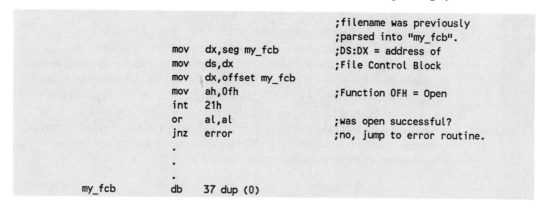

```
                                        ;filename was previously
                                        ;parsed into "my_fcb".
        mov     dx,seg my_fcb           ;DS:DX = address of
        mov     ds,dx                   ;File Control Block
        mov     dx,offset my_fcb
        mov     ah,0fh                  ;Function 0FH = Open
        int     21h
        or      al,al                   ;was open successful?
        jnz     error                   ;no, jump to error routine.
        .
        .
        .
my_fcb  db      37 dup (0)
```

Figure 6-2. Example of an FCB file operation. This sequence of code attempts to open the file whose name was previously parsed into the FCB named my_fcb.

00H	
	0FFH
01H	
	Reserved (5 bytes, must be zero)
06H	
	Attribute byte
07H	
	Drive identification
08H	
	Filename (8 characters)
10H	
	Extension (3 characters)
13H	
	Current block number
15H	
	Record size
17H	
	File size (4 bytes)
1BH	
	Date created/updated
1DH	
	Time created/updated
1FH	
	Reserved
27H	
	Current record number
28H	
	Random record number (4 bytes)

Notes (right side): note 10, note 11, notes 1,3, note 2, note 2, note 8, note 9, notes 3,6, note 7, note 8, note 5

Figure 6-3. Extended file control block. Total length is 44 bytes (2CH bytes). See notes on page 114.

can cause severe problems under MS-DOS, particularly in networking environments. At any rate, much better performance can be achieved by thoroughly rewriting the CP/M applications to take advantage of the superior capabilities of MS-DOS.

A special FCB variant called an *extended file control block* can be used to create or access files with special attributes (such as hidden or read-only files), volume labels, and subdirectories. An extended FCB has a 7-byte header followed by the 37-byte structure of a normal FCB (Figure 6-3). The first byte contains 0FFH, which could never be a legal drive code and thus indicates to MS-DOS that an extended FCB is being used. The next 5 bytes are reserved, and are unused in current versions of MS-DOS. The seventh byte contains the attribute of the special file type that is being accessed (attribute bytes are discussed in more detail in Chapter 7). Any MS-DOS function that uses a normal FCB can also use an extended FCB.

Notes for Figures 6-1 and 6-3

1. The drive identification is a binary number: 00 = default drive, 01 = drive A:, 02 = drive B:, and so on. If the drive code is supplied by the application program as zero (default drive), the code for the actual current disk drive is filled in by MS-DOS after a successful open or create call.

2. File and extension names must be left justified and padded with blanks.

3. In a normal FCB, bytes 0000H through 000FH and 0020H through 0024H are set by the user. Bytes 0010H through 001FH are used by MS-DOS and should not be modified by applications.

4. All word fields are stored with the least significant byte at the lower address.

5. The random-record field is treated as 4 bytes if the record size is less than 64 bytes; otherwise, only the first 3 bytes of this field are used.

6. The file-size field is in the same format as in the directory, with the less significant word at the lower address.

7. The date field is mapped as in the directory. Viewed as a 16-bit word (as it would appear after loading into a register), the field is broken down as:

F E D C B A 9	8 7 6 5	4 3 2 1 0
year	month	day

Bits	Contents
00–04H	Day
05–08H	Month
09–0FH	Year, relative to 1980

8. The current-block and current-record numbers are used together on sequential reads and writes. This simulates the behavior of CP/M.

9. The record-size field is set to 128 bytes by the open (0FH) and create (16H) functions, to provide compatibility with CP/M. If you want to use another record size, you must fill it in *after* the open or create function.

10. An 0FFH (255) in the first byte of the structure signifies that it is an extended file control block. Extended FCBs can be used with any of the calls that accept an ordinary FCB (see also note 11 below).

11. The attribute byte in an extended FCB allows access to files with the special characteristics hidden, system, or read-only. Extended FCBs can also be used to read volume labels and the contents of special subdirectory files.

For better understanding of the FCB file- and record-management calls, they may be gathered into the following broad classifications:

Function	Action
Common FCB file operations	
0FH	Open file
10H	Close file
16H	Create file
Common FCB record operations	
14H	Sequential read
15H	Sequential write
21H	Random read
22H	Random write
27H	Random block read
28H	Random block write
Other vital FCB operations	
1AH	Set disk transfer address
29H	Parse filename
Less commonly used FCB file operations	
13H	Delete file
17H	Rename file
Less commonly used FCB record operations	
23H	Obtain file size
24H	Set random record number

Several of these functions have special properties. For example, functions 27H (random block read) and 28H (random block write) allow reading and writing of multiple records of any size, and also update the random-record field automatically (unlike functions 21H and 22H). Function 28H can truncate a file to any desired size, and function 17H used with an extended FCB is the only way to alter a volume label or rename a subdirectory.

Detailed specifications for each of the FCB file and record functions, along with assembly-language examples, will be found in Section 2 of this book. It is also instructive to compare the preceding groups with the corresponding Handle-function groups listed on page 122.

FCB File-Access Skeleton

A typical program sequence to access a file using the FCB, or traditional, function calls (see Figure 6-4) would be:

1. Zero out the prospective file control block.

2. Obtain the filename from the user, from the default file control blocks, or from the command tail in the program segment prefix.

3. If the filename was not obtained from one of the default file control blocks, parse the filename into the new file control block using function 29H.

4. Open the file (function 0FH) or, if writing new data only, create the file or truncate any existing file by the same name to zero length (function 16H).

5. Set the record-size field in the FCB, unless the default record size is being used. Recall that it is important to do this *after* a successful open or create operation (see Figure 6-5 on page 119).

6. Set the record-number field in the FCB, if performing random record I/O.

7. Set the disk transfer area address using function 1AH, unless the buffer address has not been changed since the last call to this function. If no set DTA is ever performed by the application, the DTA address defaults to offset 0080H in the PSP.

8. Request the appropriate read or write record operation (function 14H–sequential read, 15H–sequential write, 21H– random read, 22H–random write, 27H–random block read, or 28H–random block write).

9. If not finished, go to step 6; otherwise, close the file (function 10H). If the file was used for reading only, the close operation can be skipped under early versions of MS-DOS. However, this shortcut can cause problems under MS-DOS versions 3.0 or higher, especially when files are being accessed across a network.

```
recsize         equ     1024                    ;file record size
                .
                .
                .
                mov     ah,29h                  ;parse input filename.
                mov     al,1                    ;skip leading blanks.
                mov     si,offset fname1        ;address of filename
                mov     di,offset fcb1          ;address of FCB
                int     21h
                or      al,al                   ;jump if name
                jnz     name_err                ;was bad.
                .
                .
                .
                mov     ah,29h                  ;parse output filename.
                mov     al,1                    ;skip leading blanks.
                mov     si,offset fname2        ;address of filename
                mov     di,offset fcb2          ;address of FCB
                int     21h
                or      al,al                   ;jump if name
                jnz     name_err                ;was bad.
                .
                .
                .
                mov     ah,0fh                  ;open input file.
                mov     dx,offset fcb1
                int     21h
                or      al,al                   ;open successful?
                jnz     no_file                 ;no, jump.
                .
                .
                .
                mov     ah,16h                  ;create and open
                mov     dx,offset fcb2          ;output file.
                int     21h
                or      al,al                   ;create successful?
                jnz     disk_full               ;no, jump.
                .
                .
                .                               ;set record sizes.
                mov     word ptr fcb1+0eh,recsize
                mov     word ptr fcb2+0eh,recsize
                .
                .
                .
                mov     ah,1ah                  ;set disk transfer
                mov     dx,offset buffer        ;address for reads
                int     21h                     ;and writes.
```

(continued)

Figure 6-4. Skeleton of an assembly-language program that performs file and record I/O using the FCB family of function calls.

```
next:                .                         ;process next record.
                     .
                     .
              mov    ah,14h                     ;sequential read from
              mov    dx,offset fcb1             ;input file
              int    21h
              cmp    al,01                      ;check for end of file.
              je     file_end                   ;jump if end of file.
              cmp    al,03
              je     file_end                   ;jump if end of file.
              or     al,al                      ;other read fault?
              jnz    bad_read                   ;jump if bad read.
                     .
                     .
                     .
              mov    ah,15h                     ;sequential write to
              mov    dx,offset fcb2             ;output file
              int    21h
              or     al,al                      ;write successful?
              jnz    bad_write                  ;jump if write failed.
                     .
                     .
                     .
              jmp    next                       ;process next record.
                     .
file_end:            .                         ;reached end of input
                     .
              mov    ah,10h                     ;close input file.
              mov    dx,offset fcb1
              int    21h
                     .
                     .
                     .
              mov    ah,10h                     ;close output file.
              mov    dx,offset fcb2
              int    21h
                     .
                     .
                     .
              mov    ax,4c00h                   ;exit with return
              int    21h                        ;code of zero.
                     .
                     .
                     .
fname1        db     'OLDFILE.DAT',0            ;name of input file
fname2        db     'NEWFILE.DAT',0            ;name of output file
fcb1          db     37 dup (0)                 ;FCB for input file
fcb2          db     37 dup (0)                 ;FCB for output file
buffer        db     recsize dup (?)            ;buffer for file I/O
```

Figure 6-4 continued.

byte offset	FCB before open	FCB contents	FCB after open
00H	00	Drive	03
01H	4D		4D
02H	59		59
03H	46		46
04H	49	Filename	49
05H	4C		4C
06H	45		45
07H	20		20
08H	20		20
09H	44		44
0AH	41	Extension	41
0BH	54		54
0CH	00	Current block	00
0DH	00		00
0EH	00	Record size	80
0FH	00		00
10H	00		80
11H	00	File size	3D
12H	00		00
13H	00		00
14H	00	File date	43
15H	00		0B
16H	00	File time	A1
17H	00		52
18H	00		03
19H	00		02
1AH	00		42
1BH	00	Reserved	73
1CH	00		00
1DH	00		01
1EH	00		35
1FH	00		0F
20H	00	Current record	00
21H	00		00
22H	00	Random record number	00
23H	00		00
24H	00		00

Figure 6-5. A typical file control block before and after a successful open call (Int 21H function 0FH).

Points to Remember

Here is a summary of the pros and cons of using the FCB-related file and record functions in your programs.

Advantages:

● Under MS-DOS versions 1 and 2, there is no limit on the number of files that can be open concurrently when using FCBs. (This is not true under version 3, especially if networking software is running.)

- File-access methods using FCBs are very familiar to programmers with a CP/M background, and well-behaved CP/M applications require little change in logical flow to run under MS-DOS.

- The size and date for a file are supplied to its file control block after it is opened, and can be inspected by the calling program.

Disadvantages:

- File control blocks take up room in the user's memory space.

- FCBs offer no support for the hierarchical file structure (no access to files outside the current subdirectory).

- FCBs provide no support for file locking/sharing or record locking in networking environments.

- File reads or writes using FCBs require manipulation of the file control block to set record size and record number, in addition to the read or write call itself, plus a previous separate MS-DOS function call to set the DTA address.

- Random record I/O using FCBs for a file containing variable-length records is very clumsy and inconvenient.

- Extended file control blocks, which are incompatible with CP/M anyway, are required to access or create files with special attributes such as hidden, read-only, or system.

- The FCB file functions have poor error reporting. This situation has been improved somewhat in MS-DOS version 3, since the added function 59H (get extended error) can be called after a failed FCB function to obtain additional information.

- Use of the CP/M-like calls is discouraged by Microsoft, and support for these calls may be progressively curtailed in future releases of MS-DOS. (This restriction process has already begun in version 3.)

Using the Handle File and Record Functions

The Handle file- and record-management functions are used to access files in a fashion similar to that used under the UNIX/XENIX operating system. Files are designated by an ASCIIZ string (an ASCII character string terminated by a null or zero byte) that can contain a drive designator, path, filename, and extension. For example, the file specification

C:\SYSTEM\COMMAND.COM

would appear in memory as the sequence of bytes:

43 3A 5C 53 59 53 54 45 4D 5C 43 4F 4D 4D 41 4E 44 2E 43 4F 4D 00

When a program wishes to open or create a file, the address of the ASCIIZ string specifying the file is passed to MS-DOS in registers DS:DX (Figure 6-6. If the operation is successful, a 16-bit handle is returned to the program in AX by MS-DOS. This handle must be saved for further reference.

When subsequent operations are requested on the file, the handle is usually placed in register BX before the call to MS-DOS. All the Handle functions return with the CPU's carry flag cleared if the operation was successful, or set if the operation failed; in the latter case, register AX contains a code describing the failure.

The number of handles that can be active at any one time—that is, the number of files and devices that can be open concurrently when using the Handle family of function calls—is restricted in two different ways:

- The maximum number of concurrently open files in the system, for all active processes combined, is specified by the entry

    FILES = nn

    in the CONFIG.SYS file. This entry determines the number of entries to be allocated in the *system open-file table*; under MS-DOS version 3, the default value is 8 and the maximum is 255. Once MS-DOS is booted and running, there is no way to expand this table to increase the total number of files that can be open. You must use an editor to modify the CONFIG.SYS file and then re-boot the system.

- The maximum number of concurrently open files for a single process is 20, assuming that sufficient entries are also available in the system open-file table. When a program is loaded, 5 of its potential 20 handles are pre-assigned to the standard devices. Each time the process issues an open or create function call, a handle is assigned from its private allocation of 20, until all the handles are used up or the system open-file table is full.

```
        mov    ah,3dh                  ;function 3DH = open
        mov    al,2                    ;mode 2 = read/write
        mov    dx,seg filename         ;address of ASCIIZ
        mov    ds,dx                   ;file specification
        mov    dx,offset filename
        int    21h                     ;request open from DOS.
        jc     error                   ;jump if open failed.
        mov    handle,ax               ;save file handle.
        .
        .
        .
filename  db   'C:\MYDIR\MYFILE.DAT',0
handle    dw   0
```

Figure 6-6. Example of a typical Handle file operation. This sequence of code attempts to open the file designated in the ASCIIZ string whose address is passed to MS-DOS in registers DS:DX.

For easier understanding of the Handle file- and record-management calls, they may be gathered into the following broad classifications for study:

Function	Action
Common Handle file operations	
3CH	Create file (requires ASCIIZ string)
3DH	Open file (requires ASCIIZ string)
3EH	Close file
Common Handle record operations	
42H	Set file pointer (also used to find file size)
3FH	Read record
40H	Write record
Less commonly used Handle file operations	
41H	Delete file
43H	Get or modify file attributes
56H	Rename file
57H	Get or set file date and time
5AH	Create temporary file (version 3 only)
5BH	Create file (fails if file already exists; version 3 only)

Compare the groups of Handle-type functions above with the groups of FCB functions outlined earlier, noting the degree of functional overlap. Detailed specifications for each of the Handle functions will be found in Section 2 of this book, along with assembly-language examples.

Handle File-Access Skeleton

A typical program sequence to access a file using the Handle, or UNIX/XENIX-like, family of function calls (see Figure 6-7) would be:

1. Get the filename from the user via the buffered input service (Int 21H function 0AH) or from the command tail supplied by MS-DOS in the program segment prefix.

2. Put a zero at the end of the file specification to create an ASCIIZ string.

3. Open the file using Int 21H function 3DH and mode 2 (read/write access), or create the file using function 3CH (make sure to set register CX to zero, so that you don't accidentally make a file with special attributes). Save the handle that is returned.

4. Set the file pointer using Int 21H function 42H. You may set the file-pointer position relative to one of three different locations: the start of the file, the current pointer position, or the end of the file. If you are performing sequential record I/O, you can usually skip this step, since MS-DOS will maintain the file pointer for you automatically.

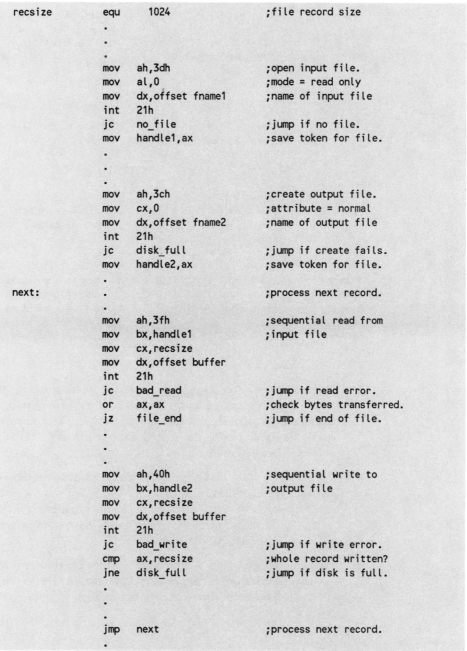

```
recsize      equ     1024                    ;file record size
             .
             .
             .
             mov     ah,3dh                  ;open input file.
             mov     al,0                    ;mode = read only
             mov     dx,offset fname1        ;name of input file
             int     21h
             jc      no_file                 ;jump if no file.
             mov     handle1,ax              ;save token for file.
             .
             .
             .
             mov     ah,3ch                  ;create output file.
             mov     cx,0                    ;attribute = normal
             mov     dx,offset fname2        ;name of output file
             int     21h
             jc      disk_full               ;jump if create fails.
             mov     handle2,ax              ;save token for file.
             .
next:        .                               ;process next record.
             .
             mov     ah,3fh                  ;sequential read from
             mov     bx,handle1              ;input file
             mov     cx,recsize
             mov     dx,offset buffer
             int     21h
             jc      bad_read                ;jump if read error.
             or      ax,ax                   ;check bytes transferred.
             jz      file_end                ;jump if end of file.
             .
             .
             .
             mov     ah,40h                  ;sequential write to
             mov     bx,handle2              ;output file
             mov     cx,recsize
             mov     dx,offset buffer
             int     21h
             jc      bad_write               ;jump if write error.
             cmp     ax,recsize              ;whole record written?
             jne     disk_full               ;jump if disk is full.
             .
             .
             .
             jmp     next                    ;process next record.
             .
```

(continued)

Figure 6-7. Skeleton of an assembly-language program that performs sequential processing on an input file and writes the results to an output file, using the Handle file and record functions. This code assumes that DS and ES have already been set to point to the segment containing the buffers and filenames.

```
file_end:        .                                   ;reached end of input
                 .
                 .
                 mov   ah,3eh                         ;close input file.
                 mov   bx,handle1
                 int   21h
                 .
                 .
                 .
                 mov   ah,3eh                         ;close output file.
                 mov   bx,handle2
                 int   21h
                 .
                 .
                 .
                 mov   ax,4c00h                       ;exit with return
                 int   21h                            ;code of zero.
                 .
                 .
                 .
fname1           db    'OLDFILE.DAT',0                ;name of input file
fname2           db    'NEWFILE.DAT',0                ;name of output file
handle1          dw    0                              ;token for input file
handle2          dw    0                              ;token for output file
buffer           db    recsize dup (?)                ;buffer for file I/O
```

Figure 6-7 continued.

5. Read from the file (function 3FH) or write to the file (function 40H).
    Both of these functions require that BX contain the file's handle, CX
    contain the length of the record, and DS:DX point to the memory
    address for the data being transferred. Both return in AX the actual
    number of bytes transferred.

    When reading, if the number of bytes read is less than the number re-
    quested, the end of the file has been reached. When writing, if the
    number of bytes written is less than the number requested, the disk
    containing the file is full. *Neither of these conditions is returned as an error
    code*; that is, the carry flag is *not* set.

6. If not finished, go to step 4; otherwise, close the file (function 3EH).
    Any normal exit from the program except function 31H (terminate
    and stay resident) will also close all active handles.

Points to Remember

Here is a summary of the pros and cons of using the Handle file and record operations in your program. Compare this list with the one given earlier in the chapter for the FCB family of functions.

Advantages:

- The Handle calls provide direct support for I/O redirection and pipes with the standard input and output devices in a manner functionally similar to that used by UNIX/XENIX.

- The Handle functions provide direct support for subdirectories (the hierarchical file structure) and special file attributes.

- The Handle calls support file sharing/locking and record locking in networking environments.

- Using the Handle functions, the programmer can open channels to character devices and treat them as files.

- The Handle calls make the use of random record access extremely easy. The current file pointer can be moved to any byte offset relative to the start of the file, the end of the file, or the current pointer position. Records of any length, up to an entire segment (65535 bytes), can be read to any memory address in one operation.

- The Handle functions have relatively good error reporting in MS-DOS version 2, and it has been enhanced even further in version 3.

- Use of the Handle family of function calls is strongly encouraged by Microsoft, to provide upward compatibility with future MS-DOS environments.

Disadvantages:

- There are definite limits on the number of concurrently open files (but these limits are also present for files opened with FCBs under MS-DOS version 3).

- Minor gaps still exist in the implementation of the Handle function calls. For example, extended FCBs must still be used to access volume labels and the contents of the special files that implement subdirectories. However, we can expect these slight inconsistencies to disappear in future versions of MS-DOS.

MS-DOS Error Codes

When one of the Handle file functions fails with the carry flag set, or when function 59H (get extended error) is called following a failed FCB function or other system service, one of the following error codes may be returned:

Code	Meaning
Version 2 file-function errors	
01	Invalid function number
02	File not found
03	Path not found
04	Too many open files (no open handles left)
05	Access denied
06	Invalid handle
07	Memory control blocks destroyed
08	Insufficient memory
09	Invalid memory block address
10	Invalid environment
11	Invalid format
12	Invalid access code
13	Invalid data
14	Reserved
15	Invalid disk drive
16	Attempt to remove current directory
17	Not same device
18	No more files
Mappings to critical error handler	
19	Disk write-protected
20	Unknown disk unit
21	Drive not ready
22	Unknown command
23	Data error (CRC)
24	Bad request structure length
25	Seek error
26	Unknown media type
27	Sector not found
28	Printer out of paper
29	Write fault
30	Read fault
31	General failure

(continued)

Version 3 additional error codes

32	Sharing violation
33	Lock violation
34	Invalid disk change
35	FCB unavailable
36	Sharing buffer overflow
37–49	Reserved
50	Network request not supported
51	Remote computer not listening
52	Duplicate name on network
53	Network name not found
54	Network busy
55	Network device no longer exists
56	Network BIOS command limit exceeded
57	Network adapter hardware error
58	Incorrect response from network
59	Unexpected network error
60	Incompatible remote adapter
61	Print queue full
62	Print queue not full
63	Print file deleted (not enough space)
64	Network name deleted
65	Access denied
66	Network device type incorrect
67	Network name not found
68	Network name limit exceeded
69	Network BIOS session limit exceeded
70	Temporarily paused
71	Network request not accepted
72	Print or disk redirection paused
73–79	Reserved
80	File already exists
81	Reserved
82	Cannot make directory entry
83	Failure on Int 24H
84	Too many redirections
85	Duplicate redirection
86	Invalid password
87	Invalid parameter
88	Network device fault

Under MS-DOS version 3, function 59H can also be used to obtain other information about the error, such as the error locus and the recommended recovery action.

Writing Well-Behaved MS-DOS Applications

Microsoft and IBM have set forth certain guidelines that should be followed whenever possible to create well-behaved MS-DOS or PC-DOS application programs. Applications that adhere to these guidelines will be likely to run correctly in future multitasking or networking versions of MS-DOS and PC-DOS, and will also be less likely to cause unexpected interactions with other programs in the current versions.

- Use the new Handle (UNIX/XENIX-like) file system calls (functions 2FH through 5CH) in preference to the older, less powerful FCB (CP/M-like) file functions.

- If you must use FCBs, close them when you are done with them, and don't move them around while they are open. Avoid reopening FCBs that are already open, or reclosing FCBs that have previously been closed—these seemingly harmless practices can cause problems in the networking environment.

- Use the environment block to check the path to your program's overlays or data files (see Chapter 9).

- Use the EXEC function call (4BH) when loading overlays or other programs, to isolate yourself from program structures and relocation requirements (see Chapter 10).

- Release any memory not used by your program. This is especially important for COM-type programs.

- Don't touch any memory not owned by your program. To set or inspect interrupt vectors, use Int 21H functions 25H and 35H (see Chapter 11).

- If you alter the contents of interrupt vectors, save their original values and restore them before the program exits (see the *TALK* program in Chapter 5 for an example).

- Avoid the use of hardware-dependent timing loops. Instead, use Int 21H function 2CH (the system get time service) whenever programmed delays are needed.

- Use buffered I/O whenever possible. The device drivers in MS-DOS versions 2.0 and above can handle strings as long as 64 Kbytes, and performance will be improved if you write fewer, larger records as opposed to many short ones.

- Take advantage of the extended error reporting (function 59H) available under MS-DOS version 3.

- Exit via Int 21H function 4CH (terminate with return code) or function 31H (terminate and stay resident with return code). The common convention is to use a zero return code for a normal exit and a nonzero return code for exits due to some kind of error or unforeseen situation. These return codes can then be inspected in batch files or by parent processes. The older methods of exit through Int 20H or Int 21H function 0 should be avoided.

Writing Hardware–Dependent IBM PC Applications

Many programmers have felt it impractical to write sophisticated high-performance applications for the IBM PC family without building some hardware dependence into the programs. IBM has taken notice of these practices and has committed to keeping certain portions of the hardware interface stable for the foreseeable future†. These portions include:

Hardware

- Sound control via port 61H

- The 8253-5 timer chip's channels 0 and 2—ports 40H, 42H, and 43H. Don't meddle with port 41H—it controls the dynamic RAM refresh. Input frequency to 8253-5 will remain at 1.9 mHz, regardless of the clock speed of the rest of the system.

- The game adapter at port 201H

- Vertical and horizontal retrace-interval status bits in ports 3BAH and 3DAH

- Control of the interrupt system via the 8259A mask register at port 21H

- The INS8250 asynchronous communications controller at ports 03F8 through 03FFH

Memory

- Interrupt vectors
  The ROM BIOS services will continue to be available on the same interrupt numbers, and will always be upwardly compatible. If you take over an interrupt, you should chain to the previous owner of the interrupt.

- Video refresh buffers at 0B0000H and 0B8000H for the original display modes (0 through 7)

- ROM BIOS data area at 00400H ("whenever reasonable")

Warning: Programs that take advantage of hardware-dependent information will not run properly under MS-DOS on machines that are not IBM PC compatible, and may behave erratically or cause system crashes in multitasking environments such as Microsoft Windows, GEM, and TopView. Sound generation and direct programming of the 8253-5 timer or 8259A interrupt controller are particularly likely to cause multitasking problems.

† *IBM Personal Computer Seminar Proceedings*. November 1983. Vol. 1, No. 3, p. 23.

Machine Identification

The byte at 0FFFFEH (F000:FFFE) designates the machine's status in the IBM PC family:

Value	Model
0FFH	PC
0FEH	PC/XT
0FDH	PCjr
0FCH	PC/AT
0F9H	PC Convertible

The content of this location on the IBM PC-compatible machines varies greatly. For example, on the original Compaq Portable with ROM Revision C, this location contains zero. On the Compaq 286 Portable, the byte contains 0FCH (which makes sense, since the machine is supposed to emulate an IBM PC/AT in every way).

In general, other methods must be resorted to when you are attempting to determine the identity of a non–IBM machine. For example, you can determine whether the host machine is a Compaq by scanning the ROM space for the Compaq Corporation's copyright notice (Figure 6-8). This turns out to be a handy piece of information to have because the Compaq video adapter does not have a snow problem, so the horizontal retrace interval can be ignored in alphanumeric display modes.

Critical Error Handlers

In Chapter 5, we discussed how an application program can take over the Ctrl-C handler vector (Int 23H) and replace the MS-DOS default handler, to avoid losing control of the computer when the operator enters a Ctrl-C or Ctrl-Break at the keyboard. Similarly, MS-DOS provides a critical error handler vector (Int 24H) that defines the routine to be called when unrecoverable hardware faults occur. The default MS-DOS critical error handler is the routine that displays a message describing the error type and the cue:

Abort, Retry, Ignore?

This message is seen after such actions as:

● Attempting to open a file on a disk drive that doesn't contain a floppy disk or whose door isn't closed.

● Trying to read a disk sector that contains a CRC error.

● Trying to print something when the printer is off line.

```
compaq          proc  near                              ;test whether host machine
                                                        ; is a Compaq computer.
                                                        ;Return AX = -1 if Compaq,
                                                        ;       AX = 0  if not.
                                                        ;
                mov   ax,0f000h                         ;search ROM BIOS for
                mov   es,ax                             ;COMPAQ copyright notice.
                mov   di,0a000h
                mov   cx,05fffh
compaq1:        mov   al,'C'                            ;look for initial C.
                repnz scasb
                jnz   compaq2                           ;ROM exhausted, string
                                                        ; "COMPAQ" not found
                push  di                                ;save current ROM pointer.
                push  cx
                push  si
                mov   cx,6                              ;found C, try & match
                mov   si,offset compaq_name             ; the string "COMPAQ".
                dec   di
                repz  cmpsb
                pop   si                                ;restore ROM pointer.
                pop   cx
                pop   di
                jnz   compaq1                           ;jump, strings don't match.
                mov   ax,-1                             ;return Compaq = True.
                ret
compaq2:        mov   ax,0                              ;return Compaq = False.
                ret
compaq          endp
compaq_name     db    'COMPAQ'
```

Figure 6-8. Routine to determine whether host machine is a member of the Compaq line of personal computers.

The unpleasant thing about MS-DOS's default critical error handler is, of course, that if the user enters an *A* for *Abort*, the application that is currently executing will be terminated abruptly, and will never get a chance to clean up and make a graceful exit. Intermediate files may be left on the disk, files that have been extended may not be properly closed so that the directory is updated, interrupt vectors may be left pointing into the transient program area, and so forth.

To write a truly bombproof MS-DOS application, you must take over the critical error handler vector and point it to your own routine, so that your program intercepts all catastrophic hardware errors and handles them appropriately. MS-DOS Int 21H function 25H can be used to alter the Int 24H vector in a well-behaved manner. When your application exits, MS-DOS will automatically restore the previous contents of the Int 24H vector from information saved in the program segment prefix.

MS-DOS calls the critical error handler for two general classes of errors: disk-related and non-disk-related. Different information is passed in the registers for each of these classes.

For disk-related errors, the registers are set up as follows:

Register	Bit(s)		Setting		
AH	7	=	0, to signify a disk error		
	1–2	=	area where disk error occurred		
			00	=	DOS area
			01	=	file allocation table
			10	=	disk directory
			11	=	files area
			0	=	0 if read error 1 if write error
AL		=	drive code (0 = A, 1 = B, etc.)		
DI		=	driver error code in lower half of register		
BP:SI		=	segment:offset of device driver header		

For non-disk-related errors, the interrupt was generated either as the result of a character-device error or because a corrupted memory image of the file allocation table was detected. In this case, the registers are set as follows:

Register	Bit		Setting
AH	7	=	1, to signify a non-disk error
DI		=	driver error code in lower half of register
BP:SI		=	segment:offset of device driver header

To determine whether the critical error was due to a character device, use the address in BP:SI to examine the device attribute word at offset 0004H in the presumed device-driver header. If bit 15 is set, then the error is indeed due to a character device and the name field of the driver's header can be inspected to determine the device.

Your critical error handler must return a code in register AL to tell
MS-DOS what action to take:

Code	Meaning
0	Ignore the error (MS-DOS pretends operation succeeded).
1	Retry the operation.
2	Terminate through the Int 23H vector.
3	Fail the system call that is in progress (version 3 only).

The actions of a critical error handler are tightly restricted. See the description of Int 24H in Section 2 for details, and see Figure 6-9 for a skeleton example of such a handler.

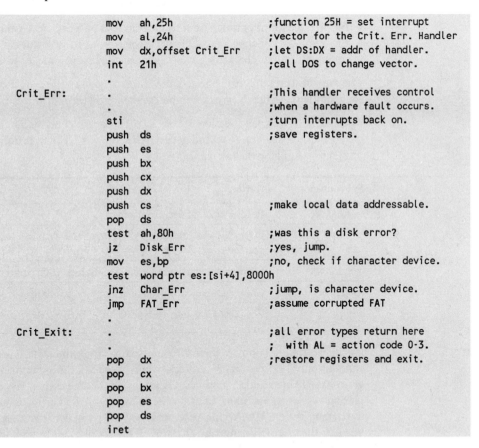

```
            mov   ah,25h                    ;function 25H = set interrupt
            mov   al,24h                    ;vector for the Crit. Err. Handler
            mov   dx,offset Crit_Err        ;let DS:DX = addr of handler.
            int   21h                       ;call DOS to change vector.
            .
Crit_Err:   .                               ;This handler receives control
            .                               ;when a hardware fault occurs.
            sti                             ;turn interrupts back on.
            push  ds                        ;save registers.
            push  es
            push  bx
            push  cx
            push  dx
            push  cs                        ;make local data addressable.
            pop   ds
            test  ah,80h                    ;was this a disk error?
            jz    Disk_Err                  ;yes, jump.
            mov   es,bp                      ;no, check if character device.
            test  word ptr es:[si+4],8000h
            jnz   Char_Err                  ;jump, is character device.
            jmp   FAT_Err                   ;assume corrupted FAT
            .
Crit_Exit:  .                               ;all error types return here
            .                               ;  with AL = action code 0-3.
            pop   dx                        ;restore registers and exit.
            pop   cx
            pop   bx
            pop   es
            pop   ds
            iret
```

Figure 6-9. An example of an application capturing the Int 24H critical error vector so that hardware faults are directed to its own handler, and a skeleton for such a handler.

Example Programs: *DUMP.ASM* and *DUMP.C*

The programs *DUMP.ASM* (Figure 6-10, on pages 135 through 141) and *DUMP.C* (Figure 6-11, on pages 142 through 144) are parallel examples of the use of the UNIX/XENIX-like file and record functions. The assembly-language version, in particular, illustrates many features of a typical and hopefully well-behaved MS-DOS utility:

- The version of MS-DOS is checked to ensure that all the functions *DUMP* is going to use are really available.

- The drive, path, and filename are parsed from the command tail in the program segment prefix.

- Buffered I/O is used for speed.

- Error messages are sent to the standard error device.

- Normal program output is sent to the standard output device, so that the dump output appears by default on the system console but can be re-directed to other character devices (such as the line printer) or to a file.

The same features are incorporated into the C version of the program, but some of them are taken care of behind the scenes by the C runtime library.

The assembly-language version of the *DUMP* program contains a number of subroutines that you may find generally useful in your own programming efforts. These include:

Subroutine	Action
read_block	Reads a block of data from a file.
get_char	Deblocks data, allowing it to be inspected character by character.
conv_word	Converts a binary word (16 bits) into hex ASCII for output.
conv_byte	Converts a binary byte (8 bits) into hex ASCII for output.
ascii	Converts 4 bits into a single hex ASCII character.

It is interesting to compare these two equivalent programs. The C program contains only 125 lines and 3 modules, whereas the assembly-language program has 340 lines and 12 modules. Clearly, the C source code is less complex and easier to maintain. On the other hand, if size and efficiency are important, the *DUMP.EXE* file generated by the C compiler is 8186 bytes, whereas the assembly-language *DUMP.EXE* file is only 1347 bytes and runs more than twice as fast.

```
1              name    dump
2              page    55,132
3              title   'DUMP --- Display File Contents'
4
5      ; DUMP --- a utility to display the contents of a file in hex
6      ; and ASCII format.  Requires DOS version 2.0 or higher.
7      ;
8      ; Used in the form:
9      ; A>dump path\filename.ext  [ >device ]
10     ; (item in square brackets is optional)
11     ;
12     ; version 1.0  March 25, 1984
13     ; Copyright (c) 1984 by Ray Duncan
14
15     cr      equ     0dh             ;ASCII carriage return
16     lf      equ     0ah             ;ASCII line feed
17     blank   equ     20h             ;ASCII space code
18
19     command equ     80h             ;buffer for command tail
20
21     blksize equ     128             ;size of input file records
22
23     output_handle equ 1            ;handle of standard output device
24                                    ;(can be redirected)
25     error_handle equ 2             ;handle of standard error device
26                                    ;(not redirectable)
27
28     cseg    segment para public 'CODE'
29
30             assume  cs:cseg,ds:data,es:data,ss:stack
31
32
33     dump    proc    far             ;entry point from DOS
34
35             push    ds              ;save DS:0000 for final
36             xor     ax,ax           ;return to DOS, in case
37             push    ax              ;function 4CH can't be used.
38             mov     ax,data         ;make our data segment
39             mov     es,ax           ;addressable via ES register.
40             mov     ah,30h          ;check version of DOS.
41             int     21h
42             cmp     al,2
43             jae     dump1           ;proceed, DOS 2.0 or greater.
44             mov     dx,offset msg3  ;DOS 1.x --- print error message;
45             mov     ax,es           ;we must use the old DOS
46             mov     ds,ax           ;string output function since
47             mov     ah,9            ;handles are not available in
48             int     21h             ;this version of DOS.
```

(continued)

Figure 6-10. The assembly-language version: DUMP.ASM.

```
49              ret
50
51    dump1:    call    get_filename        ;get path and file spec. for
52                                          ;input file from command line tail.
53              mov     ax,es               ;set DS = ES for remainder
54              mov     ds,ax               ;of program.
55              jnc     dump2               ;jump, got acceptable name.
56              mov     dx,offset msg2      ;missing or illegal filespec,
57              mov     cx,msg2_length
58              jmp     dump9               ;print error message and exit.
59
60    dump2:    call    open_input          ;now try to open input file.
61              jnc     dump3               ;jump, opened input ok.
62              mov     dx,offset msg1      ;open of input file failed,
63              mov     cx,msg1_length
64              jmp     dump9               ;print error msg and exit.
65
66    dump3:    call    read_block          ;initialize input file buffer.
67              jnc     dump4               ;jump, got a block.
68              mov     dx,offset msg4      ;empty file, print error
69              mov     cx,msg4_length
70              jmp     dump9               ;message and exit.
71
72                                          ;file successfully opened,
73    dump4:                                ;now convert and display it!
74              call    get_char            ;read 1 character from input.
75              jc      dump8               ;jump, end of file.
76              inc     input_addr          ;update relative file position.
77              or      bx,bx               ;is this 1st char of block?
78              jnz     dump5               ;no
79              call    print_heading
80    dump5:    and     bx,0fh              ;is this first byte of 16?
81              jnz     dump6               ;no, jump.
82              push    ax                  ;save the byte.
83              mov     di,offset output    ;convert relative file addr.
84              mov     ax,input_addr       ;for output string.
85              call    conv_word
86              pop     ax
87    dump6:                                ;store ASCII version of character.
88                                          ;if it is alphanumeric,
89              mov     di,offset outputb
90              add     di,bx               ;calculate output string address.
91              mov     byte ptr [di],'.'   ;if it is control character,
92              cmp     al,blank            ;just print a dot.
93              jb      dump7               ;jump, not alphanumeric.
94              cmp     al,7eh
95              ja      dump7               ;jump, not alphanumeric.
96              mov     [di],al             ;store ASCII character.
```

Figure 6-10 continued.

```
97    dump7:                              ;now convert binary byte
98                                        ;to hex  ASCII equivalent.
99            push    bx                  ;save offset 0-15 of this byte.
100                                       ;calc. its position in
101                                       ;output string.
102           mov     di,offset outputa
103           add     di,bx               ;base addr + (offset * 3)
104           add     di,bx
105           add     di,bx
106           call    conv_byte           ;convert data byte to hex.
107           pop     bx                  ;restore byte offset.
108           cmp     bx,0fh              ;16 bytes converted yet?
109           jne     dump4               ;no, get another byte.
110           mov     dx,offset output
111           mov     cx,output_length
112           call    write_std           ;yes, print the line.
113           jmp     dump4               ;get next char. from input file.
114
115   dump8:                              ;end of file detected,
116           call    close_input         ;close input file.
117           mov     ax,4c00h            ;now exit to DOS with
118           int     21h                 ;return code = zero.
119
120   dump9:                              ;come here to print message
121                                       ;on standard error device,
122           call    write_error         ;and return control to DOS
123           mov     ax,4c01h            ;with return code = 1.
124           int     21h
125
126   dump    endp
127
128
129   get_filename proc near              ;process name of input file.
130                                       ;return Carry = 0 if successful.
131                                       ;return Carry = 1 if no filename.
132                                       ;DS:SI <- addr command line
133           mov     si,offset command
134                                       ;ES:DI <- addr filespec buffer
135           mov     di,offset input_name
136           cld
137           lodsb                       ;any command line present?
138           or      al,al               ;return error status if not.
139           jz      get_filename4
140   get_filename1:                      ;scan over leading blanks
141           lodsb                       ;to file name.
142           cmp     al,cr               ;if we hit carriage return...
143           je      get_filename4       ;jump, name is missing.
144           cmp     al,20h              ;is this a blank?
```

Figure 6-10 continued.

```
145          jz      get_filename1   ;if so keep scanning.
146   get_filename2:                 ;found first char of name,
147          stosb                   ;move last char. to output
148                                  ;file name buffer.
149          lodsb                   ;check next character, found
150          cmp     al,cr           ;carriage return yet?
151          je      get_filename3   ;yes, exit with success code.
152          cmp     al,20h          ;is this a blank?
153          jne     get_filename2   ;if not keep moving chars.
154   get_filename3:                 ;exit with carry = 0
155          clc                     ;for success flag.
156          ret
157   get_filename4:                 ;exit with carry = 1
158          stc                     ;for error flag.
159          ret
160   get_filename endp
161
162   open_input proc near           ;open input file.
163                                  ;DS:DX = addr filename
164          mov     dx,offset input_name
165          mov     al,0            ;AL = 0 for read only
166          mov     ah,3dh          ;function 3DH = open
167          int     21h             ;handle returned in AX,
168          mov     input_handle,ax ;save it for later.
169          ret                     ;CY is set if error.
170   open_input endp
171
172   close_input proc near          ;close input file.
173          mov     bx,input_handle ;BX = handle
174          mov     ah,3eh
175          int     21h
176          ret
177   close_input endp
178
179   get_char proc   near         . ;get one character from input buffer.
180                                  ;return AL = char, BX = buffer offset.
181                                  ;return CY flag = 1 if end of file.
182          mov     bx,input_ptr    ;is pointer at end of buffer?
183          cmp     bx,blksize
184          jne     get_char1       ;no, jump.
185                                  ;yes, buffer is exhausted,
186          mov     input_ptr,0
187          call    read_block      ;new block must be read from disk.
188          jnc     get_char        ;got block, start routine over.
189          ret                     ;end of file detected
190                                  ;so return CY flag = True.
191   get_char1:                     ;get data byte into AL,
192          mov     al,[input_buffer+bx]
193          inc     input_ptr       ;bump input buffer pointer.
```

Figure 6-10 continued.

```
194          clc                    ;return CY flag = 0 since
195          ret                    ;not end of file.
196   get_char endp
197
198
199   read_block proc near         ;read block of data from input file
200                                 ;return CY flag = 0 if read ok.
201                                 ;       CY flag = 1 if end of file.
202          mov     bx,input_handle ;request read from DOS.
203          mov     cx,blksize
204          mov     dx,offset input_buffer
205          mov     ah,3fh
206          int     21h
207                                 ;initialize pointers.
208          inc     input_block
209          mov     input_ptr,0
210          or      ax,ax          ;was anything read in? (the OR
211                                 ; incidentally turns off the CY flag)
212          jnz     read_block1    ;yes, jump.
213          stc                    ;no, end of file so return CY = True.
214   read_block1:
215          ret
216   read_block endp
217
218   write_std proc  near         ;write string to standard output.
219                                 ;call DX = addr of output string
220                                 ;     CX = length of string.
221          mov     bx,output_handle;BX = handle for standard list device.
222          mov     ah,40h         ;function 40H = write to device.
223          int     21h            ;request service from DOS.
224          ret
225   write_std endp
226
227   write_error proc near        ;write string to standard error device.
228                                 ;call DX = addr of output string
229                                 ;     CX = length of string.
230          mov     bx,error_handle ;BX = handle for standard error device.
231          mov     ah,40h         ;function 40H = write to device.
232          int     21h            ;request service from DOS.
233          ret
234   write_error endp
235
236   print_heading proc near      ;print record number and heading
237          push    ax             ;for a block of data.
238          push    bx             ;first save registers.
239          mov     di,offset headinga
240          mov     ax,input_block
241          call    conv_word      ;convert record number to ASCII.
242          mov     dx,offset heading
```

Figure 6-10 continued.

```
243             mov     cx,heading_length
244             call    write_std           ;now print heading,
245             pop     bx                  ;restore registers,
246             pop     ax
247             ret                         ;and exit.
248     print_heading endp
249
250     conv_word proc near                 ;convert 16-bit binary word
251                                         ; to hex ASCII.
252                                         ;call with AX = binary value
253                                         ;         DI = addr to store string.
254                                         ;returns AX, DI, CX destroyed.
255             push    ax
256             mov     al,ah
257             call    conv_byte           ;convert upper byte.
258             pop     ax
259             call    conv_byte           ;convert lower byte.
260             ret
261     conv_word endp
262
263     conv_byte proc    near              ;convert binary byte to hex ASCII.
264                                         ;call with AL = binary value
265                                         ;         DI = addr to store string.
266                                         ;returns   AX, DI, CX modified.
267
268             sub     ah,ah               ;clear upper byte.
269             mov     cl,16
270             div     cl                  ;divide binary data by 16.
271             call    ascii               ;the quotient becomes the first
272             stosb                       ;ASCII character.
273             mov     al,ah
274             call    ascii               ;the remainder becomes the
275             stosb                       ;second ASCII character.
276             ret
277     conv_byte endp
278
279     ascii   proc    near                ;convert value 0-0FH in AL
280             add     al,'0'              ;into a "hex ASCII" character.
281             cmp     al,'9'
282             jle     ascii2              ;jump if in range 0-9,
283             add     al,'A'-'9'-1        ;offset it to range A-F,
284     ascii2: ret                         ;return ASCII char. in AL.
285     ascii   endp
286
287     cseg    ends
288
289
290     data    segment para public 'DATA'
291
```

Figure 6-10 continued.

```
292   input_name      db        64 dup (0)              ;buffer for input filespec
293
294   input_handle    dw        0                       ;token from DOS for input file
295
296   input_ptr       dw        0                       ;pointer to input deblocking buffer
297
298   input_addr      dw        -1                      ;relative address in file
299   input_block     dw        0                       ;current 128 byte block number
300
301   output          db        'nnnn',blank,blank
302   outputa         db        16 dup ('00',blank)
303                   db        blank
304   outputb         db        '0123456789ABCDEF',cr,lf
305   output_length   equ       $-output
306
307   heading         db        cr,lf,'Record',blank
308   headinga        db        'nnnn',blank,blank,cr,lf
309                   db        7 dup (blank)
310                   db        '0  1  2  3  4  5  6  7 '
311                   db        '8  9  A  B  C  D  E  F',cr,lf
312   heading_length  equ       $-heading
313
314   input_buffer    db        blksize dup (?) ;deblocking buffer for input file
315
316   msg1            db        cr,lf
317                   db        'Cannot find input file.'
318                   db        cr,lf
319   msg1_length     equ       $-msg1
320
321   msg2            db        cr,lf
322                   db        'Missing file name.'
323                   db        cr,lf
324   msg2_length     equ       $-msg2
325
326   msg3            db        cr,lf
327                   db        'Requires DOS version 2 or greater.'
328                   db        cr,lf,'$'
329
330   msg4            db        cr,lf,'Empty file.',cr,lf
331   msg4_length     equ       $-msg4
332
333   data    ends
334
335
336   stack   segment para stack 'STACK'
337           db        64 dup (?)
338   stack   ends
339
340           end       dump
```

Figure 6-10 continued.

```
/*

        DUMP.C              A utility to dump a file in hex and ASCII
                            to the Standard Output device (which may
                            be redirected to a file or printer).

                            This utility has been kept as simple as
                            possible for teaching purposes, and
                            makes no attempt to handle partial records
                            at end of file in an "elegant" fashion.

                            Could be changed into an MS-DOS "filter"
                            in a few minutes by substituting "stdin"
                            for "dfile", and removing fopen and fclose
                            of "dfile".

        Usage is:           C>DUMP unit:path\filename.ext

        Copyright (C) 1985 Ray Duncan

        To compile with Microsoft C:
                    C>MSC DUMP;
                    C>LINK DUMP;

*/

#include <stdio.h>

#define REC_SIZE 128            /* size of input file records */

main(argc, argv)
    int    argc;
    char   *argv[];

{   FILE *dfile;                /* control block for input file */
    int status = 0;            /* status returned from file read */
    int file_rec = 0;          /* file record number being dumped */
    long file_ptr = 0L;        /* file byte offset for current rec */
    char file_buf[REC_SIZE];   /* data block from file */

                                /* abort if no filename supplied, or
                                   more than one filename */
    if (argc != 2)
        { fprintf(stderr,"\ndump: wrong number of parameters\n");
          return(1);
        }

                                /* open specified file in raw mode,
                                   abort if open fails */
```

Figure 6-11. The C version: DUMP.C.

(continued)

```
            if ( (dfile = fopen(argv[1],"rb") ) == NULL)
                { fprintf( stderr, "\ndump: can't find file: %s \n", argv[1] );
                  return(1);
                }

                                        /* print filename on listing */
            printf( "\nDump of file: %s ", argv[1] );

                                        /* read and dump records of REC_SIZE bytes
                                           from file until stream exhausted */
            while ( (status = fread(file_buf,1,REC_SIZE,dfile) ) != 0 )
                {   dump_rec(file_buf,++file_rec,file_ptr);
                    file_ptr += REC_SIZE;
                }

            printf("\n\n");                 /* print two blank lines */
            fclose(dfile);                  /* close the input file */
            return(0);                      /* return success code */

    }


    /*
            dump REC_SIZE bytes in hex and ASCII on the Standard Output
    */

    dump_rec(file_buf,file_rec,file_ptr)
        char *file_buf;
        int file_rec;
        long file_ptr;

    {   int i;                          /* index to current record */

                                        /* print record number */
        printf("\n\nRecord %04X",file_rec);

                                        /* print heading line */
        printf("\n        0 1 2 3 4 5 6 7 8 9 A B C D E F");

                                        /* print dump of record in hex and
                                           ASCII by paragraphs (16 bytes) */
        for(i = 0; i < REC_SIZE; i += 16)
            dump_para( file_ptr+i,file_buf+i );
    }


    /*
            dump a paragraph of the current record in hex and ASCII
    */
```

Figure 6-11 continued.

```
dump_para(file_ptr,para_ptr)
    long file_ptr;                  /* file offset of current paragraph */
    unsigned char *para_ptr;        /* buffer pointer to current paragraph */

{   int j;                          /* offset within current paragraph */
    char c;                         /* current char from file buffer */

                                    /* print file offset */
    printf("\n%04lX ",file_ptr);

                                    /* print hex equivalent of each byte */
    for(j = 0; j < 16; j++)
       printf( " %02X", para_ptr[j] );
    printf("  ");
                                    /* print ASCII equivalent of each byte
                                       substituting '.' for control codes
                                       and other unprintable characters */
    for(j = 0; j < 16; j++)
       { c = para_ptr[j];
          if( (c < 32) | (c > 126) )
             c = '.' ;
          putchar(c);
       }
}
```

Figure 6-11 continued.

Directories, Subdirectories, and Volume Labels

Disk directories can be thought of as catalogs that describe the contents of a logical disk volume. On MS-DOS disks, there are two types of directories:

- The root directory, which has a fixed size

- Subdirectories, which can grow to any size

Every disk has one and only one root directory, whereas it may have from zero subdirectories to as many as the disk will hold (Figure 7-1). These subdirectories can, in turn, be nested to any number of levels. This is the hierarchical, or tree, directory structure referred to in earlier chapters.

Each file on a disk receives a unique 32-byte entry in one of the disk's directories. This entry defines the file's name and extension, specific access privileges (Figure 7-2), the time and date the file was created or last updated, the file's starting cluster, and its size. The detailed information about the location of every block of data in the file is kept in a separate control area on the disk (the file allocation table, discussed in Chapter 8).

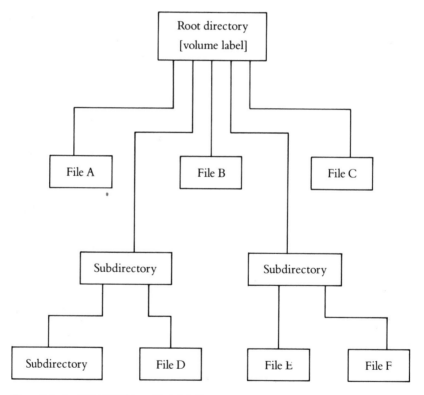

Figure 7-1. An MS-DOS hierarchical disk-directory structure.

byte offset

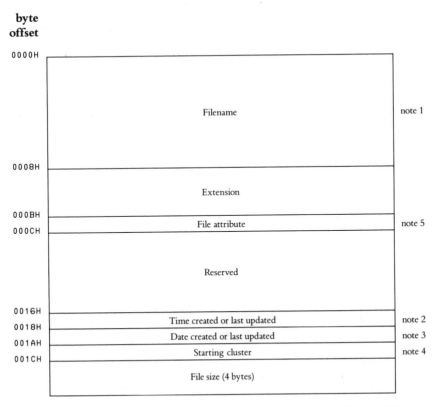

Figure 7-2. Format of a single entry in a disk directory. Total length is 32 bytes (20H bytes).

Notes for Figure 7-2

1. The first byte of the filename field of a directory entry may contain the following special information:

Value	Meaning
00	Directory entry has never been used; end of allocated portion of directory.
05H	First character of filename is actually E5H.
2EH	Entry is an alias for the current or parent subdirectory. If the next byte is also 2EH, then the cluster field contains the cluster number of the parent directory (zero, if the parent directory is the root directory; see page 149).
E5H	File has been erased.

2. The time field is encoded as:

Bits	Contents
00H–04H	Binary number of 2-second increments (0–29, corresponding to 0–58 seconds)
05H–0AH	Binary number of minutes (0–59)
0BH–0FH	Binary number of hours (0–23)

3. The date field is encoded as:

Bits	Contents
00H–04H	Day of month (1–31)
05H–08H	Month (1–12)
09H–0FH	Year (relative to 1980)

4. The file-size field is interpreted as a 4-byte integer, with the low-order 2 bytes of the number stored first.

5. The attribute byte of the directory entry is mapped as follows:

Bit	Meaning
0	Read-only; tries to open file for write or to delete file will fail.
1	Hidden file; is excluded from normal searches.
2	System file; is excluded from normal searches.
3	Volume label; can exist only in root directory.
4	Subdirectory; entry is excluded from normal searches.
5	Archive bit; is set to *on* whenever file is modified.
6	Reserved.
7	Reserved.

Files can be marked hidden when they are created, and the read-only, hidden, system, and archive attributes (but not bits 3 and 4) can be set or reset with CHMOD (43H). The MS-DOS system files (containing the BIOS and the DOS kernel) are customarily marked *read-only, hidden,* and *system.*

Disk directories can be examined, selected, created, or deleted interactively at the MS-DOS command level with the DIR, CHDIR, MKDIR, and RMDIR commands, respectively. MS-DOS also provides services to allow application programs to:

- Search for, add, delete, or modify file entries within directories.

- Select, create, and delete subdirectories.

- Move file entries between directories.

Let's look at each type of directory in greater detail.

The Root Directory

The size and position of the root directory are fixed, and are determined by the FORMAT program during disk initialization. The number of entries in the root directory, and the directory's location on the disk, can be obtained from the BIOS parameter block in the disk's boot sector (see Chapter 8).

On disks formatted under MS-DOS version 1, the root directory is the only directory. Under versions 2 and 3, the root directory can contain, in addition to the normal file descriptors, pointers to special files called subdirectories. Under these versions, the root directory can also contain a special class of entry called the *volume label*, which gives a name to the entire disk (Figure 7-3). Volume labels are described in detail later in this chapter.

If the disk is bootable, the first two entries in the root directory always describe the files containing the MS-DOS BIOS and the DOS kernel. The disk bootstrap program uses these entries to bring the operating system into memory and start it up.

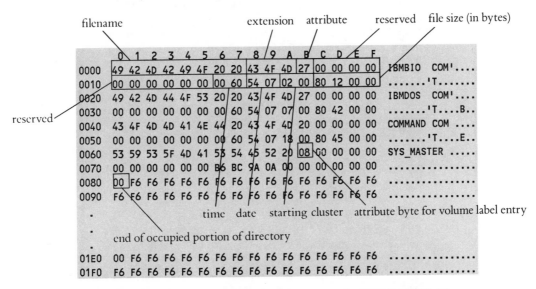

Figure 7-3. Hex and ASCII dump of the first directory sector of an IBM PC-DOS disk containing only the operating system files (IBMBIO.COM, IBMDOS.COM, and COMMAND.COM) and a volume label (SYS_MASTER).

Subdirectories

Subdirectories are a special file type whose contents are either directory descriptors for data files or pointers to other subdirectories. A directory entry that points to a subdirectory has bit 4 in the attribute byte set, carries a date and time stamp, and has a file length of zero (Figure 7-4). The cluster-number field points to the first cluster that implements the subdirectory. In current versions of MS-DOS, the additional clusters assigned to the subdirectory can be found only by tracing the chain of clusters through the file allocation table. The only limit on the size or number of subdirectories is available disk space.

Within a subdirectory file, the format of each 32-byte entry that describes either a file or another subdirectory is exactly the same as in the root directory. In addition, every subdirectory contains the two special entries . and .. at the beginning of the directory (Figure 7-5). These two special entries are put in place when the subdirectory is created, and cannot be deleted. The single-period entry refers to the current subdirectory; its cluster field points to the cluster in which the subdirectory is found. The double-period entry refers to the current subdirectory's *parent directory* (immediately above it in the tree structure), and its cluster field points to the first cluster of the parent. If the parent is the root directory, this field is zero.

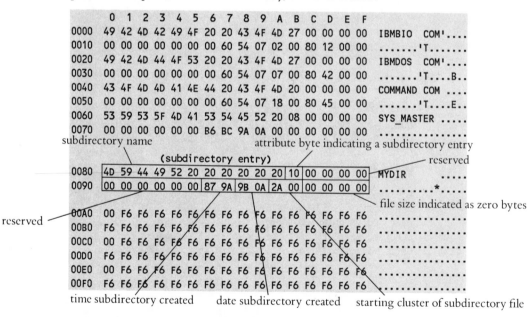

Figure 7-4. First block of a disk directory containing the three system files, a volume label (SYS_MASTER), and a subdirectory (MYDIR). The subdirectory's directory entry has bit 4 in the attribute byte set, the cluster field points to the first cluster of the subdirectory file, the date and time stamps are valid, but the file length is zero.

special entry for current subdirectory   attribute bytes indicating a subdirectory

```
        0   1   2   3   4   5   6   7   8   9   A   B   C   D   E   F
0000   2E  20  20  20  20  20  20  20  20  20  20  10  00  00  00  00    .         .....
0010   00  00  00  00  00  00  87  9A  9B  0A  2A  00  00  00  00  00    ..........*.....
0020   2E  2E  20  20  20  20  20  20  20  20  20  10  00  00  00  00    ..        .....
0030   00  00  00  00  00  00  87  9A  9B  0A  00  00  00  00  00  00    ................
0040   4D  59  46  49  4C  45  20  20  44  41  54  20  00  00  00  00    MYFILE   DAT ....
0050   00  00  00  00  00  00  98  9A  9B  0A  2B  00  15  00  00  00    ..........+.....
0060   00  00  00  00  00  00  00  00  00  00  00  00  00  00  00  00    ................
0070   00  00  00  00  00  00  00  00  00  00  00  00  00  00  00  00    ................
```

special entry for parent directory

Figure 7-5. Dump of the first block of the subdirectory MYDIR. *Note the* . *and* .. *entries. This subdirectory contains exactly one file, named* MYFILE.DAT.

Although subdirectories are really just a special class of file, they cannot, for the most part, be handled like regular files by application programs. For instance, special functions are required to make and delete subdirectories; the normal create and unlink functions cannot be used. Function 43H (CHMOD) will not turn the subdirectory bit on or off, although it can be used to toggle hidden, system, and read-only bits for an existing sub-directory (the read-only bit has no effect). The system or hidden bit can be used to block a subdirectory from being shown in a directory listing, but the subdirectory itself will still be accessible with the CHDIR and RMDIR commands.

Subdirectories cannot be opened and modified directly without the use of rather complex techniques that are not officially sanctioned and that can create havoc in multitasking or networking environments. Although procedures for the manipulation of subdirectory files have been published in *PC Tech Journal* and elsewhere, their use should be avoided.

Control of Subdirectories

MS-DOS provides three functions that enable you to modify the hierarchical file structure of a disk or select the current directory. These are:

Function	Action
Function 39H	Create subdirectory.
Function 3AH	Delete subdirectory.
Function 3BH	Select subdirectory.

All of these functions require the address of an ASCIIZ string that describes a path to the desired subdirectory. This address is passed to MS-DOS in registers DS:DX. All three functions return the carry flag clear if the operation is successful. If the operation fails, the carry flag is set and register AX contains a descriptive error code.

An additional function, 47H (get current subdirectory), allows you to obtain a string from MS-DOS that describes the current directory for a selected disk drive. The string is supplied without the drive identifier or a leading backslash (\), and is null terminated (ASCIIZ). This function can be used to obtain the identity of the working subdirectory at the time a program starts up, so that the program can restore the system to its original state with function 3BH when it terminates. Function 47H is also commonly used to build complete path and file specifications for documenting listings.

Detailed information on all four of these subdirectory functions can be found in Section 2.

Searching Disk Directories

When you request an open operation on a file, you are implicitly performing a search of a directory. MS-DOS examines each entry of the directory to match the name of the file you have given as an argument; if the file is found, MS-DOS copies certain information from the directory into a data structure that can be used to control subsequent read and write operations to the file. Thus, if you wish to test for the existence of a specific file, it is sufficient to perform an open operation and observe whether it is successful (if it is, you should, of course, perform a subsequent close operation, to avoid needless expenditure of handles).

Sometimes you may find it necessary to perform more elaborate searches of a disk directory. Perhaps you wish to find all the files with a certain extension, obtain the names of all the subdirectories of the current directory, or inspect the volume label of a disk. Although the locations of a disk's directories, and the specifics of the entries that are found in them, are of necessity somewhat hardware dependent (for example, interpretation of the field describing the starting location of the file depends upon the physical disk format), MS-DOS does provide functions that allow *examination* of a disk directory in a hardware-independent fashion.

In order to search a disk directory successfully, there are two MS-DOS services that must be understood. The first of these is the so-called "search for first" function, which accepts a file specification (which can include wildcard characters) and looks for the first matching file in the directory of interest. If a match is found, the function fills a user-designated buffer with information about the file; otherwise, it sets an error flag.

The second function, commonly called "search for next," can be called only after a successful "search for first." If the file specification that was originally passed to "search for first" included wildcard characters and at least one matching file was present, "search for next" can be called as many times as necessary to find all additional matching files. Like the "search for first" function, "search for next" returns information about the matched files in a user-designated buffer. When all matching files have been located, the function sets an error flag.

As with the MS-DOS file- and record-access functions discussed in previous chapters, there are two alternative approaches that can be used to search directories and there are parallel sets of MS-DOS services to support each approach—the FCB functions and the Handle functions:

Action	FCB function	Handle function
Search for first	11H	4EH
Search for next	12H	4FH

The FCB directory functions allow searches to match a filename and extension, both possibly containing wildcard characters, within the current subdirectory for the specified drive. Unless an extended FCB is used, only files with normal attributes will be found—that is, files that are not marked system, hidden, or read-only. The Handle directory functions, on the other hand, allow a program to perform directory searches within any subdirectory on any drive, regardless of which subdirectory is current.

Both the FCB and the Handle directory-searching functions require that the disk transfer area address be set (with function 1AH) *before* the call to "search for first," to point to a working buffer for use by MS-DOS. This DTA should not be changed between calls to "search for first" and "search for next." When a matching file is found, MS-DOS fills the working buffer with information about that file. The buffer contents are different for the FCB-like and Handle functions, so read the detailed descriptions in Section 2 of this book before attempting to interpret the returned information.

Figures 7-6 and 7-7 provide equivalent examples of searches for all files in a given directory that have the extension .*ASM*, one example using the FCB directory functions (11H and 12H) and the other using the Handle functions (4EH and 4FH). (Both programs use the Handle type of write to standard output to display the matched filenames, in order to avoid introducing tangential differences.)

```
start:          mov     dx,offset mybuff        ;set DTA to working
                mov     ah,1ah                  ;buffer for DOS.
                int     21h
                mov     dx,offset myfcb         ;Search for First.
                mov     ah,11h
                int     21h
                or      al,al                   ;any matches at all?
                jnz     exit                    ;no, quit.

display:        mov     dx,offset crlf          ;send carriage return/
                mov     cx,2                    ;linefeed sequence
                mov     bx,1                    ;to standard output.
                mov     ah,40h
                int     21h
                mov     dx,offset mybuff+1      ;display name of
                mov     cx,11                   ;matching file
                mov     bx,1                    ;on standard output.
                mov     ah,40h
                int     21h

nextfile:       mov     dx,offset myfcb         ;Search for Next.
                mov     ah,12h
                int     21h
                or      al,al                   ;any more matches?
                jz      display                 ;yes, display filename.

exit:           mov     ax,4c00h                ;return to DOS.
                int     21h

crlf            db      0dh,0ah                 ;carriage return/
                                                ;line feed string

myfcb           db      0                       ;drive = "current"
                db      8 dup ('?')             ;filename = wildcard
                db      'ASM'                   ;extension = "ASM"
                db      25 dup (0)              ;remainder of FCB = zero

mybuff          db      64 dup (0)              ;working buffer for DOS
```

Figure 7-6. Example of a directory search using the FCB functions 11H and 12H. This routine displays the names of all files in the current subdirectory that have the extension .ASM.

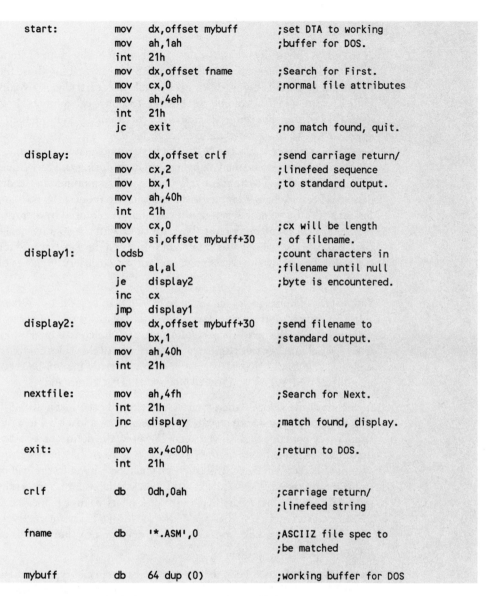

```
start:          mov     dx,offset mybuff        ;set DTA to working
                mov     ah,1ah                  ;buffer for DOS.
                int     21h
                mov     dx,offset fname         ;Search for First.
                mov     cx,0                    ;normal file attributes
                mov     ah,4eh
                int     21h
                jc      exit                    ;no match found, quit.

display:        mov     dx,offset crlf          ;send carriage return/
                mov     cx,2                    ;linefeed sequence
                mov     bx,1                    ;to standard output.
                mov     ah,40h
                int     21h
                mov     cx,0                    ;cx will be length
                mov     si,offset mybuff+30     ; of filename.
display1:       lodsb                           ;count characters in
                or      al,al                   ;filename until null
                je      display2                ;byte is encountered.
                inc     cx
                jmp     display1
display2:       mov     dx,offset mybuff+30     ;send filename to
                mov     bx,1                    ;standard output.
                mov     ah,40h
                int     21h

nextfile:       mov     ah,4fh                  ;Search for Next.
                int     21h
                jnc     display                 ;match found, display.

exit:           mov     ax,4c00h                ;return to DOS.
                int     21h

crlf            db      0dh,0ah                 ;carriage return/
                                                ;linefeed string

fname           db      '*.ASM',0               ;ASCIIZ file spec to
                                                ;be matched

mybuff          db      64 dup (0)              ;working buffer for DOS
```

Figure 7-7. Example of a directory search using the Handle functions 4EH and 4FH. This routine also displays the names of all files in the current subdirectory that have the extension .ASM.

Volume Labels

A volume is a logically self-sufficient, possibly removable, unit of storage medium. It contains complete files and a directory describing those files. For example, a single floppy disk or removable disk cartridge is a volume— in these cases, a logical volume corresponds to a physical volume. However, hard disks that are not removable are often partitioned into more than one *logical* volume to make them more manageable. On large computer systems, each removable volume of storage has a unique name, or *label*, assigned to it at the time the volume is initialized. Using this identifier, the computer's operating system can tell when one disk mounted in the disk drive has been exchanged for another, and can also request the operator to mount a specific volume when files it contains are required by a program. Frequently, other information is also associated with the volume label—the time and date the volume was created or initialized, its capacity and format type, and the read/write access privileges for various users or classes of users, for example.

Support for volume labels was added to MS-DOS in version 2.0. Whenever a disk is formatted, the user is given the option of assigning it a name. This volume label can be up to 11 characters long, and can consist of anything from a serial number to a name that is descriptive of the disk's contents, such as *PAYROLL*. A disk's label can be displayed from the MS-DOS command level with the VOL, TREE, DIR, or CHKDSK command.

In version 2, the volume labels aren't used internally at all, and no MS-DOS commands are provided to change a volume label or add a label to a disk that already contains files. In version 3, however, the definition of a device driver was extended to recognize volume labels, to enable the operating system to detect whether a disk has been changed while files are still open. If this has occurred, the disk driver can then ask the user to reinsert the proper disk in the drive, identifying the disk by its volume name. The LABEL utility function was also added at the MS-DOS command level, to allow interactive modification, creation, or deletion of volume labels on previously formatted disks.

Internally, an MS-DOS volume label is stored as a special type of entry in the disk's root directory. The entry has the attribute byte set to 8 (that is, bit 3 is turned on), the date and time fields filled in, and the starting–cluster and file-size fields zeroed (see Figure 7-3). Except for the attribute-byte setting, this is identical to the directory entry for a file that was created but never had any data written into it.

```
                    .
                    .
                    .
        mov     dx,seg buffer           ;set Disk Transfer Address
        mov     ds,dx                   ;to scratch area (DS:DX) for
        mov     dx,offset buffer        ;directory search.
        mov     ah,1ah
        int     21h
                    .
                    .
                    .
        mov     dx,offset xfcb          ;DS:DX=addr extended fcb
        mov     ah,11h                  ;search for first match.
        int     21h
        cmp     al,0ffh                 ;successful?
        je      no_label                ;no label on disk, jump.
        jmp     label_found             ;label found, jump.
                    .
no_label:           .
                    .
label_found:        .
                    .
xfcb    db      0ffh                    ;flag signifying extended fcb
        db      5 dup (0)               ;reserved (should be zeroes)
        db      8                       ;volume attribute byte
        db      0                       ;drive code (set by program)
        db      11 dup ('?')            ;wildcard filename & ext.
        db      25 dup (0)              ;remainder of fcb (not used)

buffer  db      64 dup (?)              ;buffer for directory search
```

Figure 7-8. A volume-label search under MS-DOS version 2, using an extended file control block.

The facilities provided in MS-DOS version 2 for manipulating volume labels are a bit difficult to use and contain some bugs. Furthermore, the Handle file functions cannot be used at all in version 2 to construct, alter, or search for a volume label, forcing the programmer to use extended FCB functions instead (Figure 7-8). Even then, it is still possible to get into trouble—for example, attempting to delete a volume label can damage the disk's file allocation table in an unpredictable manner.

In MS-DOS version 3, a volume identifier can be created in the expected manner, using the Handle function 3CH and an attribute of 8, and the Handle "search for first" function (4EH) can be used to obtain an existing volume label from a disk (Figure 7-9). However, extended FCB functions still must be used to change or delete a volume label.

```
                    .
                    .
                    .
          mov    dx,seg buffer              ;set Disk Transfer Address
          mov    ds,dx                      ;to scratch area (DS:DX) for
          mov    dx,offset buffer           ;directory search
          mov    ah,1ah
          int    21h
                    .
                    .
                    .
          mov    dx,offset wildcard         ;DS:DX=addr of wildcard name
                                            ;for "search for first match"
          mov    cx,8                       ;attribute for volume label
          mov    ah,4eh                     ;Function 4EH = Search for First
          int    21h
          jc     no_label                   ;no label on disk, jump
          jmp    label_found                ;label found, jump.
                    .
no_label:           .
                    .
label_found:        .
                    .
wildcard  db     '*.*',0                    ;ASCIIZ wildcard filename

buffer    db     64 dup (?)                 ;buffer for directory search
```

Figure 7-9. A volume-label search under MS-DOS version 3, using the Handle file functions. If the call to function 4EH is successful (carry flag clear), the volume name is placed at offset BUFFER + 1EH in the form of an ASCIIZ string.

Adding or Modifying Volume Labels

The following sequence will safely add or change a volume label under MS-DOS/PC-DOS versions 2.0 and higher:

1. Set the disk transfer address to a 64-byte scratch buffer, for use by DOS as a work area for the directory-search functions.

2. Using an extended file control block with the format shown in Figure 7-8, perform a function 11H (search for first match). If register AL is returned as 0FFH, then the disk has no label—go to step 5.

3. If function 11H returns register AL as zero, the buffer now contains a simulated extended file control block with the volume name stored in bytes 08H through 12H. Move your new volume name (11 characters) to BUFFER + 19H.

4. Passing the address of the scratch buffer in registers DS:DX, request a function 17H (rename file). If AL returns zero, the volume name was successfully modified and you are finished. If the return code in AL is 0FFH, you have a real problem! (If you can find a volume label with the search function but then cannot rename it, either your program or the operating system is probably corrupted.)

5. If the disk has no previous label, replace the wildcard characters shown in the extended file control block with the desired 11-character volume name. Passing the address of the extended FCB in DS:DX, request function 16H (create file). AL returned as zero means success; AL returned as 0FFH means failure (usually because the root directory is already full).

This procedure always adds the volume label to the root directory, regardless of the disk's current subdirectory.

MS-DOS Disk Internals

MS-DOS disks are organized according to a rather rigid scheme that is easily understood, and therefore easily manipulated. Although most programmers will never have a need to access the special control areas of a disk directly, an understanding of their internal structure leads to a better understanding of the behavior and performance of MS-DOS as a whole.

From the application programmer's viewpoint, MS-DOS presents disk devices as logical volumes that are associated with a drive code (A, B, C, and so on) and have a volume name (optional), a root directory, and from zero to many subdirectories and files. In addition, MS-DOS shields the programmer from the physical characteristics of the disk medium by providing a battery of disk services via Int 21H. By using these services, the programmer can create, open, read, write, close, and delete files in a uniform way, regardless of the disk drive's size, speed, number of read/write heads, number of tracks, and so forth.

Such requests for file operations actually go through two levels of translation before resulting in the physical transfer of data between the disk device and random-access memory:

- Beneath the surface of MS-DOS, each logical volume, whether it is an entire physical unit (such as a floppy disk) or only a part of a fixed disk, is viewed as a continuous sequence of logical sectors, starting at sector 0. File and record requests from application software are first translated by MS-DOS into requests for transfer of some of these logical sectors, using the information found in the volume's directories and allocation tables. Direct access to a logical sector, for those rare occasions that require it, is provided via Int 25H and Int 26H.

- Mapping of logical sectors onto actual physical addresses (head, track, and sector) is then performed by the disk device's *driver*. Any interleaving is also done at this level. The disk-device driver is extremely hardware dependent and interacts intimately with the disk device's controller. It is almost always written entirely in assembly language, and is carefully optimized for maximum performance. This driver program is created by the computer or disk-drive manufacturer, rather than by Microsoft. It is made part of the operating system either by linking it directly into the BIOS module or by installing it via a line in the CONFIG.SYS file at boot time.

Each MS-DOS logical volume is divided into several fixed-size control areas and a files area (Figure 8-1). The size of each control area may vary among disk-drive brands and computer manufacturers (except for disks formatted under MS-DOS version 1), but all of the information needed to interpret the structure of a particular disk can be found on the disk itself, in the boot sector. (A logical disk volume can also be implemented on other types of storage. For example, "RAM disks" map a disk structure onto an area of random-access memory.)

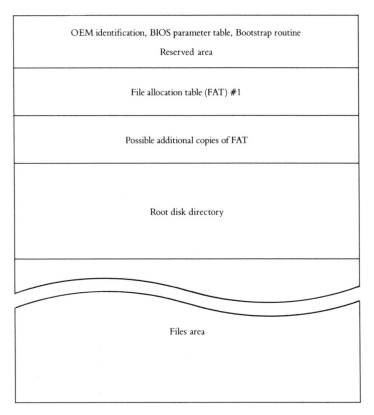

OEM identification, BIOS parameter table, Bootstrap routine
Reserved area
File allocation table (FAT) #1
Possible additional copies of FAT
Root disk directory
Files area

Figure 8-1. Map of a typical MS-DOS disk. Logical sector 0 contains the OEM identification, the BIOS parameter table, and the disk bootstrap routine. A reserved area of variable size is followed by one or more copies of the file allocation table, the root disk directory, and the files area.

The Boot Sector

Logical sector 0, known as the boot sector, contains all the critical information regarding the disk medium's characteristics (Figure 8-2). The first byte in the sector is always an 8086 jump instruction—either a normal intrasegment JMP (opcode 0E9H) followed by a 16-bit displacement or a "short jump" (opcode 0EBH) followed by an 8-bit displacement and then by an NOP (opcode 90H). If neither of these two JMP opcodes is present, the disk has not been formatted, or was not formatted for use with MS-DOS (of course, the presence of the JMP opcode does not in itself ensure that the disk has an MS-DOS format).

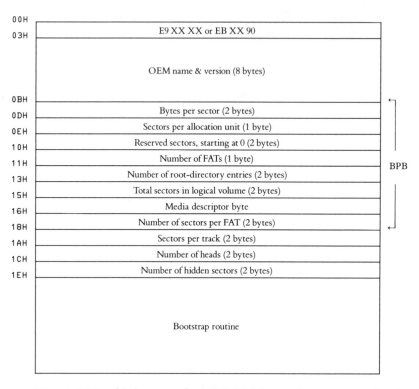

00H	
03H	E9 XX XX or EB XX 90
	OEM name & version (8 bytes)
0BH	
0DH	Bytes per sector (2 bytes)
0EH	Sectors per allocation unit (1 byte)
10H	Reserved sectors, starting at 0 (2 bytes)
11H	Number of FATs (1 byte)
13H	Number of root-directory entries (2 bytes)
15H	Total sectors in logical volume (2 bytes)
16H	Media descriptor byte
18H	Number of sectors per FAT (2 bytes)
1AH	Sectors per track (2 bytes)
1CH	Number of heads (2 bytes)
1EH	Number of hidden sectors (2 bytes)
	Bootstrap routine

Figure 8-2. Map of the boot sector of an MS-DOS disk. Note the jump at zero offset, the OEM identification field, the copy of the BIOS parameter block for this medium, three additional WORD fields to help the device driver understand the medium, and the bootstrap code. Bytes 0BH through 17H constitute the BIOS parameter block (BPB), and are read into memory by the disk driver whenever the medium is changed.

Following the initial JMP instruction, we find an 8-byte field that is reserved by Microsoft for *OEM identification*. The disk formatting program, which is specialized for each brand of computer, disk controller, and medium, fills in this area with the name of the computer manufacturer and the manufacturer's internal MS-DOS version number.

The third major component of the boot sector is the BIOS parameter block (BPB), in bytes 0BH through 17H. This data structure describes the physical disk characteristics and allows the device driver to calculate the proper physical disk address for a given logical sector number; it also contains information that is used by MS-DOS and various system utilities to calculate the address and size of each of the disk control areas (file allocation tables and root directory).

The final element of the boot sector is the disk bootstrap program. The disk bootstrap is usually read into memory by the ROM bootstrap, which is executed automatically when the computer is turned on. On most computers, the ROM bootstrap is an extremely short and primitive program, usually just smart enough to home the head of the disk drive (move it to track 0), read the first physical sector into RAM at a predetermined location, and jump to it. The disk bootstrap is slightly smarter, and can read and calculate the physical disk address of the beginning of the files storage area, read into memory the disk files containing the operating system, and transfer control to the BIOS (as described in Chapter 2).

For example, the IBM PC-DOS disk bootstrap (Figures 8-3 and 8-4) examines the first block of the disk directory to see if the files IBMBIO.COM and IBMDOS.COM are present, with the attributes *system* and *hidden*. If they are found, the disk is assumed to be bootable and the BIOS is read into memory (starting at 0070:0000) from contiguous sectors at the start of the files area, and then executed. If the two files are not found, the bootstrap displays the message:

Non-System disk or disk error

and waits for any key to be pressed, then jumps back to the ROM bootstrap routine.

```
     0  1  2  3  4  5  6  7  8  9  A  B  C  D  E  F
0000 EB 2C 90 49 42 4D 20 20 32 2E 30 00 02 02 01 00   .,.IBM  2.0.....
0010 02 70 00 D0 02 FD 02 00 09 00 02 00 00 00 00 00   .p..............
0020 0A DF 02 25 02 09 2A FF 50 F6 0F 02 CD 19 FA 33   ...%..*.P......3
0030 C0 8E D0 BC 00 7C 8E D8 A3 7A 00 C7 06 78 00 21   .....|...z...x.!
  .
  .
  .
0180 0D 0A 4E 6F 6E 2D 53 79 73 74 65 6D 20 64 69 73   ..Non-System dis
0190 6B 20 6F 72 20 64 69 73 6B 20 65 72 72 6F 72 0D   k or disk error.
01A0 0A 52 65 70 6C 61 63 65 20 61 6E 64 20 73 74 72   .Replace and str
01B0 69 6B 65 20 61 6E 79 20 6B 65 79 20 77 68 65 6E   ike any key when
01C0 20 72 65 61 64 79 0D 0A 00 0D 0A 44 69 73 6B 20   ready.....Disk
01D0 42 6F 6F 74 20 66 61 69 6C 75 72 65 0D 0A 00 69   Boot failure...i
01E0 62 6D 62 69 6F 20 20 63 6F 6D 30 69 62 6D 64 6F   bmbio  com0ibmdo
01F0 73 20 20 63 6F 6D 30 00 00 00 00 00 00 00 55 AA   s  com0.......U.
```

Figure 8-3. Dump of the boot sector (track 0, head 0, sector 1) of an IBM PC-DOS 2 floppy disk. This sector contains the OEM identification, a copy of the BIOS parameter block describing the medium, and the bootstrap program that reads the BIOS into memory and transfers control to it. See Figure 8-4.

```
0000:7c00 eb2c        jmp     7c2e            ;jump to disk
0000:7c02 90          nop                     ;bootstrap.

0000:7c03            db      'IBM  2.0'       ;8 chars OEM name

                                              ;BIOS Param Block
0000:7c0b            dw      512              ;bytes per sector
0000:7c0d            db      2                ;sectors per cluster
0000:7c0e            dw      1                ;reserved sectors
0000:7c10            db      2                ;number of FATs
0000:7c11            dw      112              ;root dir. entries
0000:7c13            dw      720              ;total sectors
0000:7c15            db      0fdh             ;media descriptor
0000:7c16            dw      2                ;sectors per FAT

0000:7c18            dw      9                ;sectors per track
0000:7c1a            dw      2                ;number of heads
0000:7c1c            dw      0                ;no. of hidden sect.

0000:7c1e            db      0
0000:7c1f            db      0                ;head
0000:7c20            db      0ah              ;length of BIOS file

0000:7c21            db      0dfh             ;disk parameter
0000:7c22            db      02               ;table (see ROM
0000:7c23            db      25h              ;BIOS listing of
0000:7c24            db      02               ;"DISK_BASE" for
0000:7c25            db      09               ;explanations)
0000:7c26            db      02ah             ;Int 1EH points
0000:7c27            db      0ffh             ;to this table.
0000:7c28            db      50h
0000:7c29            db      f6h
0000:7c2a            db      0fh
0000:7c2b            db      02

0000:7c2c cd19        int     19              ;call ROM bootstrap.

                                              ;start of disk
                                              ;bootstrap...
0000:7c2e fa          cli                     ;block interrupts
0000:7c2f 33c0        xor     ax,ax           ;set stack base
0000:7c31 8ed0        mov     ss,ax           ;to 0000:7C00.
0000:7c33 bc007c      mov     sp,7c00
                        .
                        .
                        .
```

Figure 8-4. Partial disassembly of the boot sector shown in Figure 8-3. This sector contains the OEM identification, the BIOS parameter block, and the disk bootstrap program. Since disk controllers differ, each MS-DOS OEM necessarily has a different boot program in this sector.

```
0000:7d7e          dw      0
0000:7d80          db      cr,lf
                   db      'Non-System Disk or '
                   db      'disk error.',cr,lf
                   db      'Replace and strike any '
                   db      'key when ready'
                   db      cr,lf,0
0000:7dc9          db      cr,lf
                   db      'Disk Boot failure'
                   db      cr,lf,0
0000:7ddf          db      'ibmbio  com0'
0000:7deb          db      'ibmdos  com0'
```

Figure 8-4 continued.

The Reserved Area

The boot sector is actually part of a larger reserved area that can be from one to several sectors long. The size of this area is described by the *reserved sectors* word in the BIOS parameter block, at offset 0EH in the boot sector. Remember that the number in the BPB field includes the boot sector itself, so if the value is 1 (as it is on IBM PC disks), the length of the reserved area as shown in Figure 8-1 is actually zero sectors.

The File Allocation Table

When a file is created or extended, disk sectors are assigned to it from the files area in powers of 2 known as *allocation units* or *clusters*. The number of sectors per cluster for a given medium is defined in the BIOS parameter block, and can be found at offset 0DH in the disk's boot sector. The IBM family of personal computers uses the following assignments:

Disk type	Power of 2		Sectors/cluster
Single-sided floppy disk	0	=	1
Double-sided floppy disk	1	=	2
PC/AT fixed disk	2	=	4
PC/XT fixed disk	3	=	8

The file allocation table is divided into fields that correspond directly to the assignable clusters on the disk. These fields are 12 bits long in MS-DOS versions 1 and 2, and may be either 12 bits or 16 bits long in version 3, depending upon the size of the medium (12 bits if the disk contains fewer than 4087 clusters, 16 bits otherwise).

The first two fields in the FAT are always reserved. On IBM-compatible media, the first 8 bits of the first reserved FAT entry contain a copy of the *media descriptor byte*, which is also found in the BIOS parameter block in the boot sector. The second, third, and (if applicable) fourth bytes, which constitute the remainder of the first two reserved FAT fields, always contain 0FFH. The currently defined IBM-format media descriptor bytes are:

Descriptor	Medium	MS-DOS version
0F9H	5¼″ floppy disk, 2-sided, 15-sector	3
0FCH	5¼″ floppy disk, 1-sided, 9-sector	2 3
0FDH	5¼″ floppy disk, 2-sided, 9-sector	2 3
0FEH	5¼″ floppy disk, 1-sided, 8-sector	1 2 3
0FFH	5¼″ floppy disk, 2-sided, 8-sector	1 2 3
0F8H	Fixed disk	2 3
0FEH	8″ floppy disk, 1-sided, single-density	
0FDH	8″ floppy disk, 1-sided, single-density	
0FEH	8″ floppy disk, 2-sided, double-density	

Aside from the first two reserved entries of the FAT, the remainder of the entries describe the usage of their corresponding disk clusters. The contents of the FAT fields are interpreted as follows:

Value	Meaning
(0)000H	Cluster available
(F)FF0–(F)FF6H	Reserved cluster
(F)FF7H	Bad cluster, if not part of chain
(F)FF8–(F)FFFH	Last cluster of file
(X)XXX	Next cluster in file

Each file's entry in the disk directory contains the number of the first cluster assigned to that file, which is used as an entry point into the FAT. From the entry point on, each FAT slot contains the cluster number of the next cluster in the file, until a last-cluster mark is encountered.

At the computer manufacturer's option, two or more identical copies of the FAT can be maintained by MS-DOS on each volume. All copies are updated simultaneously whenever files are extended or the directory is modified. If access to a sector in a FAT fails due to a read error, the other copies are tried until a successful disk read is obtained or all copies are exhausted. Thus, if one copy of the FAT becomes unreadable due to excessive wear or a software accident, the other(s) may still allow the files on the disk to be salvaged. As part of its procedure for checking the integrity of a disk, the CHKDSK program compares the multiple copies (usually two) of the FAT to make sure they are both readable and consistent.

The Disk Directory

Following the file allocation tables, we find an area known in MS-DOS versions 2.0 and above as the root directory (under MS-DOS 1, it was the only directory on the disk). This area contains rigidly formatted 32-byte entries that describe files, subdirectories, and the volume label (if present). The size of the root directory is determined when the disk is initialized, and is described in the BIOS parameter block, at offset 0011H of the boot sector of the disk. The structure of the disk directory was covered in detail in Chapter 7 and will not be discussed further here.

The Files Area

The remainder of the volume after the root directory is known as the files area, or data area. The disk sectors in this area are viewed as a pool of clusters, each containing one or more logical sectors, depending upon the disk format. Each cluster has a corresponding entry in the file allocation table that describes its current usage: available, reserved, assigned to a file, or unusable (due to surface defects).

When a file is extended under MS-DOS versions 1 and 2, the FAT is searched from its beginning until a free cluster (designated by a zero FAT field) is found; that FAT field is then changed to a last-cluster mark, and the previous last cluster of the file's chain is updated to point to the new last cluster. In other words, when a file is extended, the first free cluster on the disk is used, regardless of its position. Under version 3, however, a different allocation scheme is used, so the first free cluster on the disk is not necessarily the one assigned when a file is created or extended.

Because they are simply a special kind of file, subdirectories can also grow in this way, by being assigned additional clusters from the files area. This is why subdirectories are capable of containing any number of file entries, whereas the root directory has a fixed maximum size determined at the time the disk is formatted. This subject is discussed in detail in Chapter 7.

Since the first two fields of the FAT are reserved, the first cluster in the files area is assigned the number 2. If the volume is a bootable system disk, the first clusters of the files area are allocated sequentially to the files containing the MS-DOS BIOS and the DOS kernel, thus keeping the complexity of the disk bootstrap program to a minimum.

Interpreting the File Allocation Table

Now that we understand how the disk is structured, let's see how we can use this knowledge to find a FAT position from a cluster number.

If the FAT has 12-bit entries, use the following procedure:

1. Use the directory entry to find the starting cluster of the file in question.

2. Multiply the cluster number by 1.5.

3. Use the integral part of the product as the offset into the FAT and move the word at that offset into a register. Remember that a FAT position can span a physical disk-sector boundary.

4. If the product is a whole number, AND the register with 0FFFH.

5. Otherwise, "logical shift" the register right 4 bits.

6. If the result is a value from 0FF8H through 0FFFH, there are no more clusters in the file. Otherwise, the 12 bits contain the cluster number of the next cluster in the file.

On some types of MS-DOS 3 disks, where the FAT entries are 16 bits long, the extraction of a cluster number from the table is much simpler:

1. Use the directory entry to find the starting cluster of the file in question.

2. Multiply the cluster number by 2.

3. Use the product as the offset into the FAT, and move the word at that offset into a register.

4. If the result is a value from 0FFF8H through 0FFFFH, there are no more clusters in the file. Otherwise, the result is the number of the next cluster in the file.

Cluster numbers are converted to logical sectors by subtracting 2, multiplying the result by the number of sectors per cluster, then adding the logical sector number of the beginning of the data area (this can be calculated from the information in the BPB).

As an example, let's work out the disk location of the file IBMBIO.COM, which is the first entry in the directory shown in Figure 8-5. First, we need some information from the BIOS parameter block, which is found in the boot sector of the medium (see hex dump in Figure 8-3 and disassembly in Figure 8-4).

```
         0  1  2  3  4  5  6  7  8  9  A  B  C  D  E  F
0000    49 42 4D 42 49 4F 20 20 43 4F 4D 27 00 00 00 00    IBMBIO  COM'....
0010    00 00 00 00 00 00 00 60 54 07 02 00 80 12 00 00    .......'T.......
0020    49 42 4D 44 4F 53 20 20 43 4F 4D 27 00 00 00 00    IBMDOS  COM'....
0030    00 00 00 00 00 00 00 60 54 07 07 00 80 42 00 00    .......'T....B..
0040    43 4F 4D 4D 41 4E 44 20 43 4F 4D 20 00 00 00 00    COMMAND COM ....
0050    00 00 00 00 00 00 00 60 54 07 18 00 80 45 00 00    .......'T....E..
0060    53 59 53 5F 4D 41 53 54 45 52 20 08 00 00 00 00    SYS_MASTER .....
0070    00 00 00 00 00 00 B6 BC 9A 0A 00 00 00 00 00 00    ...............
0080    00 F6 F6 F6 F6 F6 F6 F6 F6 F6 F6 F6 F6 F6 F6 F6    ...............
0090    F6 F6 F6 F6 F6 F6 F6 F6 F6 F6 F6 F6 F6 F6 F6 F6    ...............
  .
  .
  .
01E0    00 F6 F6 F6 F6 F6 F6 F6 F6 F6 F6 F6 F6 F6 F6 F6    ...............
01F0    F6 F6 F6 F6 F6 F6 F6 F6 F6 F6 F6 F6 F6 F6 F6 F6    ...............
```

Figure 8-5. Dump of the first sector of the root directory for an IBM PC-DOS 2.1 disk containing the three system files and a volume label.

The BPB tells us that there are:

- 512 bytes per sector
- 2 sectors per cluster
- 2 sectors per FAT
- 2 FATs
- 112 entries in the root directory

From the BPB information, we can calculate the starting logical sector number of each of the disk's control areas and the files area by constructing a table, as follows:

Area	Length	Sector numbers
Boot sector	1 sector	00
2 FATs * 2 sectors/FAT	4 sectors	01–04
112 directory entries * 32 bytes/entry ÷ 512 bytes/sector	7 sectors	05–0BH
Total sectors occupied by bootstrap, FATs, and directory		12 sectors (0CH)

Therefore, the first sector of the files area is 12 (0CH).

The word at offset 01AH in the directory entry for IBMBIO.COM gives us the starting cluster number for that file: cluster 2. To find the logical sector number of the first block in the file, we can follow the procedure given earlier:

1. Cluster number $-2 = 2 - 2 = 0$.

2. Multiply by sectors per cluster $= 0 * 2 = 0$.

3. Add logical sector number of start of the files area $= 0 + 0CH = 0CH$.

So the calculated sector number of the beginning of the file IBMBIO.COM is 0CH, which is exactly what we expect, knowing that the FORMAT program always places the system files in contiguous sectors at the beginning of the data area.

Now let's trace IBMBIO.COM's chain through the file allocation table (Figures 8-6 and 8-7). This will be a little tedious, but a detailed understanding of the process is crucial. In an actual program, we would first read the boot sector using Int 25H, then calculate the address of the file allocation table from the contents of the BPB, and finally read the FAT into memory, again using Int 25H.

From IBMBIO.COM's directory entry, we already know that the first cluster in the file is cluster 2. To examine that cluster's entry in the FAT, we multiply the cluster number by 1.5, which gives 0003 as the FAT offset, and fetch the word at that offset (which contains 4003H). Since the product of the cluster and 1.5 is a whole number, we AND the word from the FAT with 0FFFH, yielding the number 3, which is the number of the second cluster assigned to the file.

Following the same procedure, to examine cluster 3's entry in the FAT, we multiply 3 by 1.5 to get 4.5, and fetch the word at offset 0004 (it contains 0040H). Since the product of 3 and 1.5 is not a whole number, we shift the word right 4 bits, yielding 4, which is the number of the third cluster assigned to IBMBIO.COM.

```
        0  1  2  3  4  5  6  7  8  9  A  B  C  D  E  F
0000   FD FF FF 03 40 00 05 60 00 FF 8F 00 09 A0 00 0B    ....@..'........
0010   C0 00 0D E0 00 0F 00 01 11 20 01 13 40 01 15 60    ......... ..@..'
0020   01 17 F0 FF 19 A0 01 1B C0 01 1D E0 01 1F 00 02    ................
0030   21 20 02 23 40 02 25 60 02 27 80 02 29 F0 FF 00    ! .#@.%'.'..)...
0040   00 00 00 00 00 00 00 00 00 00 00 00 00 00 00 00    ................
   .
   .
   .
01F0   00 00 00 00 00 00 00 00 00 00 00 00 00 00 00 00    ................
```

Figure 8-6. Dump of the first block of the file allocation table (track 0, head 0, sector 2) for the PC-DOS 2.1 disk whose directory is shown in Figure 8-5. Notice that the first byte of the FAT contains the media descriptor byte for a 9-sector, 2-sided disk.

```
getfat          proc  near          ;extracts the FAT field
                                     ;for a given cluster.
                                     ;call   AX = cluster #
                                     ;       DS:BX = addr of FAT
                                     ;returns AX = FAT field.
                                     ;other registers unchanged

                push  bx             ;save affected registers.
                push  cx
                mov   cx,ax
                shl   ax,1           ;cluster * 2
                add   ax,cx          ;cluster * 3
                test  ax,1
                pushf                ;save remainder in Z flag.
                shr   ax,1           ;cluster * 1.5
                add   bx,ax
                mov   ax,[bx]
                popf                 ;was cluster * 1.5 whole no.?
                jnz   getfat1        ;no, jump.
                and   ax,0fffh       ;yes, isolate bottom 12 bits.
                jmp   getfat2
getfat1:        mov   cx,4           ;shift word right 4 bits.
                shr   ax,cl
getfat2:        pop   cx             ;restore registers and exit.
                pop   bx
                ret
getfat          endp
```

Figure 8-7. *Assembly-language procedure to access the file allocation table (this example assumes 12-bit FAT fields). Given a cluster number, the procedure returns the contents of that cluster's FAT entry in AX. This simple example ignores the fact that FAT entries can span sector boundaries.*

In this manner we can follow the chain through the FAT until we come to a cluster (6, in this case), whose FAT entry contains the value 0FFFH, which is an end–of–file marker in FATs with 12-bit entries.

We have now established that the file IBMBIO.COM contains the following clusters, from which we calculate the logical sectors assigned to the file:

Cluster	Sectors	Cluster	Sectors
2	0CH, 0DH	5	12H, 13H
3	0EH, 0FH	6	14H, 15H
4	10H, 11H		

Of course, the last cluster may be only partially filled with actual data; the amount of the last cluster to use is the remainder of the file's size in bytes (found in the directory entry) divided by the bytes per cluster.

Memory Allocation

Current versions of MS-DOS can manage as much as 1 megabyte of contiguous random-access memory. On IBM PCs and compatibles, the memory occupied by MS-DOS and other programs starts at address 0000H and may reach as high as address 09FFFFH; this 640-Kbyte area of RAM is sometimes referred to as *conventional memory*. Memory above this address is reserved for ROM hardware drivers, video refresh buffers, and the like. Computers that are not IBM compatible may use other memory layouts.

The RAM area under the control of MS-DOS is divided into two major sections:

- The operating system area
- The transient program area

The operating system area starts at address 0000H—that is, it occupies the lowest portion of RAM. It holds the interrupt vector table, the operating system proper and its tables and buffers, any additional installable drivers specified in the CONFIG.SYS file, and the resident part of the COMMAND.COM command interpreter. The amount of memory occupied by the operating system area varies with the version of MS-DOS used, number of disk buffers, size of installed device drivers, and so forth.

The transient program area is the remainder of RAM above the operating system area and is dynamically allocatable memory. MS-DOS maintains a special control block for each chunk of allocated memory in the TPA, and these blocks are chained together. There are three MS-DOS functions that can be called to allocate and deallocate chunks of memory from the TPA:

Function	Action
48H	Allocate memory block
49H	Release memory block
4AH	Modify memory block

These functions are used by MS-DOS itself when a program or external command is loaded from the disk at the request of COMMAND.COM or another shell. The EXEC function, which is the MS-DOS program loader, calls function 48H to allocate a memory block for the loaded program's environment and another for the program itself and its program segment prefix. It then reads the program from the disk into the assigned memory area. When the program terminates, MS-DOS calls function 49H to release the two memory blocks, then returns control to the command interpreter.

The MS-DOS memory-management functions can also be employed by transient programs to dynamically manage the memory available in the TPA. Proper use of these functions is one of the most important criteria of whether a program is well behaved under MS-DOS. Well-behaved programs are most likely to be portable to future versions of the operating system, and least likely to cause interference with other processes under multitasking user interfaces such as Microsoft Windows.

Using the Memory Allocation Functions

The memory allocation functions are used in two common ways:

- To shrink a program's memory allocation, so that there is enough room to load and execute another program under its control.

- To dynamically allocate additional memory required by the program, and to release the same memory when it is no longer needed.

Shrinking Memory Allocation

Although many MS-DOS application programs simply assume they own all memory, this assumption is a relic of the early versions of MS-DOS (and CP/M), which could support only one active process at any given time. Well-behaved MS-DOS programs will take pains to modify only memory that they actually own, and release any memory that they don't need.

Unfortunately, under current versions of MS-DOS, the amount of memory that a program will own is not easily predicted in advance. It turns out that the amount of memory allocated to a program when it is first loaded depends upon two factors:

- The type of file the program is loaded from

- The amount of memory available in the TPA

Programs loaded from COM (memory-image) files are always allocated all of the TPA. Since COM programs contain no file header that can pass segment and memory-usage information to MS-DOS, MS-DOS simply assumes the worst case and gives such a program everything. MS-DOS will load the program as long as there is at least as much room in the TPA as the size of the file plus 256 bytes for the PSP and 2 bytes for the stack. It is the COM program's responsibility, when it receives control, to determine whether there is enough memory available to carry out its functions.

Programs loaded from EXE files are allocated memory according to more complicated rules. First, of course, enough room must be available in the TPA to hold the declared code, data, and stack segments. In addition, there are two fields in an EXE file's header that are set by the Linker to inform MS-DOS about the program's memory requirements. The first field, called MIN_ALLOC, defines the minimum number of paragraphs required by the program, in addition to those for the code, data, and stack segments. The other field, called MAX_ALLOC, defines the maximum number of paragraphs of additional memory the program would use, if available.

When loading an EXE file, MS-DOS will first attempt to allocate the number of paragraphs in MAX_ALLOC plus the number of paragraphs required by the program itself. If that much memory is not available, MS-DOS will assign the program all free memory, provided that this is at least the amount specified by MIN_ALLOC plus the size of the image file. If that condition is not satisfied, the program cannot be executed.

Once a COM or EXE program is loaded and running, it can use SETBLOCK (the modify memory block function) to release all the memory it does not immediately need. This is conveniently done right after the program receives control from MS-DOS, by calling Int 21H function 4AH with the segment of the program's PSP in register ES and the number of paragraphs that the program requires to run in BX (Figure 9-1).

```
main            proc far                        ;entry point from DOS

                                                ;both COM and EXE files
                                                ;receive control with DS
                                                ;and ES pointing to the
                                                ;Program Segment Prefix.

                mov     sp,offset stk           ;COM programs should move
                                                ;their stack to a safe
                                                ;area.

                                                ;Function 4AH =
                mov     ah,4ah                  ;Modify Memory Block

                                                ;retain 400H paragraphs
                mov     bx,400h                 ; = 16 Kbytes.

                int     21h                     ;transfer to DOS.
                jc      error                   ;jump if function failed.
                .
error:          .
                .
                dw      64 dup (?)
stk             equ     $                       ;base of new stack
                .
                .
                .
```

Figure 9-1. An example of a COM program releasing excess memory after it receives control from MS-DOS. Register ES contains the segment of the program's PSP and register BX contains the number of paragraphs of memory to which the program wishes to shrink its allocation.

Dynamic Allocation of Additional Memory

When a well-behaved program needs additional memory space—for an I/O buffer or an array of intermediate results, for example—it can call Int 21H function 48H (allocate memory block) with the desired number of paragraphs. If a sufficiently large chunk of unallocated memory is available, MS-DOS will return the segment address of the base of the assigned area and clear the carry flag (0), indicating that the function was successful.

If no unallocated chunk of sufficient size is available, MS-DOS will set the carry flag (1), return an error code in register AX, and return the size (in paragraphs) of the largest block available in register BX (Figure 9-2). In this case, no memory has yet been allocated. The program can use the value returned in register BX to determine whether it can continue in a "degraded" fashion, with less memory. If it can, it must call function 48H again to allocate the smaller memory block.

When a program is through with an allocated memory block, it should use function 49H to release the block. If it does not, MS-DOS will automatically release all memory allocations for the program when it terminates.

Memory Control Blocks

The internal structure of memory control blocks, or *arena headers* (in UNIX/XENIX terminology), is not officially documented by Microsoft for the outside world at present. This is probably to deter programmers from trying to manipulate their memory allocations directly, instead of through the MS-DOS calls provided for that purpose.

Arena headers have identical structures in MS-DOS versions 2 and 3. They are 16 bytes (one paragraph) long and are located immediately before the memory area that they control (Figure 9-3). An arena header contains:

● A byte signifying whether it is a member or the last entry in the entire chain of such headers

● A word indicating whether the area it controls is available or already belongs to a program (if the latter, the word points to the program's PSP)

● A word containing the size (in paragraphs) of the controlled memory area (*memory arena*)

MS-DOS inspects the chain of arena headers whenever a memory-block allocation, modification, or release function is requested, or when a program is EXECed or terminated. If any of the blocks appear to be corrupted or the chain is broken, MS-DOS will display the dreaded message:

Memory allocation error

and halt the system.

```
                    .
                    .
                    .
        mov     ah,48h                      ;Function 48H = Allocate Mem Block
        mov     bx,0800h                    ;800H paragraphs = 32 Kbytes
        int     21h                         ;transfer to DOS.
        jc      error                       ;jump if allocation failed.
        mov     buff_seg,ax                 ;save segment of allocated block.
                    .
                    .
                    .
        mov     es,buff_seg                 ;ES:DI = addr of block
        xor     di,di
        mov     cx,08000h                   ;store 32768 bytes.
        mov     al,0ffh                     ;fill buffer with -1s.
        cld
        rep     stosb                       ;now perform fast fill.
                    .
                    .
                    .
        mov     cx,08000h                   ;length to write, bytes
        mov     bx,handle                   ;handle for prev opened file
        push    ds                          ;save our data segment.
        mov     ds,buff_seg                 ;let DS:DX = buffer addr.
        mov     dx,0
        mov     ah,40h                      ;Function 40H = Write
        int     21h                         ;transfer to DOS.
        pop     ds                          ;restore our data segment.
        jc      error                       ;jump if write failed.
                    .
                    .
                    .
        mov     es,buff_seg                 ;ES = seg of prev allocated block
        mov     ah,49h                      ;Function 49H = release mem block
        int     21h                         ;transfer to DOS.
        jc      error                       ;jump if release failed.
                    .
                    .
                    .
error:              .
                    .
handle  dw      0
buff_seg dw     0
                    .
                    .
                    .
```

Figure 9-2. Example of dynamic memory allocation. The program requests a 32-Kbyte memory block from MS-DOS, fills it with −1s, writes it to disk, and then releases it.

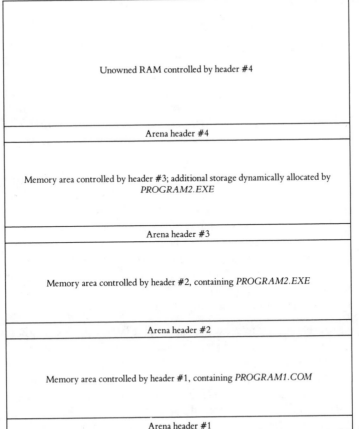

← top of RAM controlled by MS-DOS

Unowned RAM controlled by header #4

Arena header #4

Memory area controlled by header #3; additional storage dynamically allocated by *PROGRAM2.EXE*

Arena header #3

Memory area controlled by header #2, containing *PROGRAM2.EXE*

Arena header #2

Memory area controlled by header #1, containing *PROGRAM1.COM*

Arena header #1

← bottom of transient program area

Figure 9-3. An example diagram of MS-DOS arena headers (memory control blocks) and the transient program area. The environment blocks and their associated headers have been omitted from this figure to increase its clarity.

In the example in Figure 9-3, *PROGRAM1.COM* was originally loaded into the TPA by COMMAND.COM and, since it was a COM file, was allocated all of the TPA, controlled by arena header #1. *PROGRAM1.COM* then used function 4AH (modify memory block) to shrink its memory allocation to the amount it actually needed to run, and loaded and executed *PROGRAM2.EXE* with the EXEC function (Int 21H function 4BH). The EXEC function obtained a suitable amount of memory, controlled by arena header #2, and loaded *PROGRAM2.EXE* into it. *PROGRAM2.EXE*, in turn, needed some additional memory to store some intermediate results, so it called function 48H (allocate memory block) to obtain the area controlled by arena header #3. The highest arena header (#4) controls all of the remaining TPA that has not been allocated to any program.

Lotus/Intel/Microsoft Expanded Memory

When the IBM Personal Computer and MS-DOS were first released, the 640-Kbyte limit that IBM placed on the amount of RAM that could be directly managed by MS-DOS seemed almost unimaginably huge. But as MS-DOS has grown in both size and capabilities and the popular applications have become more powerful, that 640 Kbytes has begun to seem a bit crowded. Although personal computers based on the 80286 family have the potential to manage up to 16 megabytes of RAM, this is little comfort to the millions of users of 8086/8088-based computers such as the IBM PC and its compatibles.

At the Spring COMDEX in 1985, Lotus Development Corporation and Intel Corporation jointly announced the Expanded Memory Specification 3.0 (EMS), which was designed to head off rapid obsolescence of the older PCs due to limited memory. Shortly afterward, Microsoft announced that it would support the EMS and that Microsoft Windows would be enhanced to use the memory made available by EMS hardware and software. Subsequently, the Expanded Memory Specification 3.2, modified from 3.0 to add additional support for multitasking operating systems, was released as a joint effort of Lotus, Intel, and Microsoft.

As this book goes to press less than a year later, a great many hardware vendors have announced plug-in expanded-memory cards, and several of the most popular spreadsheet and integrated data-management programs have been released in new versions to take advantage of the additional fast storage provided by expanded memory. Consequently, it seems that the EMS can already be considered a success, and that it will have an impact on PC software design for some years to come.

What Is Expanded Memory?

The Intel/Lotus/Microsoft Expanded Memory Specification is a functional definition of a bank-switched memory-expansion subsystem. It is comprised of hardware expansion modules and a resident driver program specific to those modules. The expanded memory is made available to application software as 16-Kbyte pages, mapped into a contiguous 64-Kbyte area called the *page frame*, somewhere above the main memory area used by MS-DOS/PC-DOS (0–640K). The exact location of the page frame is user configurable, so it need not conflict with other hardware options.

The EMS provides a uniform means for applications to access as much as 8 megabytes of memory. The supporting software, which is called the Expanded Memory Manager (EMM), provides a hardware-independent interface between application software and the expanded memory board(s). It is supplied in the form of an installable character-device driver and is linked into the MS-DOS/PC-DOS system by adding a line to the CONFIG.SYS file on the system boot disk.

Internally, the Expanded Memory Manager is divided into two major portions, which may be referred to as the *driver* and the *manager*. The driver portion mimics some of the actions of a genuine installable device driver, in that it includes initialization and output status functions and a valid device header. The second, and major, portion of the EMM is the true interface between application software and the expanded-memory hardware. Several classes of services are provided:

- Verification of functionality of hardware and software modules

- Allocation of expanded memory pages

- Mapping of logical pages into the physical page frame

- Deallocation of expanded memory pages

- Support for multitasking operating systems

- Diagnostic routines

Application programs communicate with the EMM directly, via software Int 67H. MS-DOS versions 2 and 3 take no part in (and in fact are completely oblivious to) any expanded-memory manipulations that may occur. However, Microsoft Windows makes heavy use of expanded memory (when it is present) for program swapping, and it seems reasonable to expect that future multitasking versions of MS-DOS for the 8086/8088 family will do the same.

Expanded memory should not be confused with *extended memory*. Extended memory is the term used by IBM to refer to the memory at physical addresses above 1 megabyte that can be accessed by an 80286 CPU in protected mode. Current versions of MS-DOS run the 80286 in real mode (8086-emulation mode), and *extended* memory is therefore not directly accessible.

Checking for Expanded Memory

There are two well-behaved methods that an application program can use to test for the existence of the Expanded Memory Manager:

- Issue an open request (function 3DH) using the guaranteed device name of the EMM driver: *EMMXXXX0*. If the open succeeds, either the driver is present or there is coincidentally a file on the default disk drive with the same name. To rule out the latter, the application can issue a get output status request via the IOCTL function (44H); the status returned in register AL is 0FFH if the driver is present and zero if the driver is absent. In either case, the handle that was obtained from the open function should then be closed with function 3EH, so that it can be reused for another file or device.

- Use the address that is found in the Int 67H vector to inspect the device header of the presumed EMM. Programs that may interrupt MS-DOS during file operations or programs that are device drivers *must* use this method. If the EMM is present, the name field at offset 0AH of the device header will contain the string *EMMXXXX0*. This approach is nearly foolproof, and avoids the relatively high overhead of an MS-DOS open function. However, it is somewhat less well behaved, since it involves inspection of memory that does not belong to the application.

These two methods of testing for the existence of the Expanded Memory Manager are illustrated in Figures 9-4 and 9-5, respectively.

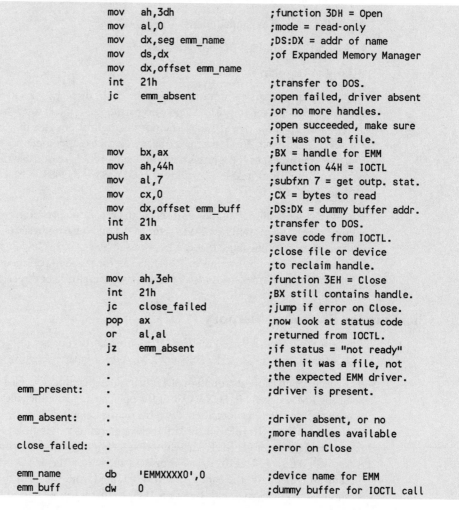

```
              mov    ah,3dh            ;function 3DH = Open
              mov    al,0              ;mode = read-only
              mov    dx,seg emm_name   ;DS:DX = addr of name
              mov    ds,dx             ;of Expanded Memory Manager
              mov    dx,offset emm_name
              int    21h               ;transfer to DOS.
              jc     emm_absent        ;open failed, driver absent
                                       ;or no more handles.
                                       ;open succeeded, make sure
                                       ;it was not a file.
              mov    bx,ax             ;BX = handle for EMM
              mov    ah,44h            ;function 44H = IOCTL
              mov    al,7              ;subfxn 7 = get outp. stat.
              mov    cx,0              ;CX = bytes to read
              mov    dx,offset emm_buff ;DS:DX = dummy buffer addr.
              int    21h               ;transfer to DOS.
              push   ax                ;save code from IOCTL.
                                       ;close file or device
                                       ;to reclaim handle.
              mov    ah,3eh            ;function 3EH = Close
              int    21h               ;BX still contains handle.
              jc     close_failed      ;jump if error on Close.
              pop    ax                ;now look at status code
              or     al,al             ;returned from IOCTL.
              jz     emm_absent        ;if status = "not ready"
                   .                   ;then it was a file, not
                   .                   ;the expected EMM driver.
emm_present:       .                   ;driver is present.
                   .
emm_absent:        .                   ;driver absent, or no
                   .                   ;more handles available
close_failed:      .                   ;error on Close
                   .
emm_name      db     'EMMXXXX0',0      ;device name for EMM
emm_buff      dw     0                 ;dummy buffer for IOCTL call
```

Figure 9-4. Testing for the Expanded Memory Manager via the MS-DOS open and IOCTL functions.

```
emm_int           equ    67h                        ;Extended Memory Manager
                   .                                 ;interrupt vector
                   .
                   .
                  mov    ah,35h                      ;DOS function 35H =
                  mov    al,emm_int                  ;get interrupt vector
                  int    21h                         ;into ES:BX
                                                     ;assume ES:0000 points
                                                     ;to the base of the EMM.
                  mov    di,10                       ;ES:DI = addr of name
                                                     ;field in Device Header
                  mov    si,seg emm_name             ;let DS:SI = addr of
                  mov    ds,si                       ;guaranteed driver name
                  mov    si,offset emm_name          ;for EMM.
                  mov    cx,8                         ;length of name field
                  cld
                  repz   cmpsb                        ;compare strings.
                  jnz    emm_absent                   ;strings didn't match.
                   .
emm_present:       .                                 ;driver present.
                   .
emm_absent:        .                                 ;driver absent.
                   .
emm_name          db     'EMMXXXX0',0                ;device name for Expanded
                                                     ;Memory Manager
```

Figure 9-5. Testing for the Expanded Memory Manager by inspection of the name field in the driver's device header.

Using Expanded Memory

After establishing that the memory-manager software is present, the application program communicates with it directly via the "user interrupt" 67H, bypassing MS-DOS/PC-DOS. The calling sequence for the EMM is as follows:

```
                  mov    ah,function                 ;AH determines service type.
                   .                                 ;load other registers with
                   .                                 ;values specific to the
                   .                                 ;requested service.
                  int    67h
```

In general, ES:DI is used to pass the address of a buffer or array, and DX is used to pass a handle. Section 4 of this book details each of the expanded memory functions and gives assembly-language examples of their use.

Upon return from an EMM function call, AH contains zero if the function was successful; otherwise, it contains an error code with the most significant bit set (Figure 9-6). Other values are typically returned in registers AL, BX, or in a user-specified buffer.

Error code	Meaning
00H	Function successful
80H	Internal error in Expanded Memory Manager software (could be caused by corrupted memory image of driver)
81H	Malfunction in expanded-memory hardware
82H	Memory manager busy
83H	Invalid handle
84H	Function requested by application not defined
85H	No more handles available
86H	Error in save or restore of mapping context
87H	Allocation request specified more logical pages than physically available in system; no pages allocated
88H	Allocation request specified more logical pages than currently available in system (request does not exceed physical pages that exist, but some are already allocated to other handles); no pages allocated
89H	Zero pages; cannot be allocated
8AH	Logical page requested to be mapped located outside range of logical pages assigned to handle
8BH	Illegal physical page number in mapping request (not in range 0–3)
8CH	Page-mapping hardware state save area full
8DH	Save of mapping context failed; save area already contains context associated with requested handle
8EH	Restore of mapping context failed; save area does not contain context for requested handle
8FH	Subfunction parameter not defined

Figure 9-6. Expanded Memory Manager error codes. After a call to the EMM, register AH will contain zero if the function was successful or an error code in the range 80H through 8FH if the function failed.

The Expanded Memory Manager relies heavily on the good behavior of application software to avoid the corruption of expanded memory. If several applications that use expanded memory are running under a multitasking manager such as Microsoft Windows and one or more of those applications does not abide strictly by the EMM's conventions, the data of some or all of the applications may be destroyed.

The MS-DOS EXEC Function

The MS-DOS EXEC function (4BH) allows a program (called the *parent*) to load any other program (called the *child*) from a storage device and execute it, then regain control when the child program is finished.

A parent program can pass information to the child in a command line, in default file control blocks, or via a set of strings called the environment block (discussed later in this chapter). All files or devices of the parent that were opened using the Handle extended file-management calls are duplicated in the newly created child task; that is, the child inherits all the active handles of the parent task. Any file operations on those handles by the child, such as seeks or file I/O, also affect the file pointers associated with the parent's handles.

When the child program finishes its work, it can pass an exit code back to the parent, indicating whether it encountered any errors. It can also, in turn, load other programs, and so on through many levels of control, until the system runs out of memory.

In MS-DOS versions 2 and 3, which do not support multitasking, the execution of the parent program is simply suspended until the child program has finished. However, it is clear that the EXEC function and the other supporting MS-DOS functions have been carefully designed to avoid address and timing dependencies. In future versions of MS-DOS, parent and child tasks will no doubt be able to execute concurrently, as they already do under other operating systems such as UNIX and iRMX.

But even without multitasking, the EXEC function has many uses. The MS-DOS command interpreter, COMMAND.COM, uses the EXEC function to run its external commands and other application programs. Many popular commercial programs, such as database managers and word processors, use EXEC to run other programs (spelling checkers, for example) or to load a second copy of COMMAND.COM, thereby allowing the user to list directories or copy and rename files without closing all the application files and stopping the main work in progress.

Making Memory Available

In order for a parent program to use the EXEC function to load a child program, there must be sufficient unallocated memory available in the transient program area.

When the parent was itself loaded, it was allocated a variable amount of memory, depending upon its original file type—COM or EXE— and any other information that was available to the loader (see Chapter 9 for further details). Since the operating system has no foolproof way of predicting how much memory any given program will require, it generally allocates far more memory to a program than is really necessary. Therefore, a prospective parent program's first action should be to release any excess memory allocation of its own to MS-DOS. The parent program's release of unneeded memory is accomplished with Int 21H function 4AH (modify memory block). In this case, function 4AH should be called with register ES pointing to the program segment prefix of the program releasing memory and register BX containing the number of paragraphs of memory to retain for that program (see Figure 9-1 for an example).

Warning: A COM program must be sure to move its stack to a safe area if it is reducing its memory allocation to less than 64 Kbytes.

Requesting the EXEC Function

Once the parent program has freed sufficient memory, it can load and execute a child program by calling the EXEC system service—performing an Int 21H, with register AH containing 4BH. Register AL contains a subfunction code of 0 to load and execute a program in unallocated memory or 3 to load an overlay at a specific address already belonging to the calling program.

When the EXEC function is invoked, the addresses of two data objects are also passed in registers:

- DS:DX points to the pathname of the program to be run.

- ES:BX points to a parameter block.

The parameter block, in turn, contains addresses of other information needed by the EXEC function.

The Program Name

The name of the program to be run, which is provided to the EXEC function by the calling program, must be an unambiguous file specification (no wildcard characters) and include an explicit *.COM* or *.EXE* extension. If the path and disk drive are not supplied in the program name, the current subdirectory and default disk drive are used. (The sequential search for COM, EXE, and BAT files in all the locations listed in the PATH variable is not a function of EXEC, but rather of the internal logic of COMMAND.COM.)

You cannot EXEC a batch file directly; instead, you must EXEC a copy of COMMAND.COM and pass the name of the batch file in the command tail, along with the /C switch.

The Parameter Block

The parameter block contains the addresses of four data objects:

- The environment block

- The command tail

- Two default file control blocks

The space reserved in the parameter block for the address of the environment block is only 2 bytes long and holds a segment address. The remaining three addresses are all double-word addresses; that is, they are 4 bytes long, with the offset in the first 2 bytes and the segment address in the last 2 bytes.

The Environment Block

Each program that is loaded by the EXEC function inherits a data structure called an *environment block* from its parent. The pointer to the segment of the block is found at offset 002CH in the program segment prefix. The environment block holds certain information used by the system's command interpreter (usually COMMAND.COM) and may also hold information to be used by transient programs. It has no effect on the operation of the operating system proper.

If the environment block pointer in the EXEC parameter block contains zero, the child program will acquire a copy of the parent program's environment block. Alternatively, a segment pointer can be provided to a different or expanded set of strings. The maximum size of the environment block is 32 Kbytes, which means that very large chunks of information can be passed between programs by this mechanism.

The environment block for any given program is static, implying that if more than one generation of child programs is resident in RAM, each one will have a distinct and separate copy of the environment block. Furthermore, the environment block for a program that terminates and stays resident will not be updated by subsequent PATH and SET commands.

More details about the environment block will be found later in this chapter.

The Command Tail

The command tail is copied into the child program's PSP at offset 0080H, as described in Chapter 3. It takes the form of a count byte followed by a string of ASCII characters, terminated by a carriage return; the carriage return is not included in the count.

The command tail can include filenames, switches, or other parameters. From the child program's point of view, the command tail should provide the same information that would be present if the program had been run by a direct user command at the MS-DOS prompt. Any I/O redirection parameters placed in the command tail for EXEC will be ignored; redirection of the standard devices must be provided for by the parent program *before* the EXEC call is made.

The Default File Control Blocks

The two default file control blocks pointed to by the EXEC parameter block are copied into the child program's PSP at offsets 005CH and 006CH. If there is no requirement for the default FCBs, they can be omitted by placing −1 (0FFFFH) in the parameter block's FCB pointers.

However, to truly emulate the function of COMMAND.COM from the child program's point of view, function 29H (the system parse-filename service) should be used to parse the first two parameters of the command tail into the default file control blocks before the EXEC function is invoked. File control blocks are not much use under MS-DOS versions 2 and 3, since they do not support the hierarchical file structure, but some application programs do inspect them as a quick way to get at the first two switches or other parameters in the command tail. File control blocks are discussed in more detail in Chapter 6.

Returning from the EXEC Function

Unlike most other MS-DOS function calls, the EXEC function destroys the contents of all registers except for the code segment (CS) and instruction pointer (IP). Therefore, *before* making the EXEC call, the parent program must push the contents of any other registers that are important onto the stack, and then save the stack segment (SS) and stack pointer (SP) registers in variables that are accessible inside the code segment. Upon return from a successful EXEC call (i.e., the child program has finished executing), the parent program should reload SS and SP from the variables where they were saved, then pop the other saved registers off the stack.

Finally, the parent can use Int 21H function 4DH (get return code) to obtain the success or failure code passed back by the child program.

The EXEC function will fail if:

- There is not enough unallocated memory available to load and execute the requested program file.

- The requested program can't be found on the disk.

- The transient portion of COMMAND.COM in highest RAM (which contains the actual loader) has been destroyed and there is not enough free memory to reload it (MS-DOS 2 version only).

Figure 10-1 summarizes the calling convention for function 4BH. A skeleton of a typical EXEC call is shown in Figure 10-2 (on page 193). This particular example uses the EXEC function to load and run the MS-DOS utility CHKDSK.COM. A more complete example that includes the use of the function 4AH to free unneeded memory is presented in the *SHELL.ASM* program listing at the end of this chapter.

Called with:

AH	= 4BH
AL	= function type
	00 = load and execute program
	03 = load overlay
ES:BX	= segment:offset of parameter block
DS:DX	= segment:offset of program specification

Returns:

If call succeeded:
Carry flag clear and, except for CS and IP, all other registers, including the stack
pointers, may be destroyed
If call failed:
Carry flag set and AX = error code

Parameter block format:
If AL = 0 (load and execute program):

Bytes 0–1	= segment pointer, environment block
Bytes 2–3	= offset of command-line tail
Bytes 4–5	= segment of command-line tail
Bytes 6–7	= offset of first file control block to be copied into new PSP + 5CH
Bytes 8–9	= segment of first file control block
Bytes 10–11	= offset of second file control block to be copied into new PSP + 6CH
Bytes 12–13	= segment of second file control block

If AL = 3 (load overlay):

Bytes 0–1	= segment address where file will be loaded
Bytes 2–3	= relocation factor to apply to loaded image

Figure 10-1. Calling convention for the EXEC function (Int 21H function 4BH).

More About the Environment Block

The environment block is always paragraph aligned (starts at an address
that is a multiple of 16 bytes) and contains a series of ASCIIZ strings. Each
of the strings takes the form:

NAME = PARAMETER

The end of the entire set of strings is indicated by an additional zero byte
(Figure 10-3 on page 194). Under MS-DOS version 3, the block of environment strings and the extra zero byte are followed by a word count and the
complete drive, path, filename, and extension used by the EXEC call to
load the program.

```
                .
                .
                .
        mov     cs:stk_seg,ss           ;save stack.
        mov     cs:stk_ptr,sp
        mov     dx,offset pgm_name
        mov     bx,offset par_block
        mov     al,0                    ;AL = 0 to run program
        mov     ah,4bh                  ;Function 4BH = EXEC
        int     21h                     ;transfer to DOS.
        mov     ss,cs:stk_seg           ;restore stack.
        mov     sp,cs:stk_ptr
                .
                .
                .
stk_seg     dw      0                   ;original SS contents
stk_ptr     dw      0                   ;original SP contents

pgm_name    db      '\CHKDSK.COM',0     ;drive, path, name of
                                        ;program to be executed
par_blk     dw      envir               ;segment address of
                                        ;environment descriptor
            dw      offset cmd_line     ;address of Command line
            dw      seg cmd_line        ;to be passed to program
            dw      offset fcb1         ;address of default File
            dw      seg fcb1            ;Control Block #1
            dw      offset fcb2         ;address of default File
            dw      seg fcb2            ;Control Block #2

cmd_line    db      4,' *.*',cr         ;actual command line to
                                        ;be passed to EXEC'd pgm
fcb1        db      0                   ;File Control Block #1
            db      11 dup ('?')
            db      25 dup (0)
fcb2        db      0                   ;File Control Block #2
            db      11 dup (' ')
            db      25 dup (0)

envir       segment    para 'ENVIR'     ;Environment Descriptor

            db      'PATH=',0           ;empty search path
                                        ;location of COMMAND.COM
            db      'COMSPEC=A:\COMMAND.COM',0
            db      0                   ;end of environment block
envir       ends
```

Figure 10-2. Brief example of the use of the MS-DOS EXEC call, with all necessary variables and command blocks. Note that the two variables used to save registers SS and SP must lie within the code segment, although the other data items may be placed in another data segment.

```
      0  1  2  3  4  5  6  7  8  9  A  B  C  D  E  F  0123456789ABCDEF
0000 43 4F 4D 53 50 45 43 3D 43 3A 5C 43 4F 4D 4D 41  COMSPEC=C:\COMMA
0010 4E 44 2E 43 4F 4D 00 50 52 4F 4D 50 54 3D 24 70  ND.COM.PROMPT=$p
0020 24 5F 24 64 20 20 20 24 74 24 68 24 68 24 68 24  $_$d   $t$h$h$h$
0030 68 24 68 24 68 20 24 71 24 71 24 67 00 50 41 54  h$h$h $q$q$g.PAT
0040 48 3D 43 3A 5C 53 59 53 54 45 4D 3B 43 3A 5C 41  H=C:\SYSTEM;C:\A
0050 53 4D 3B 43 3A 5C 57 53 3B 43 3A 5C 45 54 48 45  SM;C:\WS;C:\ETHE
0060 52 4E 45 54 3B 43 3A 5C 46 4F 52 54 48 5C 50 43  RNET;C:\FORTH\PC
0070 33 31 3B 00 00 01 00 43 3A 5C 46 4F 52 54 48 5C  31;....C:\FORTH\
0080 50 43 33 31 5C 46 4F 52 54 48 2E 43 4F 4D 00 20  PC31\FORTH.COM.
```

Figure 10-3. Dump of a typical environment block under MS-DOS version 3. This particular example contains the default COMSPEC parameter and two relatively complex PATH and PROMPT control strings that were set up by entries in the user's AUTOEXEC file. Note the path and file specification of the executing program following the double zeros at offset 0073H that denote the end of the environment block.

Under normal conditions, the environment block inherited by a program will contain at least three strings:

```
COMSPEC = variable
PATH = variable
PROMPT = variable
```

These three strings are placed into the environment block at system initialization, during the interpretation of the CONFIG.SYS and AUTOEXEC.BAT files. They tell the MS-DOS command interpreter, COMMAND.COM, the location of its executable file (to enable it to reload the transient portion), where to search for executable external commands or program files, and the format of the user prompt, respectively.

Other strings can be added to the environment block, either interactively or in batch files, by use of the SET command. These are used only for informational purposes by transient programs. For example, the Microsoft C Compiler looks in the environment block for INCLUDE, LIB, and TMP strings to tell it where to find its *#include* files and library files, and where to build its temporary working files.

Example Programs: *SHELL.C* and *SHELL.ASM*

As a practical example of use of the MS-DOS EXEC function, I have included a small command interpreter called *SHELL*, with equivalent Microsoft C (Figure 10-4) and Microsoft Macro Assembler (Figure 10-5, page 199) source code. The source code for the assembly-language version is considerably more complex, but the names and functionality of the various procedures are quite parallel.

```
/*
        SHELL.C         a simple user-extendable command
                        interpreter for MS-DOS 2.X and 3.X

        Copyright (C) 1985 Ray Duncan

        To compile with Microsoft C 3.0 and
        link into the executable file SHELL.EXE:

                        C>MSC SHELL;
                        C>LINK SHELL;
*/

#include <stdio.h>
#include <process.h>
#include <stdlib.h>
#include <signal.h>

#define dim(x) (sizeof(x)/sizeof(x[0]))  /* macro to return the number of
                                            elements in a structure */

int break_handler();                     /* handler routine for Ctrl-C */

int cls_cmd(), dos_cmd(), exit_cmd();    /* declare intrinsic processors
                                            for use in command table. */

struct cmd_table {                       /* table of intrinsic commands */
        char *cmd_name;                  /* command name entered by user */
        int  (*cmd_fxn)();               /* corresponding fxn to execute */
        }   commands[] =
            {  "CLS",   cls_cmd,
               "DOS",   dos_cmd,
               "EXIT",  exit_cmd,
            };

static char com_spec[64];                /* filespec of COMMAND.COM from
                                            Environment Block placed here */



main(argc, argv)
int    argc;
char  *argv[];

{   char inp_buf[80];                    /* operator's command placed here */

    get_comspec(com_spec);               /* get filespec for COMMAND.COM. */

                                         /* take over Break Int 23H
                                            so shell won't lose control. */
```

(continued)

Figure 10-4. SHELL.C: A simple table-driven command interpreter written in Microsoft C.

The MS-DOS EXEC Function   **195**

```
        if (signal(SIGINT,break_handler) == (int(*)()) -1)
            {   fputs("Can't capture Ctrl-C Interrupt",stderr);
                exit(1);
            }

        while(1)                            /* main command interpreter loop */
            {   get_cmd(inp_buf);           /* get a command. */
                if (! intrinsic(inp_buf) )  /* if it's an intrinsic command,
                                               run its subroutine. */
                    extrinsic(inp_buf);     /* else pass it to COMMAND.COM. */
            }
    }


    /*
            Try to match user's command with intrinsic command table.
            If a match is found, run the associated routine and return
            a True flag, else return a False flag.
    */

    intrinsic(input_string)
    char *input_string;
    {   int i, j;
                                            /* scan off leading blanks. */
        while( *input_string == '\x20') input_string++ ;
                                            /* search the command table. */
        for (i=0; i < dim(commands); i++)
            {   j = strcmp( commands[i].cmd_name,input_string );
                if  (j == 0)                /* if match found, run routine */
                    {   ( *commands[i].cmd_fxn )() ;
                        return(1);          /* and return a True flag. */
                    }
            }
        return(0);                          /* no match, return False flag. */
    }


    /*
            Process an extrinsic command by passing it
            to an EXEC'd copy of COMMAND.COM.
    */

    extrinsic(input_string)
    char *input_string;
    {   int status;
        status = system(input_string);      /* call EXEC function. */
        if (status)                         /* if failed, print error message. */
            fputs("\nEXEC of COMMAND.COM failed\n",stderr);
    }
```

Figure 10-4 continued.

```
/*
        Issue prompt, get command line from the Standard Input Device
        as a null-terminated (ASCIIZ) string, fold it to uppercase.
*/

get_cmd(buffer)
char *buffer;
{   printf("\nsh: ");                    /* display prompt. */
    gets(buffer);                        /* get line from Standard Input. */
    strupr(buffer);                      /* fold it to uppercase. */
}



/*
        Get the full path and file specification for COMMAND.COM
        from the "COMSPEC=" variable in the Environment Block
*/

get_comspec(buffer)
char *buffer;
{   strcpy( buffer, getenv("COMSPEC") );
    if ( buffer[0] == NULL )
        {   fputs("\nNo COMSPEC variable in Environment\n",stderr);
            exit(1);
        }
}



/*
        This handler for Int 23H signal keeps our shell from
        losing control when Ctrl-C is entered.  Just re-issues
        the prompt and returns.
*/

break_handler()
{   signal(SIGINT,break_handler);        /* reset handler address. */
    printf("\nsh: ");                    /* display prompt. */
}



/*
        These are the subroutines for the various intrinsic commands.
*/

cls_cmd()                    /* routine for intrinsic CLS command */
{   printf("\033[2J");       /* this is ANSI clear screen string. */
}
```

Figure 10-4 continued.

```
dos_cmd()                    /* routine for intrinsic DOS command */
{   int status;
    status = spawnlp(P_WAIT,com_spec,com_spec,NULL);
    if (status) fputs("\nEXEC of COMMAND.COM failed\n",stderr);
}

exit_cmd()                   /* routine for intrinsic EXIT command */
{   exit(0);
}
```

Figure 10-4 continued.

The *SHELL* program is table driven and can easily be extended to provide a powerful customized user interface for almost any application. When *SHELL* takes control of the system, it displays the prompt

sh:

and waits for input from the user. After the user types a line, terminated by a carriage return, *SHELL* tries to match the first token in the line against its table of internal (intrinsic) commands. If it finds a match, it calls the appropriate subroutine. If no match is found, it calls the MS-DOS EXEC function and passes the user's input to COMMAND.COM with the /C switch, essentially using COMMAND.COM as a transient command processor under its own control.

As supplied in these listings, *SHELL* "knows" exactly three internal commands:

Command	Action
CLS	Uses the ANSI standard control sequence to clear the display screen and home the cursor.
DOS	Runs a copy of COMMAND.COM.
EXIT	Exits *SHELL*, returning control of the system to the next lower command interpreter.

New intrinsic commands can be added quickly to either the C or the assembly-language version of *SHELL*. The programmer simply codes a procedure with the appropriate action and inserts the name of that procedure, along with the text string that defines the command, into the table named *COMMANDS*. In addition, *SHELL* can easily be prevented from passing certain "dangerous" commands (such as MKDIR or ERASE) to COMMAND.COM simply by putting the names of the commands to be screened out into the intrinsic command table with the address of a subroutine that prints an error message.

```
1                name    shell
2                page    55,132
3                title   'SHELL.ASM -- simple MS-DOS shell'
4       ;
5       ; SHELL.ASM       a simple user-extendable command interpreter
6       ;                 for MS-DOS 2.X or 3.X
7       ;
8       ; Copyright (C) 1985 by Ray Duncan
9       ;
10      ; To assemble and link this program into the executable SHELL.EXE:
11      ;
12      ;                 C>MASM SHELL;
13      ;                 C>LINK SHELL;
14      ;
15
16      stdin    equ     0                       ;Standard Input Device
17      stdout   equ     1                       ;Standard Output Device
18      stderr   equ     2                       ;Standard Error Device
19
20      cr       equ     0dh                     ;ASCII carriage return
21      lf       equ     0ah                     ;ASCII line feed
22      blank    equ     20h                     ;ASCII blank code
23      esc      equ     01bh                    ;ASCII escape code
24
25      cseg     segment para public 'CODE'
26
27               assume  cs:cseg,ds:data,ss:stack
28
29      shell    proc    far                     ;at entry DS = ES = PSP
30               mov     ax,data                 ;let DS point to our data segment.
31               mov     ds,ax
32               mov     ax,es:[002ch]           ;get segment of Environment Block
33               mov     env_seg,ax              ;from PSP and save it.
34                                               ;now release unneeded memory.
35               mov     bx,100h                 ;ES = segment PSP, BX = paragraphs needed
36               mov     ah,4ah                  ;Function 4AH = modify memory block
37               int     21h                     ;transfer to DOS.
38               jnc     shell1                  ;jump if request successful.
39               mov     dx,offset msg1          ;otherwise display error message
40               mov     cx,msg1_length          ;and exit.
41               jmp     shell4
42      shell1:  call    get_comspec             ;get file spec for COMMAND.COM.
43               jnc     shell2                  ;jump if it was found ok.
44               mov     dx,offset msg3          ;COMSPEC variable not found in
45               mov     cx,msg3_length          ;Environment block, print error
46               jmp     shell4                  ;message and exit.
47      shell2:  mov     dx,offset shell3        ;set Ctrl-C vector (Int 23H)
48               mov     ax,cs                   ;so that shell can keep control.
```

(continued)

Figure 10-5. SHELL.ASM: *A simple table-driven command interpreter written in Microsoft Macro Assembler.*

```
49              mov     ds,ax               ;DS:DX = addr of Ctrl-C handler
50              mov     ax,2523h            ;Function 25H = Set Interrupt
51              int     21h
52              mov     ax,data             ;make DS and ES point to our
53              mov     ds,ax               ;data segment again.
54              mov     es,ax
55      shell3:                             ;main loop of command interpreter
56              call    get_cmd             ;get a command from user.
57              call    intrinsic           ;check if intrinsic function.
58              jnc     shell3              ;yes, it was processed.
59              call    extrinsic           ;no, pass it to COMMAND.COM
60              jmp     shell3              ;then get another command.
61      shell4:                             ;come here if error detected, with
62                                          ;DS:DX = message addr, CX = length.
63              mov     bx,stderr           ;print error message on
64              mov     ah,40h              ;Standard Error Device.
65              int     21h
66              mov     ax,4c01h            ;exit to DOS with return code = 1
67              int     21h                 ;indicating an error condition.
68      shell   endp
69
70                                          ;these variables must be in Code Seg:
71      stk_seg dw      0                   ;original SS contents
72      stk_ptr dw      0                   ;original SP contents
73
74
75      intrinsic proc  near                ;Decode a user command against
76                                          ;the table "COMMANDS".  If match
77                                          ;found, run the subroutine, and
78                                          ;return Carry = False.  If no match,
79                                          ;return Carry = True.
80              mov     si,offset commands  ;let SI = start of command table.
81      intr1:  cmp     byte ptr [si],0     ;is command table exhausted?
82              je      intr7               ;jump, end of table found.
83              mov     di,offset inp_buf   ;no, let DI = addr of user input.
84      intr2:  cmp     byte ptr [di],blank ;scan off any leading blanks.
85              jne     intr3
86              inc     di
87              jmp     intr2
88      intr3:  mov     al,[si]             ;get next command char.
89              or      al,al               ;check if end of string.
90              jz      intr4               ;jump, entire string matched.
91              cmp     al,[di]             ;compare to next input char.
92              jnz     intr6               ;jump, found mismatch.
93              inc     si                  ;go to next char in strings.
94              inc     di
95              jmp     intr3
96      intr4:  cmp     byte ptr [di],cr    ;make sure user's command
```

Figure 10-5 continued.

```
 97              je      intr5              ;is the same length, next char
 98              cmp     byte ptr [di],blank ;must be blank or Return.
 99              jne     intr6
100    intr5:    call    word ptr [si+1]    ;run the command routine
101              clc                        ;then return Carry Flag = False
102              ret                        ;as success flag.
103    intr6:    lodsb                      ;look for end of this command string.
104              or      al,al
105              jnz     intr6              ;not end yet, loop.
106              add     si,2               ;skip over command routine offset.
107              jmp     intr1              ;try to match next command.
108    intr7:    stc                        ;no match on command, exit
109              ret                        ;with Carry = True.
110    intrinsic endp
111
112
113    extrinsic proc  near                 ;process an extrinsic command
114                                         ;by passing it to COMMAND.COM
115                                         ;with a " /C " command tail.
116              mov     al,cr              ;find length of the command
117              mov     cx,cmd_tail_length ;by scanning for Carriage Return.
118              mov     di,offset cmd_tail+1
119              cld
120              repnz scasb
121              mov     ax,di              ;calc length of command tail,
122              sub     ax,offset cmd_tail+2 ;not including the Carriage Return.
123                                         ;store length of synthesized
124              mov     cmd_tail,al        ;command tail for EXEC function.
125              mov     par_cmd,offset cmd_tail ;address of command tail
126              call    exec               ;call the EXEC function to pass
127              ret                        ;command line to COMMAND.COM.
128    extrinsic endp
129
130
131    get_cmd proc    near                 ;Prompt user and get a command.
132              mov     dx,offset prompt   ;display the shell prompt
133              mov     cx,prompt_length   ;on the Standard Output Device.
134              mov     bx,stdout
135              mov     ah,40h             ;Function 40H = Write file or device
136              int     21h
137              mov     dx,offset inp_buf  ;get a line from the Standard
138              mov     cx,inp_buf_length  ;Input Device and place in our
139              mov     bx,stdin           ;command line buffer.
140              mov     ah,3fh             ;Function 3FH = Read file or device
141              int     21h
142              mov     si,offset inp_buf  ;fold all lowercase characters
143              mov     cx,inp_buf_length  ;in the command line to uppercase.
144    gcmd1:    cmp     byte ptr [si],'a'
```

Figure 10-5 continued.

```
145             jb       gcmd2
146             cmp      byte ptr [si],'z'
147             ja       gcmd2
148             sub      byte ptr [si],'a'-'A'
149    gcmd2:   inc      si
150             loop     gcmd1
151             ret                           ;back to caller
152    get_cmd endp
153
154
155    get_comspec proc near                 ;Get file specification of COMMAND.COM
156                                           ;from Environment "COMSPEC=" variable.
157                                           ;Returns Carry = False if COMSPEC found.
158                                           ;Returns Carry = True if no COMSPEC.
159             mov      si,offset com_var    ;let DS:SI = string to match.
160             call     get_env              ;go search Environment Block.
161                                           ;if environment variable not found,
162             jc       gcsp2                ;return Carry = True as failure code.
163                                           ;if var found, ES:DI points past "=".
164             mov      si,offset com_spec   ;copy Env variable to our data segment.
165    gcsp1:   mov      al,es:[di]           ;transfer null-terminated string.
166             mov      [si],al
167             inc      si
168             inc      di
169             or       al,al                ;null found yet? (turns off Carry)
170             jnz      gcsp1                ;no, get next character.
171                                           ;success, return Carry Flag = False.
172    gcsp2:   ret
173    get_comspec endp
174
175
176    get_env proc     near                 ;Search Environment Block
177                                           ;Call DS:SI = "NAME=" to match.
178                                           ;Uses contents of "ENV_SEG".
179                                           ;Returns Carry = False and ES:DI
180                                           ; pointing to parameter if found,
181                                           ;Returns Carry = True if no match.
182             mov      es,env_seg           ;get segment of Environment Block.
183             xor      di,di                ;initialize offset to Env Block.
184    genv1:   mov      bx,si                ;initialize pointer to pattern.
185             cmp      byte ptr es:[di],0   ;end of Environment block?
186             jne      genv2                ;jump if end not found.
187             stc                           ;return Carry = True as failure flag.
188             ret
189    genv2:   mov      al,[bx]              ;get character from pattern.
190             or       al,al                ;end of pattern? (turns off Carry)
191             jz       genv3                ;yes, entire match succeeded.
192             cmp      al,es:[di]           ;compare to char in Environment Block.
```

Figure 10-5 continued.

```
193             jne     genv4                   ;jump if match failed.
194             inc     bx
195             inc     di
196             jmp     genv2
197     genv3:                                  ;All matched, return ES:DI pointing
198             ret                             ;to parameter, Carry Flag = False.
199     genv4:  xor     al,al                   ;scan forward in Environment Block
200             mov     cx,-1                   ;for zero byte.
201             cld
202             repnz   scasb
203             jmp     genv1                   ;go compare next string.
204     get_env endp
205
206
207     exec    proc    near                    ;call MS-DOS EXEC function
208                                             ;to run COMMAND.COM.
209             push    ds                      ;save data segments.
210             push    es
211             mov     cs:stk_seg,ss           ;save copy of SS:SP for use
212             mov     cs:stk_ptr,sp           ;after return from overlay.
213             mov     dx,offset com_spec      ;now load and execute COMMAND.COM.
214             mov     bx,offset par_blk
215             mov     ah,4bh                  ;function 4BH = EXEC
216             mov     al,0                    ;subfunction 0 = load and execute
217             int     21h
218             mov     ss,cs:stk_seg           ;restore stack segment
219             mov     sp,cs:stk_ptr           ;and stack pointer.
220             pop     es                      ;restore data segments.
221             pop     ds
222             jnc     exec1                   ;jump if no errors.
223             mov     dx,offset msg2          ;EXEC failed, print error
224             mov     cx,msg2_length          ;message.
225             mov     bx,stderr
226             mov     ah,40h
227             int     21h
228     exec1:  ret                             ;back to caller
229     exec    endp
230
231
232     cls_cmd proc    near                    ;intrinsic CLS Command
233                                             ;  = clear the screen
234             mov     dx,offset cls_str       ;send the ANSI control sequence
235             mov     cx,cls_str_length       ;to clear the screen.
236             mov     bx,stdout
237             mov     ah,40h
238             int     21h
239             ret
240     cls_cmd endp
```

Figure 10-5 continued.

```
241
242
243     dos_cmd proc    near                            ;intrinsic DOS Command
244                                                     ;   = run COMMAND.COM
245             mov     par_cmd,offset nultail  ;set command tail to null string.
246             call    exec                            ;now EXEC the COMMAND.COM.
247             ret
248     dos_cmd endp
249
250
251     exit_cmd proc   near                            ;intrinsic EXIT Command
252                                                     ;   = leave this shell
253             mov     ax,4c00h                        ;call DOS terminate function
254             int     21h                             ;with return code of zero.
255     exit_cmd endp
256
257
258     cseg    ends
259
260
261     stack   segment para stack 'STACK'      ;declare stack segment.
262             dw      64 dup (?)
263     stack   ends
264
265
266     data    segment para public 'DATA'      ;declare data segment.
267
268     commands equ $                          ;table of "intrinsic" commands
269                                             ;each entry is a null-terminated
270                                             ;string, followed by the offset
271                                             ;of the procedure to be executed
272                                             ;for that command.
273             db      'CLS',0
274             dw      cls_cmd
275             db      'DOS',0
276             dw      dos_cmd
277             db      'EXIT',0
278             dw      exit_cmd
279             db      0                       ;table terminated with null string
280
281     com_var db      'COMSPEC=',0            ;Environment Block variable to match
282
283                                             ;filespec of COMMAND.COM moved
284     com_spec db     80 dup (0)              ;here from the Environment Block
285
286     nultail db      0,cr                    ;a "Null" command tail for invoking
287                                             ;COMMAND.COM as another shell
```

Figure 10-5 continued.

```
288
289    cmd_tail db      0,' /C '                        ;command tail invoking COMMAND.COM
290                                                     ;as a transient command processor
291
292    inp_buf db       80 dup (0)                      ;command line from Standard Input
293
294    inp_buf_length equ $-inp_buf
295    cmd_tail_length equ $-cmd_tail-1
296
297    prompt db        cr,lf,'sh: '                     ;the shell's prompt to the user
298    prompt_length equ $-prompt
299
300    env_seg dw       0                               ;segment of Environment Block
301
302    msg1    db       cr,lf
303            db       'Unable to de-allocate memory.'
304            db       cr,lf
305    msg1_length equ $-msg1
306
307    msg2    db       cr,lf
308            db       'EXEC of COMMAND.COM failed.'
309            db       cr,lf
310    msg2_length equ $-msg2
311
312    msg3    db       cr,lf
313            db       'No COMSPEC variable in Environment.'
314            db       cr,lf
315    msg3_length equ $-msg3
316
317    cls_str db       esc,'[2J'                        ;this is the ANSI standard control
318    cls_str_length equ $-cls_str                      ;sequence to clear the screen.
319
320    par_blk equ      $                               ;Parameter Block for EXEC call
321            dw       0                               ;segment address, environment block
322    par_cmd dw       offset cmd_tail                 ;address of command line
323            dw       seg cmd_tail
324            dd       -1                              ;address of default FCB #1
325            dd       -1                              ;address of default FCB #2
326
327    data    ends
328
329            end      shell
```

Figure 10-5 continued.

To summarize, the basic flow of both versions of the *SHELL* program is as follows:

1. MS-DOS Int 21H function 4AH (modify memory block) is called to shrink *SHELL*'s memory allocation, so that the maximum possible space will be available for COMMAND.COM if it is run as an overlay. (This is explicit in the assembly-language version only. To keep the example code simple, the number of paragraphs to be reserved is coded as a generous literal value, rather than being figured out at runtime from the size and location of the various program segments.)

2. The environment is searched for the COMSPEC variable, which defines the location of an executable copy of COMMAND.COM. If the COMSPEC variable can't be found, *SHELL* prints an error message and exits.

3. *SHELL* puts the address of its own handler in the Ctrl-C vector (Int 23H), so that it won't lose control if the user enters a Ctrl-C or Ctrl-Break.

4. A prompt is issued to the standard output device.

5. A buffered line is read from the standard input device to get the user's command.

6. The first blank-delimited token in the line is matched against *SHELL*'s table of intrinsic commands. If a match is found, the associated procedure is executed.

7. If no match is found in the table of intrinsic commands, a command-line tail is synthesized by appending the user's input to the /C switch. A copy of COMMAND.COM is then EXECed, passing the address of the synthesized command tail in the EXEC parameter block.

8. Steps 4 through 7 are repeated until the user enters the command EXIT, which is one of the intrinsic commands and causes *SHELL* to terminate execution.

In its present form, *SHELL* allows COMMAND.COM to inherit a full copy of the current environment. However, in some applications it may be helpful, or safer, to pass a modified copy of the environment block, so that the secondary copy of COMMAND.COM will not have access to certain information.

Chapter 11

MS-DOS Interrupt Handlers

Interrupts are signals that cause the computer's central processing unit to suspend what it is doing and transfer to a special program called an *interrupt handler*. The transfer is forced by special hardware mechanisms that are carefully designed for maximum speed. The interrupt handler is responsible for determining the cause of the interrupt, taking the appropriate action, and then returning control to the original process that was suspended.

Interrupts are typically caused by events external to the central processor that require immediate attention, such as:

- Completion of an I/O process

- Detection of a hardware failure

- "Catastrophes" (power failures, and so forth)

In order to service interrupts more efficiently, most modern processors support multiple *interrupt types*, or levels. For each type, there is usually a reserved location in memory, called an *interrupt vector*, that specifies where the interrupt handler program for that interrupt type is located. This speeds processing of an interrupt, since the computer can transfer control directly to the appropriate routine; there is no need for a central routine that wastes precious machine cycles determining the cause of the interrupt. The concept of interrupt types also allows interrupts to be prioritized, so that if several interrupts occur simultaneously, the most important one can be processed first.

CPUs that support interrupts must also have the capability to block interrupts while they are executing critical sections of code. Sometimes the interrupt levels can be blocked selectively, but more frequently the effect is global. While an interrupt is being serviced, all interrupts of the same or lower priority are masked until the active handler has completed its execution; similarly, the execution of a handler can be preempted if a different interrupt with higher priority requires service. Some CPUs can even draw a distinction between selectively masking interrupts (they are recognized, but their processing is deferred) and simply disabling them (the interrupt is thrown away).

The creation of interrupt handlers has traditionally been considered one of the most arcane of programming tasks, suitable only for the elite cadre of system hackers. In reality, writing an interrupt handler is, in itself, quite straightforward. Although the exact procedure must, of course, be customized for the characteristics of the particular CPU and operating system, there are some specific guidelines that are applicable to almost any computer system.

A program preparing to handle interrupts must:

1. Disable interrupts, if they were previously enabled, to prevent them from occurring while interrupt vectors are being modified.

2. Initialize the vector for the interrupt of interest to point to the program's interrupt handler.

3. Ensure that, if interrupts were previously disabled, all other vectors point to some valid handler routine.

4. Enable interrupts again.

The interrupt handler itself must follow a very simple but rigid sequence of steps:

1. Save the system context (registers, flags, and anything else that will be modified by the handler and wasn't saved automatically by the CPU).

2. Block any interrupts that might cause interference if they were allowed to occur during this handler's processing (this is often done automatically by the computer hardware).

3. Enable any interrupts that should still be allowed to occur during this handler's processing.

4. Determine the cause of the interrupt.

5. Take the appropriate action for the interrupt: receive and store data from the serial port, set a flag to indicate the completion of a disk-sector transfer, and so forth.

6. Restore the system context.

7. Re-enable any interrupt levels that were blocked during this handler's execution.

8. Resume execution of the interrupted process.

As in writing any other program, the key to success in writing an interrupt handler is to program defensively and cover all the bases. The main reason interrupt handlers have acquired such a mystical reputation is that they are so difficult to debug when they contain obscure errors. Since interrupts can occur asynchronously—that is, they are caused by external events without regard to the state of the currently executing process—bugs in interrupt handlers can cause the system as a whole to behave quite unpredictably.

Although we can demystify the subject of interrupts and their handlers in just a few pages, it remains true that the design of interrupt handlers and the integration of the handlers with the remaining system software is a job usually best left to the operating-system implementors. In the context of a complex operating system, the analysis of the subtle interactions of many different asynchronous interrupts requires much skill, perceptiveness, and experience; and access to the complete source code for the system and detailed hardware information doesn't hurt either.

Interrupts and the Intel 8086 Family

The Intel 8086/8088/80286 family of microprocessors supports 256 levels of prioritized interrupts, which can be grouped into three basic categories:

- Internal hardware interrupts
- External hardware interrupts
- Software interrupts

Internal Hardware Interrupts

Internal hardware interrupts are generated by certain events encountered during program execution, such as an attempt to divide by zero. The assignment of such events to certain interrupt numbers is wired into the processor and is not modifiable (Figure 11-1).

Interrupt level	Vector address	Interrupt trigger	Used only by 80286
00H	00–03H	Divide by zero	
01H	04–07H	Single step	
02H	08–0BH	Nonmaskable interrupt (NMI)	
03H	0C–0FH	Breakpoint	
04H	10–13H	Overflow	
05H	14–17H	BOUND range exceeded	✔
06H	18–1BH	Invalid opcode	✔
07H	1C–1FH	Processor extension not available	✔
08H	20–23H	Double exception	✔
09H	24–27H	Segment overrun	✔
0AH	28–2BH	Invalid task state segment	✔
0BH	2C–2FH	Segment not present	✔
0CH	30–33H	Stack segment overrun	✔
0DH	34–37H	General protection fault	✔

Figure 11-1. Internal hardware interrupts on the 8086/8088 and the 80286. Interrupt types 0EH through 1FH are reserved by Intel for future expansion.

External Hardware Interrupts

External hardware interrupts are triggered by peripheral device controllers or by coprocessors such as the 8087/80287. These can be tied to either the CPU's nonmaskable interrupt (NMI) pin or its maskable interrupt (INTR) pin. The NMI line is usually reserved for interrupts caused by such catastrophic events as a memory parity error or power failure.

Instead of being wired directly to the CPU, the interrupts from external devices can be channeled through a device called the Intel 8259A Programmable Interrupt Controller (PIC). The PIC is controlled by the CPU through a set of I/O ports and, in turn, signals the CPU via the INTR pin. It allows the interrupts from specific devices to be enabled and disabled, and their priorities to be adjusted, under program control. Many 8259A PICs can be cascaded together, in a tree-like structure, to allow a huge number of peripheral devices to be tied into the CPU's interrupt system in an orderly manner.

INTR interrupts can be globally enabled and disabled with the CPU's STI and CLI instructions, respectively. As you would expect, these instructions have no effect on interrupts received on the CPU's NMI pin.

The assignment of external devices to specific interrupt levels is done by the manufacturer of the computer system and/or the manufacturer of the peripheral device. These assignments are realized as physical electrical connections and cannot be modified by software.

Software Interrupts

Software interrupts can be triggered synchronously by any program simply by executing an INT instruction. Interrupts 20H through 3FH are used by MS-DOS to communicate with its modules and with application programs (for instance, the MS-DOS function dispatcher is reached by executing an Int 21H). Other interrupts, with either higher or lower numbers, are used by the IBM PC ROM BIOS and by application software for various purposes (Figure 11-2). These assignments are simply conventions, and are not wired into the hardware in any way.

The Interrupt Vector Table

The bottom 1024 bytes of system memory are called the *interrupt vector table*. Each 4-byte position in the table corresponds to an interrupt type (0 through 0FFH), and contains the segment and offset of the interrupt handler for that level. Interrupts 0 through 1FH (the lowest levels) are used for internal hardware interrupts; Interrupts 20H through 3FH are used by MS-DOS; all the others are available for use by either external hardware devices or system drivers and application software.

Interrupt type	Usage	Used by MS-DOS
05H	Print screen	
08H	Timer tick	
09H	Keyboard input interrupt	
0BH	Asynchronous communication port controller 1	
0CH	Asynchronous communication port controller 0	
0DH	Fixed disk controller	
0EH	Floppy disk controller	
0FH	Printer controller	
10H	Video driver	
11H	Equipment configuration check	
12H	Memory size check	
13H	Floppy disk, fixed disk driver (PC/XT)	
14H	Communication port driver	
15H	Cassette I/O, PC/AT Auxiliary functions	
16H	Keyboard driver	
17H	Printer driver	
18H	ROM BASIC	
19H	Bootstrap loader	
1AH	Set/Read realtime clock	
1BH	Ctrl-Break handler	
1CH	Timer control	
1DH	#Video parameter table	
1EH	#Disk parameter table	
1FH	#Graphics character table (codes 80-FFH)	
20H	Program terminate (obsolete)	✔
21H	MS-DOS function dispatcher	✔
22H	#Terminate vector	✔
23H	#Ctrl-C vector	✔
24H	#Critical error vector	✔

(continued)

Figure 11-2. Interrupts with special significance in the IBM PC family. Note that the IBM PC's ROM BIOS uses several interrupts in the range 0 through 1FH for software purposes, although they were reserved by Intel for future expansion. This has already caused some conflicts on the 80286-based PC/AT (for example, a BOUNDS exception causes an interrupt level 5, which results in the screen being printed).

Interrupt type	Usage	Used by MS-DOS
25H	Absolute disk read	✔
26H	Absolute disk write	✔
27H	Terminate and stay resident (obsolete)	✔
28-2EH	Reserved for MS-DOS	✔
2FH	Print spooler	✔
30–3FH	Reserved for MS-DOS	✔
40H	Floppy disk driver (PC/XT)	
41H	#Fixed disk parameter table	
44H	##Graphics character table (codes 0–FFH)	

Figure 11-2 continued.

\# Contents of vector used as a pointer only; interrupt not executed directly
\#\# PCjr

When an 8259A PIC or other device interrupts the CPU via the INTR pin, it is also responsible for placing the interrupt type as an 8-bit number (0 through 0FFH) on the system bus, where the CPU can get at it. The CPU then multiplies this number by 4 to find the memory address of the interrupt vector to be used.

Servicing an Interrupt

When the CPU senses an interrupt, it pushes the program status word (which defines the various CPU flags), the code segment register (CS), and the instruction pointer (IP) onto the machine stack and disables the interrupt system. It then uses the 8-bit number that was jammed onto the system bus by the interrupting device to fetch the address of the handler from the vector table, and resumes execution at that address.

The handler usually immediately re-enables the interrupt system (to allow higher-priority interrupts to occur), saves any registers it is going to use, and then processes the interrupt as quickly as possible. Some external devices also require a special acknowledgment signal, so they will know that the interrupt has been recognized.

If the interrupt was funneled through an 8259A PIC, a special code called *end of interrupt* (EOI) must be sent to the PIC through its control port to tell it when interrupt processing is completed. (The EOI has no effect on the CPU itself.) Finally, the handler executes the special IRET (INTERRUPT RETURN) instruction that restores the original state of the CPU flags, the code segment register, and the instruction pointer (Figure 11-3).

```
pic_ctl           equ  20h                    ;control port for 8259A
                                              ;interrupt controller
                  .
                  .
                  .
                  sti                         ;turn interrupts back on.
                  push ax                     ;save registers.
                  push bx
                  push cx
                  push dx
                  push si
                  push di
                  push bp
                  push ds
                  push es

                  mov  ax,cs                  ;make local data addressable.
                  mov  ds,ax

                  .                           ;do some stuff appropriate
                  .                           ;for this interrupt here.
                  .
                  mov  al,20h                 ;send EOI to 8259A PIC.
                  mov  dx,pic_ctl
                  out  dx,al

                  pop  es                     ;restore registers.
                  pop  ds
                  pop  bp
                  pop  di
                  pop  si
                  pop  dx
                  pop  cx
                  pop  bx
                  pop  ax
                  iret                        ;resume previous processing.
```

Figure 11-3. Typical handler for hardware interrupts on the 8086/8088/80286. In real life, only the registers that were actually modified by the interrupt handler would need to be saved and restored. Also, if the handler made extensive use of the machine stack, it would need to save and restore the interrupted process's SS and SP registers, and use its own local stack.

Whether an interrupt was triggered by an external device or forced by software execution of an INT instruction, there is no discernible difference in the system state at the time the interrupt handler receives control. This is very convenient in writing and testing external interrupt handlers, since they can be debugged to a large extent simply by invoking them with software drivers.

Interrupt Handlers and MS-DOS

The introduction of an interrupt handler into your program brings with it considerable hardware dependence. It goes without saying (but we are saying it again here anyway) that it is best to avoid such hardware dependence in MS-DOS applications whenever possible, to ensure that your program will be portable to any machine running current versions of MS-DOS and that it will run properly under future versions of the operating system.

There are, however, valid reasons why you might want or need to write your own interrupt handler for use under MS-DOS:

- To supersede the MS-DOS default handler for an internal hardware interrupt (such as divide-by-zero, BOUNDS exception, and so forth).

- To supersede the MS-DOS default handler for a defined system exception, such as the critical error handler or Ctrl-C handler.

- To chain your own interrupt handler onto the default system handler for a hardware device, so that both the system's actions *and* your own will occur on an interrupt (a typical case of this is the "clock tick" interrupt).

- To service interrupts not supported by the default MS-DOS device drivers (such as the serial communications port, which can be used at much higher speeds with interrupts than with polling).

- To provide a path of communication between a program that terminates and stays resident and other application software.

MS-DOS provides facilities that enable you to install well-behaved interrupt handlers in a manner that will not interfere with operating system functions or other interrupt handlers:

Function	Action
Int 21H function 25H	Set interrupt vector
Int 21H function 35H	Get interrupt vector
Int 21H function 31H	Terminate and stay resident

These functions allow you to examine or modify the contents of the system interrupt vector table and reserve memory for the use of a handler without running afoul of other processes in the system or causing memory usage conflicts. Each of these functions is described in detail, with programming examples, in Section 2 of this book.

Handlers for external hardware interrupts under MS-DOS must operate under some fairly severe restrictions:

- Since the current versions of MS-DOS are not reentrant, the MS-DOS functions should never be called by a hardware interrupt handler during the actual interrupt processing.

- The handler must be sure to re-enable interrupts as soon as it gets control, to avoid crippling other devices or destroying the accuracy of the system clock.

- Great care should be taken in accessing the 8259A PIC. A program should not access the PIC unless that program is known to be the only process in the system concerned with that particular interrupt level. And it is vital that the handler issue an end-of-interrupt code to the 8259A PIC before performing the IRET; otherwise, the processing of further interrupts for that level or lower-priority levels will be blocked.

Handlers that replace the MS-DOS default handlers for internal hardware interrupts or system exceptions (such as Ctrl-C or critical errors) are not quite so stringently restricted, but they must still be programmed with extreme care to avoid destroying system tables or leaving the operating system in an unstable state.

Here are a few rules to keep in mind when writing an interrupt driver:

- Use Int 21H function 25H (set interrupt vector) to modify the interrupt vector, to keep MS-DOS advised of your intentions.

- Do not write directly into the vector table in low memory, or your program may cause problems in future multitasking versions of the operating system.

- If your program is not the only process in the system that uses this interrupt level, chain back to the previous handler after performing your own processing on an interrupt.

- If your program is not going to stay resident, fetch and save the current contents of the interrupt vector before modifying it, and then restore the original contents when your program exits.

- If your program is going to stay resident, use one of the terminate and stay resident functions (preferably Int 21H function 31H) to reserve the proper amount of memory for your handler.

- If you are going to process hardware interrupts, keep the time that interrupts are disabled and the total length of the service routine to an absolute minimum. Remember that even after interrupts are re-enabled with an STI instruction, interrupts of the same or lower priority remain blocked if the interrupt was received via the 8259A PIC.

ZERODIV, an Example Interrupt Handler

The listing *ZERODIV.ASM* (Figure 11-4) illustrates some of the principles and guidelines on the previous pages. It is an interrupt handler for the divide-by-zero internal interrupt (type 0). *ZERODIV* is loaded like a COM file (usually by a command in the system's AUTOEXEC file), but makes itself permanently resident in memory as long as the system is running.

The *ZERODIV* program is divided into two major portions: the initialization portion and the interrupt handler.

The initialization procedure (called *Init* in the program listing) is executed only once, when the program *ZERODIV* is executed from the MS-DOS level. *Init* takes over the type 0 interrupt vector, prints a sign-on message, then performs a terminate and stay resident exit to MS-DOS. This special exit reserves the memory occupied by the *ZERODIV* program, so that it is not overwritten by subsequent application programs.

The interrupt handler (called *Zdiv* in the program listing) receives control when a divide-by-zero interrupt occurs. The handler preserves all registers, then prints a message to the user asking whether he or she wishes to continue or to abort the program. We can use the MS-DOS console I/O functions within this particular interrupt handler because we can safely presume that the application was in control when the interrupt occurred; thus, there should be no chance of accidentally making overlapping calls upon the operating system.

If the user enters a C to continue, the handler simply restores all the registers and performs an IRET (INTERRUPT RETURN) to return control to the application (of course, the results of the divide operation will be useless). If the user enters Q to quit, the handler exits to MS-DOS. Int 21H function 4CH is particularly convenient in this case, since it allows us to pass a return code and at the same time is the only terminate function that does not rely on the contents of any of the segment registers.

For an example of an interrupt handler for external (communications port) interrupts, see the *TALK* terminal-emulator program in Chapter 5. You may also want to look again at the discussions of the Ctrl-C and critical error interrupt handlers in Chapters 5 and 6.

```
 1               name     zdivide
 2               page     55,132
 3               title    'ZERODIV.ASM --- Divide by Zero Handler'
 4       ;
 5       ; ZERODIV.ASM --- Divide-by-Zero Interrupt Handler
 6       ;
 7       ; Demonstrates a "well-behaved" interrupt handler
 8       ; that becomes resident after DOS is running.
 9       ;
10       ; Copyright (C) 1985 Ray Duncan
11       ;
12       ; To assemble, link, and convert this program into a COM file:
13       ;
14       ;       C>MASM ZERODIV;
15       ;       C>LINK ZERODIV;
16       ;       C>EXE2BIN ZERODIV.EXE ZERODIV.COM
17       ;       C>DEL ZERODIV.EXE
18       ;
19
20       cr      equ      0dh              ;ASCII carriage return
21       lf      equ      0ah              ;ASCII line feed
22       beep    equ      07h              ;ASCII bell code
23       backsp  equ      08h              ;ASCII backspace code
24
25       cseg    segment para public 'CODE'
26
27               org      100H
28
29               assume   cs:cseg,ds:cseg,es:cseg,ss:cseg
30
31       Init    proc     near
32                                         ;reset interrupt 0 vector to
33               mov      dx,offset Zdiv   ;address of new handler.
34               mov      ax,2500h         ;function 25H, interrupt 0
35               int      21h              ;transfer to DOS.
36
37                                         ;print identification message.
38               mov      dx,offset signon
39               mov      ah,9
40               int      21h
41
42                                         ;DX = paragraphs of memory
43                                         ;to reserve.
44               mov      dx,((offset Pgm_Len+15)/16)+10h
45
46               mov      ax,3100h         ;exit and stay resident, with
```

Figure 11-4. A simple example of an interrrrupt handler for use within the MS-DOS environment. ZERODIV makes itself permanently resident in memory and handles the CPU's internal divide-by-zero interrupt.

(continued)

```
47                int     21h             ;return code = 0.
48
49      Init    endp
50
51      Zdiv    proc    far             ;this is the zero-divide
52                                      ;hardware interrupt handler.
53
54                sti                     ;enable interrupts.
55                push    ax              ;save general registers.
56                push    bx
57                push    cx
58                push    dx
59                push    si
60                push    di
61                push    bp
62                push    ds
63                push    es
64
65                mov     ax,cs           ;print warning "Divide by Zero"
66                mov     ds,ax           ; and "Continue or Quit?"
67                mov     dx,offset warn
68                mov     ah,9
69                int     21h
70
71      Zdiv1:  mov     ah,1            ;read keyboard.
72                int     21h
73
74                cmp     al,'C'          ;is it C or Q?
75                je      Zdiv3           ;jump, it's a C.
76                cmp     al,'Q'
77                je      Zdiv2           ;jump, it's a Q.
78
79                mov     dx,offset bad   ;illegal entry, send
80                mov     ah,9            ;a beep, erase the bad char.
81                int     21h             ;and try again.
82
83                jmp     Zdiv1
84
85      Zdiv2:  mov     ax,4cffh        ;user wishes to abort
86                int     21h             ;program, exit with
87                                      ;return code = 255.
88
89      Zdiv3:  mov     dx,offset crlf  ;user wishes to continue,
90                mov     ah,9            ;send carriage ret-linefeed.
91                int     21h
92
93                pop     es              ;restore general registers
94                pop     ds              ;and resume execution.
```

Figure 11-4 continued.

```
95              pop     bp
96              pop     di
97              pop     si
98              pop     dx
99              pop     cx
100             pop     bx
101             pop     ax
102             iret
103
104     Zdiv    endp
105
106     signon  db      cr,lf,'Divide by Zero Interrupt '
107             db      'Handler installed.'
108             db      cr,lf,'$'
109
110     warn    db      cr,lf,lf,'Divide by Zero detected: '
111             db      cr,lf,'Continue or Quit (C/Q) ? '
112             db      '$'
113
114     bad     db      beep,backsp,' ',backsp,'$'
115
116     crlf    db      cr,lf,'$'
117
118     Pgm_Len equ     $-Init
119
120     cseg    ends
121
122             end     init
```

Figure 11-4 continued.

Installable Device Drivers

Device drivers are the modules of an operating system that control the hardware. They serve to isolate the higher levels of the operating system from the specific characteristics and idiosyncracies of the different peripheral devices interfaced to the central processor. In nearly every computer operating system that has ever existed (with the possible exception of UNIX), the device drivers have been considered to be one of the most arcane components, and have been embedded deeply within the structure in a manner that made them difficult to replace or extend (see Chapter 13).

The installable device drivers that were introduced in MS-DOS version 2 are remarkably unlike this traditional variety. They allow the user to customize and configure a particular computer for a wide range of peripheral devices, with a minimum of troublesome interactions and without having to "patch" the operating system. Even the most inexperienced user can install a new hard disk into a system by plugging in a card, copying a driver file to the boot disk, and editing the system configuration file.

For those inclined to do their own programming, the MS-DOS installable device drivers are interfaced to the hardware-independent DOS kernel through a simple and clearly defined scheme of function codes and data structures. Given adequate information about the hardware, any competent assembly-language programmer can expect to successfully interface even the most bizarre device to MS-DOS without altering the operating system in the slightest and without acquiring any special or proprietary knowledge about its innards.

In retrospect, installable device drivers can only be viewed as a stroke of genius on the part of the MS-DOS designers. I feel that they have been largely responsible for the rapid proliferation and competitive pricing of high-speed mass-storage devices for MS-DOS machines, and for the desensitization of the average user toward "tampering with" (upgrading) his or her machine.

Note: MS-DOS installable device drivers, and the terminology used in the Microsoft documentation for them, bear a strong structural and philosophical resemblance to UNIX device drivers. Readers interested in learning more about the inner details of UNIX device drivers may wish to read the article "Writing Device Drivers for XENIX Systems" by Jean McNamara, et al. in the *Uniforum Conference Proceedings*, January 1985.

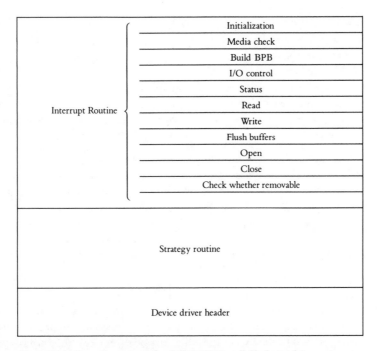

Interrupt Routine	Initialization
	Media check
	Build BPB
	I/O control
	Status
	Read
	Write
	Flush buffers
	Open
	Close
	Check whether removable
Strategy routine	
Device driver header	

Figure 12-1. General structure of an MS-DOS installable device driver.

MS-DOS Device-Driver Types

Drivers written for MS-DOS fall into two distinct classes:

- Block device drivers
- Character device drivers

A driver's class determines what functions it must support, how it is viewed by MS-DOS, and how it makes the associated physical device appear to behave when an application program makes a request for I/O.

Character Device Drivers

Character device drivers control peripheral devices that perform input and output a byte at a time, such as terminals and modems. Each character device driver can support only one hardware unit.

Character devices can be opened for input and output by name, like a file, using either the traditional FCB calls or the extended Handle calls that were added to MS-DOS in version 2, and their drivers can operate in either cooked or raw mode. The mode for a specific device can be selected with a call to the Int 21H IOCTL function, 44H (see Chapter 5), and affects MS-DOS's buffering and filtering of the input or output stream.

During cooked mode input, MS-DOS requests characters one at a time from the driver and places them into its own internal buffer, echoing each character to the screen (if the input device is the console) and checking for a Ctrl-C or carriage return. When either the requested number of characters has been received or a carriage return is detected, the input is terminated and the data are copied from MS-DOS's internal buffer into the calling program's buffer. During cooked mode output, MS-DOS checks between each character for a Ctrl-C pending at the keyboard.

In raw mode, the exact number of bytes requested is read or written. MS-DOS essentially passes the request straight through to the driver for the requested device, and the driver does not return to MS-DOS until the entire input or output is completed. Characters are read or written directly from the calling program's buffer. MS-DOS performs no checking for Ctrl-C characters, and other control characters (such as carriage returns) have no special significance.

You will recall that MS-DOS has built-in character device drivers for the console device (keyboard and video display), the serial port, and the list device (see Chapter 5). These three character devices have a unique status, even among character devices: They can be opened for input and output by name, as though they were files (like any other device); they are supported by built-in special-purpose MS-DOS function calls (01H through 0CH); and they are assigned to default handles (standard input, standard output, standard auxiliary, and standard list) that do not need to be opened to be used.

Block Device Drivers

Block device drivers usually control random-access mass-storage devices such as flexible disk drives and fixed disks, though they can also be used to control non-random-access devices such as magnetic tape drives. Block devices transfer data in chunks, rather than a byte at a time. The size of the blocks may be either fixed (disk drives) or variable (tape drives).

A block driver can support more than one hardware unit, map a single physical unit onto two or more logical units, or both. Block devices do not have file-like logical names, as character devices do. Instead, the block-device units or logical drives are assigned drive designators in an alphabetic sequence: A, B, and so forth. Each logical drive has a file allocation table and a root directory (see Chapter 8).

The first letter assigned to a given block device driver is determined by that driver's position in the chain of all drivers. The total *number* of letters assigned to the driver is determined by the number of logical drive units that the driver supports.

Unlike character device drivers, which can operate in a cooked or raw mode that may affect the appearance of the data, block device drivers always read or write exactly the number of sectors requested (barring hardware or addressing errors) and never filter or otherwise manipulate the contents of the blocks being transferred.

Structure of an MS-DOS Device Driver

A device driver consists of three major parts:

- A device header

- A strategy (*strat*) routine

- An interrupt (*intr*) routine (Figure 12-1)

We'll discuss each of these in more detail as we work through this chapter.

The Device Header

The device header (Figure 12-2) lies at the very beginning of the driver. It contains a linkage to the next driver in the chain, a set of attribute flags for the device (Figure 12-3), offsets to the executable strategy and interrupt routines for the device, and the logical device name (if it is a character device such as PRN or COM1) or the number of logical units (if it is a block device).

byte offset

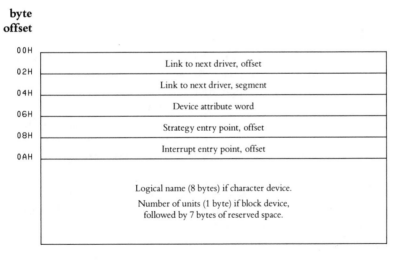

Figure 12-2. Device driver header. The offsets to the strat *and* intr *routines are offsets from the same segment used to point to the device header.*

Bit		Flag setting	Meaning
15	=	1	if character device
		0	if block device
14	=	1	if IOCTL supported
13	=	1	if non–IBM format (block devices)
	=	1	if output until busy (character devices)
12		#	
11	=	1	if open/close/RM supported*
10		#	
9		#	
8		#	
7		#	
6		#	
5		#	
4		#	(special CON driver bit, Int 29H)
3	=	1	if current clock device
2	=	1	if current NUL device
1	=	1	if current standard output (*sto*) device
0	=	1	if current standard input (*sti*) device

*MS-DOS 3.0 and above only; should be 0 for MS-DOS 2.
#Currently undefined and should be 0.

Figure 12-3. Device attribute word, found in device driver header. Only bits 11, 13, 14, and 15 have significance on block devices.

The Strategy Routine

The strategy routine (*strat*) for the device is called by MS-DOS when the driver is first loaded and installed, and again whenever an I/O request is issued for the device by an application program. MS-DOS passes the strategy routine a double-word pointer to a data structure called a *request header*. This structure contains information about the type of operation to be performed. According to MS-DOS version 2 and 3 conventions, the strategy routine never actually performs any I/O operation, but simply saves the pointer to the request header.

The first 13 bytes of the request header are the same for all device driver functions, and are therefore referred to as the *static* portion of the header. The number and contents of the subsequent bytes vary according to the type of function being requested (Figure 12-4).

The request header's most important component is a *command code*, or function number, passed in its third byte to select a driver subfunction such as *read, write,* or *status*. Other information passed to the driver in the header includes minor unit numbers, transfer addresses, and sector or byte counts.

```
;
; MS-DOS Request Header structure definition
;
Request          struc                    ;request header template structure

Rlength          db      ?                ;0  length of request header
Unit             db      ?                ;1  unit number for this request
Command          db      ?                ;2  request header's command code
Status           dw      ?                ;3  driver's return status word
Reserve          db      8 dup (?)        ;5  reserved area
Media            db      ?                ;13 media descriptor byte
Address          dd      ?                ;14 memory address for transfer
Count            dw      ?                ;18 byte/sector count value
Sector           dw      ?                ;20 starting sector value

Request          ends                     ;end of request header template
```

Figure 12-4. Format of request header. Only the first 13 bytes are common to all driver functions; the number and definition of the subsequent bytes vary, depending upon the function type. The structure shown here is the one used by the read and write subfunctions of the driver.

The Interrupt Routine

The last and most complex part of a device driver is the interrupt routine (*intr*), which is is called by MS-DOS immediately after the call to the strategy routine. The interrupt routine implements the device driver proper; it performs (or calls other resident routines to perform) the actual input or output operations based on the information passed in the request header.

When an I/O function is completed, the interrupt routine uses the return status field in the request header to inform the DOS kernel about the driver's success with the requested I/O operation. Other fields in the request header can be used to pass back such useful information as counts of the actual sectors or bytes transferred.

The interrupt routine usually consists of the following elements:

- A collection of subroutines to implement the various function types that may be requested by MS-DOS (these are sometimes called the command-code routines)

- A centralized entry point that saves all affected registers, extracts the desired function code from the request header, and branches to the appropriate command-code routine (this is typically accomplished with a jump table)

- A centralized exit point that stores status and error codes into the request header (Figures 12-5 and 12-6) and restores the previous contents of the affected registers

Bit(s)	Significance
15	Error
12–14	Reserved
9	Busy
8	Done
0–7	Error code if bit 15 = 1

Figure 12-5. Values for the return status word of the request header.

The command-code routines that implement the various functions supported by an installable device driver are discussed in detail in the following pages.

Although its name suggests otherwise, the interrupt routine is never entered asynchronously (on an I/O completion interrupt, for example). The division of function between strategy and interrupt routines is completely artificial in the current versions of MS-DOS, but will become important in later multitasking releases of the operating system.

Code	Meaning
0	Write-protect violation
1	Unknown unit
2	Drive not ready
3	Unknown command
4	Data error (CRC)
5	Bad drive request structure length
6	Seek error
7	Unknown medium
8	Sector not found
9	Printer out of paper
0AH	Write fault
0BH	Read fault
0CH	General failure
0D-0EH	Reserved
0FH	Invalid disk change (MS-DOS version 3 only)

Figure 12-6. Driver error codes returned in bits 0 through 7 of the return status word in the request header.

The Command-Code Routines

Under MS-DOS version 2, there are 13 defined functions that must be supported by an installed driver. The same 13 functions must be supported under version 3, and 4 additional functions can optionally be supported. Some of the functions are relevant only for character drivers and some only for block-device drivers, while a few are vital to both types. But regardless of driver type, there must be an executable routine present for each function code, even if it does nothing but set the done flag in the return status word of the request header.

In the command-code descriptions that follow, RH refers to the request header whose address was passed to the strategy routine in ES:BX. BYTE is an 8-bit parameter, WORD is a 16-bit unsigned integer or offset parameter, and DWORD refers to a 32-bit long address (a 16-bit offset followed by a 16-bit segment).

Function 00H (0): Driver Initialization

The initialization function (*init*) for the driver is called only once, when the driver is loaded. It is responsible for performing any necessary device hardware initialization, setup of interrupt vectors, and so forth. The initialization routine must return the address of the position where free memory begins after the driver code (the *break* address), so that MS-DOS knows where it can build certain control structures and then load the next installable driver. If this is a block-device driver, initialization must also return the number of units and the address of a BPB pointer array.

The number of units returned by a block driver in the request header is used to assign device names. For example, if the current maximum drive is D and the driver being initialized supports four units, it will be assigned the drive names E, F, G, and H. Although there is also a field in the *device* header for number of units, it is not inspected by MS-DOS.

The BPB pointer array is an array of word offsets to BIOS parameter blocks (Figure 12-7). There must be one entry in the array for each unit defined by the driver, although they can all point to the same BPB to conserve memory. During the operating system boot sequence, MS-DOS scans all the BPBs defined by all the units in all the block device drivers to determine the largest sector size that exists on any device in the system; this information is used to set MS-DOS's cache buffer size.

Byte(s)	Contents
00–01H	Bytes per sector
02H	Sectors per allocation unit (must be power of 2)
03–04H	Number of reserved sectors (starting at sector 0)
05H	Number of file allocation tables
06–07H	Maximum number of root directory entries
08–09H	Total number of sectors
0AH	Media descriptor byte
0B–0CH	Number of sectors occupied by a single FAT

Figure 12-7. Format of the BIOS parameter block. A copy of this block is always found in the boot sector of an initialized disk.

The operating system services that can be invoked by the initialization code at load time are very limited—only MS-DOS services 01 through 0CH and service 30H. These are just adequate to check the MS-DOS version number and display a driver identification or error message.

Many programmers position the initialization code at the end of the driver and return that address as the location of the first free memory, so that the memory occupied by the initializaton routine will be reclaimed after it is finished with its work. Also, if the initialization routine finds that the device is missing or defective and wants to abort the installation of the driver completely so that it does not occupy any memory, it should return the number of units as zero and set the free memory address to CS:0000H.

The initialization function is called with:

RH +2	BYTE	Command code = 0
RH +18	DWORD	Pointer to character after equal sign on CONFIG.SYS line that loaded driver (this information is read-only)
RH +22	BYTE	Drive number for first unit of this block driver (0 = A 1 = B, etc.) (MS-DOS version 3 only)

It returns:

RH + 3	WORD	Return status
RH + 13	BYTE	Number of units (block devices only)
RH + 14	DWORD	Address of first free memory above driver (break address)
RH + 18	DWORD	BPB pointer array (block devices only)

Function 01H (1): Media Check

The media check function is used on block devices only, and in character device drivers should do nothing except set the done flag. It is called when there is a pending drive access call other than a simple file read or write, and is passed the media descriptor byte for the disk that MS-DOS assumes is in the drive (Figure 12-8). If feasible, the media check routine returns a code indicating whether the disk has been changed since the last transfer. If the media check routine can assert that the disk has not been changed, MS-DOS can bypass re-reading the FAT before a directory access, which improves overall performance.

MS-DOS responds to the results of the media check function in the following ways:

- If the disk has not been changed, MS-DOS proceeds with the disk access.

- If the disk has been changed, MS-DOS invalidates all buffers associated with this unit, including buffers containing data waiting to be written (this data is simply lost), performs a BUILD BPB call, then reads the disk's FAT and directory.

- If a "Don't know" is returned, the action taken by MS-DOS depends upon the state of its internal buffers. If data that needs to be written out is present in the buffers, MS-DOS will assume no disk change has occurred and write the data (taking the risk that, if the disk really was changed, the file structure on the new disk may be damaged). If the buffers are empty or have all been previously flushed to the disk, MS-DOS will assume that the disk was changed, and then proceed as described above for the disk-changed return code.

Code	Meaning
0F9H	2-sided, 15-sector
0FCH	1-sided, 9-sector
0FDH	2-sided, 9-sector
0FEH	1-sided, 8-sector
0FFH	2-sided, 8-sector
0F8H	(fixed disk)

Figure 12-8. Current valid MS-DOS codes for the media descriptor byte of the request header (for 5¼-inch disks), assuming the non-IBM-format bit in the attribute word of the device header is zero.

Therefore, when creating a new block-device driver, it is safest to use the following strategy in the media check routine:

- If the disk is fixed and nonremovable, always return the code for "Not changed."

- If the disk is removable, return the code for "Don't know."

In the current versions of MS-DOS, and with current flexible or removable cartridge disk-drive technology, it can be very difficult for the media check routine to determine with absolute certainty that a disk has not been changed. Several methods have been suggested:

- Checking a hardware door interlock that signals when the drive door has been opened—this would suggest, but not prove, that the disk was actually changed.

- Inspecting the volume ID entry in the disk's root directory (if the volume ID has changed, the disk has certainly changed)—however, not all disks have volume labels, and there is no guarantee that they are unique, so finding the same volume label on two sequential checks would not *prove* that the disk was not changed.

- Evaluating timing constraints. It has been determined that a disk cannot be physically exchanged by a user in less than 2 seconds—therefore, if two disk accesses are less than 2 seconds apart, the disk could not have been changed.

None of these methods is completely satisfactory, for obvious reasons. The media check function is called with:

RH+1	BYTE	Unit code
RH+2	BYTE	Command code = 1
RH+13	BYTE	Media descriptor byte

It returns:

RH+3	WORD	Return status
RH+14	BYTE	Media change code
		−1 if disk has been changed
		0 if don't know whether disk changed
		1 if disk has not been changed
RH+15	DWORD	Pointer to previous volume ID, if device attribute bit 11 = 1 and disk has been changed (MS-DOS version 3 only)

Function 02H (2): Build BIOS Parameter Block (BPB)

The build BPB function is supported on block devices only, and in character-device drivers should do nothing except set the done flag. The DOS uses this function to get a pointer to the valid BIOS parameter block (see Figure 12-7) for the current disk, and calls it when the "Disk changed" code is returned by the media check routine, or if the "Don't know" code is returned and there are no dirty buffers (buffers with changed data that have not yet been written to disk). Thus, a call to this function indicates that the disk has been legally changed.

The build BPB call receives a pointer to a one-sector buffer in the request header. If the non–IBM-format bit in the device attribute word is zero, the buffer contains the first sector of the FAT (which includes the media identification byte) and should not be altered by the driver. If the non–IBM-format bit is set, the buffer can be used as scratch space.

The build BPB function is called with:

RH+1	BYTE	Unit code
RH+2	BYTE	Command code = 2
RH+13	BYTE	Media descriptor byte
RH+14	DWORD	Buffer address

It returns:

RH+3	WORD	Return status
RH+18	DWORD	Pointer to new BIOS parameter block

Under MS-DOS version 3, this routine should also read the volume identification off the disk and save it.

Function 03H (3): I/O Control Read

The I/O control read function allows control information to be passed directly from the device driver to the application program. It is called only if the IOCTL bit is set in the device header attribute word. No error check is performed on IOCTL I/O calls.

The IOCTL read function is called with:

RH + 1	BYTE	Unit code (block devices)
RH + 2	BYTE	Command code = 3
RH + 13	BYTE	Media descriptor byte
RH + 14	DWORD	Transfer address
RH + 18	WORD	Byte/sector count
RH + 20	WORD	Starting sector number (block devices)

It returns:

RH + 3	WORD	Return status
RH + 18	WORD	Actual bytes or sectors transferred

Function 04H (4): Read

The read function transfers data from the device into the specified memory buffer. If an error is encountered during the read, the function must set the error status and, in addition, report the number of bytes or sectors successfully transferred. It is not sufficient to simply report an error.

The read function is called with:

RH + 1	BYTE	Unit code (block devices)
RH + 2	BYTE	Command code = 4
RH + 13	BYTE	Media descriptor byte
RH + 14	DWORD	Transfer address
RH + 18	WORD	Byte/sector count
RH + 20	WORD	Starting sector number (block devices)

It returns:

RH + 3	WORD	Return status
RH + 18	WORD	Actual bytes or sectors transferred
RH + 22	DWORD	Pointer to volume identification if error 0FH is returned (MS-DOS version 3 only)

Under MS-DOS version 3, this routine can use the count of open files maintained by the open and close functions (0DH and 0EH) and the media descriptor byte to determine if the disk has been illegally changed.

Function 05H (5): Non-Destructive Read

The non-destructive read function is supported on character devices only, and in block-device drivers should do nothing except set the done flag. If an input status request returns the busy bit cleared (characters waiting), the next character that would be read is returned to MS-DOS, but is not removed from the input buffer. This enables MS-DOS to look ahead by one character.

The non-destructive read function is called with:

RH+2	BYTE	Command code = 5

It returns:

RH+3	WORD	Return status
RH+13	BYTE	Character

Function 06H (6): Input Status

The input status function is available on character devices only, and in block-device drivers should do nothing except set the done flag. This function returns the current input status for the device, allowing MS-DOS to test whether there are characters waiting in a type-ahead buffer. If the character device does not have a type-ahead buffer, the input status routine should always return the busy bit equal to zero, so that MS-DOS will not hang waiting.

The input status function is called with:

RH+2	BYTE	Command code = 6

It returns:

RH+3	WORD	Return status: if busy bit = 1, read request goes to physical device if busy bit = 0, characters already in device buffer and read request returns quickly

Function 07H (7): Flush Input Buffers

The flush input buffers function is available on character devices only, and in block–device drivers should do nothing except set the done flag. This function causes any data waiting in the input buffer to be discarded.

The flush input buffers function is called with:

RH+2	BYTE	Command code = 7

It returns:

RH+3	WORD	Return status

Function 08H (8): Write

The write function transfers data from the specified memory buffer to the device. If an error is encountered during the write, the write function must set the error status and, in addition, report the number of bytes or sectors successfully transferred. It is not sufficient to simply report an error.

The write function is called with:

RH+1	BYTE	Unit code (block devices)
RH+2	BYTE	Command code = 8
RH+13	BYTE	Media descriptor byte
RH+14	DWORD	Transfer address
RH+18	WORD	Byte/sector count
RH+20	WORD	Starting sector number (block devices)

It returns:

RH+3	WORD	Return status
RH+18	WORD	Actual bytes or sectors transferred
RH+22	DWORD	Pointer to volume identification if error 0FH returned (MS-DOS version 3 only)

Under MS-DOS version 3, this routine can use the reference count of open files maintained by the open and close functions (0DH and 0EH) and the media descriptor byte to determine whether the disk has been illegally changed.

Function 09H (9): Write with Verify

The write with verify function transfers data from the specified memory buffer to the device. If feasible, a read-after-write verify of the data should be performed to confirm that the data was written correctly. Otherwise, function 09H is exactly like function 08H.

Function 0AH (10): Output Status

The output status function is available on character devices only, and in block-device drivers should do nothing except set the done flag. This function returns the current output status for the device.

The output status function is called with:

RH+2	BYTE	Command code = 10 (0AH)

It returns:

RH+3	WORD	Return status: if busy bit = 1, write request waits for completion of current request if busy bit = 0, device idle and write request starts immediately

Function 0BH (11): Flush Output Buffers

The flush output buffers function is available on character devices only, and in block-device drivers should do nothing except set the done flag. This function empties the output buffer, if any, and discards any pending output requests.

The flush output buffers function is called with:

RH+2	BYTE	Command code = 11 (0BH)

It returns:

RH+3	WORD	Return status

Function 0CH (12): I/O Control Write

The I/O-control write function allows control information to be passed directly from the application program to the driver. It is called only if the IOCTL bit is set in the device header attribute word. No error check is performed on IOCTL I/O calls.

The I/O-control write function is called with:

RH+1	BYTE	Unit code (block devices)
RH+2	BYTE	Command code = 12 (0CH)
RH+13	BYTE	Media descriptor byte
RH+14	DWORD	Transfer address
RH+18	WORD	Byte/sector count
RH+20	WORD	Starting sector number (block devices)

It returns:

RH+3	WORD	Return status
RH+18	WORD	Actual bytes or sectors transferred

Function 0DH (13): Open

The open function is supported only on MS-DOS versions 3.0 and above, and is called only if the OPEN/CLOSE/RM bit is set in the device attribute word of the device header.

On block devices, the open function can be used to manage local buffering and to increment a reference count of the number of open files on the device. This capability must be used with care, however, because programs that access files through FCBs frequently fail to close them, thus invalidating the open-files count. One way to protect against this possibility is to reset the open-files count to zero, without flushing the buffers, whenever the answer to a media change call is *yes* and a subsequent build BPB call is made to the driver.

On character devices, the open function can be used to send a device initialization string (which can be set into the driver by an application program via an IOCTL write function) or to deny simultaneous access to a character device by more than one process. Note that the predefined handles for the CON, AUX, and PRN devices are always open.

The open function is called with:

RH+1	BYTE	Unit code (block devices)
RH+2	BYTE	Command code = 13 (0DH)

It returns:

RH+3	WORD	Return status

Function 0EH (14): Device Close

The close function is supported only on MS-DOS versions 3.0 and above, and is called only if the OPEN/CLOSE/RM bit is set in the device attribute word of the device header.

On block devices, this function can be used to manage local buffering and to decrement a reference count of the number of open files on the device; when the count reaches zero, all files have been closed and the driver should flush buffers, since the user may change disks.

On character devices, the close function can be used to send a device-dependent post-I/O string such as a form feed. This string can be set into the driver by an application program via an IOCTL write function. Note that the CON, AUX, and PRN devices are never closed.

The close function is called with:

RH+1	BYTE	Unit code (block devices)
RH+2	BYTE	Command code = 14 (0EH)

It returns:

RH+3	WORD	Return status

Function 0FH (15): Removable Media

The removable media function is supported only on MS-DOS versions 3.0 and above, and on block devices only; in character-device drivers it should do nothing except set the done flag. It is called only if the OPEN/CLOSE/RM bit is set in the device attribute word in the device header.

The removable media function is called with:

RH+1	BYTE	Unit code
RH+2	BYTE	Command code = 15 (0FH)

It returns:

RH+3	WORD	Return status: if busy bit = 1, medium is nonremovable if busy bit = 0, medium is removable

Function 10H (16): Output Until Busy

The output until busy function is supported only on MS-DOS versions 3.0 and above, and on character devices only; in block-device drivers it should do nothing except set the done flag. This function transfers data from the specified memory buffer to a device, continuing to transfer bytes until the device is busy. It is called only if bit 13 of the device attribute word is set in the device header.

This function is an optimization included specifically for the use of print spoolers. It is not an error for this function to return a number of bytes transferred that is less than the number of bytes requested.

The output until busy function is called with:

RH+2	BYTE	Command code = 16 (10H)
RH+14	DWORD	Transfer address
RH+18	WORD	Byte count

It returns:

RH+3	WORD	Return status
RH+18	WORD	Actual bytes transferred

The Processing of a Typical I/O Request

An application program requests an I/O operation from MS-DOS by loading registers with the appropriate values and executing an Int 21H. This results in the following sequence of actions:

1. MS-DOS inspects its internal tables and determines which device driver should receive the I/O request.

2. MS-DOS creates a request header data packet in a reserved area of memory. (Disk I/O requests are transformed from file and record information into logical-sector requests by MS-DOS's interpretation of the disk directory and file allocation table.)

3. MS-DOS calls the device driver's *strat* entry point, passing the address of the request header in registers ES:BX.

4. The device driver saves the address of the request header in a local variable and performs a FAR RETURN.

5. MS-DOS calls the device driver's *intr* entry point.

6. The interrupt routine saves all registers, retrieves the address of the request header that was saved by the strategy routine, extracts the function code, and branches to the appropriate command-code subroutine to perform the function.

7. If a data transfer on a block device was requested, the driver's read or write subroutine translates the logical-sector number into a head, track, and physical-sector address for the requested unit, then performs the I/O operation. Since a multiple-sector transfer can be requested in a single request header, a single request by MS-DOS to the driver can result in multiple read or write commands to the disk controller.

8. When the requested function is complete, the interrupt routine sets the status word and any other required information into the request header, restores all registers to their state at entry, and performs a FAR RETURN.

9. MS-DOS translates the driver's return status into the appropriate return code and carry flag status for the MS-DOS Int 21H function that was requested, and returns control to the application program.

Note that a single request by an application program can result in MS-DOS passing many request headers to the driver. For example, attempting to open a file in a subdirectory on a previously unaccessed disk drive might require:

- Reading the disk's boot sector to get the BIOS parameter block.

- Reading from one to many sectors of the root directory to find the entry for the subdirectory and obtain its starting cluster number.

- Reading from one to many sectors of both the file allocation table and the subdirectory itself to find the entry for the desired file.

The CLOCK Driver: A Special Case

The CLOCK device is used by MS-DOS for marking file control blocks and directory entries with the date and time, as well as for providing the date and time services to application programs. It has a unique type of interaction with MS-DOS—a 6-byte sequence is read or written to the driver that obtains or sets the current date and time:

0 days low byte	1 days high byte	2 minutes	3 hours	4 seconds/100	5 seconds

The value passed for *days* is a 16-bit integer representing the number of days elapsed since January 1, 1980.

The clock driver can be given any logical device name, since MS-DOS uses the CLOCK bit in the device attribute word of the driver's device header to identify the device, rather than its name. On IBM PC systems, the clock device has the logical device name $CLOCK.

Writing and Installing a Device Driver

Now that we have discussed the structure and capabilities of installable device drivers for the MS-DOS environment, we can proceed to discuss the mechanical steps of assembling and linking them.

Assembly

Device drivers for MS-DOS always have an origin of zero, but are otherwise assembled, linked, and converted into an executable module as though they were COM files. (Although MS-DOS is also capable of loading installable drivers in the EXE file format, this introduces unnecessary complexity into writing and debugging drivers, and offers no significant advantages. In addition, EXE-format drivers cannot be used with the IBM PC, since the EXE loader is located in COMMAND.COM, which is not present when the installable device drivers are being loaded.) The driver should not have a declared stack segment, and must, in general, follow the other restrictions outlined in Chapter 3 for memory-image (COM) programs. A driver can be loaded anywhere, so beware that you do not make any assumptions in your code about the driver's location in physical memory. Figure 12-9 presents a skeleton example that you can follow as you read the next few pages.

```
1              name    driver
2              page    55,132
3              title   'DRIVER --- installable driver template'
4
5      ;
6      ; This is a "template" for an MS-DOS installable device driver.
7      ;
8      ; The actual driver subroutines are stubs only and have
9      ; no effect but to return a non-error "Done" status.
10     ;
11     ; Ray Duncan, April 1985
12
13     code    segment public 'CODE'
14
15     driver  proc    far
16
17             assume  cs:code,ds:code,es:code
18
19             org     0
20
21
22     Max_Cmd equ     16            ; MS-DOS command code maximum
23                                   ; this is 16 for MS-DOS 3.x
24                                   ; and 12 for MS-DOS 2.x.
25
26
27     cr      equ     0dh           ; ASCII carriage return
28     lf      equ     0ah           ; ASCII line feed
29     eom     equ     '$'           ; end of message signal
30
31
32             page
33     ;
34     ; Device Driver Header
35     ;
36     Header  dd      -1            ; link to next device, -1 = end of list.
37
38             dw      8000h         ; Device Attribute word
39                                   ; bit 15 = 1 for character devices
40                                   ; bit 14 = 1 if driver can handle IOCTL
41                                   ; bit 13 = 1 if block device & non-IBM format
42                                   ; bit 12 = 0
43                                   ; bit 11 = 1 if OPEN/CLOSE/RM supported (DOS 3.x)
44                                   ; bit 10 = 0
45                                   ; bit 9  = 0
46                                   ; bit 8  = 0
47                                   ; bit 7  = 0
```

(continued)

Figure 12-9. DRIVER. ASM: A functional skeleton from which you can implement your own working device driver.

```
48                                      ; bit 6  = 0
49                                      ; bit 5  = 0
50                                      ; bit 4  = 0
51                                      ; bit 3  = 1 if CLOCK device
52                                      ; bit 2  = 1 if NUL device
53                                      ; bit 1  = 1 if Standard Output
54                                      ; bit 0  = 1 if Standard Input
55
56          dw      Strat               ; device "Strategy" entry point
57
58          dw      Intr                ; device "Interrupt" entry point
59
60          db      'DRIVER  '          ; character device name, 8 char, or if block
61                                      ; device, no. of units in first byte followed
62                                      ; by 7 don't care bytes.
63
64
65
66      ;
67      ; Double-word pointer to Request Header
68      ; Passed to Strategy Routine by MS-DOS
69      ;
70
71      RH_Ptr  dd      ?
72              page
73      ;
74      ; MS-DOS Command Codes dispatch table.
75      ; The "Interrupt" routine uses this table and the
76      ; Command Code supplied in the Request Header to
77      ; transfer to the appropriate driver subroutine.
78
79      Dispatch:
80              dw      Init            ;  0 = initialize driver
81              dw      Media_Chk       ;  1 = media check on block device
82              dw      Build_Bpb       ;  2 = build BIOS parameter block
83              dw      IOCTL_Rd        ;  3 = I/O control read
84              dw      Read            ;  4 = read from device
85              dw      ND_Read         ;  5 = non-destructive Read
86              dw      Inp_Stat        ;  6 = return current input status
87              dw      Inp_Flush       ;  7 = flush device input buffers
88              dw      Write           ;  8 = write to device
89              dw      Write_Vfy       ;  9 = write with verify
90              dw      Outp_Stat       ; 10 = return current output status
91              dw      Outp_Flush      ; 11 = flush output buffers
92              dw      IOCTL_Wrt       ; 12 = I/O control write
93              dw      Dev_Open        ; 13 = device open      (MS-DOS 3.X)
94              dw      Dev_Close       ; 14 = device close     (MS-DOS 3.X)
95              dw      Rem_Media       ; 15 = removable media  (MS-DOS 3.X)
```

Figure 12-9 continued.

```
96                 dw     Out_Busy          ; 16 = output until busy (MS-DOS 3.X)
97          page
98     ;
99     ; MS-DOS Request Header structure definition
100    ;
101    ; The first 13 bytes of all Request Headers are the same
102    ; and are referred to as the "Static" part of the Header.
103    ; The number and meaning of the following bytes varies.
104    ; In this "Struc" definition we show the Request Header
105    ; contents for Read and Write calls.
106    ;
107    Request struc                     ; request header template structure
108
109                                      ; beginning of "Static" portion
110
111    Rlength db      ?                 ; length of request header
112
113    Unit    db      ?                 ; unit number for this request
114
115    Command db      ?                 ; request header's command code
116
117    Status  dw      ?                 ; driver's return status word
118                                      ; bit  15   = Error
119                                      ; bits 10-14 = Reserved
120                                      ; bit  9    = Busy
121                                      ; bit  8    = Done
122                                      ; bits 0-7  = Error code if bit 15 = 1
123
124    Reserve db      8 dup (?) ; reserved area
125
126
127
128
129                                      ; end of "Static" portion, the remainder in
130                                      ; this example is for Read and Write functions.
131
132    Media   db      ?                 ; Media Descriptor byte
133
134    Address dd      ?                 ; memory address for transfer
135
136    Count   dw      ?                 ; byte/sector count value
137
138    Sector  dw      ?                 ; starting sector value
139
140    Request ends                      ; end of request header template
141            page
142
143    ; Device Driver "Strategy Routine"
```

Figure 12-9 continued.

```
144
145     ; Each time a request is made for this device, MS-DOS
146     ; first calls the "Strategy routine",  then immediately
147     ; calls the "Interrupt routine".
148
149     ; The Strategy routine is passed the address of the
150     ; Request Header in ES:BX, which it saves in a local
151     ; variable and then returns to MS-DOS.
152
153     Strat   proc    far
154                                             ; save address of Request Header.
155             mov     word ptr cs:[RH_Ptr],bx
156             mov     word ptr cs:[RH_Ptr+2],es
157
158             ret                     ; back to MS-DOS
159
160     Strat   endp
161
162             page
163
164
165     ; Device Driver "Interrupt Routine"
166
167     ; This entry point is called by MS-DOS immediately after
168     ; the call to the "Strategy Routine", which saved the long
169     ; address of the Request Header in the local variable "RH_Ptr".
170
171     ; The "Interrupt Routine" uses the Command Code passed in
172     ; the Request Header to transfer to the appropriate device
173     ; handling routine.  Each command code routine must place
174     ; any necessary return information into the Request Header,
175     ; then perform a Near Return with AX = Status.
176
177     Intr    proc    far
178
179             push    ax                      ; save general registers.
180             push    bx
181             push    cx
182             push    dx
183             push    ds
184             push    es
185             push    di
186             push    si
187             push    bp
188
189             push    cs                      ; make local data addressable.
190             pop     ds
191
```

Figure 12-9 continued.

```
192             les     di,[RH_Ptr]     ; let ES:DI = Request Header.
193
194                                     ; get BX = Command Code
195             mov     bl,es:[di.Command]
196             xor     bh,bh
197             cmp     bx,Max_Cmd      ; make sure it's legal.
198             jle     Intr1           ; jump, function code is ok.
199             mov     ax,8003h        ; set Error bit and "Unknown Command" code.
200             jmp     Intr2
201
202     Intr1:  shl     bx,1            ; form index to Dispatch table
203                                     ; and branch to driver routine.
204             call    word ptr [bx+Dispatch]
205                                     ; should return AX = status.
206
207             les     di,[RH_Ptr]     ; restore ES:DI = addr of Request Header.
208
209     Intr2:  or      ax,0100h        ; merge Done bit into status, and
210                                     ; store into Request Header.
211             mov     es:[di.Status],ax
212
213             pop     bp              ;restore general registers.
214             pop     si
215             pop     di
216             pop     es
217             pop     ds
218             pop     dx
219             pop     cx
220             pop     bx
221             pop     ax
222             ret                     ; back to MS-DOS
223
224             page
225
226     ;
227     ; Command Code subroutines called by Interrupt Routine
228     ;
229     ; These routines are called with ES:DI pointing to the
230     ; Request Header.
231     ;
232     ; They should return AX = 0 if function was completed
233     ; successfully, or AX = 8000H + Error code if function failed.
234     ;
235
236     Media_Chk proc  near            ; Function 1 = Media Check
237
238             xor     ax,ax
239             ret
```

Figure 12-9 continued.

```
240
241    Media_Chk endp
242
243
244    Build_Bpb proc    near              ; Function 2 = Build BPB
245
246            xor     ax,ax
247            ret
248
249    Build_Bpb endp
250
251
252    IOCTL_Rd proc     near              ;Function 3 = I/O Control Read
253
254            xor     ax,ax
255            ret
256
257    IOCTL_Rd endp
258
259
260    Read    proc      near              ; Function 4 = Read
261
262            xor     ax,ax
263            ret
264
265    Read    endp
266
267
268    ND_Read proc      near              ; Function 5 = Non-Destructive Read
269
270            xor     ax,ax
271            ret
272
273    ND_Read endp
274
275
276    Inp_Stat proc     near              ; Function 6 = Input Status
277
278            xor     ax,ax
279            ret
280
281    Inp_Stat endp
282
283
284    Inp_Flush proc    near              ; Function 7 = Flush Input Buffers
285
286            xor     ax,ax
287            ret
```

Figure 12-9 continued.

```
288
289   Inp_Flush endp
290
291
292   Write    proc    near            ; Function 8 = Write
293
294            xor     ax,ax
295            ret
296
297   Write    endp
298
299
300   Write_Vfy proc   near            ; Function 9 = Write with Verify
301
302            xor     ax,ax
303            ret
304
305   Write_Vfy endp
306
307
308   Outp_Stat proc   near            ; Function 10 = Output Status
309
310            xor     ax,ax
311            ret
312
313   Outp_Stat endp
314
315
316   Outp_Flush proc near            ; Function 11 = Flush Output Buffers
317
318            xor     ax,ax
319            ret
320
321   Outp_Flush endp
322
323
324   IOCTL_Wrt proc   near            ; Function 12 = I/O Control Write
325
326            xor     ax,ax
327            ret
328
329   IOCTL_Wrt endp
330
331
332   Dev_Open proc    near            ; Function 13 = Device Open
333
334            xor     ax,ax
335            ret
```

Figure 12-9 continued.

```
336
337    Dev_Open endp
338
339
340    Dev_Close proc   near              ; Function 14 = Device Close
341
342           xor      ax,ax
343           ret
344
345    Dev_Close endp
346
347
348    Rem_Media proc   near              ; Function 15 = Removable Media
349
350           xor      ax,ax
351           ret
352
353    Rem_Media endp
354
355
356    Out_Busy proc    near              ; Function 16 = Output Until Busy
357
358           xor      ax,ax
359           ret
360
361    Out_Busy endp
362           page
363
364    ; This Initialization code for the driver is called only
365    ; once, when the driver is loaded.  It is responsible for
366    ; initializing the hardware, setting up any necessary
367    ; interrupt vectors, and it must return the address
368    ; of the first free memory after the driver to MS-DOS.
369    ; If it is a block device driver, Init must also return the
370    ; address of the BIOS Parameter Block pointer array; if all
371    ; units are the same, all pointers can point to the same BPB.
372    ; Only MS-DOS services 01-0CH and 30H can be called by the
373    ; Initialization function.
374    ;
375    ; In this example, Init returns its own address to the DOS as
376    ; the start of free memory after the driver, so that the memory
377    ; occupied by INIT will be reclaimed after it is finished
378    ; with its work.
379
380    Init    proc     near              ; Function 0 = Initialize Driver
381
382           push     es                ; save address of Request Header.
383           push     di
```

Figure 12-9 continued.

```
384
385         mov     ax,cs            ; convert load address to ASCII.
386         mov     bx,offset DHaddr
387         call    hexasc
388
389         mov     ah,9             ; print sign-on message and
390         mov     dx,offset Ident  ; the load address of driver.
391         int     21h
392
393         pop     di               ; restore Request Header addr.
394         pop     es
395
396                                  ; set first usable memory addr.
397         mov     word ptr es:[di.Address],offset Init
398         mov     word ptr es:[di.Address+2],cs
399
400         xor     ax,ax            ; Return status
401         ret
402
403  Init   endp
404
405
406  Ident  db      cr,lf,lf
407         db      'Example Device Driver 1.0'
408
409
410
411         db      cr,lf
412         db      'Device Header at '
413
414
415  DHaddr db      'XXXX:0000'
416
417         db      cr,lf,lf,eom
418
419
420  Intr   endp
421
422         page
423
424  ; HEXASC --- converts a binary 16-bit number into
425  ;             a "hexadecimal" ASCII string.
426  ;
427  ; Call with   AX   = value to convert
428  ;             DS:BX = address to store 4-character string
429  ;
430  ; Returns     AX, BX destroyed, other registers preserved
431
```

Figure 12-9 continued.

```
432    hexasc    proc    near
433
434              push    cx         ; save registers.
435              push    dx
436
437              mov     dx,4       ; initialize character counter.
438
439    hexasc1:
440              mov     cx,4       ; isolate next four bits.
441              rol     ax,cl
442              mov     cx,ax
443              and     cx,0fh
444              add     cx,'0'     ; convert to ASCII.
445              cmp     cx,'9'     ; is it 0-9?
446              jbe     hexasc2    ; yes, jump.
447                                 ; add fudge factor for A-F.
448              add     cx,'A'-'9'-1
449
450    hexasc2:                     ; store this character.
451              mov     [bx],cl
452              inc     bx         ; bump string pointer.
453
454              dec     dx         ; count characters converted.
455              jnz     hexasc1    ; loop, not four yet.
456
457              pop     dx         ; restore registers.
458              pop     cx
459              ret                ; back to caller
460
461    hexasc    endp
462
463
464    Driver    endp
465
466    code      ends
467
468              end
```

Figure 12-9 continued.

The driver's device header must be located at the beginning of the file
(offset 0000H). Both words in the link field in the header should be set
to −1. The attribute word must be set up correctly for the device type and
other options. The offsets to the strategy and interrupt routines must be
relative to the same segment base as the device header itself. If the driver is
for a character device, the name field should be filled in properly with the
device's logical name. The logical name can be any legal 8-character filename, padded with spaces and without a colon. Beware of accidentally
duplicating the names of existing character devices, unless you are intentionally superseding a resident driver.

The strategy and interrupt routines for the device are called by MS-DOS via an intersegment call (CALL FAR) when the driver is first loaded and installed, and again whenever an I/O request is issued for the device by an application program. MS-DOS uses registers ES:BX to pass the *strat* routine a double-word pointer to the request header; this address should be saved internally in the driver so that it is available for use during the subsequent call to the *intr* routine.

The command-code routines for function codes 0 through 12 (0CH) must be present in *every* installable device driver, regardless of device type, whereas functions 13 (0DH) through 16 (10H) are supported only on MS-DOS version 3 systems and can be handled in one of the following ways:

● Don't implement them, and leave the OPEN/CLOSE/RM bit in the device header cleared. The resulting driver will work in either version 2 or version 3, but does not take full advantage of the augmented functionality of version 3.

● Implement them, and test the MS-DOS version during the initialization sequence, setting the OPEN/CLOSE/RM bit in the device header appropriately. Write all command-code routines so that they will test this bit and adjust their behavior to accommodate the host version of MS-DOS. Such a driver requires more work and testing, but will take full advantage of both the version 2 and the version 3 environments.

● Implement them, and just assume that all the version 3 facilities are available. With this approach, the resulting driver is useless under version 2.

Remember that device drivers must preserve the integrity of MS-DOS. All registers, including flags (especially the direction flag and interrupt enable bits), must be preserved, and if the driver makes heavy use of the stack, it should switch to an internal stack of adequate depth (the MS-DOS stack has room for only 40 to 50 bytes when a driver is called).

If you install a new CON driver, be sure to set the bits for standard input (stdin) and standard output (stdout) in the device attribute word in the device header.

You'll recall that multiple drivers can be programmed in one file. In this case, the device header link field of each driver should point to the segment offset of the next, all using the same segment base, and the link field for the last driver in the file should be set to −1, −1. The initialization routines for all the drivers in the file should return the same break address.

Linking

Use the standard MS-DOS Linker to transform the OBJ file that is output from the Assembler into a relocatable EXE module. Then, use the EXE2BIN utility (see Chapter 4) to convert the EXE file into a memory-image program. The extension on the final driver file can be anything, but BIN and SYS are most commonly used in MS-DOS systems and it is therefore wisest to follow one of these conventions.

Installation

Once the driver is assembled, linked, and converted to a BIN or SYS file, copy it to the root directory of a bootable disk. If it is a character device driver, do not use the same name for the file as you used for the logical device listed in the driver's header, or you will not be able to delete, copy, or rename the file after the driver is loaded.

Use your favorite text editor to add the line:

DEVICE = *[D:][PATH]FILENAME.EXT*

to the CONFIG.SYS file on the bootable disk. (In this line, *D:* is an optional drive designator and *FILENAME.EXT* is the name of the file containing your new device driver. A path specification can be included in the entry, if you prefer not to put the driver file in your root directory.) Now restart your computer system, to load the modified CONFIG.SYS file.

During the MS-DOS boot sequence, the SYSINIT module (which is part of IO.SYS) reads and processes the CONFIG.SYS file. It loads the driver into memory and inspects the device header. If the driver is a character-device driver, it is linked into the device chain ahead of the other character devices; if it is a block-device driver, it is placed *behind* all previously linked block devices and the resident block devices (Figures 12-10, 12-11, and 12-12). The linkage is accomplished by updating the link field in the device header to point to the segment and offset of the next driver in the chain. The link field of the last driver in the chain contains −1, −1.

Next, the *strat* routine is called with a request header that contains a command code of zero, and then the *intr* routine is called. Since the request header contains a function code of zero, the initialization routine is executed and returns the break address telling MS-DOS how much memory to reserve for this driver. Now MS-DOS can proceed to the next entry in the CONFIG.SYS file.

You cannot supersede a built-in block device driver—you can only add supplemental block devices. However, you can override the default system driver for a character device (such as CON) with an installed driver by simply giving it the same logical-device name in the device header. When processing a character I/O request, MS-DOS always scans the list of installed drivers before it scans the list of default devices and takes the first match.

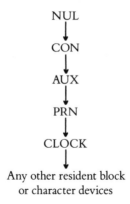

Figure 12-10. MS-DOS device-driver chain before any installable device drivers have been loaded.

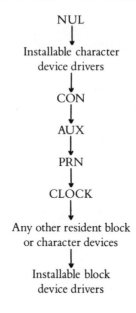

Figure 12-11. MS-DOS device-driver chain after installable device drivers are loaded.

Address	Attribute	Strategy routine	Interrupt routine	Type	Units	Name
00E3:0111	8004	0FD5	0FE0	C		NUL
0070:0148	8013	008E	0099	C		CON
0070:01DD	8000	008E	009F	C		AUX
0070:028E	8000	008E	00AE	C		PRN
0070:0300	8008	008E	00C3	C		CLOCK
0070:03CC	0000	008E	00C9	B	02	
0070:01EF	8000	008E	009F	C		COM1
0070:02A0	8000	008E	00AE	C		LPT1
0070:06F0	8000	008E	00B4	C		LPT2
0070:0702	8000	008E	00BA	C		LPT3
0070:0714	8000	008E	00A5	C		COM2

End of device chain

Figure 12-12. Example listing of device chain under MS-DOS version 2.1, "plain vanilla" IBM PC with no hard disks or user device drivers. (C = character device, B = block device.)

Debugging a Device Driver

The most important thing to remember when testing new device drivers is to maintain adequate backups and a viable fallback position. Don't modify the CONFIG.SYS file and install the new driver on your hard disk before it is proven! Be prudent—create a bootable floppy disk and put the modified CONFIG.SYS file and the new driver on that for debugging. When everything is working properly, copy the finished product to its permanent storage medium.

The easiest way to test a device driver is to write a simple assembly-language front-end routine that sets up a simulated request packet and then performs FAR CALLs to the *strat* and *intr* entry points, just as MS-DOS would. The driver and the front end can then be linked together into a COM or EXE file that can be run under the control of SYMDEB or another debugger. This arrangement makes it easy to trace each of the command-code routines individually, to observe the results of the I/O, and to examine the status codes returned in the request header.

Tracing the installed driver when it is linked into the MS-DOS system in the normal manner is more difficult. Breakpoints must be chosen carefully, to yield the maximum possible information per debugging run. Since versions 2 and 3 of MS-DOS maintain only one request header internally, the request header that was being used by the driver you are tracing will be overwritten as soon as your debugger makes an output request to display information. You will find it helpful to add a routine to your initialization subroutine that displays the driver's load address on the console when you boot MS-DOS; you can then use this address to inspect the device driver header and set breakpoints within the body of the driver.

Debugging a device driver can also be somewhat sticky when interrupt handling is involved, especially if the device uses the same interrupt request priority level (IRQ level) as other peripherals in the system. Extremely cautious and conservative programming is needed to avoid unexpected and unreproducible interactions with other device drivers and interrupt handlers. If possible, prove out the basic logic of the driver using polled I/O rather than interrupt-driven I/O, and introduce interrupt handling only when the rest of the driver's logic is known to be solid.

Typical device-driver errors or problems that can cause system crashes or strange system behavior include:

- Failure to set the linkage address of the last driver in a file to −1.

- Overflow of the MS-DOS stack by driver initialization code, corrupting the memory image of MS-DOS (can lead to unpredictable behavior during boot; remedy is to use a local stack).

- Incorrect break-address reporting by the initialization routine (can lead to a system crash if vital parts of the driver are overwritten by the next driver loaded).

- Improper BPB's supplied by the build BPB routine, or incorrect BPB pointer array supplied by the initialization routine (can lead to many confusing problems, ranging from out-of-memory errors to system boot failure).

- Incorrect reporting of the number of bytes or sectors successfully transferred at the time an I/O error occurs (can manifest itself as a system crash after you enter *R* to the prompt *Abort, Retry, Ignore?*).

Although the interface between the DOS kernel and the device driver is fairly simple, it is also quite strict. The command-code routines must perform exactly as they are defined, or the system will behave erratically. Even a very subtle discrepancy in the action of a command-code routine can have unexpectedly large global effects.

Writing MS-DOS Filters

A filter is a program that takes a stream of characters as input, processes it, and writes a transformed stream of characters as output. The source and destination of the text streams may be any character device, file, or program known to the system. The transformation may take almost any form, including:

- Sorting the input file

- Excerpting lines of text according to specific criteria

- Substituting one string of characters for another

- Encrypting and decrypting

Filters first became popular on computers running under the UNIX operating system, which pioneered redirectable I/O and pipes. Pipes allow the output of one program to be used as the input of another, so that text streams can be fed through several filters in succession to perform complex operations. Due largely to the efforts of generations of graduate-student hackers, today's UNIX systems include massive numbers of filters that do everything from paginating to finding splines for arbitrary sets of plotting coordinates.

One of the enhancements added to MS-DOS in version 2 was support for redirectable I/O very similar to that of UNIX. Two predefined I/O channels, called the *standard input* and the *standard output*, can be accessed by any program. They are ordinarily directed to the keyboard and the video display, respectively, but can be individually redirected to other devices, or to files, by parameters placed in an MS-DOS command line. Pipes are also supported, although since current versions of MS-DOS are not multitasking, the pipes are implemented as invisible intermediate files, rather than as a direct communication between programs.

Three simple filters are supplied with MS-DOS:

- SORT, which sorts text data files

- FIND, which searches an input stream to match a specified string

- MORE, which displays data one screen at a time

Many additional filters are available on PC bulletin-board systems or from PC user groups on public-domain software disks.

In this chapter, we will describe how filters work and how new ones can be constructed, so that you can take full advantage of the powerful concept of redirectable I/O in the MS-DOS environment.

How Filters Work

When MS-DOS is initialized, it establishes a system table of control blocks that relates filenames or character device names to handles. (A handle, as we have discussed before, is simply a number that identifies a device or file; it may also be called a *channel number*, a *file descriptor*, a *logical unit number*, or a *token* under other operating systems.)

MS-DOS predefines five standard handles for COMMAND.COM. These handles are always open and are assigned by default to the three standard MS-DOS character devices as follows:

Name	Logical device	Handle
Standard input	CON	0
Standard output	CON	1
Standard error	CON	2
Auxiliary	AUX	3
List device	PRN	4

When COMMAND COM loads and executes an external command or application program via the MS-DOS EXEC function (Int 21H function 4BH), the application inherits all these open handles. Therefore, it has channels to the standard input, standard output, standard error, standard auxiliary, and standard list devices available for immediate use with the Handle read and write functions.

Each time a program opens a file or device, the first free handle is assigned to that file; when a file is closed, its handle is released for re-use. The maximum number of handles available for a given task ranges from 5 (the number of default handles in the preceding list) to either the maximum defined in the CONFIG.SYS file or 20, whichever is less.

Now let's relate all this to what actually happens when COMMAND.COM parses a command line that contains redirection commands. Consider the command line:

```
SORT <ABC.DAT >XYZ.DAT
```

COMMAND.COM first scans the command line for an input redirection command, which consists of the character < followed by a filename or logical device name. If this is found, COMMAND.COM closes handle 0 (standard input), releasing that handle for re-use, and then opens the specified file or device. Since handle 0 was closed and is the first handle available, it is automatically assigned to the file *ABC.DAT* specified in the input redirection command.

Next, COMMAND.COM scans the command line for an output redirection command, which consists of the character > followed by a filename or logical device name. If this is found, COMMAND.COM closes handle 1 (standard output), and then opens the desired output file or device. Since handle 1 is now the first free handle, it is naturally assigned to the file *XYZ.DAT* specified in the output redirection command.

Finally, COMMAND.COM invokes the EXEC function (4BH) to load and execute the SORT program. Since with EXEC the child process inherits all the active handles of the parent, the new associations of the standard input and output handles with the files *ABC.DAT* and *XYZ.DAT* are automatically effective while the SORT program executes. When SORT terminates, all its active handles are automatically closed, which ensures that the disk directory is updated. When COMMAND.COM regains control from SORT, it then closes its own standard input and output handles, and re-opens them to the CON device to accept the next command from the user.

Thus, we see that redirection of input and output under MS-DOS is relatively simple in execution, following naturally from the presence of the predefined handles for the standard input and output devices and from the definition of the EXEC function.

Building a New Filter

Creating additional filters for your own requirements is a straightforward process. In its simplest form, a filter need only use the Handle read and write functions to get characters from the standard input and send them to the standard output, performing any desired alterations on the text stream on a character-by-character basis.

To demonstrate the necessary programming techniques for adding a new filter to MS-DOS, we'll compare equivalent listings for a simple but very useful filter called *CLEAN* (Figures 13-1 and 13-2). *CLEAN* processes a text file by stripping the high bit from all characters, expanding tabs, and throwing away all control codes except linefeeds, carriage returns, and form feeds. Thus, *CLEAN* can transform almost any kind of word-processed document file into a normal text file.

```
 1              name    clean
 2              page    55,132
 3              title   'CLEAN - Filter text file'
 4      ;
 5      ; CLEAN.ASM     Filter to turn document files into
 6      ;               normal text files.
 7      ;
 8      ; Usage is:     C>CLEAN  <infile  >outfile
 9      ;
10      ; All text characters are passed through with high bit stripped
11      ; off.  Form feeds, carriage returns, and linefeeds are passed
12      ; through.  Tabs are expanded to spaces.  All other control codes
13      ; are discarded.
14      ;
15      ; Copyright (c) 1984, 1985 by Ray Duncan
16      ;
17      ; To assemble and link into an EXE file for execution:
18      ;
19      ;               C>MASM CLEAN;
20      ;               C>LINK CLEAN;
21      ;
22      tab     equ     09h                     ; ASCII tab code
23      lf      equ     0ah                     ; ASCII linefeed
24      ff      equ     0ch                     ; ASCII form feed
25      cr      equ     0dh                     ; ASCII carriage return
26      eof     equ     01ah                    ; End-of-file marker
27      blank   equ     020h                    ; ASCII space code
28
29      tab_wid equ     8                       ; width of one tab stop
30
31      stdin   equ     0000                    ; standard input device handle
32      stdout  equ     0001                    ; standard output device handle
33      stderr  equ     0002                    ; standard error device handle
34
35      cseg    segment para public 'CODE'
36
37              assume  cs:cseg,ds:dseg,es:dseg,ss:sseg
38
39      clean   proc    far                     ; entry point from MS-DOS
40
41              mov     ax,dseg                 ; make our data segment addressable.
42              mov     ds,ax
43              mov     es,ax
44
45              mov     ah,30h                  ; check version of MS-DOS.
46              int     21h
47              cmp     al,2
48              jae     clean2                  ; proceed, DOS 2.0 or greater.
```

(continued)

Figure 13-1. The assembly-language version of the CLEAN filter: CLEAN.ASM.

```
49              mov     dx,offset msg1          ; if DOS 1.x print error message.
50              mov     ah,9                    ; we must use the old MS-DOS
51              int     21h                     ; string output function.
52              mov     ah,0                    ; exit via function 0.
53              int     21h
54
55    clean2: call      getchar                 ; get a character from input.
56              and     al,07fh                 ; turn off the high bit.
57              cmp     al,blank                ; is it a control char?
58              jae     clean4                  ; no.  write it to output.
59              cmp     al,eof                  ; is it end of file?
60              je      clean9                  ; yes, go write EOF mark and exit.
61              cmp     al,tab                  ; is it a tab?
62              je      clean7                  ; yes, go expand it to spaces.
63              cmp     al,cr                   ; is it a carriage return?
64              je      clean3                  ; yes, go process it.
65              cmp     al,lf                   ; is it a linefeed?
66              je      clean3                  ; yes, go process it.
67              cmp     al,ff                   ; is it a form feed?
68              jne     clean2                  ; no, discard it.
69
70    clean3: mov       column,0                ; if acceptable control character,
71              jmp     clean5                  ; we should be back at column 0.
72
73    clean4: inc       column                  ; if it's a non-ctrl char,
74                                              ; then increment column counter.
75
76    clean5: call      putchar                 ; write the char to output.
77              jnc     clean2                  ; if OK, go back for another char.
78
79              mov     dx,offset msg2          ; write failed, display error
80              mov     cx,msg2_len             ; message and exit.
81
82    clean6: mov       bx,stderr               ; issue error message to
83              mov     ah,40h                  ; standard error device.
84              int     21h
85              mov     ax,4c01h                ; then return to DOS with an
86              int     21h                     ; error code of 1.
87
88    clean7: mov       ax,column               ; tab code detected, must
89              cwd                             ; expand tabs to spaces.
90              mov     cx,tab_wid              ; divide the current column counter
91              idiv    cx                      ; by the desired tab_width.
92              sub     cx,dx                   ; tab_width minus the remainder is
93              add     column,cx               ; number of spaces to send out.
94
95    clean8: push      cx                      ; move to the next tab position.
96              mov     al,blank
```

Figure 13-1 continued.

```
 97              call     putchar              ; send an ASCII blank.
 98              pop      cx
 99              loop     clean8               ; loop until tab stop reached.
100              jmp      clean2               ; go get another character.
101
102    clean9: call     putchar              ; write out the EOF mark,
103              mov      ax,4c00h             ; and exit to DOS with
104              int      21h                  ; return code of zero.
105
106    clean    endp
107
108    getchar proc     near                 ; get a character from
109                                            ; the Standard Input device.
110              mov      bx,stdin             ; handle for Standard Input
111              mov      cx,1                 ; length to read = 1 byte
112              mov      dx,offset ibuff      ; address of input buffer
113              mov      ah,3fh               ; function 3FH = read
114              int      21h                  ; transfer to DOS.
115              or       ax,ax                ; any characters read?
116              jz       getc1                ; if none, return EOF.
117              mov      al,ibuff             ; else, return the char in AL.
118              ret
119    getc1:  mov      al,eof               ; no chars read, return
120              ret                           ; an End-of-File (EOF) mark.
121    getchar endp
122
123    putchar proc     near                 ; send a character to
124                                            ; the Standard Output device.
125              mov      obuff,al             ; save char. to be written.
126              mov      bx,stdout            ; handle for Standard Output
127              mov      cx,1                 ; length to write = 1 byte
128              mov      dx,offset obuff      ; address of output
129              mov      ah,40h               ; function 40H = write
130              int      21h                  ; transfer to DOS.
131              cmp      ax,1                 ; was char. really written?
132              jne      putc1
133              clc                           ; yes, return carry = 0
134              ret                           ; as success signal.
135    putc1:  stc                           ; write failed, return carry = 1
136              ret                           ; as error signal (device is full).
137    putchar endp
138
139    cseg     ends
140
141    dseg     segment para public 'DATA'
142
143    ibuff    db       0                    ; temporary storage for character
144                                            ; read from input stream
```

Figure 13-1 continued.

```
145
146    obuff    db      0                              ; temporary storage for character
147                                                    ; sent to output stream
148
149    column   dw      0                              ; current column counter
150
151    msg1     db      cr,lf
152             db      'clean: need MS-DOS version 2 or greater.'
153
154
155
156
157
158             db      cr,lf,'$'
159
160    msg2     db      cr,lf
161             db      'clean: disk is full.'
162
163
164             db      cr,lf
165    msg2_len equ     $-msg2
166
167    dseg     ends
168                                                    ; declare stack segment.
169    sseg     segment para stack 'STACK'
170
171             dw      64 dup (?)
172
173
174
175    sseg     ends
176
177             end     clean
```

Figure 13-1 continued.

When using the *CLEAN* filter, you must specify the source and destination files for the text stream in the command line; otherwise, *CLEAN* will simply read the default standard input device (the keyboard) and write to the default standard output device (the video display). For example, to filter the document file *MYFILE.WS* and leave the result in *MYFILE.TXT,* you would enter the command:

CLEAN <MYFILE.WS >MYFILE.TXT

(Note that the original file, *MYFILE.WS,* is unchanged.)

```
/*

        CLEAN.C          Filter to turn document files into
                         normal text files.

        Usage is:        C>CLEAN  <infile >outfile

        All text characters are passed through with high bit stripped
        off.  Form feeds, carriage returns, and linefeeds are passed
        through.  Tabs are expanded to spaces.  All other control codes
        are discarded.

        Copyright (C) 1985 Ray Duncan

        To compile with Microsoft C 3.0:
                         C>MSC CLEAN;
                         C>LINK CLEAN;

*/

#include <stdio.h>

#define TAB_WIDTH       8               /* width of a tab stop */

                                        /* misc ASCII characters */
#define TAB             '\x09'          /* Tab char.:  Control-I */
#define LF              '\x0A'          /* Linefeed or New Line */
#define FF              '\x0C'          /* Form Feed */
#define CR              '\x0D'          /* Carriage Return */
#define EOF_MARK        '\x1A'          /* End-of-File Mark: Control-Z */
#define BLANK           '\x20'          /* ASCII space code */


main(argc, argv)
int    argc;
char  *argv[];

{   char c;                             /* current character from stdin */
    int col = 0;                        /* current column counter */

    while( (c = getchar() ) != EOF )    /* read character from input stream. */
    {   c &= 0x07F;                     /* strip high bit. */
        switch(c)                       /* if not end of file, decode it. */
        {   case LF:                    /* if new line or carriage return */
            case CR:                    /* reset column count */
                col=0;                  /* and pass character through. */
            case FF:                    /* if form feed */
                writechar(c);           /* pass character through. */
```

(continued)

Figure 13-2. The C version of the CLEAN filter: CLEAN.C.

```
                          break;
                case TAB:                        /* if tab convert to spaces. */
                     do writechar(BLANK);
                     while( ( ++col % TAB_WIDTH ) != 0 );
                     break;
                default:                          /* discard other control chars */
                     if (c >= BLANK)              /* and pass text characters */
                     {   writechar(c);            /* through to the new file */
                         col++;                   /* incrementing column counter. */
                     }
                     break;
           }
     }
     writechar(EOF_MARK);                         /* send end-of-file mark */
     exit(0);                                     /* and exit with success code. */
}


/*      write a character to the standard output device;
        if the write fails display a message on the standard
        error device and abort the program.
*/

writechar(c)
char c;

{   if( (putchar(c) == EOF) && (c != EOF_MARK) )
    {   fputs("clean: disk full",stderr);
        exit(1);
    }
}
```

Figure 13-2 continued.

One valuable application of the *CLEAN* filter is to rescue assembly-
language source files. If you accidentally edit such a source file in document
mode, the resulting file may cause the Assembler to generate spurious or
confusing error messages. *CLEAN* lets you turn the source file back into
something the Assembler can cope with, without losing all those painful
hours of editing.

Another handy application for *CLEAN* is to list a word–processed document file in raw form on the printer, complete with print commands:

CLEAN <MYFILE.WS >PRN:

Contrasting the C and assembly-language versions of this filter provides some interesting lessons. The C version is 80 lines long and compiles to a 4896-byte EXE file, whereas the ASM version is 168 lines long and compiles to a 761-byte EXE file. Following the programmer's rule of thumb that the smaller of two equivalent programs is probably the more efficient, the ASM implementation appears to be clearly in the lead.

But wait! When we compare the two versions in action, we get some surprising results. The C program is nearly ten times faster. This is because the C program's *getchar* and *putchar* functions are actually macros that access 512-byte file buffers internal to the C runtime library. So, although the program appears to be processing the input stream a character at a time, in actuality it is making only two calls to MS-DOS to read and write the buffers for each 512 characters.

The assembly-language version, on the other hand, has no hidden blocking and deblocking of the data. It does just what it appears to do, which is to make two calls to MS-DOS for every character processed. As an experiment, I modified the assembly-language equivalents of the *getchar* and *putchar* routines to perform record reads and writes in 1024-byte blocks. The resulting program was about 1500 bytes long and ran three times faster than the C equivalent. However, the final ASM program (which is not shown in this book) also took about three times longer to write and debug than the C version!

As usual, the choice of a programming language is not as clear cut as it may appear at first. It is undeniable that you can always get the fastest possible program by using assembly language rather than a high-level language, even one as well-optimized as Microsoft C. But performance considerations must be balanced against the time and expense required for programming, especially if the program will not be used very often.

SECTION II

MS-DOS
Programming
Reference

Introduction to Section II

Each of the MS-DOS interrupts (20H through 2FH), and the individual functions available through Int 21H, are described in this section in detail. I've used the following standard format:

- The upper left corner of a heading gives the interrupt and function number in hexadecimal and decimal, and the upper right corner indicates which versions of MS-DOS support the function (the filled icon means that the version does support the function; the open icon means that it does not). This is followed by the body of the entry, which includes . . .
- The name of the function;
- A clear English description of the function's purpose;
- The input parameters to the function;
- The values or status codes returned by the function;
- Notes giving information or warnings about the function;
- An example invoking the function in assembly language.

Comparisons to CP/M and UNIX are included where appropriate.

For purposes of clarity, the examples may include code that would not always be necessary in an application (such as code that explicitly sets the segment registers before each call to MS-DOS—these are frequently initialized at the first entrance to a program and then left unchanged). Also, please keep in mind that error codes may differ, depending upon the version of MS-DOS you are using.

One of several methods that a program can use to perform a final exit. Informs the operating system that the program is completely finished and that the memory it occupied can be released. MS-DOS then takes the following actions:

- Restores the termination handler vector from PSP:000AH.
- Restores the Ctrl-C vector from PSP:000EH.
- **2** **3** Restores the critical error handler vector from PSP:0012H.
- Flushes the file buffers.
- Transfers to the termination handler address.

If the program is returning to COMMAND.COM, control transfers to COMMAND.COM's resident portion and the transient portion of COMMAND.COM is reloaded (if necessary) and receives control. If a batch file is in progress, the next line of the file is fetched and interpreted; otherwise, a prompt is issued for the next user command.

Call with: **CS**   = segment address of program segment prefix
                        (thus, cannot be used from an EXE file)

Returns: **Nothing**

Notes: ● Any files that have been written to by the program using FCBs should be closed before performing this exit call; otherwise, data may be lost.

● **2** **3** This is the traditional way to exit from an application program, for those programmers who have been with MS-DOS since its earliest incarnations. However, under versions 2 and 3, the preferred method of termination is via Int 21H function 31H (terminate and stay resident) or function 4CH (terminate with return code).

● This function is equivalent to the CP/M BDOS function 00H. However, when a program exits under MS-DOS version 2.0 or above, control may return via the EXEC call (function 4BH) to a parent program that "spawned" the exiting program, rather than to the operating system.

Example: Perform a final exit.

```
        int    20h              ;transfer to DOS.
```

Int 21H (33)
General

Most of the MS-DOS operating-system services are invoked through software interrupt 21H. Using these services, a program can inspect disk directories, make or delete files, read or write records within files, set or read the real-time clock, and perform many other functions in a hardware-independent manner.

The MS-DOS functions available through Int 21H are well standardized and available on any MS-DOS system. Programs that perform all I/O through these functions will run on any machine that supports MS-DOS.

Calling sequence:	MS-DOS services can be invoked in several different ways: – Load the AH register with the function number and other registers with the call-specific parameters, then execute an Int 21H. This is the recommended method and produces the cleanest, most compact object code.

```
mov    ah,function_number
  .
  .
  .
int    21h
```

- 2 3 Load the AH register with the function number and other registers with the call-specific parameters, then execute a long call to offset 0050H in the program segment prefix. This linkage is available only with MS-DOS version 2.0 and above.
- Load the CL register with the function number and other registers with the call-specific parameters, then execute an intrasegment call to offset 0005H in the PSP, which contains a long call to the MS-DOS function dispatcher. This method is valid only for function calls 00H through 24H. Register AX is always destroyed if this method is used; otherwise, the results are the same as for the first two methods discussed above. The precursor to MS-DOS, the 86-DOS originally sold by Seattle Computer Products (see Chapter 1), included this linkage mechanism to facilitate easy conversion of CP/M-80 programs, and its use should now be avoided.

The contents of all registers are preserved across MS-DOS calls, except for those registers that are used to return results. The only exceptions are function 63H, which was added in MS-DOS version 2.25 to support extended character sets, and function 4BH (EXEC).

For those functions that are comparable to CP/M functions (00H through 24H), success or failure codes are typically returned in register AL. For those functions that were added in MS-DOS version 2.0 and above, the carry flag is cleared to indicate success or set to indicate failure, and in the latter case a more specific error code is also returned in register AX.

Int 21H (33)
Function summary

Hex	Dec	Function name	Input type	MS-DOS version
0	0	Program terminate		1 2 3
1	1	Character input with echo		1 2 3
2	2	Character output		1 2 3
3	3	Auxiliary input		1 2 3
4	4	Auxiliary output		1 2 3
5	5	Printer output		1 2 3
6	6	Direct console I/O		1 2 3
7	7	Unfiltered character input without echo		1 2 3
8	8	Character input without echo		1 2 3
9	9	Output character string		1 2 3
0A	10	Buffered input		1 2 3
0B	11	Get input status		1 2 3
0C	12	Reset input buffer and then input		1 2 3
0D	13	Disk reset		1 2 3
0E	14	Set default disk drive	D	1 2 3
0F	15	Open file	F	1 2 3
10	16	Close file	F	1 2 3
11	17	Search for first match	F	1 2 3
12	18	Search for next match	F	1 2 3
13	19	Delete file	F	1 2 3
14	20	Sequential read	F	1 2 3
15	21	Sequential write	F	1 2 3
16	22	Create or truncate file	F	1 2 3
17	23	Rename file	F	1 2 3

*Key to input type:
A = ASCIIZ string
D = drive number
F = file control block
H = handle

(continued)

Hex	Dec	Function name	Input type	MS-DOS version
18	24	Reserved		1 2 3
19	25	Get default disk drive		1 2 3
1A	26	Set disk transfer area address		1 2 3
1B	27	Get allocation information for default drive		1 2 3
1C	28	Get allocation information for specified drive	D	1 2 3
1D	29	Reserved		1 2 3
1E	30	Reserved		1 2 3
1F	31	Reserved		1 2 3
20	32	Reserved		1 2 3
21	33	Random read	F	1 2 3
22	34	Random write	F	1 2 3
23	35	Get file size	F	1 2 3
24	36	Set random record number	F	1 2 3
25	37	Set interrupt vector		1 2 3
26	38	Create program segment prefix		1 2 3
27	39	Random block read	F	1 2 3
28	40	Random block write	F	1 2 3
29	41	Parse filename		1 2 3
2A	42	Get system date		1 2 3
2B	43	Set system date		1 2 3
2C	44	Get system time		1 2 3
2D	45	Set system time		1 2 3
2E	46	Set verify flag		1 2 3
2F	47	Get disk transfer area address		1 2 3
30	48	Get MS-DOS version number		1 2 3
31	49	Terminate and stay resident		1 2 3
32	50	Reserved		1 2 3
33	51	Get or set Ctrl-Break flag		1 2 3
34	52	Reserved		1 2 3
35	53	Get interrupt vector		1 2 3
36	54	Get free disk space	D	1 2 3
37	55	Reserved		1 2 3
38	56	Get or set country		1 2 3

(continued)

Hex	Dec	Function name	Input type	MS-DOS version
39	57	Create subdirectory	A	1 2 3
3A	58	Delete subdirectory	A	1 2 3
3B	59	Set current directory	A	1 2 3
3C	60	Create or truncate file	A	1 2 3
3D	61	Open file	A	1 2 3
3E	62	Close file	H	1 2 3
3F	63	Read file or device	H	1 2 3
40	64	Write to file or device	H	1 2 3
41	65	Delete file	A	1 2 3
42	66	Move file pointer	H	1 2 3
43	67	Get or set file attributes	A	1 2 3
44	68	Device driver control (IOCTL)	H, D	1 2 3
45	69	Duplicate handle	H	1 2 3
46	70	Force duplicate of handle	H	1 2 3
47	71	Get current directory	D	1 2 3
48	72	Allocate memory		1 2 3
49	73	Release memory		1 2 3
4A	74	Modify memory allocation		1 2 3
4B	75	Execute program		1 2 3
4C	76	Terminate with return code		1 2 3
4D	77	Get return code		1 2 3
4E	78	Search for first match	A	1 2 3
4F	79	Search for next match	A	1 2 3
50	80	Reserved		1 2 3
51	81	Reserved		1 2 3
52	82	Reserved		1 2 3
53	83	Reserved		1 2 3
54	84	Get verify flag		1 2 3
55	85	Reserved		1 2 3
56	86	Rename file	A	1 2 3
57	87	Get or set file date and time	H	1 2 3
58	88	Get or set allocation strategy		1 2 3
59	89	Get extended error information		1 2 3

(continued)

Hex	Dec	Function name	Input type	MS-DOS version
5A	90	Create temporary file	A	1 2 3
5B	91	Create new file	A	1 2 3
5C	92	Record locking	H	1 2 3
5D	93	Reserved		1 2 3
5E	94	Get machine name/printer setup		1 2 3
5F	95	Assign list entry		1 2 3
60	96	Reserved		1 2 3
61	97	Reserved		1 2 3
62	98	Get program segment prefix address		1 2 3
63	99	Get lead byte table*		1 **2** 3

*MS-DOS 2.25 only

Int 21H (33)
Functions by class

Hex	Dec	Function name	Input type	MS-DOS version
Program termination				
0	0	Terminate		**1 2 3**
31	49	Terminate and stay resident		1 **2 3**
4C	76	Terminate with return code		1 **2 3**
Character input				
1	1	Character input with echo		**1 2 3**
3	3	Auxiliary input		**1 2 3**
6	6	Direct console I/O		**1 2 3**
7	7	Unfiltered character input without echo		**1 2 3**
8	8	Character input without echo		**1 2 3**

*Key to input type:
A = ASCIIZ string
D = drive number
F = file control block
H = handle

(continued)

Hex	Dec	Function name	Input type	MS-DOS version
0A	10	Buffered input		1 2 3
0B	11	Get input status		1 2 3
0C	12	Reset input buffer and then input		1 2 3
Character output				
2	2	Character output		1 2 3
4	4	Auxiliary output		1 2 3
5	5	Printer output		1 2 3
6	6	Direct console I/O		1 2 3
9	9	Output character string		1 2 3
Disk control				
0D	13	Disk reset		1 2 3
0E	14	Set default disk drive	D	1 2 3
19	25	Get default disk drive		1 2 3
1B	27	Get allocation information for default drive		1 2 3
1C	28	Get allocation information for specified drive	D	1 2 3
2E	46	Set verify flag		1 2 3
36	54	Get free disk space	D	1 2 3
54	84	Get verify flag		1 2 3
58	88	Get or set allocation strategy		1 2 3
File operations				
0F	15	Open file	F	1 2 3
10	16	Close file	F	1 2 3
11	17	Search for first match	F	1 2 3
12	18	Search for next match	F	1 2 3
13	19	Delete file	F	1 2 3
16	22	Create or truncate file	F	1 2 3
17	23	Rename file	F	1 2 3
23	35	Get file size	F	1 2 3
3C	60	Create or truncate file	A	1 2 3
3D	61	Open file	A	1 2 3
3E	62	Close file	H	1 2 3

(continued)

Hex	Dec	Function name	Input type	MS-DOS version
41	65	Delete file	A	1 2 3
43	67	Get or set file attributes	A	1 2 3
45	69	Duplicate handle	H	1 2 3
46	70	Force duplicate of handle	H	1 2 3
4E	78	Search for first match	A	1 2 3
4F	79	Search for next match	A	1 2 3
56	86	Rename file	A	1 2 3
57	87	Get or set file date and time	H	1 2 3
5A	90	Create temporary file	A	1 2 3
5B	91	Create new file	A	1 2 3

Record operations

Hex	Dec	Function name	Input type	MS-DOS version
14	20	Sequential read	F	1 2 3
15	21	Sequential write	F	1 2 3
21	33	Random read	F	1 2 3
22	34	Random write	F	1 2 3
24	36	Set random record number	F	1 2 3
27	39	Random block read	F	1 2 3
28	40	Random block write	F	1 2 3
3F	63	Read file or device	H	1 2 3
40	64	Write to file or device	H	1 2 3
42	66	Move file pointer	H	1 2 3
5C	92	Record locking	H	1 2 3

Directory operations

Hex	Dec	Function name	Input type	MS-DOS version
39	57	Create subdirectory	A	1 2 3
3A	58	Delete subdirectory	A	1 2 3
3B	59	Set current directory	A	1 2 3
47	71	Get current directory	D	1 2 3

Disk transfer area address

Hex	Dec	Function name	Input type	MS-DOS version
1A	26	Set disk transfer area address		1 2 3
2F	47	Get disk transfer address		1 2 3

(continued)

Hex	Dec	Function name	Input type	MS-DOS version
System date and time				
2A	42	Get system date		1 2 3
2B	43	Set system date		1 2 3
2C	44	Get system time		1 2 3
2D	45	Set system time		1 2 3
Dynamic memory allocation				
48	72	Allocate memory		1 2 3
49	73	Release memory		1 2 3
4A	74	Modify memory allocation		1 2 3
58	88	Get or set allocation strategy		1 2 3
Network functions				
44	68	Device driver control (IOCTL)		1 2 3
5E	94	Get machine name/printer setup		1 2 3
5F	95	Assign list entry		1 2 3
Miscellaneous system functions				
25	37	Set interrupt vector		1 2 3
26	38	Create program segment prefix		1 2 3
29	41	Parse filename		1 2 3
30	48	Get MS-DOS version number		1 2 3
33	51	Get or set Ctrl–Break flag		1 2 3
35	53	Get interrupt vector		1 2 3
38	56	Get or set country		1 2 3
44	68	Device driver control	H, D	1 2 3
4B	75	Execute program		1 2 3
4D	77	Get return code		1 2 3
59	89	Get extended error information		1 2 3
62	98	Get program segment prefix address		1 2 3
63	99	Get lead byte table*		1 2 3
Reserved functions (not implemented or not documented)				
18	24	Reserved		1 2 3
1D	29	Reserved		1 2 3
1E	30	Reserved		1 2 3

(continued)

Hex	Dec	Function name	Input type	MS-DOS version
1F	31	Reserved		▮ 2 3
20	32	Reserved		▮ 2 3
32	50	Reserved		▯ 2 3
34	52	Reserved		▯ 2 3
37	55	Reserved		▯ 2 3
50	80	Reserved		▯ 2 3
51	81	Reserved		▯ 2 3
52	82	Reserved		▯ 2 3
53	83	Reserved		▯ 2 3
55	85	Reserved		▯ 2 3
5D	93	Reserved		▯ 2 3
60	96	Reserved		▯ 2 3
61	97	Reserved		▯ 2 3

*MS-DOS 2.25 only.

Int 21H (33)
Function 00H (0)
Program terminate

1 2 3

One of several methods that a program can use to make a final exit.

Equivalent to performing an Int 20H. Informs the operating system that the program is completely finished and that the memory it occupied can be released. MS-DOS then takes the following actions:

- Restores the termination handler vector from PSP:000AH.
- Restores the Ctrl–C vector from PSP:000EH.
- **2 3** Restores the critical error handler vector from PSP:0012H.
- Flushes the file buffers.
- Transfers to the termination handler address.

If the program is returning to COMMAND.COM, control transfers to COMMAND.COM's resident portion and the transient portion of COMMAND.COM is reloaded (if necessary) and receives control. If a batch file is in progress, the next line of the file is fetched and interpreted; otherwise, a prompt is then issued for the next user command.

(continued)

| Call with: | AH | = 00 |
| | CS | = segment address of program segment prefix |

| Returns: | Nothing |

Notes:	•	Any files that have been written to by the program using FCBs should be closed before performing this exit call; otherwise, data may be lost.
	•	Other methods of performing a final exit are: – Int 20H (should be avoided); – Int 21H function 31H; – Int 21H function 4CH; – Int 27H (should be avoided).
	•	**2 3** Functions 31H and 4CH are the preferred methods of making a final exit, since they allow the terminating program to pass a return code to the command processor or parent program.
	•	This function is logically equivalent to CP/M BDOS function 00H. However, when a program exits under MS-DOS, control may return via the EXEC call (function 4BH) to a parent program that "spawned" the exiting program, rather than to the operating system.

| Example: | Perform a final exit. |

```
        mov   ah,0          ;function number
        int   21h           ;transfer to DOS.
```

Int 21H (33)
Function 01H (1)
Character input with echo

1 Inputs a character from the keyboard, then echoes it to the display. If no character is ready, waits until one is available.

2 3 Reads a character from the standard input device and echoes the character to the standard output device. If no character is ready, waits until one is available. I/O can be redirected. (If I/O has been redirected, there is no way to detect EOF.)

| Call with: | AH | = 01 |

| Returns: | AL | = 8-bit data (input) |

(continued)

Notes:
- If the character read is a Ctrl-C, an Int 23H is executed.

- To read extended ASCII codes (such as the special function keys F1 through F10) on the IBM PCs and compatibles, you must call this function twice. The first call returns zero, to signal the presence of an extended code.

- See also functions 06H, 07H, and 08H, which provide character input with various combinations of echo and/or Ctrl-C sensing.

- **2 3** You can also read the keyboard by performing a read (function 3FH) using the predefined handle for the standard input device (0000), if input has not been redirected.

- This function is logically equivalent to CP/M BDOS function 01H, except for the Ctrl-C handling.

Example: Read one character from the keyboard into register AL, echo it to the display, and store it in the variable *input_char*.

```
            mov    ah,1              ;function number
            int    21h               ;transfer to DOS.
            mov    input_char,al     ;save character.
            .
            .
            .
input_char  db     0
```

Int 21H (33)
Function 02H (2)
Character output

1 Outputs a character to the currently active video display.

2 3 Outputs a character to the standard output device. Output can be redirected. (If I/O has been redirected, there is no way to detect disk full.)

Call with:	AH	= 02
	DL	= 8-bit data (usually an ASCII character code)

Returns: Nothing

Notes:
- When writing to the video display, a backspace code (08H) causes the cursor to move left one position, then remain at that position.

- If a Ctrl-C or Ctrl-Break is detected by MS-DOS after the requested character is output, an Int 23H is executed.

(continued)

- You can also send strings to the display by performing a write (function 40H) using the predefined handle for the standard output device (0001) or the predefined handle for the standard error device (0002), if output has not been redirected.

- This function is logically equivalent to CP/M BDOS function 02H, except for the Ctrl-C handling.

Example: Transmit the character * to the standard output device.

```
mov   ah,2          ;function number
mov   dl,'*'        ;character to output
int   21h           ;transfer to DOS.
```

Int 21H (33)
Function 03H (3)
Auxiliary input

▨ Reads a character from the first serial port.

▨ ▨ Reads a character from the standard auxiliary device. This defaults to the first serial port (COM1), unless explicitly redirected with the MS-DOS MODE command.

Call with: **AH** = 03

Returns: **AL** = 8-bit data (input)

Notes:
- In most MS-DOS systems, the serial device is unbuffered and is not interrupt driven. If the auxiliary device is sending data faster than your program can process it, characters may be lost.

- At startup on the IBM PC, PC-DOS initializes the first serial port to 2400 baud, no parity, 1 stop bit, and 8 data bits. Other implementations of MS-DOS may initialize the auxiliary device differently.

- There is no way for your program to read the status of the auxiliary device or to detect I/O errors (such as lost characters) through this function call. On the IBM PC, more precise control can be obtained by calling ROM BIOS Int 14H (see Section 3), or by driving the communications controller directly.

- ▨ ▨ You can also input from the auxiliary device by performing a read (function 3FH) using the predefined handle for the standard auxiliary device (0003), or by opening a channel to the AUX device.

- If a Ctrl-C or Ctrl-Break is detected by MS-DOS, an Int 23 is executed.

- This function is logically equivalent to CP/M BDOS function 03H.

(continued)

Example: Read a character from the standard auxiliary input device into register AL, and store it in the variable *input_char.*

```
        mov   ah,3              ;function number
        int   21h              ;transfer to DOS.
        mov   input_char,al    ;save character.
        .
        .
        .
input_char   db   0
```

Int 21H (33)
Function 04H (4)
Auxiliary output

■ Outputs a character to the first serial port.

② ③ Outputs a character to the standard auxiliary device. This defaults to the first serial port (COM1), unless explicitly redirected with the MS-DOS MODE command.

Call with:	AH	= 04
	DL	= 8-bit data (output)

Returns:	Nothing

Notes:	●	If the output device is busy, this function waits until the device is ready to accept a character.
	●	There is no way to poll the status of the auxiliary output device using this function. On the IBM PC, more precise control can be obtained by calling ROM BIOS Int 14H (see Section 3), or by driving the communications controller directly.
	●	② ③ You can also send strings to the auxiliary device by performing a write (function 40H) using the predefined handle for the standard auxiliary device (0003), or by opening a channel to the AUX device.
	●	If a Ctrl-C or Ctrl-Break is detected by MS-DOS, an Int 23 is executed.
	●	This function is logically equivalent to CP/M BDOS function 04H.

Example: Output the character * to the auxiliary device.

```
        mov   ah,4             ;function number
        mov   dl,'*'           ;character to output
        int   21h             ;transfer to DOS.
```

Int 21H (33)
Function 05H (5)
Printer output

1 **2** **3**

1 Sends a character to the first list device (PRN or LPT1).

2 **3** Sends a character to the standard list device. This defaults to the printer on the first parallel port (LPT1), unless explicitly redirected with the MS-DOS MODE command.

| Call with: | AH | = 05 |
| | DL | = 8-bit data (output) |

| Returns: | Nothing |

Notes:	•	If the printer is busy, this function waits until the printer is ready to accept the character.
	•	If a Ctrl-C or Ctrl-Break is detected by MS-DOS, an Int 23H is executed.
	•	There is no standardized way to poll the status of the printer under MS-DOS.
	•	**2** **3** You can obtain more flexible list-device output by performing a write (function 40H) using the predefined handle for the standard list device (0004), or by opening the PRN logical device as a file.
	•	This function is logically equivalent to CP/M BDOS function 05H.

Example: Send the character ∗ to the list device.

```
mov   ah,5          ;function number
mov   dl,'*'        ;character to output
int   21h           ;transfer to DOS.
```

Int 21H (33)
Function 06H (6)
Direct console I/O

1 **2** **3**

Used by programs that need to read and write all possible characters and control codes without any interference from the operating system.

1 Reads a character from the keyboard or returns zero if none is ready; or writes a character to the display.

2 **3** Reads a character from the standard input device or returns zero if no character is ready; or writes a character to the standard output device. I/O can be redirected. (If I/O has been redirected, there is no way to detect EOF or disk full.)

(continued)

Call with:	AH	= 06
	DL	= function requested
		00H–0FEH	*if output request (i.e., DL contains character to be output)*
		0FFH	*if input request*

Returns: If call was output request:
Nothing

If call was input request and a character is ready:
Zero flag   = clear
AL   = 8-bit data (input)

If call was input request and no character is ready:
Zero flag   = set

Notes:
- When this function is used, no special action is taken if a Ctrl-C or Ctrl-Break is detected.

- To read extended ASCII codes (such as the special function keys F1 through F10) on the IBM PCs and compatibles, you must call this function twice. The first call returns zero, to signal the presence of an extended code.

- See also functions 01H, 07H, 08H, and 0AH, which can be used to read data from the standard input device, and functions 02H and 09H, which can be used to write characters to the standard output device.

- 2 3 You can also read and write the keyboard by performing a read (function 3FH) or write (function 40H) using the predefined handle for the standard input or output device (0000 and 0001, respectively), if they have not been redirected.

- This function is logically equivalent to CP/M BDOS function 06H. BDOS function 06H as implemented in MP/M II, CP/M-86, and MP/M-86 added other status and data-read services invoked by passing parameters 0FDH and 0FEH in register DL.

Examples: Send the character * to the standard output device.

```
        mov   ah,6          ;function number
        mov   dl,'*'        ;character to output
        int   21h           ;transfer to DOS.
```

Read one character from the standard input device. If no character is waiting, wait until one is available.

```
wait:   mov   ah,6          ;function number
        mov   dl,0ffh       ;parameter for read
        int   21h           ;transfer to DOS.
        jz    wait          ;wait until character ready.
```

Int 21H (33)
Function 07H (7)
Unfiltered character input without echo

◼ Reads a character from the keyboard without echoing it to the display. If no character is ready, waits until one is available.

▨ ▣ Reads a character from the standard input device without copying it to the standard output device. If no character is ready, waits until one is available. I/O can be redirected.

Call with:	AH	= 07

Returns:	AL	= 8-bit data (input)

Notes:	•	When this function is used, no special action is taken if a Ctrl-C or Ctrl-Break is detected. If such detection is required, use function 08H. (Reads of the standard input using function 3FH will also detect Ctrl-C and Ctrl-Break.)
	•	To read extended ASCII codes (such as the special function keys F1 through F10) on the IBM PCs and compatibles, you must call this function twice. The first call returns zero, to signal the presence of an extended code.
	•	▨ ▣ You can also read the keyboard by performing a read (function 3FH) using the predefined handle for the standard input device (0000), if input has not been redirected.
	•	There is no logical equivalent for this function under CP/M.

Example: Read one character from the keyboard into register AL without echoing the character to the display, and store it in the variable *input_char*.

```
            mov    ah,7              ;function number
            int    21h               ;transfer to DOS.
            mov    input_char,al     ;save character.
            .
            .
            .
input_char  db     0
```

Int 21H (33)
Function 08H (8)
Character input without echo

■ Reads a character from the keyboard without echoing it to the display. If no character is ready, waits until one is available.

② ③ Reads a character from the standard input device without copying it to the standard output device. If no character is ready, waits until one is available. I/O can be redirected. (If I/O has been redirected, there is no way to detect EOF.)

Call with:	AH	= 08

Returns:	AL	= 8-bit data (input)

Notes:
- If a Ctrl-C or Ctrl-Break is detected, an Int 23H is executed. If you require input without this possible interference, use function 07H.
- See functions 01H, 06H, 0AH, and 0CH for other character-input services.
- To read extended ASCII codes (such as the special function keys F1 through F10) on the IBM PCs and compatibles, you must call this function twice. The first call returns zero, to signal the presence of an extended code.
- ② ③ You can also read the keyboard by performing a read (function 3FH) using the predefined handle for the standard input device (0000), if it has not been redirected.
- There is no logical equivalent for this function under CP/M.

Example: Read one character from the standard input device into register AL, allowing detection of Ctrl-C or Ctrl-Break, and store the character in the variable *input_char*.

```
          mov    ah,8                  ;function number
          int    21h                   ;transfer to DOS.
          mov    input_char,al         ;save character.
          .
          .
          .
input_char    db    0
```

Int 21H (33)
Function 09H (9)
Output character string

■ Sends a string of characters to the display.

② ③ Sends a string of characters to the standard output device. Output can be redirected.

| Call with: | AH | = 09 |
| | DS:DX | = segment:offset of string |

| Returns: | Nothing |

Notes:

- This is the string equivalent of function 02H.

- The string must be terminated with the character $ (24H), which is not transmitted. Any other ASCII codes, including control codes, can be embedded in the string.

- See functions 02H and 06H for single-character output to the video display or standard output device.

- ② ③ You can also send strings to the display by performing a write (function 40H) using the predefined handle for the standard output device (0001), if it has not been redirected.

- This function is logically equivalent to CP/M BDOS function 09H.

Example: Send the string *Hello there*, followed by a carriage return and linefeed, to the standard output device.

```
cr          equ     0dh
lf          equ     0ah
            .
            .
            .
            mov     ah,9                ;function number
            mov     dx,seg mystring     ;address of string
            mov     ds,dx               ;to be output
            mov     dx,offset mystring
            int     21h                 ;transfer to DOS.
            .
            .
            .
mystring    db      'Hello there',cr,lf,'$'
```

1 Reads a line from the keyboard and places it in a user-designated buffer.

2 **3** Reads a string of bytes from the standard input device, up to and including an ASCII carriage return (0DH), and places them in a user-designated buffer. Input can be redirected. (If I/O has been redirected, there is no way to detect EOF.)

| Call with: | AH | = 0AH |
| | DS:DX | = segment:offset of buffer |

| Returns: | Nothing |

Notes:	•	The first byte of the buffer specifies the maximum number of characters it can hold (1 through 255); this value must be supplied by the user. The second byte of the buffer is filled in by MS-DOS to signal the number of characters actually read, excluding the carriage return. If the buffer fills to one less than the maximum number of characters it can hold, subsequent input is ignored and the bell is sounded until a carriage return is detected.
	•	This input function is buffered with type-ahead capability, and all of the standard keyboard editing commands are active.
	•	If a Ctrl-C or Ctrl-Break is detected, an Int 23 is executed.
	•	See functions 01H, 06H, 07H, and 08H for single-character input.
	•	**2** **3** You can also read complete strings from the keyboard by performing a read (function 3FH) using the predefined handle for the standard input device (0000), if input has not been redirected.
	•	This function is logically equivalent to CP/M BDOS function 0AH, except for the keyboard editing commands.

| Example: | Read one string containing a maximum of 80 characters, plus a carriage-return byte, from the standard input device, and place it in *my_buffer*. |

```
                mov    ah,0ah                ;function number
                mov    dx,seg my_buffer      ;address of input
                mov    ds,dx                 ;buffer
                mov    dx,offset my_buffer
                int    21h                   ;transfer to DOS
                .
                .
my_buffer       db     81                    ;max. len. of string, including CR.
                db     0                     ;actual len. of string read.
                db     81 dup (0)            ;string buffer
```

Int 21H (33)
Function 0BH (11)
Get input status

1 Checks whether a character is available from the keyboard.

2 **3** Checks whether a character is available from the standard input device. Input can be redirected.

Call with:	AH	= 0BH	

Returns:	AL	= 00	if no character available
		0FFH	if character available

Notes:	●	If an input character is waiting, this function continues to return a true flag until the character is actually input by the program with a call to function 01H, 06H, 07H, 08H, or 0AH.
	●	If a Ctrl-C or Ctrl-Break is detected, an Int 23H is executed. (This function is the same as IOCTL—Int 21H function 44H, service 6.)
	●	This function is logically equivalent to CP/M BDOS function 0BH.

Example: Check whether a character is available from the standard input device.

```
        mov   ah,0bh          ;function number
        int   21h             ;transfer to DOS.
        or    al,al           ;character waiting?
        jnz   char_ready      ;jump if character ready.
                .
char_ready:     .
                .
```

Int 21H (33)
Function 0CH (12)
Reset input buffer and then input

1 Clears the type-ahead buffer and then invokes one of the keyboard input functions.

2 **3** Clears the standard input buffer and then invokes one of the character input functions. Input can be redirected.

(continued)

Call with:	AH	= 0CH
	AL	= number of input function to be invoked after resetting buffer; must be 01H, 06H, 07H, 08H, or 0AH
	If function 0AH:	
	DS:DX	= segment:offset of input buffer

Returns:	If function 0AH: Nothing	
	If function 01H, 06H, 07H, or 08H:	
	AL	= 8-bit data (input)

Notes:
- The intent of this function is to discard any input characters that have been stored in the type-ahead buffer within MS-DOS, forcing the program to wait for an input character (usually a keyboard entry) that is truly entered after the program's request.
- There is no logical equivalent for this function under CP/M.

Example: Clear the type-ahead buffer, then wait for a character to be entered, echoing it and then returning it in AL. Store the character in the variable *input_char*.

```
        mov   ah,0ch          ;function number
        mov   al,1            ;subfunction = input character
        int   21h            ;transfer to DOS.
        mov   input_char,al   ;save character.
        .
        .
        .
input_char   db   0
```

Int 21H (33)
Function 0DH (13)
Disk reset

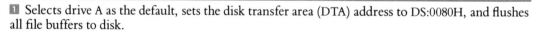

1 Selects drive A as the default, sets the disk transfer area (DTA) address to DS:0080H, and flushes all file buffers to disk.

2 3 Flushes all file buffers; i.e., all data for which a write has been requested by your programs, but which has been buffered within MS-DOS, is physically written to the disk.

| Call with: | AH | = 0DH |

| Returns: | Nothing |

(continued)

Notes: • This function does *not* update the disk directory for any files that are still open. If your program fails to properly close all files before the disk is removed, and the files have changed size, the data forced out to the disk by this function may still be inaccessible because the directory entries will not be correct.

• When running 3Com Ethernet, calling this function after closing all files forces a new copy of the file allocation table (FAT) for a network volume to be read from the server. This allows applications to share files that can be extended; however, only one application should be allowed to write to such a file.

• ▣ This function has a documented effect that is equivalent to that of CP/M BDOS function 0DH.

• ▢ ▣ The effects on the default drive and DTA address are not documented.

Example: Flush all MS-DOS internal disk buffers.

```
mov   ah,0dh         ;function number
int   21h            ;transfer to DOS.
```

Int 21H (33)
Function 0EH (14)
Set default disk drive

Selects a specified drive to be the current, or default, disk drive, and returns the total number of logical drives in the system.

| Call with: | AH | = 0EH |
| | DL | = drive code (0 = A, 1 = B, etc.) |

| Returns: | AL | = number of logical drives in system |

Notes: • ▣ 16 drive designators (0 through 0FH) are available.

• ▢ 63 drive designators (0 through 3FH) are available.

• ▣ 26 drive designators (0 through 19H) are available.

• To preserve upward compatibility, new applications should limit themselves to the drive letters A through Z (A = 0, B = 1, etc.).

• *Logical drives* means the total number of block devices: floppy-disk drives, simulated disk drives (RAM disks), and hard-disk drives. Sometimes a single physical hard-disk drive is partitioned into two or more logical drives.

• In a single-drive IBM PC-compatible system, AL will return 2, because the drive can be accessed as either drive A or drive B and the system therefore has two logical drives.

(continued)

- On the IBM PC, if you need to know the actual number of physical floppy-disk drives in the system, you can use ROM BIOS software Int 11H.

- This function is logically equivalent to CP/M BDOS function 0EH, except for the added capability of returning the number of drives.

Example: Make logical drive B the current, or default, disk drive. Store the number of logical drives in the system in the variable *drives*.

```
        mov     ah,0eh          ;function number
        mov     dl,1            ;drive 1 = B
        int     21h             ;transfer to DOS.
        mov     drives,al       ;save total drives in system.
          .
          .
          .
drives  db      0
```

Int 21H (33)
Function 0FH (15)
Open file

Opens a file and makes it available for subsequent read/write operations.

Call with:	AH	= 0FH
	DS:DX	= segment:offset of file control block

Returns: If function successful (file found):
AL = 00

FCB filled in by MS-DOS as follows:

drive-code field (offset 0000H)	= specified drive (1 = A, 2 = B, etc.), if original drive code = 0 (default drive)
current-block field (offset 000CH)	= 00
record-size field (offset 000EH)	= 0080H (128)
2 3 file-size field (offset 0010H)	= file size from directory
2 3 date field (offset 0014H)	= date from directory
2 3 time field (offset 0016H)	= time from directory

If function failed (file not found):
AL = 0FFH

(continued)

Notes:	●	If your program is going to use a record size other than 128 bytes, it should set the record-size field at FCB offset 000EH *after* the file is successfully opened and *before* any disk operation.
	●	If random access is to be performed, the calling program must also set the random-record field after successfully opening the file.
	●	This function is logically equivalent to CP/M BDOS function 0FH, except for the differences in FCB formats.

Example:	Attempt to open the file named *QUACK.DAT* on the disk in the default drive.

```
          mov   ah,0fh            ;function number
          mov   dx,seg my_fcb     ;address of file control
          mov   ds,dx             ;block
          mov   dx,offset my_fcb
          int   21h               ;transfer to DOS.
          cmp   al,0ffh           ;check status.
          je    no_file           ;jump if file not found.
                .
no_file:        .
                .
my_fcb    db    0                 ;use default drive.
          db    'QUACK    '       ;filename, 8 characters
          db    'DAT'             ;extension, 3 characters
          db    25 dup (0)        ;remainder of FCB
```

Int 21H (33)
Function 10H (16)
Close file

Closes a file, and updates the disk directory if the file has been modified or extended.

Call with:	AH	= 10H
	DS:DX	= segment:offset of file control block

Returns:	AL	= 00	if directory update successful
		0FFH	if file not found in directory

Notes:	●	**2** MS-DOS manuals document that the function will return an error code if the disk has been changed while a file is open. However, in real life, MS-DOS version 2 usually fails to detect this condition. Instead, the directory and file allocation table of the previous disk may be written onto the new disk, making it thoroughly unusable.
	●	This function is logically equivalent to CP/M BDOS function 10H.

(continued)

Example: Close the file that was previously opened using the FCB named *my_fcb*.

```
mov   ah,10h              ;function number
mov   dx,seg my_fcb       ;address of file
mov   ds,dx               ;control block
mov   dx,offset my_fcb
int   21h                 ;transfer to DOS.
cmp   al,0ffh             ;check status.
je    error               ;jump, close failed.
         .
error:   .
         .
```

Int 21H (33)
Function 11H (17)
Search for first match

Searches the current directory on the disk in the designated drive for a matching filename.

Call with: AH   = 11H
             DS:DX   = segment:offset of file control block

Returns: If function successful (matching filename found):
             AL   = 00
             Buffer at current disk transfer area (DTA) address set up as an unopened normal FCB or extended FCB, depending upon which type of FCB was input to function

             If function failed (matching filename not found):
             AL   = 0FFH

Notes: •   It is very important to use function 1AH to set the DTA to point to a buffer of adequate size before using this call.

         •   The wildcard character ? is allowed in the filename. If ? is used, this function will return the first matching filename.

         •   An extended FCB must be used to search for files that are marked with the system, hidden, read-only, subdirectory, or volume-label attributes.

         •   If an extended FCB is used, its attribute byte determines the type of search that will be performed. If the attribute byte (byte 0) contains zero, only ordinary files are found. If the volume-label attribute bit is set, only volume labels will be returned (if any are present). If any other attribute or combination of attributes is set (such as hidden, system, or read-only), those files and all ordinary files will be matched.

(continued)

- This function derives from CP/M function 11H and does not provide access to other subdirectories. For full access to the hierarchical file structure, use function 4EH.

Example: Search for the first file in the current subdirectory with the extension *COM*.

```
        mov     ah,1ah              ;function = set DTA
        mov     dx,seg buffer       ;address of scratch area
        mov     ds,dx
        mov     dx,offset buffer
        int     21h                 ;transfer to DOS.
        mov     ah,11h              ;function = search
        mov     dx,offset my_fcb    ;address of FCB
        int     21h                 ;transfer to DOS.
        cmp     al,0ffh             ;check status.
        je      no_match            ;jump if no match.
                .
                .
no_match:       .
                .
buffer  db      37 dup (0)

my_fcb  db      0
        db      '????????'          ;wildcard filename
        db      'COM'               ;extension = COM
        db      25 dup (0)
```

Int 21H (33)
Function 12H (18)
Search for next match

Given that a previous call to function 11H has been successful, returns the next matching filename (if any).

Call with: AH   = 12H
            DS:DX   = segment:offset of file control block

Returns: If function successful (matching filename found):
          AL   = 00
          Buffer at current disk transfer area (DTA) address set up as an unopened normal FCB or extended FCB, depending upon which type of FCB was input to function

          If function failed (no more matching filenames in current directory):
          AL   = 0FFH

(continued)

Notes:

- This function assumes that the FCB used as input has been properly initialized by a previous call to function 11H (and possible subsequent calls to function 12H), and that the filename or extension being searched for contained at least one *?* wildcard character.

- As with function 11H, it is very important to use function 1AH to set the DTA to a buffer of adequate size before using this function.

- This function is equivalent to CP/M function 12H and does not provide access to other subdirectories. For full access to the hierarchical file structure, use functions 4EH and 4FH.

Example: Assuming a previous successful call to function 11H, search for the next file in the current subdirectory with the extension *.COM*.

```
                  mov    ah,1ah              ;function = set DTA
                  mov    dx,seg buffer       ;address of scratch
                  mov    ds,dx               ;area
                  mov    dx,offset buffer
                  int    21h                 ;transfer to DOS.
                  mov    ah,12h              ;function = search next
                  mov    dx,offset my_fcb    ;address of FCB
                  int    21h                 ;transfer to DOS.
                  cmp    al,0ffh             ;check status.
                  je     no_match            ;jump if no match.
                         .
no_match:                .
                         .
buffer            db     37 dup (0)

my_fcb            db     0
                  db     '????????'          ;wildcard filename
                  db     'COM'               ;extension = COM
                  db     25 dup (0)
```

Deletes all matching files from the current subdirectory.

| Call with: | AH | = 13H |
| | DS:DX | = segment:offset of file control block |

| Returns: | AL | = 00 | if file(s) deleted |
| | | 0FFH | if no matching file(s) found, or all matching files were read-only |

Notes:
- The wildcard character *?* is allowed in the filename; if *?* is present and there is more than one matching filename, all matching files will be deleted.
- This function is equivalent to CP/M BDOS function 13H and does not provide full access to the hierarchical file structure under MS-DOS version 2.0 or above. To delete files in other subdirectories, use function 41H.

Example: Delete the file named *MYFILE.DAT* from the current subdirectory on the disk in the current drive.

```
            mov   ah,13h              ;function number
            mov   dx,seg my_fcb       ;address of file
            mov   ds,dx               ;control block
            mov   dx,offset my_fcb
            int   21h                 ;transfer to DOS.
            cmp   al,0ffh             ;check status.
            je    error               ;jump, delete failed.
                  .
error:            .
                  .
my_fcb      db    0                   ;drive = default
            db    'MYFILE  '          ;filename, 8 characters
            db    'DAT'               ;extension, 3 characters
            db    25 dup (0)          ;remainder of FCB
```

Reads the next sequential block of data from a file, then increments the file pointer appropriately.

Call with:	AH	= 14H	
	DS:DX	= segment:offset of previously opened file control block	

Returns:	AL	= 00	if read successful
		01	if end of file
		02	if segment wrap
		03	if partial record read at end of file

Notes:
- The record is read into memory at the current disk transfer area (DTA) address, specified by the most recent call to function 1AH. If the size of the record and location of the DTA are such that a segment overflow or wraparound would occur, the function fails with a return code of 2.

- The size of the block of data to be read is specified by the record-size field (offset 000EH) of the file control block (FCB).

- The file location of the block to be read is specified by the combination of the current-block field (offset 000CH) and the current-record field (offset 0020H) of the FCB. These fields are also automatically incremented by this function.

- If a partial record is read at the end of the file, it is padded to the requested record length with zeros.

- This function is logically equivalent to CP/M BDOS function 14H, except for the added capability of user-specified record sizes.

Example: Read a block of data 1024 bytes long from the current position in the file specified by the previously opened FCB named *my _fcb*.

```
            mov     ah,14h                  ;function number
            mov     dx,seg my_fcb           ;address of file
            mov     ds,dx                   ;control block
            mov     dx,offset my_fcb
            mov     word ptr ds:my_fcb+0eh,1024  ;set record size.
            int     21h                     ;transfer to DOS.
            or      al,al                   ;check status.
            jnz     error                   ;jump, read failed.
            .
error:      .
            .
my_fcb      db      0                       ;drive = default
            db      'QUACK   '              ;filename, 8 characters
            db      'DAT'                   ;extension, 3 characters
            db      25 dup (0)              ;remainder of FCB
```

Int 21H (33)
Function 15H (21)
Sequential write

Writes the next sequential block of data into a file, then increments the file pointer appropriately.

| Call with: | AH | = 15H | |
| | DS:DX | = segment:offset of previously opened file control block | |

Returns	AL	= 00	if write successful
		01	if disk full
		02	if segment wrap

Notes:

- The record is written (logically, not necessarily physically) to the file from memory at the current disk transfer area (DTA) address, specified by the most recent call to function 1AH. If the size of the record and location of the DTA are such that a segment overflow or wraparound would occur, the function fails with a return code of 2.

- The size of the block of data to be written is specified by the record-size field (offset 000EH) of the file control block (FCB).

- The file location of the block that will be written is specified by the combination of the current-block field (offset 000CH) and the current-record field (offset 0020H) of the FCB. These fields are also automatically incremented by this function.

- This function is logically equivalent to CP/M BDOS function 15H, except for the added capability of user-specified record sizes.

Example: Write a block of data 1024 bytes long to the current position in the file specified by the previously opened FCB named *my_fcb*.

```
          mov   ah,15h                        ;function number
          mov   dx,seg my_fcb                 ;address of file
          mov   ds,dx                         ;control block
          mov   dx,offset my_fcb
          mov   word ptr ds:my_fcb+0eh,1024   ;set record size.
          int   21h                           ;transfer to DOS.
          or    al,al                         ;check status.
          jnz   error                         ;jump if write failed.
             .
error:       .
             .
my_fcb    db    0                             ;drive = default
          db    'QUACK   '                    ;filename, 8 characters
          db    'DAT'                          ;extension, 3 characters
          db    25 dup (0)                    ;remainder of FCB
```

Creates a new directory entry in the current subdirectory, or truncates any existing file with the specified name to zero length. Opens the file for subsequent read/write operations.

Call with:	AH	= 16H	
	DS:DX	= segment:offset of unopened file control block	

Returns:	AL	= 00	if file created successfully
		0FFH	if file not created (no directory space)

Notes:
- Since an existing file with the specified name is truncated to zero length by this function (i.e., all data in the file is irretrievably lost), this function must be used with caution.

- If this function is called with an extended file control block (FCB), the new file may be assigned an attribute during its creation by setting the appropriate bit in the extended FCB's attribute byte.

- Since this function also opens the file, a subsequent call to function 0FH is not required.

- 2 3 This function is logically equivalent to CP/M BDOS function 16H, and does not provide full access to the hierarchical file structure. To create files in other subdirectories, use function 3CH, 5AH, or 5BH.

Example: Create a file in the current subdirectory with the name found in the FCB named *my_fcb*.

```
            mov     ah,16h              ;function number
            mov     dx,seg my_fcb       ;address of file
            mov     ds,dx               ;control block
            mov     dx,offset my_fcb
            int     21h                 ;transfer to DOS.
            cmp     al,0ffh             ;check status.
            je      error               ;jump, create failed.
            .
error:      .
            .
my_fcb      db      0                   ;drive = default
            db      'QUACK   '          ;filename, 8 characters
            db      'DAT'               ;extension, 3 characters
            db      25 dup (0)          ;remainder of FCB
```

Int 21H (33)
Function 17H (23)
Rename file

Alters the name of all matching files in the current subdirectory on the disk in the specified drive.

| Call with: | AH | = 17H |
| | DS:DX | = segment:offset of "special" file control block |

| Returns: | AL | = 00 | if file(s) renamed |
| | | 0FFH | if no matching file(s) found, or if new name matched that of existing file |

Notes:
- The special file control block (FCB) has a drive code, filename, and extension in the customary position, and a second filename starting 6 bytes after the first (offset 0011H).
- The ? wildcard character can be used in the first filename. Every file matching the first file specification will be renamed to match the second file specification.
- If the second file specification contains any occurrences of ?, those letters in the original name are left unchanged.
- The function terminates if the new name matches that of an existing file.
- ■2 ■3 This function is logically equivalent to CP/M BDOS function 17H, and does not provide full access to the hierarchical file structure. To rename files in other subdirectories, use function 56H.

Example: Rename the file *OLDNAME.DAT* as *NEWNAME.DAT*.

```
              mov   ah,17h              ;function number
              mov   dx,seg rename_fcb   ;address of file
              mov   ds,dx               ;control block
              mov   dx,offset rename_fcb
              int   21h                 ;transfer to DOS.
              cmp   al,0ffh             ;check status.
              je    no_match            ;jump, rename failed.
              .
no_match:     .
              .
rename_fcb    db    0                   ;drive = default
              db    'OLDNAME '          ;old file name, 8 characters
              db    'DAT'               ;old extension, 3 characters
              db    5 dup (0)           ;reserved area
              db    'NEWNAME '          ;new file name, 8 characters
              db    'DAT'               ;new extension, 3 characters
              db    15 dup (0)          ;reserved area
```

Int 21H (33)
Function 18H (24)
Reserved

Int 21H (33)
Function 19H (25)
Get default disk drive

Returns the drive code of the current or default disk drive.

Call with:	AH	= 19H

Returns:	AL	= drive code (0 = A, 1 = B, etc.)

Note:
- To set the default drive, use function 0EH.
- Some other MS-DOS functions use drive codes beginning at 1 (that is, 1 = A, etc.), and reserve drive code zero for the default drive.
- This function is logically equivalent to CP/M BDOS function 19H.

Example: Get the current disk-drive code and store it in the variable *drive*.

```
        mov   ah,19h          ;function number
        int   21h             ;transfer to DOS.
        mov   drive,al        ;save drive code.
        .
        .
        .
drive         db    0
```

Int 21H (33)
Function 1AH (26)
Set disk transfer area address

Specifies the memory address to be used for subsequent FCB disk operations.

Call with: AH   = 1AH
           DS:DX = segment:offset of disk transfer area

Returns: Nothing

Notes:
- If this function is never called by the program, the disk transfer area (DTA) defaults to a 128-byte buffer at offset 0080H in the program segment prefix.

- In general, it is the programmer's responsibility to ensure that the buffer area specified is large enough for any disk operation that will use it. The only exception to this is that MS-DOS will detect and abort disk transfers that would wrap around within the current segment or overflow into the next segment.

- Use function 2FH to determine the current DTA address.

- As well as being required before normal FCB record reads or writes, this function must also be used before calling function 11H, 12H, 4EH, or 4FH, to provide a scratch area for use by MS-DOS during directory searches.

- This function is logically equivalent to CP/M BDOS function 1AH. Under CP/M-86, the segment of the DTA address must be passed using a separate call (function 33H).

Example: Set the current DTA address to point to an area of memory whose first byte is labeled *my_buffer.*

```
          mov   ah,1ah              ;function number
          mov   dx,seg my_buffer    ;address of disk
          mov   ds,dx               ;transfer area
          mov   dx,offset my_buffer
          int   21h                 ;transfer to DOS.
          .
          .
          .
my_buffer db    128 dup (?)
```

Obtains selected information about the default disk drive, and a pointer to the identification byte from its file allocation table (FAT).

Call with:	AH	= 1BH

Returns:	AL	= number of sectors per cluster
	DS:BX	= segment:offset of FAT identification byte
	CX	= size of physical sector (in bytes)
	DX	= number of clusters for default drive

Notes:
- The first byte (the identification byte) of the FAT designates the type of disk and has the following meanings for 5¼-inch disks:

0FFH	Dual-sided, 8 sectors per track, floppy disk
0FEH	Single-sided, 8 sectors per track, floppy disk
0FDH	Dual-sided, 9 sectors per track, floppy disk
0FCH	Single-sided, 9 sectors per track, floppy disk
0F9H	Dual-sided, 15 sectors per track, floppy disk (PC/AT high-capacity drives)
0F8H	Fixed disk (any size)

- To obtain information about disks other than the one in the default drive, use function 1CH. See also function 36H, which returns similar information.

- **1** The address returned in DS:BX points to the actual FAT.

  2 **3** The address returned in DS:BX points only to a copy of the FAT's identification byte; the memory above that address cannot be assumed to contain the FAT or any other useful information. If direct access to the FAT is required, use Int 25H (absolute disk read) to transfer the FAT from the disk.

- There is no equivalent for this function under CP/M.

Example: Use function 1BH to determine whether the current disk drive is fixed or removable.

```
                mov     ah,1bh              ;function number
                int     21h                 ;transfer to DOS.
                cmp     byte ptr ds:[bx],0f8h  ;compare ID byte.
                je      fixed               ;jump, fixed disk.
                jmp     floppy              ;else assume floppy.
        fixed:  .
                .
        floppy: .
```

Int 21H (33)
Function 1CH (28)
Get allocation information for specified drive

Obtains selected information about the specified disk drive, and a pointer to the identification byte from its file allocation table (FAT).

| Call with: | AH | = 1CH |
| | DL | = drive code (0 = default, 1 = A, etc.) |

Returns:	AL	= number of sectors per cluster
	DS:BX	= segment:offset of FAT identification byte
	CX	= size of physical sector (in bytes)
	DX	= number of clusters for default or specified drive

Notes:
- The first byte (the identification byte) of the FAT designates the type of disk and has the following meanings for the 5¼-inch disks:

0FFH	Dual-sided, 8 sectors per track, floppy disk
0FEH	Single-sided, 8 sectors per track, floppy disk
0FDH	Dual-sided, 9 sectors per track, floppy disk
0FCH	Single-sided, 9 sectors per track, floppy disk
0F9H	Dual-sided, 15 sectors per track, floppy disk (PC/AT high-capacity drives)
0F8H	Fixed disk (any size)

- In general, this call is identical to function 1BH except for the ability to designate a specific disk drive. It is not available under MS-DOS version 1. See also function 36H, which returns similar information.

- The address returned in DS:BX points only to a copy of the FAT's identification byte; the memory above that address cannot be assumed to contain the FAT or any other useful information. If direct access to the FAT is required, use Int 25H (absolute disk read) to transfer the FAT from the disk.

- There is no equivalent for this function under CP/M.

Example: Use function 1CH to determine whether disk drive C is fixed or removable.

```
        mov   ah,1ch              ;function number
        mov   dl,03               ;drive code, 3 = C
        int   21h                 ;transfer to DOS.
        cmp   byte ptr ds:[bx],0f8h   ;compare ID byte.
        je    fixed               ;jump, fixed disk.
        jmp   floppy              ;else assume floppy.
fixed:  .
        .
        .
floppy: .
```

Int 21H (33)
Function 1DH (29)
Reserved
          ■1 ■2 ■3

Int 21H (33)
Function 1EH (30)
Reserved
          ■1 ■2 ■3

Int 21H (33)
Function 1FH (31)
Reserved
          ■1 ■2 ■3

Int 21H (33)
Function 20H (32)
Reserved
          ■1 ■2 ■3

Int 21H (33)
Function 21H (33)
Random read

Reads a selected record from a file into memory.

Call with:	AH	= 21H	
	DS:DX	= segment:offset of previously opened file control block	

Returns:	AL	= 00	if read successful
		01	if end of file
		02	if segment wrap
		03	if partial record read at end of file

Notes:
- The record is read into memory at the current disk transfer area (DTA) address, specified by the most recent call to function 1AH. It is the programmer's responsibility to ensure that this area is large enough for any record that will be transferred. If the size of the record and location of the DTA are such that a segment overflow or wraparound would occur, the function fails with a return code of 2.

- The file location of the data to be read is specified by the combination of the random-record field (offset 0021H) and the record-size field (offset 000EH) of the FCB. The current-block and current-record fields are updated to agree with the random-record field as a side effect of the function.

- The current file pointers are not advanced after this function; i.e., if the random-record field in the FCB is not altered by the application program before another random-read call is issued, the same file location will be accessed. This is in contrast to functions 27H and 28H.

- If a partial record is read at the end of the file, it is padded to the requested record length with zeros.

- This function is logically equivalent to CP/M BDOS function 21H, except for the added capability of user-specified record sizes.

(continued)

Example: Open the file *MYFILE.DAT*, set the record length to 1024 bytes, then read record
           number 4 from the file into the memory area named *buffer*.

```
               mov    ah,0fh                      ;function = open
               mov    dx,seg my_fcb               ;address of file
               mov    ds,dx                       ;control block
               mov    dx,offset my_fcb
               int    21h                         ;transfer to DOS.
               or     al,al                       ;check open status.
               jnz    no_file                     ;jump if not found.
               mov    ah,1ah                      ;function = set DTA
               mov    dx,offset buffer            ;buffer address for read
               int    21h                         ;transfer to DOS.
                                                  ;set record size.
               mov    word ptr my_fcb+0eh,1024
               mov    word ptr my_fcb+21h,4       ;set random record no.
               mov    ah,21h                      ;function = random read
               mov    dx,offset my_fcb            ;address of file
                                                  ;control block
               int    21h                         ;transfer to DOS.
               or     al,al                       ;check status.
               jnz    no_read                     ;jump, read failed.
                      .
 no_read:             .
                      .
 no_file:             .
                      .
 my_fcb        db     0                           ;drive = default
               db     'MYFILE  '                  ;filename, 8 characters
               db     'DAT'                       ;extension, 3 characters
               db     25 dup (0)                  ;remainder of FCB

 buffer        db     4096 dup (?)
```

Int 21H (33)
Function 22H (34)
Random write

① ② ③

Writes data from memory into a selected record in a file.

Call with:	AH	= 22H	
	DS:DX	= segment:offset of previously opened file control block	

Returns:	AL	= 00		if write successful
		01		if disk full
		02		if segment wrap

(continued)

Notes:	•	The record is written (logically, not necessarily physically) to the file from memory at the current disk transfer area (DTA) address, specified by the most recent call to function 1AH. If the size of the record and location of the DTA are such that a segment overflow or wraparound would occur, the function fails with a return code of 2.
	•	The file location of the data to be written is specified by the combination of the random-record field (offset 0021H) and the record-size field (offset 000EH) of the FCB. The current-block and current-record fields are updated to agree with the random-record field as a side effect of the function.
	•	The current file pointers are not advanced after this function; i.e., if the random-record field in the FCB is not altered by the application program before another random-write call is issued, the same file location will be accessed. This is in contrast to functions 27H and 28H.
	•	This function is logically equivalent to CP/M BDOS function 22H, except for the added capability of user-specified record sizes.

Example: Open the file *MYFILE.DAT*, set the record length to 1024 bytes, write record number 4 in the file from the memory area named *buffer*, then close the file.

```
            mov    ah,0fh              ;function = open
            mov    dx,seg my_fcb       ;address of FCB
            mov    ds,dx
            mov    dx,offset my_fcb
            int    21h                 ;transfer to DOS.
            or     al,al               ;check status.
            jnz    no_file             ;jump, file not found.
            mov    ah,1ah              ;function = set DTA
            mov    dx,offset buffer    ;buffer address for write
            int    21h                 ;transfer to DOS.
                                       ;set record size.
            mov    word ptr my_fcb+0eh,1024
            mov    word ptr my_fcb+21h,4 ;set random record no.
            mov    ah,22h              ;function = random write
            mov    dx,offset my_fcb    ;address of FCB
            int    21h                 ;transfer to DOS.
            or     al,al               ;check status.
            jnz    no_write            ;jump, write failed.
            mov    ah,10h              ;function = close
            int    21h                 ;transfer to DOS.
            or     al,al               ;check status.
            jnz    no_close            ;jump, close failed.
            .
no_write:   .
            .
no_file:    .
            .
no_close:   .
            .
```

(continued)

```
my_fcb          db      0                       ;drive = default
                db      'MYFILE  '              ;filename, 8 characters
                db      'DAT'                   ;extension, 3 characters
                db      25 dup (0)              ;remainder of FCB
                .
                .
                .
buffer          db      4096 dup (?)            ;buffer for record
                                                ;being written
```

Int 21H (33)
Function 23H (35)
Get file size in records

Searches for a matching file in the current subdirectory; if one is found, fills a file control block (FCB) with file size information in terms of record count.

Call with:	AH	= 23H
	DS:DX	= segment:offset of unopened file control block

Returns:	If matching file found:
	AL = 00
	FCB's random-record field (offset 0021H) set to corresponding number of records in file, rounded up to next even record
	If no matching file found:
	AL = 0FFH

Notes:	●	Before calling this function, you must set the appropriate value in the FCB's record-size field (offset 000EH). Note that the way this function is used contrasts with normal file open or create functions, which use FCBs wherein the record size must be set *after* the function is successful.
	●	This function is similar to CP/M BDOS function 23H.

Example:	Determine the size in bytes of the file *MYFILE.DAT*, and leave the result in registers DX:AX.

(continued)

```
            mov    ah,23h                    ;function number
            mov    dx,seg my_fcb             ;address of FCB
            mov    ds,dx
            mov    dx,offset my_fcb
            mov    word ptr my_fcb+0eh,1     ;set record size = 1 byte.
            int    21h                       ;transfer to DOS.
            or     al,al                     ;check status.
            jnz    no_file                   ;jump, file not found.
                                             ;load file size in bytes.
            mov    ax,word ptr my_fcb+21h
            mov    dx,word ptr my_fcb+23h
                   .
no_file:           .
                   .
my_fcb      db     0                         ;drive = default
            db     'MYFILE  '                ;filename, 8 characters
            db     'DAT'                     ;extension, 3 characters
            db     25 dup (0)                ;remainder of FCB
```

Int 21H (33)
Function 24H (36)
Set random record number

Sets the random-record field of a file control block (FCB) to correspond to the current file position as recorded in the opened FCB.

Call with:	AH	= 24H
	DS:DX	= segment:offset of previously opened file control block

Returns:	Register contents not affected
	Random-record field modified in file control block

Notes:	•	This function is used when switching from sequential to random I/O within a file. The current random-record position is derived from the record-size, current-block, and current-record fields of the FCB.
	•	This function is logically equivalent to CP/M BDOS function 24H.

Example:	After a series of sequential record transfers have been performed using the FCB named *my_fcb*, find the current random-record position in the file, then leave the record number in DX.

(continued)

```
                    mov     ah,24h                      ;function number
                    mov     dx,seg my_fcb               ;address of FCB
                    mov     ds,dx
                    mov     dx,offset my_fcb
                    int     21h                         ;transfer to DOS.
                                                        ;get random record no.
                    mov     dx,word ptr my_fcb+21h
                    .
                    .
                    .
        my_fcb      db      0                           ;drive = default
                    db      'MYFILE '                   ;filename, 8 characters
                    db      'DAT'                       ;extension, 3 characters
                    db      25 dup (0)                  ;remainder of FCB
```

Int 21H (33)
Function 25H (37)
Set interrupt vector

Initializes a machine interrupt vector to point to an interrupt handling routine.

Call with:	AH	= 25H
	AL	= machine interrupt number
	DS:DX	= segment:offset of interrupt handling routine

| Returns: | Nothing |

| Notes: | • | This is the approved way to modify machine interrupt vectors under MS-DOS. It will help ensure proper operation under Microsoft Windows, TopView and other multitasking systems that run on top of MS-DOS. |
| | • | If an interrupt vector is going to be modified, the original contents of the vector should first be obtained using function 35H and saved, then restored using function 25H when your program exits. The only exceptions to this are Interrupts 22H, 23H, and 24H, which are automatically restored by MS-DOS from information in the program segment prefix. |

| Example: | Force any divide-by-zero machine faults to transfer to an interrupt handler named *zero_div*. |

(continued)

```
                mov    ah,25h                 ;function number
                mov    al,0                   ;interrupt number
                mov    dx,seg zero_div        ;address of interrupt
                mov    ds,dx                  ;handler
                mov    dx,offset zero_div
                int    21h                    ;transfer to DOS.
                       .
zero_div:              .
                       .
```

Int 21H (33)
Function 26H (38)
Create program segment prefix

Copies the program segment prefix (PSP) of the currently executing program to a specified segment address in free memory, then updates the new PSP to make it usable by another program.

| Call with: | AH | = 26H |
| | DX | = segment of new program segment prefix |

Returns: **Nothing**

Notes:
- After the executing program's PSP is copied into the new segment, the memory-size information in the new segment is updated appropriately and the current contents of the termination handler (Int 22H), Ctrl–Break handler (Int 23H), and critical error handler (Int 24H) interrupt vectors are saved starting at offset 000AH.

- This function does not load another program, or in itself cause one to be executed.

- **2** **3** This call has been rendered obsolete in MS-DOS versions 2.0 and above by function 4BH (EXEC), and its use should be avoided.

Example: Create a new PSP 64K above the currently executing program. (This example assumes that the running program was loaded as a COM file, so that the CS register points to its PSP throughout its execution. If the running program was loaded as an EXE file, the address of the PSP must be obtained by saving the original contents of the DS and ES registers at entrance, or, under MS-DOS version 3, through function 62H.)

```
                mov    ah,26h                 ;function number
                mov    dx,cs                  ;segment current program
                                              ;is running at.
                add    dx,1000h               ;add 64 kbytes as
                                              ;paragraph address.
                int    21h                    ;transfer to DOS.
```

Reads one or more sequential records from a file into memory, starting at a designated file location.

Call with:	AH	= 27H	
	CX	= number of records to be read	
	DS:DX	= segment:offset of previously opened file control block	

Returns:	AL	= 00	if all requested records read
		01	if end of file
		02	if segment wrap
		03	if partial record read at end of file
	CX	= actual number of records read	

Notes:

- The records are read into memory starting at the current disk transfer area (DTA) address, specified by the most recent call to function 1AH. It is the programmer's responsibility to ensure that this area is large enough for the group of records that will be transferred. If the size of the record and location of the DTA are such that a segment overflow or wraparound would occur, the function may read one or more records before failing with a return code of 2.

- This function assumes that the FCB's record-size field (offset 000EH) and random-record field (offset 0021H) are appropriately set. The record size defaults to 128 bytes after a successful open or create, if the user does not otherwise modify it.

- If a partial record is read at the end of the file, the remainder of the record is padded with zeros.

- After the disk transfer is performed, the random-record, current-block, and current-record fields of the FCB are updated to point to the next record in the file.

- This function is similar to function 21H (random read), except that it allows you to transfer multiple records with one call to MS-DOS.

Example: Read four 1024-byte records, starting at record number 8, into the memory area named *buffer*, using the FCB named *my_fcb*.

(continued)

```
                  mov    ah,1ah                    ;function = set DTA
                  mov    dx,seg buffer             ;address of buffer
                  mov    ds,dx                     ;for records
                  mov    dx,offset buffer
                  int    21h                       ;transfer to DOS.
                  mov    ah,27h                    ;function = block read
                  mov    dx,seg my_fcb             ;address of FCB
                  mov    ds,dx
                  mov    dx,offset my_fcb
                  mov    word ptr my_fcb+21h,8     ;set random record no.
                                                   ;set record size.
                  mov    word ptr my_fcb+0eh,1024
                  mov    cx,4                      ;number of blocks to read
                  int    21h                       ;transfer to DOS.
                  or     al,al                     ;check status.
                  jnz    error                     ;jump if partial read
                  .                                ; or read failed.
        error:    .
                  .
        my_fcb    db     0                         ;drive = default
                  db     'MYFILE  '                ;filename, 8 characters
                  db     'DAT'                     ;extension, 3 characters
                  db     25 dup (0)                ;remainder of FCB
                  .
                  .
                  .
        buffer    db     4096 dup (?)
```

Int 21H (33)
Function 28H (40)
Random block write

■1 ■2 ■3

Writes one or more sequential records from memory to a file, starting at a designated file location.

Call with:	AH	= 28H	
	CX	= number of records to be written	
	DS:DX	= segment:offset of previously opened file control block	

Returns:	AL	= 00	if all requested records written
		01	if disk full
		02	if segment wrap
	CX	= actual number of records written	

(continued)

Notes:
- The records are written from memory starting at the current disk transfer area (DTA) address, specified by the most recent call to function 1AH. If the size of the record and location of the DTA are such that a segment overflow or wrap-around would occur, the function may write one or more records before failing with a return code of 2.

- This function assumes that the FCB's record-size field (offset 000EH) and random-record field (offset 0021H) are appropriately set. The record size defaults to 128 bytes after a successful open or create, if the user does not otherwise modify it.

- After the disk transfer is performed, the random-record, current-block, and current-record fields of the FCB are updated to point to the next record in the file.

- If this function is called with CX = zero, no data is written to the disk, but the file is extended or truncated to the length specified by the combination of the random-record field and the record-size field.

- This function is similar to function 22H (random write), except that it allows you to transfer multiple records with one call to MS-DOS.

Example: Write four 1024-byte records, starting at record number 8, to the disk from the memory area named *buffer*, using the FCB named *my_fcb*.

```
            mov     ah,1ah                  ;function = set DTA
            mov     dx,seg buffer           ;address of buffer
            mov     ds,dx                   ;for write
            mov     dx,offset buffer
            int     21h                     ;transfer to DOS.
            mov     ah,28h                  ;function = block write
            mov     cx,4                    ;number of records
            mov     dx,seg my_fcb           ;address of FCB
            mov     ds,dx
            mov     dx,offset my_fcb
            mov     word ptr my_fcb+21h,8   ;set random record no.
                                            ;set record size.
            mov     word ptr my_fcb+0eh,1024
            int     21h                     ;transfer to DOS.
            or      al,al                   ;check status.
            jnz     error                   ;jump if write error.
                    .
error:              .
                    .
my_fcb      db      0                       ;drive = default
            db      'MYFILE  '              ;filename, 8 characters
            db      'DAT'                   ;extension, 3 characters
            db      25 dup (0)              ;remainder of FCB
                    .
                    .
                    .
buffer      db      4096 dup (?)
```

Int 21H (33)
Function 29H (41)
Parse filename

Parses a text string into the various fields of a file control block (FCB).

Call with:	AH	= 29H		
	AL	= flags to control parsing		
		Bit 3	*= 1*	*if extension field in an existing FCB will be modified only if an extension is specified in string being parsed*
			0	*if extension field will be modified regardless; if no extension in parsed string, extension field is set to ASCII blanks*
		Bit 2	*= 1*	*if default filename in an existing FCB will be modified only if a filename is specified in string being parsed*
			0	*if filename will be modified regardless; if no filename in parsed string, filename field is set to ASCII blanks*
		Bit 1	*= 1*	*if drive ID byte in resulting FCB will be modified only if a drive is specified in string being parsed*
			0	*if drive ID byte will be modified regardless; if no drive specifier in parsed string, drive-code field is set to 0 (default)*
		Bit 0	*= 1*	*if leading separators will be scanned off (ignored)*
			0	*if leading separators will not be scanned off*
	DS:SI	= segment:offset of text string		
	ES:DI	= segment:offset of file control block		

Returns:	AL	= 00	if no global (wildcard) characters encountered
		01	if parsed string contains global characters
		0FFH	if drive specifier invalid
	DS:SI	= segment:offset of first character after parsed filename	
	ES:DI	= segment:offset of formatted unopened file control block	

Notes:
- This call regards the following characters as separator characters:
  1   : . ; , = + tab space / " [ ]
  2 3   : . ; , = + tab space

- This call regards all control characters and the following as terminator characters:
  : . ; , = + tab space < > | / " [ ]

- If no valid filename is present in the string to be parsed, upon return ES:DI + 1 points to an ASCII blank.

- If the character * occurs in a filename or extension, it and all remaining characters in the corresponding field in the FCB are set to ?.

- This function (and file control blocks in general) cannot be used with file specifications that include a path.

(continued)

Example: Parse the string *my_name* into the FCB named *my_fcb*.

```
                mov   ah,29h              ;function number
                mov   al,01               ;skip leading separators.
                mov   si,seg my_name      ;address of text string
                mov   ds,si               ;to be parsed
                mov   si,offset my_name
                mov   di,seg my_fcb       ;address of FCB
                mov   es,di               ; to be initialized
                mov   di,offset my_fcb
                int   21h                 ;transfer to DOS.
                cmp   al,0ffh             ;check status.
                je    error               ;jump, drive invalid.
                  .
        error:    .
                  .
        my_name   db    'D:QUACK.DAT',0   ;string to be parsed.
                                          ;0 terminates filename.
        my_fcb    db    37 dup (0)        ;becomes file control block.
```

Int 21H (33)
Function 2AH (42)
Get system date

Obtains the system day of the month, day of the week, month, and year.

Call with:	AH	= 2AH

Returns:	CX	= year (1980 through 2099)
	DH	= month (1 through 12)
	DL	= day (1 through 31)
	Under MS-DOS version 1.10 and above:	
	AL	= day of week (0 = Sunday, 1 = Monday, etc.)

Note: • This function's register format is the same as that required for function 2BH (set system date).

(continued)

Example: Obtain the system date and store its components in the variables *year*, *day*, and *month*.

```
        mov   ah,2ah          ;function number
        int   21h             ;transfer to DOS.
        mov   year,cx         ;save year (word).
        mov   month,dh        ;save month (byte).
        mov   day,dl          ;save day (byte).
        .
        .
        .
year    dw    0
month   db    0
day     db    0
```

Int 21H (33)
Function 2BH (43)
Set system date

Initializes the system-clock driver to a specific date. The system time is not affected.

Call with:	AH	= 2BH
	CX	= year (1980 through 2099)
	DH	= month (1 through 12)
	DL	= day (1 through 31)

Returns:	AL	= 00	if date set successfully
		0FFH	if date not valid (ignored)

Note: • This function's register format is the same as that for function 2AH (get system date).

Example: Set the system date according to the contents of the variables *year*, *day*, and *month*.

```
        mov   ah,2bh          ;function number
        mov   cx,year         ;get year (word).
        mov   dh,month        ;get month (byte).
        mov   dl,day          ;get day (byte).
        int   21h             ;transfer to DOS.
        or    al,al           ;check status.
        jnz   error           ;jump, date was invalid.
        .
error:  .
        .
year    dw    0
month   db    0
day     db    0
```

Obtains the time of day from the system real-time clock driver, converted to hours, minutes, seconds, and hundredths of seconds.

Call with:	AH	= 2CH

Returns:	CH	= hour (0 through 23)
	CL	= minutes (0 through 59)
	DH	= seconds (0 through 59)
	DL	= hundredths of seconds (0 through 99)

Notes:
- This function's register format is the same as that required for function 2DH (set system time).
- In many systems, the real-time clock does not have a resolution of single hundredths of seconds. As a result, the values returned in DL may be discontinuous on some machines.

Example: Obtain the system time and store its two major components in the variables *hours* and *minutes*.

```
        mov   ah,2ch           ;function number
        int   21h              ;transfer to DOS.
        mov   hours,ch         ;save hours (byte).
        mov   minutes,cl       ;save minutes (byte).
        .
        .
        .
hours   db    0
minutes db    0
```

Int 21H (33)
Function 2DH (45)
Set system time

Initializes the system real-time clock to a specified hour, minute, second, and hundredth of second. The system date is not affected.

Call with:	AH	= 2DH	
	CH	= hour (0 through 23)	
	CL	= minutes (0 through 59)	
	DH	= seconds (0 through 59)	
	DL	= hundredths of seconds (0 through 99)	

Returns:	AL	= 00	if time set successfully
		0FFH	if time not valid (ignored)

Note:	●	The register format is the same as that for function 2CH (get system time).

Example:	Set the system time according to the contents of the variables *hours* and *minutes*. Force the current seconds and hundredths of seconds to zero.

```
              mov   ah,2dh         ;function number
              mov   ch,hours        ;get hours (byte).
              mov   cl,minutes      ;get minutes (byte).
              mov   dx,0            ;force seconds and
                                    ;hundredths to zero.
              int   21h            ;transfer to DOS.
              or    al,al          ;check status.
              jnz   error          ;jump, time was invalid.
                    .
error:              .
                    .
hours         db    0
minutes       db    0
```

Int 21H (33)
Function 2EH (46)
Set verify flag

Turns off or turns on the operating-system flag for automatic read-after-write verification of data.

Call with:	AH	= 2EH	
	AL	= 00	if turning off verify flag
		01	if turning on verify flag
	DL **1** **2**	= 00	

Returns:	Nothing

Notes:
- This function provides increased data integrity by allowing the user to force a read-after-write verification of all data written to the disk, if that capability is supported by the manufacturer's BIOS disk driver.
- The state of the verify flag is also controlled by the MS-DOS commands VERIFY OFF and VERIFY ON.
- The current state of the verify flag can be determined using function 54H.

Example: Save the current state of the system verify flag in the variable *vflag*, then force all subsequent disk writes to be verified.

```
        mov    ah,54h          ;function = get verify flag
        int    21h             ;transfer to DOS.
        mov    vflag,al        ;save verify flag.
        mov    ah,2eh          ;function = set verify flag
        mov    al,1            ;turn verify on.
        mov    dl,0            ; for DOS 1 and 2 compatibility
        int    21h             ;transfer to DOS.
        .
        .
        .
vflag   db     0
```

Int 21H (33)
Function 2FH (47)
Get disk transfer area address

Obtains the current address of the disk transfer area (DTA) for FCB file read/write operations.

(continued)

Call with:	AH	= 2FH

Returns:	ES:BX	= segment:offset of disk transfer area

Note:
- The DTA address is set through function 1AH. The default DTA address is a 128-byte buffer at offset 0080H in that program's program segment prefix.

Example: Determine the current DTA address and leave the result in ES:BX.

```
        mov   ah,2fh                    ;function number
        int   21h                       ;transfer to DOS.
        mov   word ptr cur_dta,bx        ;offset
        mov   word ptr cur_dta+2,es      ;segment
        .
        .
        .
cur_dta dd    0                          ;double word variable to
                                         ; hold current DTA address
```

Int 21H (33)
Function 30H (48)
Get MS-DOS version number

Returns the version number of the host MS-DOS operating system. This function is used by application programs to determine the capabilities of their environment.

Call with:	AH	= 30H

Returns:	AL ② ③	= major version number (MS-DOS 3.1 = 3, etc.)
	AH	= minor version number (MS-DOS 3.10 = 0AH (10), etc.)

Note:
- If AL returns zero, the system is a version 1 environment.
- If the MS-DOS version 1 environment is detected and version 2 or version 3 functions are required to continue, extreme care must be taken to prevent the program from terminating in an unacceptable fashion when it encounters a function that cannot be used. For example, function 4CH (terminate with return code) is not available, nor is the standard error output channel. A program requiring MS-DOS version 2.0 or above that detects an MS-DOS version 1 environment should display an error message with function 9 and then terminate with Int 21H function 0 or with Int 20H.

(continued)

Example: Get the MS-DOS version number and exit with an error message if it is not MS-DOS
version 2.0 or above.

```
            mov     ah,30h                  ;function = get version
            int     21h                     ;transfer to DOS.
            cmp     al,2                    ;is it version 2 or higher?
            jae     version_ok              ;jump, it's version 2+

                                            ;DOS 1, print message and exit.
            mov     ah,09                   ;function = display string
            mov     dx,offset message       ;address of error message
            int     21h                     ;transfer to DOS.
            mov     ah,0                    ;function = exit
            int     21h                     ;transfer to DOS.
                    .
version_ok:         .
                    .
message     db      0dh,0ah,'Wrong DOS version',0dh,0ah,'$'
```

Int 21H
Function 31H (49)
Terminate and stay resident (KEEP process)

[1] [2] [3]

Terminates a process without releasing its memory. If the program is returning to
COMMAND.COM, control transfers to COMMAND.COM's resident portion and the transient
portion of COMMAND.COM is reloaded (if necessary) and receives control. If a batch file is in
progress, the next line of the file is fetched and interpreted; otherwise, a prompt is issued for the
next user command.

Call with:	AH	= 31H
	AL	= return code
	DX	= memory size to reserve (in paragraphs)

| Returns: | Nothing |

Notes:
- This function is typically used by resident drivers or subroutine libraries that
  are called once from the MS-DOS command level and then provide services to
  other applications via a software interrupt.
- This function attempts to set the initial memory allocation block to the length
  in paragraphs specified in register DX.
- This function deals only with memory allocated when the program was
  loaded. Memory blocks requested by the application via function 48H are
  not affected.

(continued)

- The return code can be retrieved by a parent process through function 4DH (get return code). It can also be tested in batch files though the ERRORLEVEL subcommands.

- This function should be used in preference to Int 27H, since this function allows a return code to be passed, and allows more than 64k bytes to remain resident.

Example: Terminate with a return code of 1 but stay resident, reserving 16K of memory starting at the task's program segment prefix.

```
mov    ah,31h          ;function number
mov    al,1            ;return code for command
                       ;processor or parent
mov    dx,0400h        ;paragraphs to reserve
int    21h             ;transfer to DOS.
```

Int 21H (33)
Function 32H (50)
Reserved

Int 21H (33)
Function 33H (51)
Get or set Ctrl–Break flag

Determines the current status of the operating system's Ctrl–Break or Ctrl–C checking flag.

Call with:	AH	= 33H	
	If getting status of Ctrl-Break flag:		
	AL	= 00	
	If setting status of Ctrl-Break flag:		
	AL	= 01	
	DL	= 00	to turn Ctrl-Break checking off
	DL	= 01	to turn Ctrl-Break checking on

Returns:	DL	= 00	if Ctrl-Break checking off
		01	if Ctrl-Break checking on

(continued)

- When Ctrl-Break checking is in effect, the keyboard is examined for a Ctrl-Break or Ctrl-C entry whenever any operating-system input or output is requested; if one is found, control is transferred to the Ctrl-C handler (Int 23H).

- The Ctrl-Break checking flag is not part of the local environment of the process, but affects all programs. An application that alters the flag should first save the flag's original status, and then restore the original status before terminating.

Example: Save the current status of the Ctrl-Break flag in the variable *check*, then turn off Ctrl-Break checking, so that disk I/O operations will not be interrupted at an inopportune time by user's entry of a Ctrl-Break.

```
        mov     ah,33h          ;function = get
        mov     al,0            ; Control-Break flag
        int     21h             ;transfer to DOS.
        mov     check,dl        ;save flag.
        mov     ah,33h          ;now alter Control-Break
        mov     al,01           ;flag.
        mov     dl,0            ;set checking OFF.
        int     21h             ;transfer to DOS.
        .
        .
        .
check   db      0
```

Int 21H (33)
Function 34H (52)
Reserved

Int 21H (33)
Function 35H (53)
Get interrupt vector

Obtains the address of the current interrupt handler routine for the specified machine interrupt.

| Call with: | AH | = 35H |
| | AL | = interrupt number |

| Returns: | ES:BX | = segment:offset of interrupt handler |

(continued)

Note: •   Together with function 25H (set interrupt vector), this function is used by
                well-behaved application programs to modify or inspect the machine interrupt
                vector table. Use of these two functions, rather than reading and writing the
                interrupt vectors directly, is vital for proper operation under multitasking en-
                vironments such as Microsoft Windows and TopView.

Example: Obtain the address of the current interrupt handler for machine interrupt 0 (divide by
            zero). Store the segment of the interrupt handler in the variable *int0seg* and the offset
            in the variable *int0off.*

```
        mov    ah,35h           ;function number
        mov    al,0             ;interrupt type
        int    21h             ;transfer to DOS.
        mov    int0seg,es      ;segment of handler
        mov    int0off,bx      ;offset of handler
        .
        .
        .
int0seg    dw    0
int0off    dw    0
```

Int 21H (33)
Function 36H (54)
Get free disk space

Obtains selected information about a disk drive, from which the drive's capacity can be calculated.

Call with: AH   = 36H
             DL   = drive code (0 = default, 1 = A, etc.)

Returns: If specified drive valid:
             AX   = sectors per cluster
             BX   = number of available clusters
             CX   = bytes per sector
             DX   = clusters (allocation units) per drive

             If specified drive invalid:
             AX   = FFFFH

Note: •   Similar information is returned by functions 1BH and 1CH.

(continued)

Example: Calculate the capacity of disk drive C in bytes, leaving the result in registers DX:AX (this assumes that the result of *sectors/cluster* * *bytes/sector* will not be larger than 16 bits).

```
            mov    ah,36h              ;function number
            mov    dl,3                ;drive code 3 = C
            int    21h                 ;transfer to DOS.
            cmp    ax,0ffffh           ;was drive invalid?
            je     error               ;yes, jump.
            mul    cx                  ;sectors/cluster * bytes/sector
            mul    bx                  ; * available clusters
            .                          ;result is now in DX:AX.
error:      .
            .
```

Int 21H (33)
Function 37H (55)
Reserved

1 2 3

Int 21H (33)
Function 38H (56)
Get or set country

1 2 3

2 3 Obtains current-country information.

3 Sets current-country code.

Call with: AH   = 38H

If getting current-country information:
AL 2 3   = 00
DS:DX   = segment:offset of buffer for returned information

AL 3   = 00   for current country
AL   = 01 through 0FEH   for specific country with code < 255
               0FFH   for specific country with code >= 255
BX   = 16-bit country code if AL = 0FFH
DS:DX   = segment:offset of buffer for returned information

If setting current-country code:
AL 3   = 01 through 0FEH   for country code < 255
               0FFH   for country code >= 255
BX   = 16-bit country code if AL = 0FFH
DX   = 0FFFFH

(continued)

Returns: If no error while getting current-country information:
             BX   = country code
             Buffer at DS:DX filled in as follows:

▨2

Bytes 0–1   = date format
                   0   = USA   m d y
                   1   = Europe   d m y
                   2   = Japan   y m d
Byte 2   = currency symbol
Byte 3   = zero
Byte 4   = thousands separator character
Byte 5   = zero
Byte 6   = decimal separator character
Byte 7   = zero
Bytes 8–31   = reserved

▨3

Bytes 0–1   = date format
                   0   = USA   m d y
                   1   = Europe   d m y
                   2   = Japan   y m d
Bytes 2–6   = currency-symbol string, null terminated
Byte 7   = thousands separator character
Byte 8   = zero
Byte 9   = decimal separator character
Byte 10   = zero
Byte 11   = date separator character
Byte 12   = zero
Byte 13   = time separator character
Byte 14   = zero
Byte 15   = currency format
                   Bit 1 = number of spaces between value and currency symbol
                            (0 or 1)
                   Bit 0 = 0   if currency symbol precedes value
                            1   if currency symbol follows value
Byte 16   = number of digits after decimal in currency
Byte 17   = time format
                   Bit 0 = 0   if 12-hour clock
                            1   if 24-hour clock
Bytes 18–21 = case map call address
Byte 22   = data-list separator character
Byte 23   = zero
Bytes 24–33 = reserved

If error while getting current-country information:
Carry flag   = set
AX   = error code
                   2   if country code invalid

(continued)

If no error while setting current-country code:
Carry flag   = clear

If error while setting current-country code:
Carry flag   = set
AX   = error code
              2   *if country code invalid*

Notes: •   ▣ The fact that DX does not contain 0FFFFH is the signal to the operating system that country information is being requested, rather than the country code being set. The country code is usually the international telephone prefix code.

          •   When getting current-country information, the buffer must be 2 bytes larger under MS-DOS version 3 than under version 2. It is the programmer's responsibility to supply a buffer large enough for the operating-system version, so that segment overflow or wraparound will not occur.

          •   The case-map call address is the segment:offset of a FAR procedure that performs country-specific lowercase to uppercase mapping on character values from 80H through 0FFH. Before the procedure is called, the character to be mapped must be in AL. If an uppercase value exists for that character, it is returned in AL; otherwise AL remains unchanged.

Example: Assuming your program is running in the United States under MS-DOS version 2.1, use function 38H to obtain current-country information, specifying that the returned information be stored in the buffer *country_buf*.

```
            mov     ah,38h                      ;function number
            mov     al,0                        ;get current country
            mov     dx,seg country_buf          ;address of buffer
            mov     ds,dx                       ;for country information
            mov     dx,offset country_buf
            int     21h                         ;transfer to DOS.
            jc      error                       ;jump if function failed.
                    .
                    .
error:              .
                    .
country_buf db      32 dup (0)
```

After the call completes, the buffer is filled in as follows:

Byte	Contents	Byte	Contents
0–1	Zero	5	Zero
2	$	6	.
3	Zero	7–31	Zero
4	,		

Creates a subdirectory using the specified drive and path.

| Call with: | AH | = 39H |
| | DS:DX | = segment:offset of ASCIIZ path specification |

Returns:	If function successful:
	Carry flag	= clear
	If function failed:
	Carry flag	= set
	AX	= error code
		3	*if path not found*
		5	*if access denied*

Notes:
- The function fails if:
  - any element of the pathname does not exist.
  - a subdirectory with the same name at the end of the same path already exists.
  - the parent subdirectory for the new subdirectory is the root directory and is full.
- This function is sometimes referenced as MKDIR in the Microsoft documentation, to point out its similarity to the UNIX command of the same name. The analogous UNIX system function is called *mknod* and requires superuser privileges.

Example: Create a subdirectory named *MYSUB* in the root directory of disk drive C.

```
            mov     ah,39h              ;function number
            mov     dx,seg dirname      ;address of path
            mov     ds,dx               ;specification
            mov     dx,offset dirname
            int     21h                 ;transfer to DOS.
            jc      failure             ;jump, couldn't create
                                        ;the subdirectory.
                    .
failure:            .
                    .
dirname     db      'C:\MYSUB',0
```

Int 21H (33)
Function 3AH (58)
Delete subdirectory

Removes a subdirectory using the specified drive and path.

Call with:	AH	= 3AH
	DS:DX	= segment:offset of ASCIIZ path specification

Returns:	If function successful:		
	Carry flag	= clear	
	If function failed:		
	Carry flag	= set	
	AX	= error code	
		3	*if path not found*
		6	*if current directory*
		5	*if access denied*
		16	*if current directory*

Notes:	●	The function fails if:

- any element of the pathname does not exist.
- the specified subdirectory is also the current subdirectory.
- the specified subdirectory still contains files.

    ●   This function is sometimes referenced as RMDIR in the Microsoft documentation, to point out its similarity to the UNIX command of the same name.

Example: Remove the subdirectory named *MYSUB* in the root directory of disk drive C.

```
            mov    ah,3ah              ;function number
            mov    dx,seg dirname      ;address of path
            mov    ds,dx               ;specification
            mov    dx,offset dirname
            int    21h                 ;transfer to DOS.
            jc     failure             ;jump if couldn't
                   .                   ;delete subdirectory.
failure:           .
                   .
dirname     db     'C:\MYSUB',0
```

Int 21H (33)
Function 3BH (59)
Set current directory

Sets the current or default directory using the specified drive and path.

| Call with: | AH | = 3BH |
| | DS:DX | = segment:offset of ASCIIZ path specification |

Returns:	If function successful:
	Carry flag	= clear
	If function failed:
	Carry flag	= set
	AX	= error code
		3	*if path not found*

Notes:
- The function fails if any element of the pathname does not exist.
- You can use function 47H to determine the current directory or subdirectory before selecting a new one, so that the original directory or subdirectory can be restored later.
- This function is sometimes referenced as CHDIR in the Microsoft documentation, to point out its similarity to the UNIX command and function of the same name.

Example: Change the current subdirectory to the subdirectory named *MYSUB* in the root directory of disk drive C.

```
                mov     ah,3bh              ;function number
                mov     dx,seg dirname      ;address of path
                mov     ds,dx               ;specification
                mov     dx,offset dirname
                int     21h                 ;transfer to DOS.
                jc      failure             ;jump if couldn't
                    .                       ;set current subdirectory.
failure:            .
                    .
dirname         db      'C:\MYSUB',0
```

Int 21H (33)
Function 3CH (60)
Create or truncate file

Given an ASCIIZ file specification, creates a new file in the designated or default directory on the designated or default disk drive. If the specified file already exists, it is truncated to zero length. In either case, the file is opened and a 16-bit token, or handle, is returned, which is used by the program for further access to the file.

Call with:	AH	= 3CH	
	CX	= file attribute	
		00H	*if normal*
		01H	*if read-only*
		02H	*if hidden*
		04H	*if system*
	DS:DX	= segment:offset of ASCIIZ file specification	

Returns:	If function successful:		
	Carry flag	= clear	
	AX	= file handle	
	If function failed:		
	Carry flag	= set	
	AX	= error code	
		3	*if path not found*
		4	*if no handle available*
		5	*if access denied*

Notes:
- The function fails if:
  - any element of the pathname does not exist.
  - the file is being created in the root directory, and the root directory is already full.
  - a file with the same name and the read-only attribute already exists in the specified subdirectory.
- If the volume or subdirectory bits are set in the file attribute passed in register CX, they are ignored by MS-DOS.
- The file is normally given the read/write attribute when it is created, and is opened for both read and write operations. The attribute can subsequently be modified with function 43H.
- See also function 5BH, which protects against the inadvertent destruction of existing file data, and function 5AH, which aids in the creation of temporary working files.
- This function is sometimes referenced as CREAT in Microsoft documentation, to point out its similarity to the UNIX function of the same name.

(continued)

Example: Create and open, or truncate to zero length and open, the file described by the string *fname*, and save the handle for future use by other file I/O routines.

```
            mov   ah,3ch            ;function number
            xor   cx,cx             ;file attribute = normal
            mov   dx,seg fname      ;address of file
            mov   ds,dx             ;specification
            mov   dx,offset fname
            int   21h               ;transfer to DOS.
            jc    failure           ;jump, create failed.
            mov   handle,ax         ;create successful,
            .                       ;save file handle.
failure:    .
            .
fname       db    'C:\MYDIR\MYFILE.DAT',0
handle      dw    0
```

Int 21H (33)
Function 3DH (61)
Open file

Given an ASCIIZ file specification, opens the specified file in the designated or default directory on the designated or default disk drive. A 16-bit token, or handle, is returned, which is used by the program for further access to the file.

Call with:

AH	= 3DH			
AL ②	= access mode			
	Bits 0–2	*= 000*	*if read access*	
		001	*if write access*	
		010	*if read/write access*	
DS:DX	= segment:offset of ASCIIZ file specification			
AL ③	= access and file-sharing modes			
	Bit 7	*= inheritance flag*		
		0	*if file inherited by child processes*	
		1	*if file private to current process*	
	Bits 4–6	*= sharing mode*		
		000	*if compatibility mode (compatible with the way FCBs open files)*	
		001	*if read/write access denied (exclusive)*	
		010	*if write access denied*	
		011	*if read access denied*	
		100	*if full access permitted*	
	Bit 3	*= reserved (should be 0)*		
	Bits 0–2	*= 000*	*if read access*	
		001	*if write access*	
		010	*if read/write access*	
DS:DX	= segment:offset of ASCIIZ file specification			

(continued)

If function successful:
Carry flag = clear
AX   = file handle

If function failed:
Carry flag = set
AX   = error code

1	*if function number invalid (file-sharing must be loaded)*
2	*if file not found*
3	*if path not found or file doesn't exist*
4	*if no handle available*
5	*if access denied*
0CH	*if file access code invalid*

Notes:

- Any normal, system, or hidden file with a matching name will be opened by this function. After opening the file, the read/write pointer is set to offset zero (the first byte of the file).

- **2** Only bits 0 through 2 of register AL are significant; the remaining bits should be zero.
  3 When file-sharing routines are loaded, register AL contains four bits that control access by other programs (the sharing mode—bits 4 through 6—and the inherit bit—bit 7).

- The function fails if:
  - any element of the pathname does not exist.
  - the file is opened with an access mode of read/write and the file has the read-only attribute.

- After a successful open call, the file's date and time stamp can be accessed using function 57H.

- The file's attribute can be accessed using function 43H.

- If the file handle was inherited from a parent process or was duplicated by DUP or FORCEDUP, all sharing and access restrictions are also inherited.

- A file-sharing error causes an Int 24H to execute, with an error code of 2. Function 59H can be used to return the sharing violation.

(continued)

Example: Open the file described by the string *fname* for both reading and writing, and save the handle in the variable *handle* for future use by other file I/O routines.

```
        mov   ah,3dh              ;function number
        mov   al,2                ;access mode = read/write
        mov   dx,seg fname        ;address of ASCIIZ
        mov   ds,dx               ;file specification
        mov   dx,offset fname
        int   21h                 ;transfer to DOS.
        jc    failure             ;jump if open failed.
        mov   handle,ax           ;open was successful,
          .                       ;save file handle.
failure:
          .
          .
fname   db    'C:\MYDIR\MYFILE.DAT',0
handle  dw    0
```

Int 21H (33)
Function 3EH (62)
Close file

Given a file token, or handle, that was returned by a previous successful open (function 3DH) or create (function 3CH, 5AH, or 5BH) operation, flushes all internal buffers to disk, closes the file, and releases the handle for reuse. If the file was modified or extended, the time and date stamp and the file size are updated in the directory entry.

Call with:	AH	= 3EH
	BX	= file handle

Returns:	If function successful:		
	Carry flag	= clear	
	If function failed:		
	Carry flag	= set	
	AX	= error code	
		6	*if handle invalid or not open*

Note: ● If you accidentally call function 3EH with a zero handle, you will get the unexpected result of closing the standard input device, and the keyboard will appear to go dead. Make sure you always call this close function with a valid, previously opened handle.

(continued)

Example: Close the file whose handle is stored in the variable *handle*.

```
            mov    ah,3eh              ;function number
            mov    bx,handle           ;handle of previously
                                       ;opened file
            int    21h                 ;transfer to DOS.
            jc     failure             ;jump, close failed.
                   .
failure:           .
                   .
handle      dw     0
```

Int 21H (33)
Function 3FH (63)
Read file or device

1 2 3

Given a valid file token, or handle, from a previous successful open (function 3DH) or create (function 3CH, 5AH, or 5BH) operation, a buffer address, and a length in bytes, transfers data at the current file-pointer position from the file into the buffer, and then updates the file-pointer position.

Call with: AH   = 3FH
              BX   = file handle
              CX   = number of bytes to read
              DS:DX   = segment:offset of buffer area

Returns: If function successful:
              Carry flag   = clear
              AX   = number of bytes read
                      0   *if end of file*

              If function failed:
              Carry flag   = set
              AX   = error code
                      5   *if access denied*
                      6   *if handle invalid or not open*

Notes: •   If reading from a character device (such as the standard input device) in cooked mode, at most one line of input will be read (i.e., up to a carriage-return character).

          •   If the carry flag is returned clear but AX = 0, then the file pointer was already at the end of the file when the program requested the read.

          •   If the carry flag is returned clear but AX < CX, then a partial record was read at the end of the file or there is an error.

(continued)

Starting at the current file-pointer location, read 1024 bytes from the file whose handle was previously stored in the variable *file1* into the buffer *databuf.*

```
          mov   ah,3fh              ;function number
          mov   bx,file1            ;handle of previously
                                    ;opened file
          mov   cx,1024             ;length to read
          mov   dx,seg databuf      ;address of read buffer
          mov   ds,dx
          mov   dx,offset databuf
          int   21h                 ;transfer to DOS.
          jc    failure             ;jump, read failed.
          .
failure:  .
          .
databuf   db    1024 dup (?)        ;buffer for read
file1     dw    0                   ;contains file handle.
```

Int 21H (33)
Function 40H (64)
Write to file or device

Given a file token, or handle, from a previous successful open (function 3DH) or create (function 3CH, 5AH, or 5BH) operation, a buffer address, and a length in bytes, transfers data from the buffer into the file, and then updates the file-pointer position.

Call with: AH   = 40H
              BX   = file handle
              CX   = number of bytes to write
              DS:DX   = segment:offset of buffer area

Returns: If function successful:
              Carry flag   = clear
              AX   = number of bytes written
                   0   *if disk full*

              If function failed:
              Carry flag   = set
              AX   = error code
                   5   *if access denied*
                   6   *if handle invalid or not open*

(continued)

Note:	•	If the carry flag is clear but AX < CX, then a partial record was written or there is an error.
	•	If CX = 0, this function truncates or extends the file size to the current file pointer position.

Example: Starting at the current file-pointer location, write 1024 bytes from the buffer *databuf* into the file whose handle was previously stored in the variable *file1*.

```
          mov   ah,40h              ;function number
          mov   bx,file1            ;handle of previously
                                    ;opened file
          mov   cx,1024             ;length to write
          mov   dx,seg databuf      ;address of buffer for
          mov   ds,dx               ;record to be written
          mov   dx,offset databuf
          int   21h                 ;transfer to DOS.
          jc    failure             ;jump, write failed.
          cmp   ax,1024             ;was entire record written?
          jne   diskfull            ;no, jump.
                .
diskfull:       .
                .
                .
failure:        .
                .
databuf   db    1024 dup (?)        ;buffer for write
file1     dw    0                   ;contains file handle.
```

Int 21H (33)
Function 41H (65)
Delete file

Deletes a file from the specified or default disk and directory.

Call with:	AH	= 41H
	DS:DX	= segment:offset of ASCIIZ file specification

Returns:	If function successful:	
	Carry flag	= clear
	If function failed:	
	Carry flag	= set
	AX	= error code
	2	*if file not found*
	5	*if access denied*

(continued)

Notes:	•	This function deletes a file by deleting its directory entry.
	•	Unlike function 13H (which deletes a file or files using a file control block), the file specification for this function cannot include the wildcard characters * and ?.
	•	The function fails if:

- any element of the pathname does not exist.
- the designated file exists but has the read-only attribute (you can use function 43H to examine and modify a file's attribute before you try to delete it).

- This function is sometimes referenced as UNLINK in the Microsoft documentation, to point out its similarity to the UNIX function of the same name. However, the functions are not completely equivalent, since under UNIX a file may have entries in one or more directories, and the file itself is deleted only when the very last directory entry has been deleted.

Example: Delete the file named *MYFILE.DAT* from the subdirectory *MYDIR* on drive C.

```
          mov   ah,41h            ;function number
          mov   dx,seg fname      ;address of ASCIIZ file
          mov   ds,dx             ;specification
          mov   dx,offset fname
          int   21h               ;transfer to DOS.
          jc    failure           ;jump, delete failed.
          .
failure:  .
          .
fname     db    'C:\MYDIR\MYFILE.DAT',0
```

Int 21H (33)
Function 42H (66)
Move file pointer

Sets the file-pointer location relative to the start of the file, the end of the file, or the current file position.

Call with:	AH	= 42H
	AL	= method code
		0 = *absolute byte offset from beginning of file (always positive double integer)*
		1 = *byte offset from current location (positive or negative double integer)*
		2 = *byte offset from end of file (positive or negative double integer)*
	BX	= file handle
	CX	= most significant half of offset
	DX	= least significant half of offset

(continued)

Returns:	If function successful:	
	Carry flag	= clear
	DX	= most significant part of new pointer location
	AX	= least significant part of new pointer location
	If function failed:	
	Carry flag	= set
	AX	= error code

	1	*if function number invalid*
	6	*if handle invalid or not open*

Notes:
- This function uses a method code and a double-precision value (a 32-bit integer) to set the current file-pointer location. The next record read or written in the file will begin at the new file-pointer location.

- Method 2 can be used to find the size of the file by calling function 42H with an offset of zero and examining the pointer location that is returned.

- Using method 1 or 2, it is possible to set the file pointer to a location that is before the start of the file. If this is done, no error code is returned by function 42H, but an error will be encountered upon subsequent attempts to read or write to the file.

- No matter what method code is used in the call to function 42H, the file-pointer location returned in DX:AX is always the resulting absolute byte offset from the start of the file.

- This function is sometimes referenced as LSEEK in the Microsoft documentation, to point out its similarity to the UNIX function of the same name.

Examples: Set the current file-pointer location for the file whose handle is stored in the variable *fhandle* to 1024 bytes from the start of the file.

```
                mov     ah,42h          ;function number
                mov     al,0            ;method = absolute offset
                mov     bx,fhandle      ;handle of previously
                                        ;opened file
                mov     cx,0            ;upper part of offset
                mov     dx,1024         ;lower part of offset
                int     21h             ;transfer to DOS.
                jc      error           ;jump, function failed.
                .
error:          .
                .
fhandle         dw      0               ;file handle
```

(continued)

In most programs, it is very useful to have a single subroutine that accepts a record number, record size, and handle, and then sets the file pointer of the corresponding I/O stream appropriately, as this one does:

```
; call this routine with bx = handle
;                        ax = record number
;                        cx = record size
; returns all registers unchanged.
;
set_ptr         proc  near
                push  ax                ;save record number.
                push  cx                ;save record size.
                push  dx                ;save whatever's in DX.
                mul   cx                ;size * record number
                mov   cx,ax
                xchg  cx,dx             ;CX:DX = offset in file
                mov   ax,4200h          ;function number & method
                int   21h               ;transfer to DOS.
                pop   dx                ;restore previous DX.
                pop   cx                ;restore record size.
                pop   ax                ;restore record number.
                ret                     ;back to caller
set_ptr         endp
```

Int 21H (33)
Function 43H (67)
Get or set file attributes

1 2 3

Obtains or alters the attribute of a file (read-only, hidden, system, or archive).

Call with:	AH	= 43H	
	AL	= 00H	if getting file attribute
		01H	if setting file attribute
	CX	= new attribute	if AL = 01
		Bit 5 = *archive*	
		Bit 2 = *system*	
		Bit 1 = *hidden*	
		Bit 0 = *read-only*	
	DS:DX	= segment:offset of ASCIIZ file specification	

(continued)

Returns:	If function successful:		
	Carry flag	= clear	
	If AL = 00 on call:		
	CX	= attribute	
	If function failed:		
	Carry flag	= set	
	AX	= error code	
		1	*if function code invalid*
		2	*if file not found*
		3	*if path not found or file doesn't exist*
		5	*if attribute can't be changed*

Notes:
- Bit 0 of the attribute byte is the least significant, or rightmost, bit.
- This function cannot be used to set a file's volume label bit (bit 3) or subdirectory bit (bit 4). These bits must be manipulated using an extended file control block.
- This function is sometimes referenced as CHMOD in the Microsoft documentation, to point out its similarity to the UNIX function of the same name.

Example: Change the attribute of the file *D:\MYDIR\MYFILE.DAT* to read-only, so that it cannot be modified or deleted by other application programs.

```
read_only    equ    01h
hidden       equ    02h
system       equ    04h
volume       equ    08h
subdir       equ    10h
archive      equ    20h
             .
             .
             .
             mov    ah,43h              ;function number
             mov    al,01               ;call is modify attribute.
             mov    cx,read_only        ;load desired attribute.
             mov    dx,seg fname        ;address of ASCIIZ
             mov    ds,dx               ;file specification
             mov    dx,offset fname
             int    21h                 ;transfer to DOS.
             jc     failure             ;jump, function failed.
             .
failure:     .
             .
fname        db     'D:\MYDIR\MYFILE.DAT',0
```

Passes control information directly between an application and a device driver.

Call with:	AH	= 44H	
	AL	= 00H	if getting device information
		01H	if setting device information
		02H	if reading from device control channel to buffer (character device)
		03H	if writing from buffer to device control channel (character device)
		04H	same as 02H, but using drive number in BL (block device)
		05H	same as 03H, but using drive number in BL (block device)
		06H	if getting input status
		07H	if getting output status
3		08H	if testing whether block device changeable
3		09H	if testing whether drive local (Microsoft Networks) or remote (redirected to a server) (version 3.1)
3		0AH	if testing whether handle local (Microsoft Networks) or remote (redirected to a server) (version 3.1)
3		0BH	if changing sharing retry count
	BX	= handle, if function code 00H, 01H, 02H, 03H, 06H, 07H, or 0AH	
	or:		
	BL	= drive code (0 = default, 1 = A, etc.), if function code 04H, 05H, 08H, or 09H	
	CX	= number of bytes to read or write	
	DS:DX	= segment:offset of buffer area, if function code 02H through 05H	
	DX	= device information, if function code 01H (bits 8–15 must be zero when called)	

If character device:

	Bit 15	= 0	*(reserved)*
	Bit 14	= 1	*if this device can process control strings sent with function codes 02H and 03H (This bit can only be read; it cannot be set.)*
	Bit 8-13	= 0	*(reserved)*
	Bit 7	= 1	*indicates character device*
	Bit 6	= 0	*if end of file on input*
	Bit 5	= 1	*if operating in binary or "raw" mode*
		0	*if operating in "cooked" mode*

(continued)

Bit 4	= 0	*(reserved)*	
Bit 3	= 1	*if CLOCK device*	
Bit 2	= 1	*if NUL device*	
Bit 1	= 1	*if console output device*	
Bit 0	= 1	*if console input device*	

If disk file:

Bit 8-15	= 0	*(reserved)*
Bit 7	= 0	*indicates disk file*
Bit 6	= 0	*if file has been written*
Bits 0–5	= *drive number (0 = A, 1 = B, etc.)*	

Returns: If function successful:

Carry flag	= clear
AX	= number of bytes transferred, if function codes 02H through 05H/AL
AL	= status, if function codes 06H through 07H

0	*if not ready*
0FFH	*if ready*

AX	= value, if function code 08H

0	*if removable*
1	*if fixed*

DX	= device information, if function code 00H (see above for mapping of device-information word)

If function failed:

Carry flag	= set
AX	= error code

1	*if function number invalid*
4	*if no handle available*
5	*if access denied*
6	*if handle invalid or not open*
0DH	*if data invalid*
0FH	*if drive number invalid*

Notes:
- If this function is used on an ordinary file rather than a logical device, only subfunction codes 00H, 06H, and 07H are valid.

- For subfunction code 0BH, CX = the number of delay loops (i.e., the pause between retries) and DX = the number of times MS-DOS should retry a disk operation that fails because of a file-sharing operation. The default is: delay loops = 1, and retries = 3.

- This function is sometimes referenced as IOCTL in the Microsoft documentation, to point out its similarity to the UNIX function of the same name.

(continued)

Set raw output mode for the standard output device. With all MS-DOS console drivers, this speeds up output by disabling checking for Ctrl-C, Ctrl-S, and Ctrl-P.

```
mov     ax,4400h          ;get current device information.
mov     bx,1              ;std output = handle 1
int     21h               ;transfer to DOS.
mov     dh,0              ;force DH = 0.
or      dl,20h            ;set raw mode bit.
mov     ax,4401h          ;set current device information.
int     21h               ;transfer to DOS.
```

Int 21H (33)
Function 45H (69)
Duplicate handle

Given a handle for a currently open device or file, returns a new handle that refers to the same device or file (at the same position).

Call with:	AH	= 45H
	BX	= file handle

Returns:

If function successful:

Carry flag	= clear
AX	= new file handle

If function failed:

Carry flag	= set	
AX	= error code	
	4	*if no handle available*
	6	*if handle invalid or not open*

Notes:

- If you move the file pointer of one handle using a seek, read, or write operation, the file pointer attached to the other handle will also be moved.

- This function is sometimes referenced as DUP in Microsoft documentation, to point out its similarity to the UNIX function of the same name.

- One use for this admittedly obscure function is to force an update of the directory for a file that has changed length, without incurring the overhead of re-opening the file. The file's handle is duplicated with function 45H, and the new handle that is returned is closed with function 3EH, leaving the original handle open for further read/write operations.

(continued)

Ensure that the disk directory entry is updated for the file whose handle is found in the variable *my_file*, without incurring the overhead of a file open.

```
        mov   ah,45h          ;function 45H = DUP handle,
                              ;i.e. get another handle
                              ;referring to the same file.
        mov   bx,my_file      ;handle for previously opened file
        int   21h             ;transfer to DOS.
        jc    error           ;jump if DUP failed.
        mov   bx,ax           ;now close the DUP'd handle.
        mov   ah,3eh          ;function 3EH = close file
        int   21h             ;transfer to DOS.
        jc    error           ;jump if close failed, otherwise
                              ;directory is updated, continue
                              ;processing with a light heart.
error:        .
              .
              .
my_file dw    0               ;handle from previous successful
                              ;file "open" operation
```

Int 21H (33)
Function 46H (70)
Force duplicate of handle

Given two handles, makes the second handle refer to the same opened file at the same location as the first handle.

Call with:	AH	= 46H
	BX	= first file handle
	CX	= second file handle

Returns:	If function successful:		
	Carry flag	= clear	
	If function failed:		
	Carry flag	= set	
	AX	= error code	
		4	*if no handles available*
		6	*if handle invalid or not open*

Notes:
- If the handle passed in CX refers to an open file, that file is closed first.
- If the file pointer for one handle is moved by a seek, read, or write operation, the file pointer for the other handle will be changed identically.
- This function is sometimes referenced as CDUP in the Microsoft documentation, to point out its similarity to the UNIX function of the same name.

(continued)

Example: Redirect everything written to the standard output device to the standard list device. Later, restore the original meaning of the handle for the standard output device.

```
stdin       equ     0
stdout      equ     1
stderr      equ     2
stdaux      equ     3
stdprn      equ     4
            .
            .
            .
            mov     ah,45h          ;function 45H = dup handle
            mov     bx,stdout       ;first, dup handle of Standard
                                    ;Output so we can restore it later.
            int     21h             ;transfer to DOS.
            jc      error           ;jump if dup failed.
            mov     old_han,ax      ;save dup'd handle of Std Out.
                                    ;now redirect Standard Output to
                                    ;the Standard List device.
            mov     ah,46h          ;function 46H = force dup
            mov     bx,stdprn       ;BX = handle for Std List
            mov     cx,stdout       ;CX = handle for Standard Output
            int     21h             ;transfer to DOS.
            jc      error           ;jump if force dup failed.
            .
            .                       ;now remove redirection of
            .                       ;Standard Output device...
            mov     ah,46h          ;function 46H = force dup
            mov     bx,old_han      ;force Std Out to track the
            mov     cx,stdout       ;duplicate that was made earlier.
            int     21h             ;transfer to DOS.
            jc      error           ;jump if force dup failed.
                                    ;
                                    ;now duplicate is no longer needed.
            mov     ah,3eh          ;function 3EH = close
            mov     bx,old_han      ;dup'd handle
            int     21h             ;transfer to DOS.
            jc      error           ;jump if close failed.
            .
error:      .
            .
old_han     dw      0
```

Obtains an ASCIIZ string that describes the path from the root to the currently active directory, and the name of that directory.

Call with:	AH	= 47H
	DL	= drive code (0 = default, 1 = A, etc.)
	DS:SI	= segment:offset of 64-byte scratch buffer

Returns:	If function successful:
	Carry flag = clear
	Buffer is filled in with full pathname from root to current directory
	If function failed:
	Carry flag = set
	AX = error code
	0FH *if drive specification invalid*

Notes:
- The returned pathname does not include the drive identifier or a leading \. It is terminated with a null (zero) byte. Consequently, if the current directory is the root directory, the first byte in the buffer will be a zero.

- The function fails if the drive code is invalid.

- The current directory may be set with function 3BH.

Example: Get the name of the current directory on the disk in drive C and store it in the buffer named *dir_buff*.

```
          mov   ah,47h              ;function number
          mov   dl,03              ;drive code = 3 for C
          mov   si,seg dir_buff     ;address of buffer
          mov   ds,si              ;for path string
          mov   si,offset dir_buff
          int   21h                ;transfer to DOS.
          jc    failure            ;jump, function failed.
                .
failure:        .
                .
dir_buff  db    64 dup (0)
```

Allocates a block of memory, and returns a pointer to the beginning of the allocated area.

| Call with: | AH | = 48H |
| | BX | = number of paragraphs of memory needed |

Returns:	If function successful:	
	Carry flag	= clear
	AX	= initial segment of allocated block
	If function failed:	
	Carry flag	= set
	AX	= error code
	7	*if memory control blocks destroyed*
	8	*if insufficient memory*
	BX	= size of largest available block

Notes:
- If the function succeeds, it returns the segment address of the newly allocated memory area; i.e., the base address of the allocated area is AX:0000.

- When a COM program is loaded in a non-multitasking MS-DOS environment, it already "owns" all of memory when it is loaded and therefore this function will always fail. In multitasking environments such as Windows and TopView, the apparent top of memory as seen by the application may not be the same as the physical top of memory, and this function may be used to obtain additional memory resources.

- This function is similar to the XENIX function *malloc*.

Example: Request a 64K block of memory for use as a buffer.

```
        mov     ah,48h          ;function number
        mov     bx,1000h        ;block size in paragraphs
        int     21h             ;transfer to DOS.
        jc      failure         ;jump, not enough memory
                                ;to allocate block.
        mov     buf_seg,ax      ;save segment address
                                ;of new block.
                .
failure:        .
                .
buf_seg         dw      0
```

Int 21H (33)
Function 49H (73)
Release memory

Releases a memory block and makes it available for use by other programs.

Call with:	AH	= 49H
	ES	= segment of block to be released

Returns: If function successful:
Carry flag   = clear

If function failed:
Carry flag   = set
AX   = error code

	7	*if memory control blocks destroyed*
	9	*if incorrect segment in ES*

Notes:

- This function assumes that the memory block being released was previously obtained by a successful call to function 48H.

- The function will fail or cause unpredictable system errors if:
  - the program tries to release a memory block that does not belong to it.
  - the segment address provided in ES does not correspond to a memory block that was previously allocated via function 48H.

- This function is similar to the XENIX function *free*, described in the Microsoft documentation under *malloc*.

Example: Release the memory block that was previously allocated in the example for function 48H.

```
              mov   ah,49h           ;function number
              mov   es,buf_seg       ;segment of memory block
              int   21h              ;transfer to DOS.
              jc    failure          ;jump, release failed.
                    .
failure:            .
                    .
buf_seg       dw    0                ;contains segment of
                                     ;previously allocated
                                     ;block.
```

Dynamically shrinks or extends a memory block, according to the needs of an application program.

Call with:	AH	= 4AH
	BX	= new requested block size in paragraphs
	ES	= segment of block to be modified

Returns:	If function successful:	
	Carry flag	= clear
	If function failed:	
	Carry flag	= set
	AX	= error code
		7 *if memory control blocks destroyed*
		8 *if insufficient memory*
		9 *if incorrect segment in ES*
	BX	= maximum block size available

Notes:

- This function modifies the size of a memory block that was previously allocated through a call to function 48H.

- This call *must* be used by a COM program to release all possible memory before performing an EXEC function (4BH) to run another program (see Chapter 8). EXE programs may also use this function if desired.

- This function is sometimes referenced as SETBLOCK in the Microsoft documentation. It is similar to the XENIX function *realloc*, which is described in the documentation under *malloc*.

Example: Modify the memory block that was allocated in the example for function 48H so that the block is only 32K long.

```
                mov     ah,4ah          ;function number
                mov     bx,0800h        ;new size of block
                                        ;in paragraphs
                mov     es,buf_seg      ;segment of memory block
                int     21h             ;transfer to DOS.
                jc      failure         ;jump, reallocation failed.
                .
failure:        .
                .
buf_seg         dw      0               ;contains segment of
                                        ;previously allocated
                                        ;memory block.
```

Allows an application program to run another program, regaining control when it is finished and optionally examining the child program's return code. Can also be used to load overlays, but this use is uncommon.

Call with:	AH	= 4BH	
	AL	= 00	if loading and executing program
		03	if loading overlay
	ES:BX	= segment:offset of parameter block	
	DS:DX	= segment:offset of program specification	

Returns: If function successful:
Carry flag = clear
All registers except CS and IP are destroyed, including the stack pointers

If function failed:
Carry flag = set
AX = error code

	1	*if function invalid*
	2	*if file not found or path invalid*
	5	*if access denied*
	8	*if insufficient memory to load the program*
	0AH	*if environment invalid*
	0BH	*if format invalid*

Notes: ● The parameter-block format is as follows:

Byte	Contents
0–1	Segment pointer to environment block
2–3	Offset of command tail
4–5	Segment of command tail
6–7	Offset of first FCB to be copied into new PSP + 5CH
8–9	Segment of first FCB
10–11	Offset of second FCB to be copied into new PSP + 6CH
12–13	Segment of second FCB

(continued)

- The environment block must be paragraph aligned. It consists of a sequence of ASCIIZ strings in the form

  db 'COMSPEC = A:\COMMAND.COM',0

  The entire set of strings is terminated by an extra zero byte.

- The command-tail format consists of a count byte, followed by an ASCII string terminated by a carriage return (which is not included in the character count); for example:

  db 6,' *.DAT',0dh

- Before a program uses function 4BH to run another program, it must release all memory it is not actually using with a call to function 4AH, passing the segment address of its own program segment prefix (PSP) and the number of paragraphs to retain.

- All active handles (open files and standard devices) of the parent program are inherited by the child program. If the parent redirects standard input and/or output to other devices or files, the child will inherit the same environment and will read its input from the redirected source.

- The environment block can be used to pass information to the child process. If the environment-block pointer in the parameter block is zero, a copy of the environment block for the parent program is inherited by the child program. In any case, the segment address of the environment block is found at offset 002CH in the child program's PSP.

- This function is sometimes referenced as EXEC in the Microsoft documentation, to point out its similarity to the UNIX function of the same name.

- Upon return from the child process, the only registers that are valid are CS:IP. All the remaining registers may be (and probably have been) destroyed, including the stack pointer and segment. Before issuing an EXEC call, the parent program must store SS and SP in variables that are addressable from inside the code segment, and must then restore them from those variables after the return, using a code-segment override.

- SS and SP should be loaded after the return in such a way that an interrupt cannot occur before the restoration of stack addressing is complete (for example, after SS is loaded but before SP is loaded).

Example: See Chapter 10.

Int 21H (33)
Function 4CH (76)
Terminate with return code

Performs a final exit to MS-DOS or to a parent task, passing back a return code. MS-DOS then takes the following actions:

1. Restores the termination handler vector from PSP:000AH.
2. Restores the Ctrl-Break vector from PSP:000EH.
3. ② ③ Restores the critical error handler vector from PSP:0012H.
4. Flushes the file buffers.
5. Transfers to the termination handler address.

If the program is returning to COMMAND.COM rather than to another program, control transfers to COMMAND.COM's resident portion and the transient portion of COMMAND.COM is reloaded (if necessary). If COMMAND.COM then determines that a batch file is in progress, the next line of the file is fetched and interpreted; otherwise, a prompt is issued for the next user command.

| Call with: | AH | = 4CH |
| | AL | = return code |

| Returns: | Nothing |

Notes:
- ② ③ This is the approved way to terminate a program. It is the only way that does not rely on the contents of any segment register, and it is thus particularly appropriate for large EXE files. Other methods of terminating a program are:
  - Int 20H (should be avoided)
  - Int 21H function 00H
  - Int 21H function 31H
  - Int 27H (should be avoided)

- When this function is called, all files with active handles are closed and the disk directory is updated.

- The return code can be interrogated by the parent process with function 4DH (get return code). It can also be inspected by the batch subcommands IF and ERRORLEVEL.

- This function is sometimes referenced as EXIT in the Microsoft documentation, to point out its similarity to the UNIX function of the same name.

Example: Perform a final exit, passing a return code of 1.

```
        mov   ah,4ch          ;function number
        mov   al,01           ;return code
        int   21h             ;transfer to DOS.
```

Int 21H (33)
Function 4DH (77)
Get return code

Used by a parent task, after the successful completion of an EXEC call (function 4BH), to obtain the return code of the child task.

Call with:	AH	= 4DH

Returns:	AH	= exit type
		00 = *normal termination*
		01 = *termination by Ctrl-C*
		02 = *termination by critical device error*
		03 = *termination by call to interrupt 21H function 31H or interrupt 27H*
	AL	= return code (passed by child process)

Notes:	●	This function will yield the return code of a child process only once.
	●	UNIX contains a similar function named *wait*; however, the two are not really equivalent because MS-DOS does not support the concurrent, asynchronous execution of parent and child programs.

Example:	Get the return code of a program that was previously run using the EXEC service (function 4BH).

```
            mov     ah,4dh          ;function number
            int     21h             ;transfer to DOS.
            mov     retcode,ax      ;save return code.
              .
              .
              .
retcode     dw      0
```

Int 21H (33)
Function 4EH (78)
Search for first match

Given a file specification in the form of an ASCIIZ string, searches the default or specified directory on the default or specified disk drive for the first matching file.

Call with:	AH	= 4EH
	CX	= attribute to use in search
	DS:DX	= segment:offset of ASCIIZ file specification

(continued)

Returns:	If function successful:

Carry flag = clear
Current disk transfer area filled in as follows:

Bytes	0–20	= reserved for use by MS-DOS on subsequent calls
Byte	21	= attribute of matched file
Bytes	22–23	= file time
Bytes	24–25	= file date
Bytes	26–27	= least significant word of file size
Bytes	28–29	= most significant word of file size
Bytes	30–42	= filename and extension in form of ASCIIZ string

If function failed:
Carry flag = set
AX = error code

2	if path invalid
12H	if no matching directory entry found

Notes:
- This function assumes that you have previously used function 1AH to set the address of the disk transfer area (DTA).

- The wildcard characters ? and * are allowed in the filename. If wildcard characters are present, this function will return only the first matching filename.

- If the attribute is zero, only ordinary files are found. If the volume-label attribute bit is set, only volume labels will be returned (if any are present). Any other attribute or combination of attributes (hidden, system, and directory) results in those files *and* all normal files being matched.

Example: Find the first COM file in the subdirectory \ *MYDIR* on the disk in drive C.

```
              mov    ah,1ah               ;function = set DTA
              mov    dx,seg dir_buff      ;set disk transfer
              mov    ds,dx                ;to scratch buffer.
              mov    dx,offset dir_buff
              int    21h                  ;transfer to DOS.
              mov    ah,4eh               ;function = search
              mov    cx,0                 ;attribute "normal"
              mov    dx,seg sch_str       ;address of ASCIIZ
              mov    ds,dx                ;file specification
              mov    dx,offset sch_str
              int    21h                  ;transfer to DOS.
              jc     no_match             ;jump, no file
              .                           ;matched specification.
no_match:     .
              .
sch_str       db     'C:\MYDIR\*.COM',0
dir_buff      db     43 dup (0)           ;scratch area for use
                                          ;by DOS search function
```

Int 21H (33)
Function 4FH (79)
Search for next match

Assuming a successful previous call to function 4EH, finds the next file in the current or specified directory on the current or specified disk drive that matches the original file specification.

Call with:	AH	= 4FH

Returns: If function successful (another match found):
Carry flag   = clear
Current disk transfer area filled in as follows:

Bytes	0–20	= reserved for use by MS-DOS on subsequent calls
Byte	21	= attribute of matched file
Bytes	22–23	= file time
Bytes	24–25	= file date
Bytes	26–27	= least significant word of file size
Bytes	28–29	= most significant word of file size
Bytes	30–42	= filename and extension in form of ASCIIZ string

If function failed (no match found):
Carry flag   = set
AX   = error code

12H	if no matching directory entry found

Notes:
- Use of this call assumes that the original file specification contained one or more * or ? wildcard characters.

- When this function is called, the current disk transfer area (DTA) must contain information from a previous successful function 4EH or 4FH.

- The IBM PC-DOS version 3.0 manual states that this call requires DS:DX to point to the information from a previous function 4EH or 4FH. This is not correct and should be ignored.

Example: Using the results of the example for function 4EH, find the next COM file in the \MYDIR subdirectory on the disk in drive C.

```
                mov    ah,4fh          ;function number
                int    21h             ;transfer to DOS.
                jc     no_match        ;jump, no more files
                .                      ;matched specification.
no_match:       .
                .
sch_str         db     'C:\MYDIR\*.COM',0
dir_buff        db     43 dup (0)      ;scratch area for use
                                       ;by DOS search functions
```

Int 21H (33)
Function 50H (80)
Reserved

1 2 3

Int 21H (33)
Function 51H (81)
Reserved

1 2 3

Int 21H (33)
Function 52H (82)
Reserved

1 2 3

Int 21H (33)
Function 53H (83)
Reserved

1 2 3

Int 21H (33)
Function 54H (84)
Get verify flag

1 2 3

Obtains the current value of the system verify (read-after-write) flag.

Call with:	AH	= 54H

Returns:	AL	= current verify flag value
		00 *if verify off*
		01 *if verify on*

(continued)

Note: ● The state of the system verify flag can be changed through a call to function 2EH or by the MS-DOS commands VERIFY ON and VERIFY OFF.

Example: Test the state of the system verify flag.

```
        mov     ah,54h          ;function number
        int     21h             ;transfer to DOS.
        cmp     al,01           ;is verify on?
        je      verify_on       ;yes, jump.
        or      al,al           ;is verify off?
        jz      verify_off      ;yes, jump.
        jmp     fatal_error     ;otherwise something
                                ;terrible is wrong.
                .
verify_on:      .
                .
                .
verify_off:     .
                .
```

Int 21H (33)
Function 55H (85)
Reserved

1 2 3

Int 21H (33)
Function 56H (86)
Rename file

1 2 3

Renames a file and/or moves its directory entry to a different directory on the same disk.

Call with:

AH	= 56H
DS:DX	= segment:offset of current ASCIIZ filename
ES:DI	= segment:offset of new ASCIIZ filename

Returns: If function successful:

Carry flag	= clear

If function failed:

Carry flag	= set
AX	= error code

2	if file not found
3	if path not found or file doesn't exist
5	if access denied
11H	if not same device

(continued)

Notes:
- The function fails if:
  - any element of the pathname does not exist.
  - the current filename specification contains a different disk drive than the new filename.
  - the file is being moved to the root directory, and the root directory is already full.
  - a file with the new path and filename specification already exists.
- Wildcard characters are not allowed in either the current or the new filename specifications.

Example: Change the name of the file *MYFILE.DAT* in the subdirectory *MYDIR* on disk drive C to *MYTEXT.DAT*, and move it into the subdirectory *SYSTEM* on the same disk in the same drive.

```
          mov    ah,56h              ;function number
          mov    dx,seg old_name     ;address of ASCIIZ
          mov    ds,dx               ;specification for
          mov    dx,offset old_name  ;old file name
          mov    di,seg new_name     ;address of ASCIIZ
          mov    es,di               ;specification for
          mov    di,offset new_name  ;new file name
          int    21h                 ;transfer to DOS.
          jc     failure             ;jump, rename failed.
                 .
failure:         .
                 .
old_name  db     'C:\MYDIR\MYFILE.DAT',0

new_name  db     'C:\SYSTEM\MYTEXT.DAT',0
```

Int 21H (33)
Function 57H (87)
Get or set file date and time

Reads or modifies the date and time stamp in a file's directory entry.

Call with: If getting date and time:
AH   = 57H
AL   = 00
BX   = file handle

If setting date and time:
AH   = 57H
AL   = 01

(continued)

BX	= file handle	
CX	= time	
	Bits 0BH–0FH = hours (0 through 23)	
	Bits 05–0AH = minutes (0 through 59)	
	Bits 00–04H = number of 2-second increments (0 through 29)	
DX	= date	
	Bits 09–0FH = year (relative to 1980)	
	Bits 05–08H = month (1 through 12)	
	Bits 00–04H = day of month (1 through 31)	

Returns: If function successful:
Carry flag   = clear

If getting date and time:
CX   = time (time-information map given above)
DX   = date (date-information map given above)

If function failed:
Carry flag   = set
AX   = error code
                1   if function code invalid
                6   if handle invalid

Notes: • The file must have been previously opened or created via a successful call to function 3CH, 3DH, 5AH, or 5BH.

            • The date and time are in the format used in the directory, with bit 0 the least significant, or rightmost, bit.

Example: Get the date that the file *MYFILE.DAT* was last modified; then decompose the packed date into its constituent parts in the variables *month*, *day*, and *year*.

```
        mov     ah,3dh          ;function 3DH = open file
        mov     al,0            ;mode = read-only
        mov     dx,seg fname    ;DS:DX = filename
        mov     ds,dx
        mov     dx,offset fname
        int     21h             ;transfer to DOS.
        jc      op_err          ;jump if open failed.
        mov     bx,ax           ;BX = file handle
        mov     ah,57h          ;function 57H = get date/time
        mov     al,0            ;AL = 0 to get date/time
        int     21h             ;transfer to DOS.
        jc      get_err         ;jump if get failed.
        mov     day,dx          ;decompose date into parts.
        and     day,01fh        ;day of month
        mov     cl,5
        shr     dx,cl
        mov     month,dx        ;month of year
        and     month,0fh
```

(continued)

```
                    mov    cl,4
                    shr    dx,cl
                    and    dx,03fh           ;year relative to 1980
                    add    dx,1980           ;correct it to real year
                    mov    year,dx           ;and save it.
                                             ;release file handle in BX.
                    mov    ah,3eh            ;function 3EH = close file
                    int    21h               ;transfer to DOS.
                    jc     cl_err            ;jump if close failed.
                    .
op_err:             .
                    .
get_err:            .
                    .
cl_err:             .
                    .
month               dw     0
day                 dw     0
year                dw     0
fname               db     'MYFILE.DAT',0
```

Int 21H (33)
Function 58H (88)
Get or set allocation strategy

⬜1⬜ ⬜2⬜ ■3■

Obtains or changes the code indicating the current MS-DOS strategy for allocating memory blocks.

Call with:	If getting strategy code:		
	AH	= 58H	
	AL	= 00	
	If setting strategy code:		
	AH	= 58H	
	AL	= 01	
	BX	= strategy code	
		00	*if first fit*
		01	*if best fit*
		02	*if last fit*

Returns:	If function successful:		
	Carry flag	= clear	
	If getting strategy code:		
	AX	= strategy code	
	If function failed:		
	Carry flag	= set	
	AX	= error code	
		1	*function code invalid*

(continued)

Note:
- The memory allocation strategies are:
  - First fit—MS-DOS searches the available memory blocks from low addresses to high addresses, assigning the first one large enough to satisfy the block allocation request. (This is the default strategy.)
  - Best fit—MS-DOS searches all available memory blocks and assigns the smallest available block that will satisfy the request, regardless of its position.
  - Last fit—MS-DOS searches the available memory blocks from high addresses to low addresses, assigning the highest one large enough to satisfy the block allocation request.

Example: Save the code indicating the current memory allocation strategy in the variable *strat*, then force the system's strategy to be "best fit."

```
           mov     ah,58h          ;function 58H = get/set strategy
           mov     al,0            ;mode = 0 for "get strategy"
           int     21h             ;transfer to DOS.
           jc      error           ;jump if get strategy failed.
           mov     strat,ax        ;save old strategy code.
           mov     bx,1            ;strategy = 1 for "best fit"
           mov     ah,58h          ;function 58H = get/set strategy
           mov     al,1            ;mode = 1 to "set strategy"
           int     21h             ;transfer to DOS.
           jc      error           ;jump if set strategy failed.
                   .
error:             .
                   .
strat      dw      0               ;save code for system's previous
                                   ;allocation strategy here.
```

Int 21H (33)
Function 59H (89)
Get extended error information

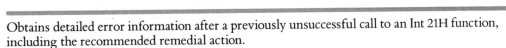

Obtains detailed error information after a previously unsuccessful call to an Int 21H function, including the recommended remedial action.

| Call with: | AH | = 59H |
| | BX | = 00 |

Returns:	AX	= extended error code
		1	*if function number invalid*
		2	*if file not found*
		3	*if path not found*
		4	*if too many open files*
		5	*if access denied*
		6	*if handle invalid*

(continued)

	7	if memory control blocks destroyed
	8	if insufficient memory
	9	if memory block address invalid
	0AH	if environment invalid
	0BH	if format invalid
	0CH	if access code invalid
	0DH	if data invalid
	0EH	reserved
	0FH	if disk drive invalid
	10H	if attempted to remove current directory
	11H	if not same device
	12H	if no more files
	13H	if disk write-protected
	14H	if unknown unit
	15H	if drive not ready
	16H	if unknown command
	17H	if data error (CRC)
	18H	if bad request structure length
	19H	if seek error
	1AH	if unknown medium type
	1BH	if sector not found
	1CH	if printer out of paper
	1DH	if write fault
	1EH	if read fault
	1FH	if general failure
	20H	if sharing violation
	21H	if lock violation
	22H	if disk change invalid
	23H	if FCB unavailable
	24-4FH	reserved
	50H	if file already exists
	51H	reserved
	52H	if cannot make directory
	53H	if fail on Int 24H (critical error interrupt)
BH	= error class	
	1	if out of resource (such as storage or channels)
	2	if not error, but temporary situation (such as locked region in file) that can be expected to end
	3	if authorization problem
	4	if internal error in system software
	5	if hardware failure
	6	if system software failure not the fault of active process (such as missing configuration files)
	7	if application program error
	8	if file or item not found
	9	if file or item of invalid format or type
	0AH	if file or item interlocked
	0BH	if wrong disk in drive, bad spot on disk, or storage-medium problem
	0CH	if other error

(continued)

BL		= recommended action
	1	*retry reasonable number of times, then prompt user to select* abort *or* ignore
	2	*retry reasonable number of times with delay between retries, then prompt user to select* abort *or* ignore
	3	*get corrected information from user (typically caused by incorrect filename or drive specification)*
	4	*abort application with cleanup (i.e., terminate program in as orderly manner as possible, releasing locks, closing files, etc.)*
	5	*perform immediate exit without cleanup (system is probably corrupted and attempts to close files, etc., may do more harm than good)*
	6	*ignore error*
	7	*retry after user intervention to remove cause of error*
CH		= error locus
	1	*unknown*
	2	*block device (disk or disk emulator)*
	3	*network related*
	4	*serial device*
	5	*memory related*

Notes:

- The contents of registers CL, DX, SI, DI, BP, DS, and ES are destroyed by this function.

- The error routines for MS-DOS function calls fall into two general classes:
  - An error code, usually 255 (0FFH), is returned in AL. This method is used by file and record functions in the range 0 through 2EH, and is present for historical reasons and for compatibility with CP/M.
  - The error status is returned with the carry flag, and a descriptive error code is returned in AX if the carry flag is set. This method is used by file, directory, and record functions in the range 2FH through 62H.

- Function 59H can be used after any MS-DOS Int 21H or Int 24H function that returns an error status, in order to obtain more detailed information about the error type and the recommended action. If function 59H is called when the previous Int 21H or Int 24H function had no error, it will return 0000 in AX.

- Note that extended error codes 13H (19) through 1FH (31) correspond exactly to error codes 0 through 0CH (12) returned by Int 24H.

- The Microsoft documentation explicitly warns that new error codes will be added in future versions of MS-DOS, and that you should not code your programs to recognize only specific error numbers, if you wish to ensure upward compatibility.

(continued)

Example: Attempt to open the file named NOSUCH.DAT using a file control block; when the open request fails, get the extended error code.

```
start:      mov     dx,offset my_fcb        ;address of FCB
            mov     ds,dx
            mov     dx,offset my_fcb
            mov     ah,0fh                  ;function = open
            int     21h                     ;transfer to DOS.
            or      al,al
            jz      success                 ;jump, file opened.
            mov     ah,59h                  ;function = get
                                            ;extended error code
            xor     bx,bx                   ;BX must = 0 for
                                            ;use with DOS 3.
            int     21h                     ;transfer to DOS.
            or      ax,ax                   ;double check for
                                            ;error return.
            jz      success                 ;jump, no error.
            cmp     bl,2                    ;should we retry?
            jle     start                   ;yes, jump.
            jmp     error                   ;no, give up.
            .
error:      .
            .
success:    .
            .
my_fcb      db      0                       ;drive = default
            db      'NOSUCH  '              ;filename, 8 characters
            db      'DAT'                   ;extension, 3 characters
            db      25 dup (0)              ;remainder of FCB
```

Int 21H (33)
Function 5AH (90)
Create temporary file

Creates a temporary or working file with a unique name, in a specified directory on the default or specified disk drive, and opens the file for subsequent read/write operations.

Call with:	AH	= 5AH	
	CX	= attribute	
		00H	if normal
		01H	if read-only
		02H	if hidden
		04H	if system
	DS:DX	= segment:offset of ASCIIZ path specification	

(continued)

Returns:	If function successful:		
	Carry flag	= clear	
	AX	= handle	
	DS:DX	= segment:offset of complete ASCIIZ file specification	
	If function failed:		
	Carry flag	= set	
	AX	= error code	
		3	*if path not found*
		5	*if access denied*

Notes:
- Files created with this function are not automatically deleted when the calling program terminates.
- The function fails if:
  - any element of the pathname does not exist.
  - the file is being created in the root directory, and the root directory is already full.
- See also functions 3CH and 5BH, which provide additional facilities for creating files.

Example: Create a file with a unique name and normal attribute in the *TEMP* directory on disk drive C for use as a temporary storage area. Typically, the directory to use for temporary files would be obtained by the program from a variable in the environment block. Note that you must save room for MS-DOS to fill in the filename and extension behind the path you supply. The complete file specification must be preserved and used to delete the temporary file before your program terminates.

```
            mov     ah,5ah          ;function 5AH = create temporary
            mov     cx,0            ;file attribute = "normal"
            mov     dx,seg tfile    ;set DS:DX = address of path
            mov     ds,dx           ;for the temporary file.
            mov     dx,offset tfile
            int     21h             ;transfer to DOS.
            jc      error           ;jump if create failed.
                                    ;temporary file created.
                                    ;since it was also opened,
            mov     thandle,ax      ;save its handle and
            .                       ;continue processing.
    error:  .
            .
    tfile   db      'C:\TEMP',0     ;path to be used for
                                    ;temporary file

            db      13 dup (0)      ;room for \filename.ext
                                    ;to be filled in by DOS

    thandle dw      0               ;handle for temporary file
```

Int 21H (33)
Function 5BH (91)
Create new file

Given an ASCIIZ file specification, creates a file in the designated or default directory on the designated or default drive. The file is opened and a 16-bit token, or handle, is returned, which is used by the program for further access to the file.

Call with:	AH	= 5BH	
	CX	= attribute	
		00H	*if normal*
		01H	*if read-only*
		02H	*if hidden*
		04H	*if system*
	DS:DX	= segment:offset of ASCIIZ file specification	

Returns:	If function successful:		
	Carry flag	= clear	
	AX	= file handle	
	If function failed:		
	Carry flag	= set	
	AX	= error code	
		3	*if path not found*
		4	*if no handle available*
		5	*if access denied*
		50H	*if file already exists*

Notes:
- The function fails if:
  - any element of the pathname does not exist.
  - the file is being created in the root directory and the root directory is already full.
  - a file with the same name already exists in the specified directory.

- The file is usually given the *normal* (read/write) attribute when it is created, and is opened for both read and write operations. The attribute can subsequently be modified with function 43H.

- See also function 3CH. The two calls are identical except that function 5BH fails if a file by the same name already exists, rather than truncating the file to zero length. Function 5AH provides an additional facility for creating temporary working files.

(continued)

- This function can be used to implement semaphores in the form of files across a local area network. The program can simultaneously test the semaphore and lock it, by simply attempting to create a file with a predetermined name using function 5BH. If the create operation succeeds, the program has acquired the semaphore and can proceed with its operations, releasing the semaphore when it finishes by simply deleting the file. If the create operation fails, the program can wait and retry the operation at suitable intervals until it succeeds.

Example: Create and open the file described by the string *fname*, and store the handle for future use by other file I/O routines.

```
          mov    ah,5bh              ;function number
          xor    cx,cx               ;attribute = normal
          mov    dx,seg fname        ;address of ASCIIZ
          mov    ds,dx               ;file specification
          mov    dx,offset fname
          int    21h                 ;transfer to DOS.
          jc     failure             ;jump, create failed.
          mov    handle,ax           ;save file handle for
           .                         ;future use.
failure:   .
           .
fname     db     'C:\MYDIR\MYFILE.DAT',0
handle    dw     0                   ;handle returned by
                                     ;successful create
```

Int 21H (33)
Function 5CH (92)
Control record access

Locks or unlocks a specified region of a file in systems that support multitasking or networking.

Call with:	AH	= 5CH
	AL	= function code
		00 *if locking*
		01 *if unlocking*
	BX	= file handle
	CX	= high part of region offset
	DX	= low part of region offset
	SI	= high part of region length
	DI	= low part of region length

(continued)

Returns:	If function successful:		
	Carry flag	= clear	
	If function failed:		
	Carry flag	= set	
	AX	= error code	
		1	*if function code invalid*
		6	*if handle invalid*
		21H	*if all or part of region already locked*

Notes:	
●	This function is useful for file and record synchronization in a multitasking environment or network. Access to the file as a whole is controlled by the attribute and file-sharing parameters passed in open or create calls, and by the file's attributes, which are stored in its directory entry.
●	This function must be used on a file that has previously been successfully opened or created via functions 3CH, 3DH, 5AH, or 5BH.
●	The beginning location in the file to be locked or unlocked is supplied as a positive double-precision integer, which is a byte offset into the file. The length of the region to be locked or unlocked is similarly supplied as a positive, double-precision integer.
●	For every call to lock a region of a file, there must be an unlock call with exactly the same file offset and length.
●	Locking beyond the current end of file is not an error.
●	If a process terminates without releasing active locks on a file, the result is undefined.
●	Programs that are spawned with the EXEC call (function 4BH) inherit the handles of their parent but not any active locks.

Example: Assuming that a file was previously opened and its handle was stored in the variable *handle*, lock a 4096-byte region of the file, starting 32768 bytes from the beginning of the file, so that it cannot be accessed by other programs.

```
        mov     ah,5ch          ;function number
        mov     al,0            ;request lock of region.
        mov     bx,handle       ;file token
        mov     cx,0            ;upper part of offset
        mov     dx,32768        ;lower part of offset
        mov     si,0            ;upper part of length
        mov     di,4096         ;lower part of length
        int     21h             ;transfer to DOS.
        jc      error           ;jump if lock failed.
        .
error:  .
        .
handle  dw      0               ;contains handle from previous
                                ;successful open or create.
```

Int 21H (33)
Function 5DH (93)
Reserved

Int 21H (33)
Function 5EH (94) Subfunction 00H
Get machine name

Returns the address of an ASCIIZ (null-terminated) string identifying the local computer. Microsoft Networks must be running to use this function request.

Call with:	AH	= 5EH	
	AL	= 00	
	DS:DX	= segment:offset of user buffer to receive string	

Returns:	If function successful:		
	Carry flag	= clear	
	CH	= 00	if name not defined
		> 00	if name defined
	CL	= NETBIOS name number, if CH < > 00	
	DS:DX	= segment:offset of identifier, if CH < > 00	
	If function failed:		
	Carry flag	= set	
	AX	= error code	
		1	*if function code invalid*

Notes:
- The computer identifier is a 15-byte string, padded with spaces and terminated with a null (zero) byte.
- This call is available only in MS-DOS version 3.1 or later, and the effect of this call is unpredictable if the file-sharing support module is not loaded.

(continued)

Example: Get the name of the local computer into the buffer named *machine*.

```
            mov     ax,5e00h                ;function 5EH subfunction 0
                                            ;   = get machine name
            mov     dx,seg machine          ;DS:DX = address of buffer
            mov     ds,dx
            mov     dx,offset machine
            int     21h                     ;transfer to DOS.
            jc      error                   ;jump, function failed.
            or      ch,ch
            jz      error                   ;jump, no name defined.
            .
error:      .
            .
machine     db      16 dup (?)
```

Int 21H (33)
Function 5EH (94) Subfunction 02H
Set printer setup

① ② ③

Specifies a string to be sent in front of all files directed to a particular network printer, allowing users at different network nodes to specify individualized operating modes on the same printer. Microsoft Networks must be running to use this function request.

Call with:		
	AH	= 5EH
	AL	= 02
	BX	= redirection list index
	CX	= length of setup string
	DS:SI	= segment:offset of setup string

Returns:		
	If function successful:	
	Carry flag	= clear
	If function failed:	
	Carry flag	= set
	AX	= error code
		1 *if function code invalid*

Notes:
- The redirection list index passed in register BX is obtained with function 5FH subfunction 02H (get redirection list entry).
- See also function 5EH subfunction 03H (get printer setup string), which can be used to obtain the existing setup string for a particular network printer.
- This call is available only in MS-DOS version 3.1 or later, and the call will fail if the file-sharing support module is not loaded.

(continued)

Example: Initialize the setup string for the printer designated by redirection list index number 2 so that the printer is put into boldface mode before printing a file requested by this network node.

```
        mov   ax,5e02h          ;function 5EH subfunction 2
                                ;   = printer setup string
        mov   bx,2              ;use redirection list index 2.
        mov   cx,2              ;length of setup string
        mov   si,seg setup      ;DS:DX = address of buffer
        mov   ds,si
        mov   si,offset setup
        int   21h               ;transfer to DOS.
        jc    error             ;jump, function failed.
        .
error:  .
        .
setup   db    01bh,045h         ;puts printer into boldface mode.
```

Int 21H (33)
Function 5EH (94) Subfunction 03H
Get printer setup

Obtains the printer setup string for a particular network printer. Microsoft Networks must be running to use this function request.

Call with:
AH	= 5EH
AL	= 03
BX	= redirection list index
ES:DI	= segment:offset of buffer to receive setup string

Returns:
If function successful:
Carry flag	= clear
CX	= length of printer setup string
ES:DI	= address of buffer holding setup string

If function failed:
Carry flag	= set	
AX	= error code	
	1	*if function code invalid*

Notes:
- The redirection list index passed in register BX is obtained with function 5FH subfunction 02H (get redirection list entry).
- See also function 5EH subfunction 02H (set printer setup string), which can be used to specify a setup string for a particular network printer.
- This call is available only in MS-DOS version 3.1 or later, and the call will fail if the file-sharing support module is not loaded.

(continued)

Example: Get the setup string for the network node associated with the printer designated by
            redirection list index number 2.

```
            mov    ax,5e03h            ;function 5EH subfunction 3
                                       ;   = get printer setup string
            mov    bx,2                ;use redirection list index 2.
            mov    di,seg setup        ;DS:DX = address of buffer
            mov    es,di
            mov    di,offset setup
            int    21h                 ;transfer to DOS.
            jc     error               ;jump, function failed.
                                       ;now buffer holds setup string
                   .                   ;and CX holds its length.
error:             .
                   .
setup       db     64 dup (?)          ;buffer to receive setup string
```

Int 21H (33)
Function 5FH (95) Subfunction 02H
Get redirection list entry

Allows inspection of the system redirection list, which associates local logical names with network
files, directories, or printers. Microsoft Networks must be running to use this function request.

Call with:	AH	= 5FH
	AL	= 02
	BX	= redirection list index
	DS:SI	= segment:offset of 16-byte buffer to hold device name
	ES:DI	= segment:offset of 128-byte buffer to hold network name

Returns:	If function successful:			
	Carry flag	= clear		
	BH	= device status flag		
		Bit 0	= 0	if device valid
			1	if device invalid
	BL	= device type		
		03	if printer	
		04	if drive	
	CX	= stored parameter value		
	DX	= destroyed		
	BP	= destroyed		
	DS:SI	= address of ASCIIZ local device name		
	ES:DI	= address of ASCIIZ network name		

(continued)

If function failed:
Carry flag = set
AX = error code

1	*if function code invalid*
12H	*if no more files*

Notes: ●   This call is available only in MS-DOS version 3.1 or later, and the call will fail if the file-sharing support module is not loaded.

       ●   The parameter returned in register CX is a value that was previously passed to MS-DOS in register CX with function 5FH subfunction 03H (redirect device).

Example: Get the local and network names for the device specified by the first redirection list entry.

```
        mov   ax,5f02h              ;function 5FH subfunction 2
        mov   bx,0                  ;redirection list entry # 0
        mov   si,seg local          ;DS:SI = buffer for local name
        mov   ds,si
        mov   si,offset local
        mov   di,seg network        ;ES:DI = buffer for network name
        mov   es,di
        mov   di,offset network
        int   21h                   ;transfer to DOS.
        jc    error                 ;jump if call failed.
        test  bh,1
        jnz   error                 ;jump if device not valid.
        .
error:  .
        .
local       db   16 dup (?)         ;buffer to hold local device name

network     db   128 dup (?)        ;buffer to hold network name
```

Int 21H (33)
Function 5FH (95) Subfunction 03H
Redirect device

Establish redirection across the network by associating a local device name with a network name. Microsoft Networks must be running to use this function request.

Call with:	AH	= 5FH	
	AL	= 03	
	BL	= device type	
		03	*if printer*
		04	*if drive*
	CX	= parameter to save for caller	
	DS:SI	= segment:offset of ASCIIZ local device name	
	ES:DI	= segment:offset of ASCIIZ network name, followed by ASCIIZ password	

Returns:	If function successful:		
	Carry flag	= clear	
	If function failed:		
	Carry flag	= set	
	AX	= error code	
		1	*if function code invalid*
			if source or destination string in wrong format
			if source device already redirected
		3	*if path not found*
		5	*if access denied*
		8	*if insufficient memory*

Notes:	•	This call is available only in MS-DOS version 3.1 or later, and the call will fail if the file-sharing support module is not loaded.
	•	The parameter passed in register CX can be retrieved by later calls to function 5FH subfunction 02H (get redirection list entry).
	•	The local device name can be a drive designator (a letter followed by a colon, such as *D:*), a printer name, or a null string. Printer names must be one of the following: PRN, LPT1, LPT2, or LPT3. If a null string followed by a password is used, MS-DOS attempts to grant access to the network directory with the specified password.

(continued)

Example: Redirect the local drive *E:* to the directory *pcforth* on the server named *LMI*, using the password *fred*.

```
                mov    ax,5f03h              ;function 5FH subfunction 3
                mov    bl,4                  ;code 4 = disk drive
                mov    si,seg locname        ;DS:SI = local name
                mov    ds,si
                mov    si,offset locname
                mov    di,seg netname        ;ES:DI = network name
                mov    es,di
                mov    di,offset netname
                int    21h                   ;transfer to DOS.
                jc     error                 ;jump, redirection failed.
                .
error:          .
                .
locname         db     "e:",0
netname         db     "\lmi\pcforth",0,"fred",0
```

Int 21H (33)
Function 5FH (95) Subfunction 04H
Cancel redirection

Cancels a previous redirection request by removing the association of a local device name with a network name. Microsoft Networks must be running to use this function request.

Call with:	AH	= 5FH
	AL	= 04
	DS:SI	= segment:offset of ASCIIZ local device name

Returns:	If function successful:	
	Carry flag	= clear
	If function failed:	
	Carry flag	= set
	AX	= error code
	1	*if function code invalid*
		if ASCIIZ string doesn't name an existing source device
	0FH	*if redirection paused on server*

Notes:
- This call is available only in MS-DOS version 3.1 or later, and the call will fail if the file-sharing support module is not loaded.

- The local device name can be a drive designator (a letter followed by a colon, such as *D:*), a printer name, or a string starting with two backslashes (\ \). Printer names must be one of the following: PRN, LPT1, LPT2, or LPT3. If the string with two backslashes is used, the connection between the local machine and the network directory is terminated.

(continued)

Example: Cancel the redirection of the local drive *E:* to the network server.

```
            mov   ax,5f04h              ;function 5FH subfunction 4
            mov   si,seg locname        ;DS:SI = local drive name
            mov   ds,si
            mov   si,offset locname
            int   21h                   ;transfer to DOS.
            jc    error                 ;jump if cancel failed.
error:        .
              .
locname     db    'e:',0
```

Int 21H (33)
Function 60H (96)
Reserved

1   2   3

Int 21H (33)
Function 61H (97)
Reserved

1   2   3

Int 21H (33)
Function 62H (98)
Get program segment prefix address

1   2   3

Obtains the segment (paragraph) address of the PSP for the currently executing program.

Call with:	AH	= 62H

Returns:	BX	= segment address of program segment prefix

Note: ● Before a program receives control from MS-DOS, the PSP is set up to contain certain vital information, such as the segment address of the environment block, the command line originally entered by the user, the original contents of the Ctrl-Break and critical error handler interrupt vectors, the top address of available RAM, and so forth. The segment address of the PSP is normally passed to the executing program in the DS and ES registers when it first gets control. This function allows a program to conveniently recover the PSP address at any given point, without having to save it at program entrance.

(continued)

Get the address of the PSP and copy the MS-DOS command tail into a local working buffer named *my_buff*.

```
psp_fcb         equ     05ch
psp_cmd         equ     080h
                .
                .
                .
                mov     ah,62h                  ;function number
                int     21h                     ;transfer to DOS.
                mov     ds,bx                   ;"from" segment
                mov     si,offset psp_cmd       ;offset of command tail
                mov     di,seg my_buff          ;address of destination
                mov     es,di                   ;buffer
                mov     di,offset my_buff
                mov     cl,[si]                 ;length of command tail
                inc     cl                      ;point to string
                xor     ch,ch
                cld                             ;and move it to
                rep     movsb                   ;local buffer.
                .
                .
                .
my_buff         db      80 dup (?)              ;buffer for copy of command tail
```

Int 21H (33)
Function 63H (99)
Get lead byte table

Obtains the address of the system table of legal lead byte ranges for extended character sets, or sets or obtains the interim console flag. Function 63H is available only in MS-DOS version 2.25; it is not supported in MS-DOS version 3.

Call with:	AH	= 63H	
	AL	= subfunction	
		00	*if getting address of system lead byte table*
		01	*if setting or clearing interim console flag*
		02	*if obtaining value of interim console flag*
	If AL = 01:		
	DL	= 01	if setting interim console flag
		00	if clearing interim console flag

Returns:	If getting address of lead byte table:	
	DS:SI	= segment:offset of table
	If getting value of interim console flag:	
	DL	= value of flag

Int 22H (34)
Terminate address

The machine interrupt vector for Int 22H (memory locations 0000:0088H through 0000:008BH) contains the address of the routine that receives control when the currently executing program terminates via Int 20H or Int 21H function 00H, 31H, or 4CH. This address is also copied into bytes 0AH through 0DH of the program segment prefix when a program is loaded but before it begins executing, and is restored from the program segment prefix (in case it was modified by the application) as part of MS-DOS's termination handling.

This interrupt should never be issued directly.

Int 23H (35)
Ctrl-C handler address

The machine interrupt vector for Int 23H (memory locations 0000:008CH through 0000:008FH) contains the address of the routine that receives control when a Ctrl-C (also Ctrl-Break on IBM PC compatibles) is detected during any character I/O function and, if the break flag is ON, during most other MS-DOS function calls. The address in this vector is also copied into bytes 0EH through 11H of the program segment prefix when a program is loaded but before it begins executing, and is restored from the program segment prefix (in case it was modified by the application) as part of MS-DOS's termination handling.

This interrupt should never be issued directly.

Notes:	•	The initialization code for an application can use Int 21H function 25H to reset the Int 23H vector to point to its own routine for Ctrl-C handling. When set up in this way, the program will not lose control of the machine as a result of any keyboard entry.
	•	When a Ctrl-C is detected and the user's Int 23H handler receives control, all registers are set to the original values they had when the function call that is being interrupted was made. The user's interrupt handler can then do any of the following:

           — Set a local flag for later inspection by the application, or take any other appropriate action, and then perform a RETURN FROM INTERRUPT (IRET) to give control back to MS-DOS. All registers must be preserved. The MS-DOS function in progress will be restarted from scratch, then proceed to completion, and control will finally return to the application in the normal manner.

           — Take appropriate action and then perform a FAR RETURN (RET FAR) to give control back to MS-DOS. The state of the carry flag is used by MS-DOS to determine what action to take. If the carry flag is set, the application will be aborted; if the carry flag is clear, it will continue in the normal manner.

(continued)

- Retain control by transferring to an error handling routine within the application and then resume execution or take other appropriate action, never performing a RET FAR or IRET to end the interrupt handling sequence. This option will cause no harm to the system.

- Any MS-DOS function call can be used within the body of an Int 23H handler.

Example: See Chapter 5 for a detailed example.

Int 24H (36)
Critical error handler address

The machine interrupt vector for Int 24H (memory locations 0000:0090H through 0000:0093H) contains the address of the routine that receives control when a critical error (usually a hardware error) is detected. This address is also copied into bytes 12H through 15H of the program segment prefix when a program is loaded but before it begins executing, and is restored from the program segment prefix (in case it was modified by the application) as part of MS-DOS's termination handling.

This interrupt should never be issued directly.

Notes:
- On entry to the critical error interrupt handler, bit 7 of register AH is clear (0) if the error was a disk I/O error; otherwise, it is set (1). BP:SI contains the address of a device-header control block from which additional information can be obtained. Interrupts are disabled. The registers will be set up for a retry operation, and an error code will be in the lower byte of the DI register, with the upper byte undefined.

  The lower byte of DI contains:

00H	if write-protect error
01H	if unknown unit
02H	if drive not ready
03H	if unknown command
04H	if data error (bad CRC)
05H	if bad request structure length
06H	if seek error
07H	if unknown media type
08H	if sector not found
09H	if printer out of paper
0AH	if write fault
0BH	if read fault
0CH	if general failure

  Note that these are the same error codes returned by the device drivers in the request header.

- On a disk error, MS-DOS will retry the operation three times before transferring to the Int 24H handler.

(continued)

- Int 24H handlers must preserve the SS, SP, DS, ES, BX, CX, and DX registers. Only Int 21H functions 01 through 0CH can be used by an Int 24H handler; other calls will destroy the MS-DOS stack and its ability to retry or ignore an error.

- When the Int 24H handler issues a RETURN FROM INTERRUPT (IRET), it should return an action code in AL that will be interpreted by MS-DOS as follows:

0	Ignore error.
1	Retry operation.
2	Terminate program through Int 23H.
3	▨ Fail system call in progress.

- If an Int 24H routine returns to the user program rather than to MS-DOS, it must restore the user program's registers, removing all but the last three words from the stack, and issue an IRET. Control returns to the statement immediately following the I/O function request that resulted in an error. This will leave MS-DOS in an unstable state until a call to an Int 21H function higher than 0CH is made.

Example: See Chapter 6 for a detailed example.

Int 25H (37)
Absolute disk read

▨   ▨   ▨

Provides direct linkage to the MS-DOS BIOS module to read data from a logical disk sector into a specified memory location.

Call with:		
	AL	= drive number (0 = A, 1 = B, etc.)
	CX	= number of sectors to read
	DX	= starting relative (logical) sector number
	DS:BX	= segment:offset of disk transfer area

Returns:		
	If operation successful:	
	Carry flag	= clear
	If operation failed:	
	Carry flag	= set
	AX	= error code (see notes)

Notes:
- All registers except the segment registers may be destroyed.
- When this interrupt returns, the CPU flags originally pushed onto the stack by the Int 25H instruction are *still* on the stack. The stack must be cleared by a POPF or ADD SP,2 to prevent uncontrolled stack growth, and to make accessible any other values that were pushed onto the stack before the call to Int 25H.

(continued)

- Logical sector numbers are obtained by numbering each disk sector sequentially from track 0, head 0, sector 1, and continuing until the last sector on the disk is counted. The head number is incremented before the track number. Logically adjacent sectors may not be physically adjacent, due to interleaving that occurs at the physical device-driver level for some types of disks.

- The error code is interpreted as follows. The lower byte (AL) is the same error code that is returned in the lower byte of DI when an Int 24H is issued. The upper byte (AH) contains:

80H	if attachment failed to respond
40H	if seek operation failed
20H	if controller failed
10H	if data error (bad CRC)
08H	if direct memory access (DMA) failure
04H	if requested sector not found
03H	if write-protect fault
02H	if bad address mark
01H	if bad command

Example: Read logical sector 1 of drive A into the memory area named *buff* (on most MS-DOS floppy disks, this sector contains the beginning of the file allocation table).

```
                mov    al,0              ;drive A:
                mov    cx,1              ;number of sectors
                mov    dx,1              ;beginning sector number
                mov    bx,seg buff       ;address of buffer
                mov    ds,bx
                mov    bx,offset buff
                int    25h               ;request disk read.
                jc     error             ;jump if read failed.
                add    sp,2              ;clear stack.
                  .
error:            .
                  .
buff            db     512 dup (?)
```

Int 26H (38)
Absolute disk write

Provides direct linkage to the MS-DOS BIOS module to write data from a specified memory buffer to a logical disk sector.

Call with:		
	AL	= drive number (0 = A, 1 = B, etc.)
	CX	= number of sectors to write
	DX	= starting relative (logical) sector number
	DS:BX	= segment:offset of disk transfer area

(continued)

Returns:	If operation successful:
	Carry flag = clear
	If operation failed:
	Carry flag = set
	AX = error code (see notes)

Notes:	•	When this interrupt returns, the CPU flags originally pushed onto the stack by the Int 26H instruction are *still* on the stack. The stack must be cleared by a POPF or ADD SP,2 to prevent uncontrolled stack growth, and to make accessible any other values that were pushed on the stack before the call to Int 26H.
	•	Logical sector numbers are obtained by numbering each disk sector sequentially from track 0, head 0, sector 1, and continuing until the last sector on the disk is counted. The head number is incremented before the track number. Logically adjacent sectors may not be physically adjacent due to interleaving that occurs at the physical device-driver level for some types of disks.
	•	The error code is interpreted as follows: The lower byte (AL) is the same error code that is returned in the lower byte of DI when an Int 24H is issued. The upper byte (AH) contains:

80H	if attachment failed to respond
40H	if seek operation failed
20H	if controller failed
10H	if data error (bad CRC)
08H	if direct memory access (DMA) failure
04H	if requested sector not found
03H	if write-protect fault
02H	if bad address mark
01H	if bad command

Example: Write the contents of the memory area named *buff* into logical sector 3 of drive C.

WARNING: Verbatim use of this code could damage the file structure of your hard disk. It is meant only as a general guide. There is, unfortunately, no way to give a really safe example of this interrupt.

```
                mov    al,2                  ;drive C:
                mov    cx,1                  ;number of sectors
                mov    dx,3                  ;beginning sector number
                mov    bx,seg buff           ;address of buffer
                mov    ds,bx
                mov    bx,offset buff
                int    26h                   ;request disk write.
                jc     error                 ;jump if write failed.
                add    sp,2                  ;clear stack.
                .
error:          .
                .
buff            db     512 dup (?)           ;data to be written to disk
```

Int 27H (39)
Terminate and stay resident

Terminates execution of the currently executing program, but reserves part or all of its memory so that it will not be overlaid by the next transient program to be loaded. MS-DOS then takes the following actions:

1. Restores the terminate vector (Int 22H) from PSP:000AH.

2. Restores the Ctrl–C vector (Int 23H) from PSP:000EH.

3. ② ③ Restores the critical error handler vector (Int 24H) from PSP:0012H.

4. Transfers to the terminate address.

If the program is returning to COMMAND.COM rather than to another program, control transfers to COMMAND.COM's resident portion and the transient portion of COMMAND.COM is reloaded (if necessary). If COMMAND.COM then determines that a batch file is in progress, the next line of the file is fetched and interpreted; otherwise, a prompt is issued for the next user command.

| Call with: | DX | = offset of last byte plus 1 (relative to the program segment prefix) of program to be protected |
| | CS | = segment of program segment prefix |

| Returns: | Nothing |

Notes:	•	This interrupt is typically used to allow user-written drivers or interrupt handlers to be loaded as ordinary COM or EXE programs, then remain resident. Subsequent entrance to the code is via a hardware or software interrupt.
	•	① The maximum amount of memory that can be reserved with this interrupt is 64 Kbytes. Therefore, the Int 27H call should be used only for applications that must run under MS-DOS version 1. ② ③ The preferred method to terminate and stay resident is to use Int 21H function 31H, which allows you to reserve any amount of memory.
	•	This interrupt should not be called by EXE programs that are loaded into the high end of memory (i.e., linked with the /HIGH switch), since this would reserve the memory that is normally used by the transient part of COMMAND.COM. If COMMAND.COM cannot be reloaded, the system will fail.
	•	Since execution of this interrupt results in the restoration of the terminate (Int 22H), Ctrl–C (Int 23H), and critical error (Int 24H) vectors, it cannot be used to permanently install a user-written critical error handler.

(continued)

- Open files are not automatically closed upon execution of Int 27H.
- This interrupt does not work correctly when DX contains values in the range 0FFF1H through 0FFFFH. In this case, MS-DOS discards the high bit of the contents of DX, resulting in 32 Kbytes less resident memory than was actually requested by the programmer.

Example: Exit and stay resident, reserving enough memory to protect the program's code and data.

```
start:          .
                .
                .
                mov   dx,offset pgm_end     ;DX = bytes to reserve
                int   27h                   ;terminate, stay resident
                .
                .
                .
pgm_end         equ   $

                end   start
```

Int 28H (40)
Reserved

1 2 3

Int 29H (41)
Reserved

1 2 3

Int 2AH (42)
Reserved

1 2 3

Int 2BH (43)
Reserved

1 2 3

Int 2CH (44)
Reserved

1 2 3

Int 2DH (45)
Reserved

1 2 3

Int 2EH (46)
Reserved

1 2 3

Int 2FH (47)
Print spool control

1 2 3

Submits a file to the print spooler, removes a file from the print spooler's queue of pending files, or obtains the status of the printer.

Call with:	AH	= 01H	
	AL	= 00H	if getting installed status
		01H	if submitting file to be printed
		02H	if removing file from print queue
		03H	if canceling all files in queue
		04H	if holding print jobs for status read
		05H	if ending hold for status read
	DS:DX	= segment:offset of packet address if function 01H	
		= segment:offset of ASCIIZ file specification if function 02H	

Returns:	If function successful:		
	Carry flag	= clear	
	For function 00H:		
	AL	= status	
		00H	*if not installed, OK to install*
		01H	*if not installed, not OK to install*
		0FFH	*if installed*
	For function 04H:		
	DX	= error count	
	DS:SI	= segment:offset of print queue	

(continued)

```
If function failed:
Carry flag    = set
AX            = error code
                    1          if function invalid
                    2          if file not found
                    3          if path not found
                    4          if too many open files
                    5          if access denied
                    8          if queue full
                    9          if spooler busy
                  0CH          if name too long
                  0FH          if drive invalid
```

Notes:

- For function 01H, the packet consists of 5 bytes. The first byte contains the level (zero for MS-DOS versions 3.1 through 3.3), the next four bytes contain the double-word address (segment and offset) of an ASCIIZ file specification (the filename cannot contain wildcard characters). If the file exists, it is added to the end of the print queue.

- For function 02H, wildcard characters (* and ?) are allowed in the file specification, making it possible to delete multiple files from the print queue with one call.

- For function 04H, the address returned for the print queue points to a series of filename entries. Each entry in the queue is 64 bytes long and contains an ASCIIZ string that is a file specification. The first file specification in the queue is the one currently being printed. The last slot in the queue has a null (zero) in the first byte.

SECTION III

IBM PC
BIOS Reference

Int 10H (16)
IBM PC ROM BIOS video driver services

The IBM Personal Computer's ROM software contains a complete set of text and graphics drivers. These routines are accessed through Int 10H and provide display-mode selection, cursor addressing, display of text, scrolling, and point plotting.

Under PC-DOS versions 1.0 or 1.1, the ROM video driver routines must be used to perform screen-oriented I/O with cursor addressing and color control. Under PC-DOS versions 2.0 and above, these capabilities are also available via ANSI-standard escape sequences, using the MS-DOS display output functions. Under any version, calls to the ROM BIOS should be avoided whenever possible, to ensure portability among IBM PC-compatible machines and compatibility with future versions of MS-DOS.

The most elegant feature of the ROM BIOS video support is that most of the routines can be called by user software without regard for the display controller or video mode in use—Monochrome Adapter, Color/Graphics Adapter, or Enhanced Graphics Adapter. The video support routines determine the current type of display and perform all necessary address translation, including fetching bit patterns from a resident table if the program wishes to display text in graphics mode. Naturally, one must exchange some speed for this flexibility; where the video display mode is known in advance, the user can readily write much faster drivers for dedicated application programs.

More detailed information on the various video driver functions can be obtained by direct reference to the ROM BIOS listings in the PC/XT, PCjr, and PC/AT technical reference manuals.

Int 10H (16)
Calling sequence

The common calling sequence for the video driver routines is as follows:

```
mov   ah,function            ;AH contains function type.
.                            ;other registers are loaded
.                            ;with call-specific parameters.
.
int   10h                    ;transfer to ROM BIOS.
```

(continued)

Although each ROM BIOS video function has different arguments and returns different results, some general rules may be applied:

- The contents of register AH determine the call type. If the number in register AH falls outside the legal range of video driver function numbers, no action is taken (the legal range varies according to the type of machine and display adapter).

- The character or pixel value to be written is usually passed in register AL.

- The BX, CX, and DX registers and the segment registers are preserved across all video driver calls. The contents of all other registers, especially SI and DI, may be destroyed.

- The x coordinate (column number) is passed in CX for graphics functions or DL for text functions.

- The y coordinate (row number) is passed in DX for graphics functions or DH for text functions.

- The display page, if applicable, is passed in register BH.

Int 10H (16)
Function 00H (0)
Set video mode

Selects the current video display mode. Also selects the active video controller, if more than one video adapter is present.

Call with:	AH	= 00H	
	AL	= display mode	
		00H	for 40 x 25 black-and-white text, color adapter
		01H	for 40 x 25 color text
		02H	for 80 x 25 black-and-white text
		03H	for 80 x 25 color text
		04H	for 320 x 200 4-color graphics
		05H	for 320 x 200 4-color graphics (color burst off)
		06H	for 640 x 200 2-color graphics
		07H	for Monochrome Adapter or EGA text display
		08H	for 160 x 200 16-color graphics (PCjr)
		09H	for 320 x 200 16-color graphics (PCjr)
		0AH	for 640 x 200 4-color graphics (PCjr)
		0DH	for 320 x 200 16-color graphics (EGA)
		0EH	for 640 x 200 16-color graphics (EGA)
		0FH	for 640 x 350 monochrome graphics (EGA)
		10H	for 640 x 350 4-color or 16-color graphics (EGA) (depends upon amount of RAM available)

Returns:	Nothing

(continued)

- For RGB monitors, there is no functional difference between modes 00H and 01H or between modes 02H and 03H. Two palettes are available in mode 04H and only one in mode 05H.

- On the PCjr, modes 00H through 0AH, with the exception of mode 07H, are legal. On the EGA, modes 00H through 06H and 0DH through 10H are legal. If the high bit in AL is set, the display buffer is not cleared when the new mode is selected. When used carefully, this feature allows creation of some interesting effects (such as characters of different sizes within the same display frame).

Example: Set the current display mode to 02H (80 x 25 black-and-white text).

```
mov    ah,0        ;function 0 = select mode
mov    al,2        ;mode 2 = 80 x 25 A/N
int    10h         ;transfer to ROM driver.
```

Int 10H (16)
Function 01H (1)
Set cursor type

Selects the starting and ending lines for the blinking hardware cursor (text modes).

Call with: AH   = 01H
CH bits 0–4 = starting line for cursor (see notes)
CL bits 0–4 = ending line for cursor (see notes)

Returns: Nothing

Notes:
- The hardware causes the cursor to blink and cannot be disabled (text modes).
- Setting bit 4 or 5 in register CH will have an unpredictable effect on the cursor.
- The maximum legal starting and ending lines for the cursor depend upon the type of display adapter in use. The default values set by the ROM BIOS mode selection function are:

Display	Start	End
Monochrome mode 07H	11	12
Text modes 00H–03H	6	7

- The cursor can be turned off by several methods. The methods that involve setting illegal starting and ending lines for the cursor under the current display mode tend to be unreliable. An alternative method is to position the cursor to a nondisplayable address such as:

$(x,y) = (0,25)$

(continued)

Example: Set the starting line for the cursor to 6, and the ending line to 7.

```
mov   ah,1          ;function 1 = set cursor size
mov   ch,6          ;cursor starting line
mov   cl,7          ;cursor ending line
int   10h           ;transfer to ROM driver.
```

Int 10H (16)
Function 02H (2)
Set cursor position

Positions the cursor on the display, using text coordinates.

Call with:	AH	= 02H
	BH	= page number (must be zero in graphics modes)
	DH	= row (y coordinate)
	DL	= column (x coordinate)

| Returns: | Nothing |

Notes:
- Text coordinates (x, y) = (0,0) are the upper left corner of the screen.
- Text coordinates (x, y) = (79,24) are the lower right corner of the screen for the Monochrome Adapter and the Color/Graphics Adapter in 80 by 25 text display modes (mode 02H or 03H) or high-resolution graphics mode (mode 06H).
- Text coordinates (x, y) = (39,24) are the lower right corner of the screen for the Color/Graphics Adapter in 40 by 25 text display modes (modes 00H and 01H) or medium-resolution graphics modes (modes 04H and 05H).
- Attempts to position the cursor outside the limits of the current display mode will have unpredictable results.

Example: Position the cursor to (x, y) = (0,11) of display page 0 (the leftmost character in line 11 of display page 0).

```
mov   ah,2          ;function 2 = position cursor
mov   bh,0          ;select page 0.
mov   dl,0          ;X
mov   dh,11         ;Y
int   10h           ;transfer to ROM driver.
```

Int 10H (16)
Function 03H (3)
Read cursor position

Obtains the current position of the cursor on the display, in text coordinates.

| Call with: | AH | = 03H |
| | BH | = page number |

Returns:	CH	= starting line for cursor
	CL	= ending line for cursor
	DH	= row (y coordinate)
	DL	= column (x coordinate)

Notes:
- The Monochrome Adapter has only one display page.
- The Color/Graphics Adapter has four display pages in 80 by 25 text modes and eight display pages in 40 by 25 text modes. A separate cursor is maintained for each page, and each can be examined with this function, regardless of which page is actually being shown on the screen. Switching between pages is done with Int 10H function 05H.

Example: Read the current cursor position for display page 0, returning the coordinates in registers DH and DL.

```
mov   ah,3        ;function 3 = read cursor pos'n.
mov   bh,0        ;select page 0.
int   10h         ;transfer to ROM driver.
```

Int 10H (16)
Function 04H (4)
Read light pen position

Obtains the current status and position of the light pen.

Call with:	AH	= 04H	

Returns:	AH	= 0	if light pen not down/not triggered
		1	if light pen down/triggered
	CH	= pixel row (y coordinate, 0–199)	
	BX	= pixel column (x coordinate, 0–319 or 0–639, depending upon graphics mode—see notes)	
	DH	= character row (y coordinate, 0–24)	
	DL	= character column (x coordinate, 0–79 or 0–39)	

Notes:
- Although the light pen returns x and y pixel coordinates that span the full range of the currently selected graphics mode, the coordinates are not evenly distributed across the range. The y coordinate is always a multiple of 2, while the x coordinate is either a multiple of 4 for the 320 by 200 graphics mode, or a multiple of 8 for the 640 by 200 graphics mode. This lack of precision severely limits the usefulness of the light pen in graphics applications.

- Depending upon your brand of light pen, you may need to use one of the brighter background colors (such as light blue or green) to obtain maximum sensitivity from the light pen across the full screen width, because the intensity of light varies from the edge to the center of the screen.

Example: Monitor the status of the light pen until it has been triggered to read its current position.

```
wait:       mov     ah,4        ;function 4 = LP status
            int     10h         ;transfer to ROM driver.
            and     ah,1        ;pen triggered?
            jz      wait        ;loop if pen not triggered.
```

Int 10H (16)
Function 05H (5)
Select display page

Selects the active display page for the video display.

Call with:	AH	= 05H	
	AL	= page number	
		0 through 7	for modes 00H and 01H (CGA)
		0 through 3	for modes 02H and 03H (CGA)
		0 through 7	for modes 02H and 03H (EGA)
		0 through 7	for mode 0DH (EGA)
		0 through 3	for mode 0EH (EGA)
		0 through 1	for mode 0FH (EGA)
		0 through 1	for mode 10H (EGA)
	Or (on PCjr only):		
	AH	= 05H	
	AL	= 80H	if reading CRT/CPU page registers
		81H	if setting CPU page register
		82H	if setting CRT page register
		83H	if setting both CPU and CRT page registers
	BH	= CRT page for subfunctions 82H and 83H	
	BL	= CPU page for subfunctions 81H and 83H	

Returns:	On standard PC:	
	Nothing	
	On PCjr, if AL bit 7 = 1 on call:	
	BX	= CRT page register
	BL	= CPU page register

Notes:

- Function 05H is legal only in text modes on the standard Color/Graphics Adapter.

- Switching between pages does not affect their contents. In addition, text can be written to any of the video pages via functions 02H, 09H, and 10H, regardless of which page is active (currently being displayed).

- On the PCjr, the CPU page determines which part of the physical memory region 0000-1FFFFH will be hardware-mapped onto 16 Kbytes of memory addresses, starting at segment B800H. The CRT page determines the starting address of the physical memory used by the video controller to refresh the display. Smooth animation effects can be achieved by manipulation of these registers. Programs that write directly to the B800H segment can reach only the first 16 Kbytes of the video refresh buffer. Programs that require direct access to the entire 32-Kbyte buffer in modes 09H and 0AH can obtain the current CRT page from the reserved word PAGDAT at offset 008AH in the ROM BIOS's data area.

(continued)

Example: Select video page 2 to be the current display page.

```
mov    ah,5                    ;function 5 = select page
mov    al,2                    ;choose page 2.
int    10h                     ;transfer to ROM driver.
```

Int 10H (16)
Function 06H (6)
Initialize window or scroll window contents up

Initializes a specified window of the display to ASCII blank characters with a given attribute, or scrolls the contents of a window up by a specified number of lines.

Call with: AH   = 06H
              AL   = number of lines to scroll (if AL = zero, entire window is blanked)
              BH   = attribute to be used for blanked area
              CH   = y coordinate, upper left corner of window
              CL   = x coordinate, upper left corner of window
              DH   = y coordinate, lower right corner of window
              DL   = x coordinate, lower right corner of window

Returns: Nothing

Notes: •   If the Color/Graphics Adapter is in use in text mode, this function affects only the currently active display page.

          •   If AL contains a number other than zero, the area within the specified window is scrolled upward by the requested number of lines. Text scrolled beyond the top of the window is lost. The new lines that appear at the bottom of the window are filled with blanks carrying the attribute specified by register BH.

          •   To scroll the contents of a window downward, see Int 10H function 07H.

Example: Assume a window with the upper left corner at (0,0) and the lower right corner at (79,12)—equivalent to the upper half of the screen in 80 by 25 text mode. Scroll the contents of the window up by one line, filling the new line at the bottom of the window with blanks carrying a normal video attribute.

```
mov    ah,6                    ;function 6 = scroll up
mov    al,1                    ;scroll by 1 line.
mov    bh,7                    ;normal video attribute
mov    ch,0                    ;upper left Y
mov    cl,0                    ;upper left X
mov    dh,12                   ;lower right Y
mov    dl,79                   ;lower right X
int    10h                     ;transfer to ROM driver.
```

Int 10H (16)
Function 07H (7)
Initialize window or scroll window contents down

Initializes a specified window of the display to ASCII blank characters with a given attribute, or scrolls the contents of a window down by a specified number of lines.

Call with:	AH	= 07H
	AL	= number of lines to scroll (if AL = zero, entire window is blanked)
	BH	= attribute to be used for blanked area
	CH	= y coordinate, upper left corner of window
	CL	= x coordinate, upper left corner of window
	DH	= y coordinate, lower right corner of window
	DL	= x coordinate, lower right corner of window

Returns:	Nothing

Notes:	•	If the Color/Graphics Adapter is in use in text mode, this function affects only the currently active display page.
	•	If AL contains a number other than zero, the area within the specified window is scrolled downward by the requested number of lines. Text scrolled beyond the bottom of the window is lost. The new lines that appear at the top of the window are filled with blanks carrying the attribute specified by register BH.
	•	To scroll the contents of a window upward, use Int 10H function 06H.

Example:	Clear a window with the upper left corner at (0,0) and the lower right corner at (39,24), initializing it to reverse video (white background). This window is equivalent to the left half of the screen in 80 by 25 text mode.

```
        mov    ah,7         ;function 7 = scroll down or init.
        mov    al,0         ;scroll 0 lines = initialize
        mov    bh,70h       ;"reverse" video attribute
        mov    ch,0         ;upper left Y
        mov    cl,0         ;upper left X
        mov    dh,24        ;lower right Y
        mov    dl,39        ;lower right X
        int    10h          ;transfer to ROM driver.
```

For an example of scrolling, see the example for function 06H. To scroll down, enter the code given in that example, but substitute 07H in register AH.

Int 10H (16)
Function 08H (8)
Read attribute and character at cursor

Obtains the ASCII character and its attribute at the current cursor position for the specified display page.

| Call with: | AH | = 08H |
| | BH | = display page (on CGA, must be 0 in graphics modes) |

| Returns: | AH | = attribute byte |
| | AL | = ASCII character code |

| Note: | • | When using the Color/Graphics Adapter, attributes and characters can be read from any of the legal display pages, regardless of which page is currently active. |

| Example: | Read the character and attribute present at display position $(x, y) = (0, 11)$ on display page 0 (the leftmost position of line 11 on page 0). |

```
                                 ;first position the cursor...
        mov    ah,2              ;function 2 = set cursor position
        mov    bh,0              ;select page 0.
        mov    dh,11             ;Y = 11
        mov    dl,0              ;X = 0
        int    10h               ;transfer to ROM driver.
                                 ;now read character and attribute.
        mov    ah,8              ;function 8 = read character
        mov    bh,0              ;select display page.
        int    10h               ;transfer to ROM driver.
```

Int 10H (16)
Function 09H (9)
Write attribute and character at cursor

Writes a specified ASCII character and its attribute to the video display at the current cursor position.

Call with:	AH	= 09H
	AL	= ASCII character code
	BH	= display page
	BL	= attribute (alpha modes) or color (graphics modes)
	CX	= count of characters to write (replication factor)

(continued)

Returns:	Nothing

Notes:	•	The replication factor in CX produces a valid result only for the current row. If more characters are written than there are remaining columns in the current row, the result is unpredictable.
	•	All values of AL result in some sort of display; control characters, including bell, backspace, carriage return, and linefeed, are not recognized as special characters and do not affect the cursor position.
	•	After a character is written, the cursor must be moved explicitly with Int 10H function 02H to the next desired position.
	•	To write a character without changing the attribute at the current cursor position, use Int 10H function 0AH.
	•	If this function is used to write characters in graphics mode, and bit 7 of BL is set to 1, the character will be exclusive-ORed (XOR) with the current display contents. This feature can be used to write characters and then "erase" them.
	•	In graphics modes, the bit patterns for ASCII character codes 80H through 0FFH are obtained from a table whose segment and offset are found in the vector for Int 01FH (location 0000:007CH). This vector can be modified by the user to install modified character sets. On the standard IBM PC, the bit table for ASCII character codes 00H through 7FH is contained in the ROM BIOS and is not replaceable by the user; on the PCjr, the pointer to the table for those codes is in interrupt vector 44H (location 0000:00110H) and can be replaced by the user.

Example: Position the cursor to $(x, y) = (25, 20)$ of display page 0 (line 20, column 25) and write an asterisk (*) with a normal video attribute.

```
                          ;first position the cursor...
        mov    ah,2       ;function 2 = position cursor
        mov    bh,0       ;select page 0.
        mov    dh,20      ;Y = 20
        mov    dl,25      ;X = 25
        int    10h        ;transfer to ROM driver.
                          ;now write the character.
        mov    ah,9       ;function 9 = write character
        mov    al,'*'     ;this is the character itself.
        mov    bh,0       ;select page 0.
        mov    bl,7       ;normal video attribute
        mov    cx,1       ;character count
        int    10h        ;transfer to ROM driver.
```

Int 10H (16)
Function 0AH (10)
Write character only at cursor

Writes an ASCII character to the video display at the current cursor position. The character receives the attribute of the previous character displayed at the same position.

Call with:
	AH	= 0AH
	AL	= ASCII character code
	BH	= display page
	BL	= color (graphics modes, PCjr)
	CX	= count of characters to write (replication factor)

Returns: Nothing

Notes:
- The replication factor in CX produces a valid result only for the current row. If more characters are written than there are remaining columns in the current row, the result is unpredictable.

- All values of AL result in some sort of display; control characters, including bell, backspace, carriage return, and linefeed, are not recognized as special characters and do not affect the cursor position.

- After a character is written, the cursor must be moved explicitly with Int 10H function 02H to the next desired position.

- To write a character and change the attribute at the current cursor position, use Int 10H function 09H.

- If this function is used to write characters in graphics mode, and bit 7 of BL is set to 1, the character will be exclusive-ORed (XOR) with the current display contents. This feature can be used to write characters and then "erase" them.

- In graphics modes, the bit patterns for ASCII character codes 80H through 0FFH are obtained from a table whose segment and offset are found in the vector for Int 01FH (location 0000:007CH). This vector can be modified by the user to install modified character sets. On the standard IBM PC, the bit table for ASCII character codes 00H through 7FH is contained in the ROM BIOS and is not replaceable by the user; on the PCjr, the pointer to the table for those codes is in interrupt vector 44H (location 0000:00110H) and can be replaced by the user.

Example: Position the cursor to (x, y) = (25, 20) of display page 0 (line 20, column 25) and write an ASCII X. The X takes on the attribute of the character previously present at that position.

```
        mov     ah,2            ;function 2 = position cursor
        mov     bh,0            ;select page zero.
        mov     dh,20           ;Y = 20
```

(continued)

```
        mov   dl,25              ;X = 25
        int   10h               ;transfer to ROM driver.
                                ;now write the character.
        mov   ah,0ah            ;function 0AH = write character only
        mov   al,'X'            ;character to display
        mov   bh,0              ;page 0
        mov   cx,1              ;character count
        int   10h               ;transfer to ROM driver.
```

Int 10H (16)
Function 0BH (11)
Set color palette

Selects a palette, or sets the contents of a color palette.

Call with:	AH	= 0BH
	BH	= color palette ID being set
	BL	= color value to be used with that color ID

Returns:	Nothing

Notes:
- This function is valid only in medium-resolution color-graphics display mode (mode 04H) on the standard Color/Graphics Adapter, and in modes 04H through 06H and 08H through 0AH on the PCjr.

- If register BH contains zero, BL contains the background and border color (0 through 15) in graphics modes. In alphanumeric (text) modes, the contents of BL controls the border color only; the background color of each individual character is controlled by the high 4 bits of its attribute byte.

- If register BH = 1, BL contains the palette being selected (0 or 1 on the standard Color/Graphics Adapter).

Palette	Pixel value	Color
0	0	Same as background
	1	Green
	2	Red
	3	Brown
1	0	Same as background
	1	Cyan
	2	Magenta
	3	White

(continued)

- In 16-color modes on the PCjr, the following default palette is set up:

Pixel value	Color	Pixel value	Color
01H	Blue	08H	Dark grey
02H	Green	09H	Light blue
03H	Cyan	0BH	Light cyan
04H	Red	0CH	Light red
05H	Magenta	0DH	Light magenta
06H	Brown	0EH	Yellow
07H	Light grey	0FH	White

Examples: Select palette 0 for color-graphics display on the standard Color/Graphics Adapter.

```
mov   ah,0bh          ;function 0BH = select palette
mov   bh,1            ;color set id
mov   bl,0            ;request palette zero.
int   10h            ;transfer to ROM driver.
```

Select background color 5 for graphics display on the standard Color/Graphics Adapter.

```
mov   ah,0bh          ;function 0BH = select palette
mov   bh,0            ;color set id of 0
mov   bl,5            ;background color of 5
int   10h            ;transfer to ROM driver.
```

Int 10H (16)
Function 0CH (12)
Write graphics pixel

Plots a point on the video display at the specified graphics coordinates.

Call with:	AH	= 0CH
	AL	= pixel value (see notes for legal values)
	BH	= graphics page
	CX	= column number (x coordinate)
	DX	= row number (y coordinate)

Returns: Nothing

Notes:
- In display modes 04H and 05H (medium-resolution 4-color graphics), legal pixel values are 0 through 3.

(continued)

- In display mode 06H (high-resolution 2-color graphics), legal pixel values are 0 or 1.

- If bit 7 of AL is set, the new pixel value will be exclusive-ORed (XOR) with the current contents of the pixel.

- The range of x for this function depends upon the currently selected graphics mode (0 through 319 for modes 04H, 05H, and 0DH; 0 through 639 for modes 06H and 0EH through 10H). The value of y is always in the range 0 through 199 for modes 04H through 06H and 0DH through 0EH, or in the range 0 through 349 for modes 0FH through 10H.

Example: Write the pixel value 3 at coordinates $(x, y) = (200, 100)$.

```
mov   ah,0ch          ;function OCH = write pixel
mov   al,3            ;pixel value
mov   cx,200          ;X coordinate
mov   dx,100          ;Y coordinate
int   10h             ;transfer to ROM driver.
```

Int 10H (16)
Function 0DH (13)
Read graphics pixel

Obtains the current value of the pixel on the video display at the specified graphics coordinates.

Call with:	AH	= 0DH
	BH	= graphics page
	CX	= column number (x coordinate)
	DX	= row number (y coordinate)

| Returns: | AL | = pixel value (range depends on graphics mode—see function 0C) |

Note:
- The range of x for this function depends upon the currently selected graphics mode (0 through 319 for modes 04H, 05H, and 0DH; 0 through 639 for modes 06H and 0EH through 10H). The value of y is always in the range 0 through 199 for modes 04H through 06H and 0DH through 0EH, or in the range 0 through 349 for modes 0FH and 10H.

Example: Read the current value of the pixel at $(x, y) = (100, 25)$.

```
mov   ah,0dh          ;function 0DH = read pixel
mov   cx,100          ;X coordinate
mov   dx,25           ;Y coordinate
int   10h             ;transfer to ROM driver.
```

Int 10H (16)
Function 0EH (14)
Write text in teletype mode

Writes an ASCII character to the video display at the current cursor position, using the specified color (if in graphics modes); then increments the cursor position appropriately.

Call with:	AH	= 0EH
	AL	= ASCII character code
	BH	= display page in alpha modes
	BL	= foreground color in graphics modes

Returns:	Nothing

Notes:
- The special ASCII codes for bell, backspace, carriage return, and linefeed are recognized, and the appropriate action is taken. All other characters are written to the display (even if they are control characters) and the cursor is moved to the next position.

- If the Color/Graphics Adapter is in use in one of the text modes, characters can be written to any of the legal display pages, regardless of which page is currently active.

- Automatic line wrapping and scrolling are provided by this function. If the cursor is at the end of a line, it is automatically moved to the start of the next line. If the cursor is at the end of the screen, the screen is automatically scrolled up by one line and the cursor is placed at the beginning of a new blank line. The display attribute for the entire new line is taken from the last character that was written on the preceding line.

- This is the function used by the MS-DOS console driver (CON) to write text to the screen. There is no way to specify the attribute of a text character using this output function. The easiest method for writing a character to the screen with a specific attribute is to first write an ASCII blank (20H) with the desired attribute at the current cursor location using function 09H, then write the actual character with function 0EH. This technique, although somewhat clumsy, will not require you to explicitly handle line wrapping and screen scrolling.

Example: Write an ASCII *X* to the screen at the current cursor position on page 0. The *X* takes on the attribute of the character that was previously displayed at this location. The cursor is automatically incremented to the next legal character position.

```
        mov     ah,0eh          ;function 0EH = write character
        mov     al,'X'          ;ASCII X
        mov     bh,0            ;select page zero.
        int     10h             ;transfer to ROM driver.
```

Int 10H (16)
Function 0FH (15)
Get current display mode

Obtains the current display mode of the active video controller.

Call with:	AH	= 0FH

Returns:	AH	= number of character columns on screen
	AL	= display mode
		00H *for 40 x 25 black-and-white text, color adapter*
		01H *for 40 x 25 color text*
		02H *for 80 x 25 black-and-white text*
		03H *for 80 x 25 color text*
		04H *for 320 x 200 4-color graphics*
		05H *for 320 x 200 4-color graphics (color burst off)*
		06H *for 640 x 200 2-color graphics*
		07H *for Monochrome Adapter or EGA text display*
		08H *for 160 x 200 16-color graphics (PCjr)*
		09H *for 320 x 200 16-color graphics (PCjr)*
		0AH *for 640 x 200 4-color graphics (PCjr)*
		0DH *for 320 x 200 16-color graphics (EGA)*
		0EH *for 640 x 200 16-color graphics (EGA)*
		0FH *for 640 x 350 monochrome graphics (EGA)*
		10H *for 640 x 350 4-color or 16-color graphics (EGA) (depends upon amount of RAM available)*
	BH	= active display page

Notes:
- For RGB monitors, there is no functional difference between modes 00H and 01H or between modes 02H and 03H. Two palettes are available in mode 04H; only one is available in mode 05H.

- This function is usually called before clearing the screen with function 06H or 07H, in order to find the width of the screen in the current display mode.

Example: Obtain the current video display mode.

```
        mov    ah,0fh          ;function 0FH = get mode
        int    10h             ;transfer to ROM driver.
```

Int 10H (16)
Function 10H (16)
Set palette registers

Controls the correspondence of colors to pixel values (PCjr and Enhanced Graphics Adapter only).

Call with:	AH	= 10H	
	AL	= 00H	if setting palette register
		01H	if setting border color register
		02H	if setting all palette registers and border register
		03H	if toggling blink/intensity bit (EGA only)
	BH	= color value	
	BL	= palette register to set (00H through 0FH) if AL = 00	
		blink/intensity bit if AL = 03	
		0	*enable intensity*
		1	*enable blinking*
	ES:DX	= segment:offset of color list (if AL = 02)	

Returns:	Nothing

Note:
- For subfunction 02H (AL = 02), ES:DX points to a 17-byte list; bytes 0 through 0FH are the color values to be loaded into palette registers 0 through 0FH, and byte 10H (the 17th byte) becomes the new value in the border color register.

Example: Set the border color to blue.

```
mov    ah,10h       ;function 10H = set palette
mov    al,1         ;set overscan color.
mov    bh,1         ;blue = color #1
int    10h          ;transfer to ROM driver.
```

Int 10H (16)
Function 11H (17)
Reserved

Int 10H (16)
Function 12H (18)
Reserved

Int 10H (16)
Function 13H (19)
Write string

Transfers a string to the video buffer for the currently active display.

Call with:	AH	= 13H		
	AL	= write mode		
		0		*attribute in BL*
				string contains character codes only
				cursor position is not updated after write
		1		*attribute in BL*
				string contains character codes only
				cursor position is updated after write
		2		*string contains alternating character codes and attribute bytes*
				cursor position is not updated after write
		3		*string contains alternating character codes and attribute bytes*
				cursor position is updated after write
	BH	= page		
	BL	= attribute (write modes 0 and 1)		
	CX	= length of character string		
	DH	= y coordinate (row) for string to be written		
	DL	= x coordinate (column) for string to be written		
	ES:BP	= segment:offset of source string		

Returns:	Nothing

Notes:
- This function is documented for the IBM PC/AT's ROM BIOS video driver only; it does not apply to the PC, PC/XT, or PCjr.

- This function can be thought of as an extension to Int 10H function 0EH (write text in teletype mode). The string is scanned for ASCII carriage returns, linefeeds, backspaces, and bell codes; these are treated as control codes and properly acted upon. This function is not particularly fast or efficient, since it is coded using a combination of calls to Int 10 functions 02H, 09H, and 0EH. The only real advantage to using this function is that it will save a small amount of space in the calling program.

(continued)

Example: Write the string *Hello* using the normal video attribute at the lower left corner of the display, (x, y) = (0, 24). Update the cursor position.

```
        mov     ah,13h              ;function 13H = write string
        mov     al,1                ;write mode 1 = simple char.
                                    ;string with cursor update
        mov     bl,07h              ;"normal" video attribute
        mov     bh,0                ;select page zero.
        mov     cx,5                ;length of string
        mov     dl,0                ;X coordinate
        mov     dh,24               ;Y coordinate
        mov     bp,seg string       ;ES:BP = addr of string
        mov     es,bp
        mov     bp,offset string
        int     10h                 ;transfer to ROM driver.
        .
        .
        .
string  db      'Hello'
```

Int 10H (16)
Function 0FEH (254)   (TopView)
Get video buffer

Obtains the memory address of the video buffer for the currently executing task under TopView.

| Call with: | AH | = 0FEH |
| | ES:DI | = segment:offset of assumed video buffer (see notes) |

| Returns: | ES:DI | = segment:offset of actual video buffer for current process |

Notes:
- Under TopView, each process is assigned a shadow buffer that is used to capture display output from the program. Portions (or all) of the shadow buffer are copied to the process's screen windows when an update (function 0FFH) is requested. This function is provided for applications that update the video refresh buffer directly, for performance reasons, rather than calling MS-DOS or ROM BIOS video output functions.
- The assumed address should be supplied as follows:

Display	Address
Monochrome Adapter	ES:DI = 0B000:0000H
Standard Color/Graphics Adapter	ES:DI = 0B800:0000H

(continued)

- If TopView is not running, this function is ignored by the ROM BIOS video driver, so the assumed buffer address is returned as the address to be used by the application. The application should inspect the address returned to determine whether function 0FFH (update video display) will be required after an alteration of the contents of the video buffer.

- This function cannot be used in graphics modes.

Example: Obtain the memory address of the video display buffer for the task currently executing.

```
                mov   ah,0fh        ;first obtain the current
                int   10h           ;display mode with function 0FH.
                cmp   al,7          ;is it monochrome display?
                je    label1        ;yes, jump.
                mov   di,0b800h     ;no, assume color graphics adapter.
                jmp   label2
label1:         mov   di,0b000h
label2:         mov   es,di         ;set segment of presumed buffer
                push  di            ;and save copy for later.
                mov   di,0          ;offset
                mov   ah,0feh
                int   10h           ;now request actual buffer address.
                mov   ax,es         ;get segment of display buffer
                mov   vseg,ax       ;and save it.
                pop   bx            ;recover presumed segment.
                sub   ax,bx         ;are they the same?
                mov   upd_flag,ax   ;flag = 0 if no update calls required
                .
                .
                .
vseg            dw    0             ;segment of task's display buffer
upd_flag        dw    0             ;<> 0 if update calls required
                .                   ; (TopView is running)
                .
```

Int 10H (16)
Function 0FFH (255)   (TopView)
Update video buffer

Copies the contents of the application's shadow video buffer to the true video refresh buffer under TopView.

Call with:
AH = 0FFH
CX = number of sequential characters that have been modified
DI = offset of first character that has been modified within shadow video buffer
ES = segment of shadow video buffer

(continued)

Returns:	Nothing

Notes:	•	This function is used by the application to notify TopView that the contents of its display have been altered, and that the portions of that display that lie within windows allocated to the application should be updated.
	•	The count in CX is of character positions only; however, the attribute bytes in the display buffer will also be updated.
	•	If TopView is not running, this function has no effect.
	•	If only a few characters in the buffer are updated at a time and the characters are at widely scattered locations, single-character requests to update each position should be issued, rather than one large request. If several characters that are close together or a very large number of scattered characters are modified, it is probably more efficient to issue a single update call with a range in CX that will include all of the altered positions.
	•	This function can not be used in graphics modes.

Int 13H (19)
IBM PC ROM BIOS floppy disk services

An entire hierarchy of disk-access services is available on the IBM Personal Computer under PC-DOS. From the most powerful and hardware independent to the most primitive or hardware dependent, they are:

1. Extended file-handling services with handles and pathname support. Available under PC-DOS version 2.0 or higher only, via Int 21H functions 3CH through 46H. Provided by the DOS kernel.

2. Traditional file-handling services (compatible with those available under CP/M on 8-bit microcomputers). Available under PC-DOS versions 1 and 2, via Int 21H functions 12H through 24H and 27H through 29H. Provided by the DOS kernel.

3. Device-independent absolute disk read and write functions, available via Int 25H and Int 26H. Provided by the MS-DOS BIOS.

4. Device-dependent absolute read and write, available for floppy disks via Int 13H. A service of the ROM BIOS, and therefore usable under all operating systems.

5. Floppy disk I/O by direct access to the disk controller chip. Used by many copy-protected programs to read nonstandard sectoring schemes.

Use of Int 13H is a compromise between portability and hardware dependence. Although it can be safely used across all models of the PC family, it is not necessarily portable to other 8086/8088 microcomputers running MS-DOS.

Int 13H (19)
Calling sequence

A total of six different functions are available through ROM BIOS Int 13H to access floppy disks. (Most hard disks can also be accessed with this interrupt.) They are summarized on the following pages. The general calling sequence is:

```
mov    ah,function          ;AH contains a function code.
  .                         ;load other registers with
  .                         ;function-specific values.
  .
int    13h                  ;transfer to ROM driver.
```

The segment registers are preserved, as are registers BX, CX, DX, SI, DI, and BP. Register AX is used to return results or status.

Int 13H (19)
Function 00H (0)
Reset floppy disk system

Resets the disk controller and prepares for floppy disk I/O.

Call with:	AH	= 00H

Returns:	Nothing

Example:

```
mov    ah,0               ;function 0 = reset
int    13h               ;transfer to ROM driver.
```

Int 13H (19)
Function 01H (1)
Get floppy disk system status

Obtains the status of the floppy disk drive controller.

Call with:	AH	= 01H

Returns:	AH	= status byte
		If set:
		Bit 7 = *disk timed-out (failed to respond)*
		Bit 6 = *seek failure*
		Bit 5 = *controller error*
		Bit 4 = *data error on disk read (CRC)*
		Bit 3 = *DMA overrun on operation*
		Bit 2 = *requested sector not found*
		Bit 1 = *disk write-protected*
		Bit 0 = *illegal command passed to driver*

Example: Obtain the current status of the floppy disk controller, branching to an error routine if there was an error on the most recent operation.

```
        mov   ah,1          ;function 1 = read status
        int   13h           ;transfer to ROM driver.
        or    al,al         ;was there an error?
        jz    error         ;yes, jump.
        .
error:  .
        .
```

Int 13H (19)
Function 02H (2)
Read floppy disk

Transfers a sector or sectors from the floppy disk into memory.

Call with:	AH	= 02H
	AL	= number of sectors to transfer (1–9)
	ES:BX	= segment:offset of user's disk I/O buffer
	CH	= track number (0–39)
	CL	= sector number (1–9)
	DH	= head number (0–1)
	DL	= drive number (0–3)

(continued)

Returns:	If function successful:		
	Carry flag	= clear	
	AH	= 0	
	AL	= number of disk sectors actually transferred	
	If function failed:		
	Carry flag	= set	
	AH	= status byte	
		If set:	
		Bit 7	= *disk timed-out (failed to respond)*
		Bit 6	= *seek failure*
		Bit 5	= *controller error*
		Bit 4	= *data error on disk read (CRC)*
		Bit 3	= *DMA overrun on operation*
		Bit 2	= *requested sector not found*
		Bit 1	= *disk write-protected*
		Bit 0	= *illegal command passed to driver*

Example: Read one sector from drive A, head 0, track 0, sector 1 (the boot sector of a normal PC-DOS disk) into the buffer named *mybuff*.

```
                mov     ax,seg mybuff       ;ES:BX = buffer address
                mov     es,ax
                mov     bx,offset mybuff
                mov     al,1                ;transfer 1 sector.
                mov     dl,0                ;use first floppy drive.
                mov     dh,0                ;head 0
                mov     ch,0                ;track 0
                mov     cl,1                ;sector 1
                mov     ah,2                ;function 2 = Read disk
                int     13h                 ;transfer to ROM driver.
                jc      error               ;jump if error.
                .
error:          .
                .
mybuff          db      512 dup (?)
```

Int 13H (19)
Function 03H (3)
Write disk

Writes a sector or sectors from memory to the floppy disk.

Call with:		
	AH	= 03H
	AL	= number of sectors to transfer (1–9)
	ES:BX	= segment:offset of user's disk I/O buffer
	CH	= track number (0–39)
	CL	= sector number (1–9)
	DH	= head number (0–1)
	DL	= drive number (0–3)

Returns: If function successful:

Carry flag	= clear
AH	= 0
AL	= number of disk sectors actually transferred

If function failed:

Carry flag	= set
AH	= status byte

If set:

Bit 7	*= disk timed-out (failed to respond)*
Bit 6	*= seek failure*
Bit 5	*= controller error*
Bit 4	*= data error on disk read (CRC)*
Bit 3	*= DMA overrun on operation*
Bit 2	*= requested sector not found*
Bit 1	*= disk write-protected*
Bit 0	*= illegal command passed to driver*

Example: Write one sector from the buffer named *mybuff* to drive B, head 1, track 5, sector 8.

```
        mov     ax,seg mybuff       ;ES:BX = buffer address
        mov     es,ax
        mov     bx,offset mybuff
        mov     al,1                ;transfer 1 sector.
        mov     dl,1                ;use second floppy drive.
        mov     dh,1                ;head 1
        mov     ch,5                ;track 5
        mov     cl,8                ;sector 8
        mov     ah,3                ;function 3 = Write disk
```

(continued)

```
                    int    13h              ;transfer to ROM driver.
                    jc     error            ;jump if error.
                           .
        error:             .
                           .
        mybuff      db     512 dup (?)
```

Int 13H (19)
Function 04H (4)
Verify disk sectors

Verifies the address fields of the specified sectors on the floppy disk. No data is transferred to or from memory by this operation.

Call with:	AH	= 04H
	AL	= number of sectors to verify (1–9)
	CH	= track number (0–39)
	CL	= sector number (1–9)
	DH	= head number (0–1)
	DL	= drive number (0–3)

Returns: If function successful:

Carry flag	= clear
AH	= 0

If function failed:

Carry flag	= set
AH	= status byte

If set:

Bit 7	= *disk timed-out (failed to respond)*
Bit 6	= *seek failure*
Bit 5	= *controller error*
Bit 4	= *data error on disk read (CRC)*
Bit 3	= *DMA overrun on operation*
Bit 2	= *requested sector not found*
Bit 1	= *disk write-protected*
Bit 0	= *illegal command passed to driver*

Note: ●   This function can be used to test whether a readable disk is in the disk drive on an IBM PC or PC/XT. It has unpredictable results on the PC/AT family.

(continued)

Example: Determine if a properly formatted disk is present in disk drive 0 (drive A).

```
              mov    ah,4            ;function 4 = verify disk
              mov    dl,0            ;drive 0
              mov    dh,0            ;head 0
              mov    ch,0            ;track 0
              mov    cl,1            ;sector 1
              mov    al,1            ;sectors to verify = 1
              int    13h             ;transfer to BIOS driver.
              jc     error           ;jump if bad or no diskette.
                     .
       error:        .
                     .
```

Int 13H (19)
Function 05H (5)
Format disk track

Performs initialization of floppy disk address fields and data sectors.

Call with: **AH**   **= 05H**
             ES:BX   **= segment:offset of address field list**

Returns: **Nothing**

Note: ●   The proper use of function 05H is beyond the scope of this book. It requires a
                detailed understanding of the disk controller chip and of the physical floppy
                disk formats.

Int 14H (20)
IBM PC ROM BIOS serial port services

Four different functions are available via Int 14H to access the serial communications port controllers. These functions are summarized on the following pages. The general calling sequence is:

```
mov    ah,function        ;AH contains a function type.
mov    dx,portnumber      ;DX selects communications port.
 .                        ;load other registers with
 .                        ;function-specific values.
 .
int    14H                ;call the ROM BIOS.
```

The segment registers are preserved, as are registers BX, CX, DX, SI, DI, and BP. Register AX is used to return results or status.

Note that the communications port numbers selected with Int 14H begin with zero, although at the MS-DOS level they are numbered starting at one (COM1, COM2, etc.).

Int 14H (20)
Function 00H (0)
Initialize communications port

Initializes the specified serial communications port to a desired baud rate, parity, word length, and number of stop bits.

Call with:	AH	= 00H
	AL	= initialization parameter (see note)
	DX	= communications port number (COM1 = 0, COM2 = 1, etc.)

Returns:	AH	= port status
		If set:
		Bit 7	= *timed-out*
		Bit 6	= *transmission shift register empty*
		Bit 5	= *transmission hold register empty*
		Bit 4	= *break detected*
		Bit 3	= *framing error*
		Bit 2	= *parity error*
		Bit 1	= *overrun error*
		Bit 0	= *data ready*

(continued)

AL   = modem status
          If set:

Bit 7   = *receive line signal detected*
Bit 6   = *ring indicator*
Bit 5   = *data-set ready*
Bit 4   = *clear to send*
Bit 3   = *change in receive line signal detected*
Bit 2   = *trailing edge ring indicator*
Bit 1   = *change in data-set ready status*
Bit 0   = *change in clear-to-send status*

Note: • The initialization parameter byte for the communications port is defined as follows:

7,6,5 baud rate	4,3 parity	2 stop bits	1,0 word length
000 = 110 baud	X0 = none	0 = 1 bit	10 = 7 bits
001 = 150 baud	01 = odd	1 = 2 bits	11 = 8 bits
010 = 300 baud	11 = even		
011 = 600 baud			
100 = 1200 baud			
101 = 2400 baud			
110 = 4800 baud			
111 = 9600 baud			

Example: Set the the first communications port to 9600 baud, 8-bit word, 1 stop bit, no parity.

```
mov    ah,0          ;function 0 = configure comm port
mov    al,0e3h       ;9600,8,N,1
mov    dx,0          ;use first communications port.
int    14h           ;transfer to ROM driver.
```

Int 14H (20)
Function 01H (1)
Write character to communications port

Writes a character to the specified serial communications port, returning the current status of the port.

Call with: AH   = 01H
              AL   = character to be written
              DX   = communications port number (COM1 = 0, COM2 = 1, etc.)

(continued)

If function successful:
AH bit 7   = 0
AL   = unchanged

If function failed:
AH bit 7   = 1
AH bits 0–6 = port status
              If set:
              Bit 6   = *transmission shift register empty*
              Bit 5   = *transmission hold register empty*
              Bit 4   = *break detected*
              Bit 3   = *framing error*
              Bit 2   = *parity error*
              Bit 1   = *overrun error*
              Bit 0   = *data ready*
AL   = unchanged

Example: Write an ASCII asterisk character to the first communications port.

```
mov   ah,1          ;function 1 = write character
mov   al,'*'        ;register AL = character
mov   dx,0          ;use first communications port.
int   14h           ;transfer to ROM driver.
```

Int 14H (20)
Function 02H (2)
Read character from communications port

Reads a character from the specified serial communications port, also returning the port's status.

Call with: AH   = 02H
             DX   = communications port number (COM1 = 0, COM2 = 1, etc.)

Returns: If function successful:
AH bit 7   = 0
AL   = character

If function failed:
AH bit 7   = 1

(continued)

AH bits 0–6 = port status
    If set:

        Bit 6   = *transmission shift register empty*
        Bit 5   = *transmission hold register empty*
        Bit 4   = *break detected*
        Bit 3   = *framing error*
        Bit 2   = *parity error*
        Bit 1   = *overrun error*
        Bit 0   = *data ready*

AL   = unchanged

Example: Read a character from communications port 0. This example assumes that an Int 14H function 03H call has previously been made to determine that a character is ready.

```
mov   ah,2              ;function 2 = read character
mov   dx,0              ;use first communications port.
int   14h               ;transfer to ROM driver.
```

Int 14H (20)
Function 03H (3)
Communications port status request

Returns the status of the specified serial communications port.

Call with:	AH	= 03H
	DX	= communications port number (COM1 = 0, COM2 = 1, etc.)

Returns:	AH	= port status
		If set:

        Bit 7   = *timed-out*
        Bit 6   = *transmission shift register empty*
        Bit 5   = *transmission hold register empty*
        Bit 4   = *break detected*
        Bit 3   = *framing error*
        Bit 2   = *parity error*
        Bit 1   = *overrun error*
        Bit 0   = *data ready*

(continued)

AL	= modem status
	If set:
	Bit 7 = *receive line signal detected*
	Bit 6 = *ring indicator*
	Bit 5 = *data-set ready*
	Bit 4 = *clear to send*
	Bit 3 = *change in receive line signal detected*
	Bit 2 = *trailing edge ring indicator*
	Bit 1 = *change in data-set ready status*
	Bit 0 = *change in clear-to-send status*

Example: Read a character from communications port 0. If no character is ready, wait until one is available.

```
wait:       mov   ah,3        ;function 3 = read status
            mov   dx,0        ;use first communications port.
            int   14h         ;transfer to ROM driver.
            and   ah,1        ;character ready yet?
            jz    wait        ;no, keep checking.
            mov   ah,2        ;yes, read it with function 2.
            mov   dx,0        ;use communications port 0.
            int   14h         ;transfer to ROM driver.
            and   ah,08eh     ;check for errors
            jc    error       ;and branch if error detected.
            .
error:      .
            .
```

Int 16H (22)
IBM PC ROM BIOS keyboard services

Three different functions are available via ROM BIOS Int 16H to access the keyboard controller and its status flags. The general calling sequence is:

```
            mov   ah,function   ;AH contains a function type.
            .                   ;load other registers with
            .                   ;function-specific values.
            .
            int   16H           ;call the ROM BIOS.
```

The segment registers are preserved, as are registers BX, CX, DX, SI, DI, and BP. Register AX and the CPU's zero flag are used to return results or status.

Use of the ROM BIOS keyboard driver is rarely necessary when writing programs to run under MS-DOS.

Int 16H (22)
Function 00H (0)
Read character from keyboard

Reads a character from the keyboard, also returning the keyboard scan code.

Call with:	AH	= 00H

Returns:	AH	= keyboard scan code
	AL	= ASCII character

Example: Wait until a character is ready for input from the keyboard, then return it in register AL.

```
            mov    ah,0            ;function 0 = read character
            int    16h             ;transfer to ROM driver.
```

Int 16H (22)
Function 01H
Read keyboard status

Determines if a character is ready for input, returning a flag and also the character itself, if one is waiting.

Call with:	AH	= 01H

Returns:	If key waiting to be input:	
	Zero flag	= clear
	AH	= scan code
	AL	= ASCII character
	If no key waiting:	
	Zero flag	= set

Note: •   If the zero flag is returned cleared and a character is returned in register AL, the character also remains in the buffer (this is a one-character look-ahead). The same character will be retrieved by the next call to Int 16H function 00H.

(continued)

Example: Wait until a character is ready for input from the keyboard.

```
wait:           mov   ah,1        ;function 1 = keyboard status
                int   16h         ;transfer to ROM driver.
                jz    wait        ;loop if no key waiting.
                .
                .
                .
```

Int 16H (22)
Function 02H (2)
Return keyboard flags

Returns the BIOS flags byte that describes the state of the various keyboard toggles and shift keys.

Call with:	AH	= 02H

Returns:	AL	= ROM BIOS keyboard flags byte (from 0000:0417H)
		If set:
		Bit 7 = *Insert on*
		Bit 6 = *Caps Lock on*
		Bit 5 = *Num Lock on*
		Bit 4 = *Scroll Lock on*
		Bit 3 = *Alt key down*
		Bit 2 = *Ctrl key down*
		Bit 1 = *Left-shift key down*
		Bit 0 = *Right-shift key down*

Example: Obtain the current keyboard flags byte, branching to the insert routine if the insert toggle is set.

```
                mov    ah,2        ;function 2 = get flags byte
                int    16h         ;transfer to BIOS driver.
                test   al,80h      ;check insert flag.
                jnz    insert      ;jump, insert toggle is on.
                .
insert:         .
                .
```

Int 17H (23)
IBM PC ROM BIOS printer controller services

Three different functions are available via ROM BIOS Int 17H to access the parallel printer port controllers. These are summarized on the following pages. The general calling sequence is:

```
mov    ah,function          ;AH contains a function type.
mov    dx,portnumber        ;DX selects printer port.
  .                         ;load other registers with
  .                         ;function-specific values.
  .
int    17H                  ;call the ROM BIOS.
```

The segment registers are preserved, as are registers BX, CX, DX, SI, DI, and BP. Register AH is used to return the printer status.

Note that the parallel port numbers selected with Int 17H begin with zero, although at the MS-DOS level they are numbered starting at one (LPT1, LPT2, etc.). Use of the ROM BIOS printer services is rarely necessary or justifiable when writing programs to run under MS-DOS.

Int 17H (23)
Function 00H (0)
Write character to printer

Sends a character to the specified parallel printer interface port, and returns the current status of the port.

Call with:	AH	= 00H
	AL	= character to be written
	DX	= printer number (0–2)

Returns:	AH	= printer status
		If set:
		Bit 7	= *printer not busy*
		Bit 6	= *acknowledge*
		Bit 5	= *out of paper*
		Bit 4	= *printer selected*
		Bit 3	= *I/O error*
		Bit 2	= *unused*
		Bit 1	= *unused*
		Bit 0	= *timed-out*

(continued)

Example: Send an ASCII form-feed character to the printer.

```
        mov   ah,0          ;function 0 = write character
        mov   al,0ch        ;0CH = ASCII Form Feed control char.
        mov   dx,0          ;use the first printer port.
        int   17h           ;transfer to ROM driver.
        test  ah,1          ;was there a time-out?
        jnz   error         ;yes, jump.
              .
error:        .
              .
```

Int 17H (23)
Function 01H (1)
Initialize printer port

Initializes the specified parallel printer interface port, and returns its status.

| Call with: | AH | = 01H |
| | DX | = printer number (0–2) |

Returns:	AH	= printer status
		If set:
		Bit 7	= *printer not busy*
		Bit 6	= *acknowledge*
		Bit 5	= *out of paper*
		Bit 4	= *printer selected*
		Bit 3	= *I/O error*
		Bit 2	= *unused*
		Bit 1	= *unused*
		Bit 0	= *timed-out*

Example: Initialize the first printer port, returning the status for that printer in register AH.

```
        mov   ah,1          ;function 1 = initialize printer port
        mov   dx,0          ;use the first printer port.
        int   17h           ;transfer to ROM driver.
```

Int 17H (23)
Function 02H (2)
Printer status request

Returns the current status of the specified parallel printer interface port.

| Call with: | AH | = 02H |
| | DX | = printer number (0–2) |

Returns:	AH	= printer status
		If set:
		Bit 7	= *printer not busy*
		Bit 6	= *acknowledge*
		Bit 5	= *out of paper*
		Bit 4	= *printer selected*
		Bit 3	= *I/O error*
		Bit 2	= *unused*
		Bit 1	= *unused*
		Bit 0	= *timed-out*

Example: Obtain the status of the first printer port, returning it in register AH. Branch to an error routine if the printer attached to that port is out of paper.

```
        mov   ah,2          ;function 2 = get status
        mov   dx,0          ;use the first printer port.
        int   17h           ;transfer to ROM driver.
        test  ah,020h       ;check out of paper bit.
        jnz   error         ;jump if bit set.
          .
error:    .
          .
```

SECTION IV

Lotus/Intel/ Microsoft Expanded Memory Specification Reference

Int 67H
Lotus/Intel/Microsoft Expanded Memory

The Lotus/Intel/Microsoft Expanded Memory Specification (EMS) defines a hardware/software subsystem, compatible with 8086/8088/80286-based microcomputers running MS-DOS, that allows applications to access as much as 8 megabytes of bank-switched random access memory.

After ensuring that the Expanded Memory Manager (EMM) is present by using one of the techniques demonstrated in Chapter 9, an application program communicates with the Manager directly via a software interrupt. The calling sequence for the Manager is:

```
mov     ah,function         ;AH contains the function number
 .                          ;other registers are loaded with
 .                          ;function-specific arguments.
 .
int     67h                 ;transfer to Expanded Memory Manager.
```

If an EMM call is successful, the value zero is returned in register AH; otherwise, AH will contain an error code.

Expanded memory resources are acquired and released by application programs using a process that is similar to opening and closing a file; similarly, memory resources owned by a program are referred to by a handle.

The material in this section has been verified against the Lotus/Intel/Microsoft EMS document, version 3.2, dated September 1985. A copy of this documentation (Part number 300275-003) can be obtained from Intel Corporation, 3065 Bowers Avenue, Santa Clara, CA 95051.

Int 67H
EMS Function 01H (1)
Get manager status

Tests whether the expanded memory hardware is functional.

Call with:	AH	= 40H	

Returns:	AH	= status	
		00H	if function successful
		80H	if internal error in EMM software (possibly caused by corrupted memory image of driver)
		81H	if malfunction in expanded memory hardware
		84H	if function requested by application not defined

(continued)

Note: • This call can be used only after the application has established that the Expanded Memory Manager is in fact present, using one of the techniques presented in Chapter 9.

Example: Determine whether expanded memory hardware is available and functioning correctly.

```
        mov   ah,40h        ;40H = EMM Function 1
        int   67h           ;transfer to Manager.
        or    ah,ah         ;test status.
        jnz   emm_error     ;AH <> 0 if error
              .
emm_error:    .
              .
```

Int 67H (103)
EMS Function 02H (2)
Get page frame segment

Obtains the segment address of the page frame used by the Expanded Memory Manager.

Call with: **AH** = 41H

Returns: If function successful:
AH = 00H
BX = segment of the page frame
If function failed:
AH = error code
80H   *if internal error in EMM software (possibly caused by corrupted memory image of driver)*
81H   *if malfunction in expanded memory hardware*
84H   *if function requested by application not defined*

Notes: • The page frame is divided into four 16-Kbyte pages, which are used to map logical expanded memory pages into the physical memory space of the CPU.

• The application need not have already acquired an EMM handle to use this function.

Example: Get the segment of the page frame used by the EMS in this system.

(continued)

```
                    mov    ah,41h           ;41H = EMM Function 2
                    int    67h              ;transfer to Manager.
                    or     ah,ah            ;test status.
                    jnz    emm_error        ;AH <> 0 if error
                    mov    page_frame,bx    ;save segment of page frame.
                    .
    emm_error:      .
                    .
    page_frame      dw     0
```

Int 67H (103)
EMS Function 03H (3)
Get number of pages

Obtains the total number of logical expanded memory pages present in the system, and the number of those pages that are not already allocated.

Call with:	AH	= 42H	

Returns:	If function successful:		
	AH	= 00H	
	BX	= unallocated pages	
	DX	= total number of pages in the system	
	If function failed:		
	AH	= error code	
		80H	if internal error in EMM software (possibly caused by corrupted memory image of driver)
		81H	if malfunction in expanded memory hardware
		84H	if function requested by application not defined

Note:	•	The application need not have already acquired an EMM handle to use this function.

Example: Get the total number of logical EMS pages and the remaining pages available, saving the values for later reference.

```
                    mov    ah,42h           ;42H = EMM Function 3
                    int    67h              ;transfer to Manager.
                    or     ah,ah            ;test status.
                    jnz    emm_error        ;AH <> 0 if error
                    mov    total_pages,dx   ;save total EMM pages.
                    mov    avail_pages,bx   ;save pages available.
                    .
    emm_error:      .
                    .
    total_pages     dw     0
    avail_pages     dw     0
```

Int 67H (103)
EMS Function 04H (4)
Get handle and allocate memory

Notifies the EMM that a program will be using extended memory, obtains a handle, and allocates a certain number of logical pages of extended memory to be controlled by that handle.

Call with:	AH	= 43H
	BX	= number of logical pages to allocate

Returns: If function successful:

	AH	= 00H
	DX	= handle

If function failed:

	AH	= error code	
		80H	*if internal error in EMM software (possibly caused by corrupted memory image of driver)*
		81H	*if malfunction in expanded memory hardware*
		84H	*if function requested by application not defined*
		85H	*if no more handles available*
		87H	*if allocation request specified more logical pages than are physically available in system; no pages allocated*
		88H	*if allocation request specified more logical pages than are currently available in system (request does not exceed physical pages that exist, but some are already allocated to other handles); no pages allocated*
		89H	*if zero pages requested*

Notes:
- This is the equivalent of a file open function for the Expanded Memory Manager. The handle that is returned is analogous to a file handle, and owns a certain number of EMM pages. The handle must be used with every subsequent request to map memory, and must be released by a close operation when the application is finished.

- Function 04H can fail either because there are no handles left to allocate or because there is an insufficient number of available logical pages of extended memory to satisfy the request. In the latter case, function 03H can be called by the application to determine the actual number of pages available.

- On the Intel Above Board implementation of the EMS, the handles are assigned in the sequence FF00H, FE01H, FD02H, etc.

Example: Attempt to open the Expanded Memory Manager for subsequent memory paging operations, and allocate 10 logical pages (16 Kbytes each) of expanded memory.

(continued)

```
                    mov     ah,43h            ;43H = EMM Function 4
                    mov     bx,10             ;BX = pages to allocate
                    int     67h               ;transfer to Manager.
                    or      ah,ah             ;test status.
                    jnz     emm_error         ;AH <> 0 if error
                    mov     handle,dx         ;allocation successful,
                            .                 ;save handle.
        emm_error:          .
                            .
        handle      dw      0                 ;save EMM handle.
```

Int 67H (103)
EMS Function 05H (5)
Map memory

Maps one of the logical pages of expanded memory assigned to a handle onto one of the four physical pages within the EMM's page frame.

Call with:	AH	= 44H
	AL	= physical-page number (0–3)
	BX	= logical-page number
	DX	= handle

Returns:	AH	= status	
		00H	*if function successful*
		80H	*if internal error in EMM software (possibly caused by corrupted memory image of driver)*
		81H	*if malfunction in expanded memory hardware*
		83H	*if invalid handle*
		84H	*if function requested by application not defined*
		8AH	*if logical page requested to be mapped is outside range of logical pages assigned to handle*
		8BH	*if illegal physical-page number in mapping request (not in range 0–3)*

Notes:
- The handle used in this function is the token returned by function 04H.
- The logical-page number must be in the range $\{0 \ldots n-1\}$, where n was the number of logical pages previously allocated to the EMM handle with function 04H.
- In order to actually access the memory once it has been mapped to a physical page, the application needs the segment address of the EMM's page frame. This segment address would typically be obtained by a call to EMM function 02H during the application's initialization sequence.

(continued)

Map logical page 4 of expanded memory assigned to this EMM handle onto physical page 2, then load the first byte of the page into register AL.

```
        mov     ah,44h              ;44H = EMM Function 5
        mov     al,2                ;AL = physical page number
        mov     bx,4                ;BX = logical page number
        mov     dx,handle           ;DX = handle owning page
        int     67h                 ;transfer to Manager.
        or      ah,ah               ;test status.
        jnz     emm_error           ;AH <> 0 if error
        mov     es,page_frame       ;get segment of page frame.
        mov     bx,8000h            ;page 2 is at offset 2 * 16K.
        mov     al,es:[bx]          ;read byte from EMM page.
                .
emm_error:      .
                .
handle      dw      0               ;EMM handle from Function 4
page_frame  dw      0               ;Page Frame segment from
                                    ;EMM Function 2
```

Int 67H (103)
EMS Function 06H (6)
Release handle and memory

Deallocates (releases) the logical pages of expanded memory currently assigned to a handle, and then releases the handle itself.

| Call with: | AH | = 45H |
| | DX | = EMM handle |

Returns:	AH	= status	
		00H	if function successful
		80H	if internal error in EMM software (possibly caused by corrupted memory image of driver)
		81H	if malfunction in expanded memory hardware
		83H	if invalid handle
		84H	if function requested by application not defined
		86H	if error in save or restore of mapping context

Notes:
- This is the equivalent of a close operation on a file. It notifies the Expanded Memory Manager that the application will not be making further use of the data it may have stored within expanded memory pages. This function would typically be called by an application just before it was going to perform a final exit.

- The EMM handle was obtained by a previous call to function 04H.

(continued)

- If an error condition is returned, it should not be ignored in the application's headlong rush toward task termination. For example, if the "busy" error condition is returned, the logical pages assigned to the application have not been released; if the task does not retry function 06H until it is successful, those pages will be lost to use by other programs until the system is reset.

Example: Release the EMM logical pages and the EMM handle assigned to the executing program.

```
            mov    ah,45h          ;45H = EMM Function 6
            mov    dx,handle       ;DX = EMM handle to release
            int    67h             ;transfer to Manager.
            or     ah,ah           ;test status.
            jnz    emm_error       ;AH <> 0 if error
            .                      ;otherwise close succeeded.
emm_error:  .
            .
handle      dw     0
```

Int 67H (103)
EMS Function 07H (7)
Get EMM version

Returns the version number of the Expanded Memory Manager software.

Call with: | AH | = 46H |

Returns:
If function successful:
| AH | = 00H |
| AL | = EMM version number |

If function failed:
AH	= error code
	80H	*if internal error in EMM software (possibly caused by corrupted memory image of driver)*
	81H	*if malfunction in expanded memory hardware*
	84H	*if function requested by application not defined*

Notes:
- The version number is the version number of the EMS that the driver software complies with. It is returned encoded as BCD, with the integer part of the version number in the upper 4 bits of AL, and the fractional part of the version number in the lower 4 bits.

- Applications should check the EMM version number to ensure that all EMM functions they use are available.

(continued)

Example: Obtain the Expanded Memory Manager version number and save it.

```
            mov   ah,46h              ;46H = EMM Function 7
            int   67h                 ;transfer to Manager.
            or    ah,ah               ;test status.
            jnz   emm_error           ;AH <> 0 if error
            mov   emm_version,al      ;otherwise save version.
                  .
emm_error:        .
                  .
emm_version db    0
```

Int 67H (103)
EMS Function 08H (8)
Save mapping context

Saves the contents of the expanded memory page-mapping registers on the expanded memory boards, associating those contents with a specific EMM handle.

| Call with: | AH | = 47H |
| | DX | = handle |

Returns:	AH	= status	
		00H	*if function successful*
		80H	*if internal error in EMM software (possibly caused by corrupted memory image of driver)*
		81H	*if malfunction in expanded memory hardware*
		83H	*if invalid handle*
		84H	*if function requested by application not defined*
		8CH	*if page-mapping hardware state save area is full*
		8DH	*if save of mapping context failed; save area already contains context associated with requested handle*

Notes:
- The EMM handle was obtained by a previous call to function 04H.
- This function is designed for use by interrupt handlers or resident drivers that must access expanded memory. The handle supplied to the function is the handle that was assigned to the interrupt handler during its initialization sequence, not to the program that was interrupted.
- The mapping context is restored by a subsequent call to EMM function 09H.

(continued)

Example: Save the EMS mapping state for the currently executing program.

```
            mov   ah,47h        ;47H = EMM Function 8
            mov   dx,handle      ;EMM handle from Function 4
            int   67h            ;transfer to Manager.
            or    ah,ah          ;test status.
            jnz   emm_error      ;AH <> 0 if error
                  .
emm_error:        .
                  .
handle      dw    0              ;EMM handle from function 4.
```

Int 67H (103)
EMS Function 09H (9)
Restore mapping context

Restores the contents of all expanded memory hardware page-mapping registers to the values associated with the given handle by a previous function 08H (save mapping context).

Call with:	AH	= 48H
	DX	= EMM handle

Returns:	AH	= status	
		00H	if function successful
		80H	if internal error in EMM software (possibly caused by corrupted memory image of driver)
		81H	if malfunction in expanded memory hardware
		83H	if invalid handle
		84H	if function requested by application not defined
		8EH	if restore of mapping context failed; save area does not contain context for requested handle

Note: ●   Use of this function must be balanced with a previous call to EMM function 08H. It is designed to allow an interrupt handler or driver that used expanded memory to restore the mapping context to its state at the point of interrupt.

Example: Restore the EMS mapping state for the currently executing program.

```
            mov   ah,48h        ;48H = EMM Function 9
            mov   dx,handle      ;DX = handle from Function 4
            int   67h            ;transfer to Manager.
            or    ah,ah          ;test status.
            jnz   emm_error      ;AH <> 0 if error
                  .
emm_error:        .
                  .
handle      dw    0
```

Int 67H (103)
EMS Function 0AH (10)
Reserved

This function was defined in the EMS 3.0 specification, but is no longer documented in EMS version 3.2.

Int 67H (103)
EMS Function 0BH (11)
Reserved

This function was defined in the EMS 3.0 specification, but is no longer documented in EMS version 3.2.

Int 67H (103)
EMS Function 0CH (12)
Get number of EMM handles

Obtains the number of active expanded memory handles.

Call with:	AH	= 4BH

Returns:	If function successful:		
	AH	= 00H	
	BX	= number of EMM handles	
	If function failed:		
	AH	= error code	
		80H	*if internal error in EMM software (possibly caused by corrupted memory image of driver)*
		81H	*if malfunction in expanded memory hardware*
		83H	*if invalid handle*
		84H	*if function requested by application not defined*

Notes:
- If the returned number of EMM handles is zero, the Expanded Memory Manager is idle and none of the expanded memory is in use.
- The value returned by this function is not the same as the number of active programs using expanded memory, since a single program can make several allocation requests and therefore own several EMM handles.
- The number of active EMM handles will never exceed 255.

(continued)

Example: Get the number of active EMM handles.

```
            mov   ah,4BH         ;4BH = EMM Function 12
            int   67h            ;transfer to Manager.
            or    ah,ah          ;test status.
            jnz   emm_error      ;AH <> 0 if error
            mov   actives,bl     ;save active handles.
                  .
emm_error:        .
                  .
actives     db    0
```

Int 67H (103)
EMS Function 0DH (13)
Get pages owned by handle

Returns the number of logical expanded memory pages allocated to a specific EMM handle.

| Call with: | AH | = 4CH |
| | DX | = EMM handle |

Returns: If function successful:
AH   = 00H
BX   = number of logical pages

If function failed:
AH   = error code

80H	if internal error in EMM software (possibly caused by corrupted memory image of driver)
81H	if malfunction in expanded memory hardware
83H	if invalid handle
84H	if function requested by application not defined

Note: •   The number of pages returned will always be in the range 1 through 512, if the function is successful. An EMM handle never has zero pages of memory allocated to it.

(continued)

Get the number of logical EMS pages associated with the EMM handle for the currently executing program.

```
          mov   ah,4CH              ;4CH = EMM Function 13
          mov   dx,handle           ;DX = handle from Function 4
          int   67h                 ;transfer to Manager.
          or    ah,ah               ;test status.
          jnz   emm_error           ;AH <> 0 if error
          mov   pages,bx            ;save assigned pages.
                .
emm_error:      .
                .
handle    dw    0                   ;EMM handle from function 4
pages     dw    0                   ;number of pages assigned
```

Int 67H (103)
EMS Function 0EH (14)
Get pages for all handles

Returns an array that contains all the active handles and the number of logical expanded memory pages associated with each handle.

Call with:	AH	= 4DH
	ES:DI	= segment:offset of array to receive information

Returns:	If function successful:	
	AH	= 00H
	BX	= number of active EMM handles
	Array is filled in as described in notes	
	If function failed:	
	AH	= error code
		80H — *if internal error in EMM software (possibly caused by corrupted memory image of driver)*
		81H — *if malfunction in expanded memory hardware*
		84H — *if function requested by application not defined*

Notes:
- The array is filled in with 2-word entries. The first word of each entry contains a handle, and the next word contains the number of pages associated with that EMM handle. The value returned in BX gives the number of valid 2-word entries in the array.

- Since the maximum number of active EMM handles is 255, the array need not be larger than 1024 bytes.

(continued)

Example: Get an array describing the active EMM handles and their associated EMS logical pages.

```
                mov    ah,4Dh                ;4DH = EMM Function 14
                                             ;ES:DI = address of array
                                             ;to receive information
                mov    di,segment proc_array
                mov    es,di
                mov    di,offset proc_array
                int    67h                   ;transfer to Manager.
                or     ah,ah                 ;test status.
                jnz    emm_error             ;AH <> 0 if error
                mov    actives,bx            ;save no. of active handles.
                .
emm_error:      .
                .
actives         dw     0                     ;number of active EMM handles

proc_array      dw     512 dup (0)           ;array of EMM information:
                                             ;EMM handles in even words,
                                             ;number of allocated pages
                                             ;in odd words.
```

Int 67H (103)
EMS Function 0FH (15)
Get or set page map

Saves or sets the contents of the EMS page-mapping registers on the expanded memory boards.

Call with:	AH	= 4EH	
	AL	= 00H	if getting mapping registers into array
		01H	if setting mapping registers from array
		02H	if getting and setting mapping registers in one operation
		03H	if returning size of page-mapping array
	DS:SI	= segment:offset of array holding information (subfunction 01H, 02H)	
	ES:DI	= segment:offset of array to receive information (subfunction 00H, 02H)	

(continued)

If function successful:

AH   = 00H
AL   = bytes in page-mapping array (subfunction 03H only)
Array pointed to by ES:DI receives mapping information (subfunctions 00H and 02H)

If function failed:

AH   = error code

80H	*if internal error in EMM software (possibly caused by corrupted memory image of driver)*
81H	*if malfunction in expanded memory hardware*
84H	*if function requested by application not defined*
8FH	*if subfunction parameter not defined*

Notes:

- This function was added in EMS version 3.2 and is designed to be used by multitasking operating systems. It should not ordinarily be used by standard application software.

- The user must ensure that a segment wrap will not occur when the array is accessed by the Expanded Memory Manager.

- The contents of the array are hardware and EMM-software dependent. Besides the contents of the mapping registers themselves, the array also contains any additional information that is necessary to restore the expanded memory subsystem to its previous state.

Index

Ctrl-C
 checking, 67
 handler, 22, 89, 317, 386 (*see also* Int 23H and Int 1BH)
  example in SHELL.ASM, 199
  example in SHELL.C, 195
  vector restoration, 273, 282, 360, 391
 system flag, 329 (*see also* Int 24H)
Currency format, 333
Current block, 114, 302, 303, 311, 313, 318
Current record, 114, 302, 303, 311, 313, 318
Cursor position, 69, 108, 402
 get current, 403
 text modes, 77
Cursor type, setting, 401

D

Data area. *See* Files area
Date
 CLOCK device, 242
 directory, 147
 FCB, 113-14
 file, 366
 format, 333
 get system date, 322
 set system date, 323
DEBUG.COM, 56
Default
 disk drive, 295, 306
 file control blocks, 112, 191
 record size, 111
Delete
 directory, 151, 336
 file, 301, 344
Destination operand, 41
Device attribute word. *See* Device information word
Device chain, 255
 example, 256
Device driver. *See* Driver
Device header, 184, 225. *See also* Driver
Device information word, 72. *See also* Driver
 get or set, 349
Device redirection, 380-84
Direct console I/O, 287
Directory, 146, 169
 create, 335
 date field, 366
 delete, 336

Directory (*continued*)
 example hex dump, 149, 171
 format of entry, 147
 get current, 354
 move file between directories, 365
 searching, 152, 298, 361
  example using FCB calls, 154
  example using handle calls, 155
 select current, 337
 volume label, 156
Disabling interrupts, 208
Disk
 allocation information, 308, 309, 331
 bootstrap, 165
 buffer cache, 17
 device driver, 162
 drive, default, 295, 306
 get available space, 331
 read logical sector, 388
 sector buffer, 16
 write logical sector, 389
Disk Toolkit (Morgan Computing), 57
Disk Transfer Address (DTA)
 default, 22-23, 307
 get current, 326
 set current, 307
 use in directory searches, 153
 use with read function, 302, 311, 318
 use with search functions, 298
 use with write function, 303, 313
Disk Transfer Area. *See* Disk Transfer Address
Diskette
 format track, 426
 read absolute, 422
 reset controller, 421
 system status, 422
 types, 168
 verify sectors, 425
 write absolute, 424
Display output, 69, 291
 active page, 78
 get video mode, 415
 graphics modes, 80
 Handle functions, 70
 hardware dependent, 73
 memory mapped, 75
 set video mode, 400
 traditional functions, 71, 284, 287
Display page. *See* Active page
Divide by zero interrupt, 210, 216
Document files, 268

S

Save Expanded Memory mapping
      context, 448
Scan codes, 69
Screen control, 69
Screen output. *See* Display output
Scroll window, 406-7
Search for first, 152, 157
    FCB function, 298
    Handle function, 361
Search for next, 153
    FCB function, 299
    Handle function, 363
Search order, 13, 189
Seattle Computer Products, 4
Seek (move file pointer), 345
SEGMENT directive, 27
Select directory, 151
Select display page, 405
Semaphores, 375
Separator characters, 321, 333
Sequential read, 116, 302
Sequential write, 116, 303
Serial port, 86
    default settings, 285
    Handle functions, 86
    initialization, 427
    input (MS-DOS), 86-87, 285
    input (ROM BIOS), 429
    interrupts, 212
    output (MS-DOS), 86-87, 286
    output (ROM BIOS), 428
    status (ROM BIOS), 430
    traditional functions, 87
Sessions, example. *See* Example sessions
SETBLOCK, 357
Set color palette, 411
Set Ctrl-Break flag, 329
Set country code, 332
Set current directory, 337
Set cursor position, 402
Set cursor type, 401
Set default disk drive, 295
Set Disk Transfer Address, 307
Set Expanded Memory page map, 453
Set file attributes, 347
Set file date and time, 366
Set interrupt vector, 215, 316
Set memory allocation strategy, 368
Set palette registers, 416
Set printer setup string, 378

Set random record number, 315
Set system date, 323
Set system time, 325
Set verify flag, 326
Set video mode, 400
Sharing modes, file, 339
Sharing retry count, 349
Shell, 188. *See also* Command processor
SHELL.ASM, 199
SHELL.C, 195
Shrinking memory allocation, 177, 189
    example program skeleton, 178
Single step interrupt, 210
Small model, 20
Snow (video controller), 79
Software interrupts, 211
Source file
    assembly language, 39
    C language, 44
Source operand, 41
Spooler. *See* Print spooler
Stack
    overflow, 257
    segment, 29, 31, 34
Standard auxiliary device, 18, 65, 87,
        224, 261
    via traditional functions, 285, 286
Standard error device, 65, 71, 261
Standard input device, 18, 65, 224,
        253, 260-61
    buffered, 292
    device driver flag, 226
    via traditional functions, 283, 287, 289-90
Standard list device, 18, 65, 84, 224, 261
    via traditional functions, 287
Standard output device, 18, 65, 70, 224, 253,
        260-61
    device driver flag, 226
    via traditional functions, 284, 287, 291
Status
    Expanded Memory Manager, 441
    extended error code, 369
    FCB functions, 112
    floppy disk controller, 422
    Handle functions, 121, 126
    input function (driver), 235
    via IOCTL, 349
    keyboard, 67, 293, 433
    modem, 428
    output (driver), 237
    printer, 85, 436
    request header, 227
    serial port, 427, 430
Stop bits, 427

Write (*continued*)
    file or device (Handle), 70, 343
    pixel, 412
    random, 312
    random block, 319
    sequential, 303
    serial port, 428
    string (ROM BIOS), 417
    with verify (driver), 237

Z

ZERODIV.ASM, 217-20

Ray Duncan

Ray Duncan is a member of that rare species, the California native. He received a B.A. in Chemistry at the University of California, Riverside and an M.D. at the University of California, Los Angeles, and subsequently received specialized training in Pediatrics and Neonatology at the Cedars-Sinai Medical Center in Los Angeles. Ray has been involved with microcomputers since the Altair days and has written many articles for personal computer magazines including monthly columns for *Softalk/PC* and *Dr. Dobb's Journal*. He is the founder of Laboratory Microsystems Incorporated, a software house specializing in FORTH interpreters and compilers.

Colophon

The manuscript for this book was prepared and submitted to Microsoft Press in electronic form. Text files were processed and formatted using Microsoft Word.

Cover design by Ted Mader & Associates
Interior text design by The NBBJ Group

Text composition by Microsoft Press in Bembo with display in Bembo Bold, using the CCI composition system and the Mergenthaler Linotron 202 digital phototypesetter.

Other Titles from Microsoft Press

Supercharging MS-DOS The Microsoft guide to high-performance computing for the experienced PC user
Van Wolverton $18.95

Running MS-DOS, 2nd Edition The Microsoft guide to getting the most out of the standard operating system for the IBM PC and 50 other personal computers *Van Wolverton* $21.95

Quick Reference Guide to MS-DOS Commands
Van Wolverton $4.95

Windows The official guide to Microsoft's operating environment *Nancy Andrews* $17.95

The Peter Norton Programmer's Guide to the IBM PC The ultimate reference guide to the entire family of IBM personal computers *Peter Norton* $19.95

Command Performance: Lotus 1-2-3 The Microsoft desktop dictionary and cross-reference guide *Eddie Adamis* $24.95

Variations in C Programming techniques for developing efficient professional applications *Steve Schustack* $19.95

CD ROM 2: Optical Publishing A practical approach to developing CD ROM applications *Edited by Suzanne Ropiequet with John Einberger and Bill Zoellick* $22.95

Presentation Graphics on the IBM PC How to use Microsoft Chart to create dazzling graphics for corporate and professional applications *Steve Lambert* $19.95

XENIX at Work *Edited by JoAnne Woodcock and Michael Halvorson* $21.95

Available wherever fine books are sold.